Group Dynamics and Problem Solving Process

Group Dynamics and Problem Solving Process

Presented to
Shunumunu (Kaveri)
&
Soumitra
As a gift of surprise for both of them.

RANDOM PUBLICATIONS

NEW DELHI (INDIA)

Group Dynamics and Problem Solving Process

ISBN 978-93-5111-464-2

Published in 2014 in India by

RANDOM PUBLICATIONS

Reprint : 2016

4376-A/4B, Gali Murari Lal, Ansari Road
New Delhi-110 002
Phone : +9111-43580356, 011-23289044
e-mail : sales@randompublications.com
info@randompublications.com

Type Setting by : Shah Computer Graphics, Delhi-110094
Digitally Printed at : Replika Press Pvt. Ltd.

Preface

This book is about maximizing the performance of groups, academic or professional, but more importantly, smaller groups. In other words, the direction is towards team building. The team members are usually groups of diverse individuals having separate and distinctive goals, needs and aspirations. They have to work together effectively to achieve a set of objectives. This book primarily aims to fulfil these aims to encourage each individual to cooperate and participate in team building functions and performance. As management guru Tom Peters had so meaningfully said that the word TEAM stands for "Together Everyone Achieves More".

In all professional courses today, group exercises and group problem solving processes are a major activity relating to all management, media and career studies. Understandably, the faculty members and the students have long been feeling the absence of such publications in totality to equip the students appropriately well. Similarly, in the organsiational environment also, group exercises have come up as a useful medium of brainstorming and finding solutions to problems. This book, therefore, is expected to fill a long felt gap in this direction.

In each chapter, distinctive queries in the form of Concept Development Questions, Analytical Exercises and Examples are provided which should be helpful to students and any reader interested in self-development tasks. In the same way, both for organsiational and their personal selves, professionals should find the book significantly useful to move on in their career developments.

Additionally, apart from Indian cases and examples, number of international instances have been cited in the book. We presume that such material will be largely applicable to other countries as well.

Sailesh Sengupta
Susmita Sengupta

Acknowledgements

We feel immensely happy to see that our book on "Group Dynamics and Problem Solving Process" is now in print for the benefit of the professionals, students and general readers.

We are glad to acknowledge that the original manuscript had received support and cooperation from many people together with their critical suggestions and well - founded recommendations. This has allowed the book to be much more meaningful and desirably better. We must record our sincere thanks and gratitude to those friends and well-wishers who, through their guidance, counseling and enthusiasm, helped us enormously.

The first named author (Sailesh Sengupta) feel indebted to Apeejay Institute of Mass Communication and particularly to its Director, Mr. Ashok Ogra and Associate Professor Dr. Puja Mahesh for their unstinted support. Grateful thanks are due to YMCA Institute for Media Studies and IT and specially its Director Mr. Dalip MacCune. Similarly, the first author fondly remembers his close association as a visiting faculty with Institute of Marketing Management , EMPI Business School, Delhi Productivity Council Institute of Management and Bharatiya Vidya Bhavan's College of Communication and Management. In all these reputed institutes of professional learning, the author had conducted series of group exercises, case study discussions and problem solving sessions to the benefit of the participating students. The two authors, the team of the father and his daughter, worked together to finalize the manuscript containing the material for the book. The final judgement will rest in the hands of faculty members, professionals and the student groups as a whole.

My wife Ruby(and mother of Susmita) deserves a word of praise and appreciation for her silent services to help us to proceed with the task. She was a great source of encouragement at all times.

We are, like the previous occasions, thankful to young Ashutosh Anand who carried out the computer processing for this book. He had to provide us with the final manuscript after series of revisions and corrections from our end. We must also express grateful thanks to several institutes for providing us with the required photographs for this book.

Finally, our thanks to Random Publications and their senior most executives who accepted our proposal for the publication of the book. They ensured a very smooth process while dealing with us and, as a result, the actual bringing out the final print took much less time than usual.

Sailesh Sengupta
Susmita Sengupta

Contents

Part—I

Part—II

Part—I

1

Group Formations and Group Process in Solving Problems

LEARNING OBJECTIVES

To begin with, the first chapter intends to make the concept of the entire book clear and understandable by discussing the following:-

- Fundamentals of group system and defining a group.
- Characteristics of a group.
- Why groups are formed and types of groups.
- Barriers in group activity
- Seminar method in group process.
- Checklist for success and failure.
- What is groupthink and how to strive against groupthink.

Human beings are social animals. We spend most of our waking hours in groups, large or small. But a group for our purpose is more than a collection of individuals. When we talk about group communication, we actually mean that the individuals belonging to such groups are distinctly different from any unstructured formation of people. And, to fulfill our requirements, organized group activities are a planned and systematic process. Even so, group dynamics have to be frequently reflected upon and have to face challenges of success and survival.

Defining a Group and Characteristics

The concept of a group, indeed, is very abstract. Although difficult to make it specific, we may try to identity a group and group communication in the following ways.

1. A small number of people jointly focus their combined knowledge, experience, information, and critical thinking on matters of mutual interest and importance.
2. Individuals in a group communicate or interact directly or indirectly with one another, thus creating the group.
3. A communication system in which a series of interactions among members establish the identity and structure of the group. The group exists for the specific purpose of accomplishing a job or a set of tasks.

The group identity, however, involves an individual in accepting and being accepted. The social needs of individuals, therefore, are related to acceptance, belonging and conformity in a group environment. The other aspects are: recognition, interaction, approval, association and, finally, achievement.

At the cost of repetition, we may refer to A.H. Maslow's universally acknowledged theory of the "Hierarchy of Needs". Indeed, the mainspring of all human behavior is the satisfaction of individual needs and aspirations.

Group Process: Planning and Systematic

MASLOW'S HIERARCHY OF NEEDS

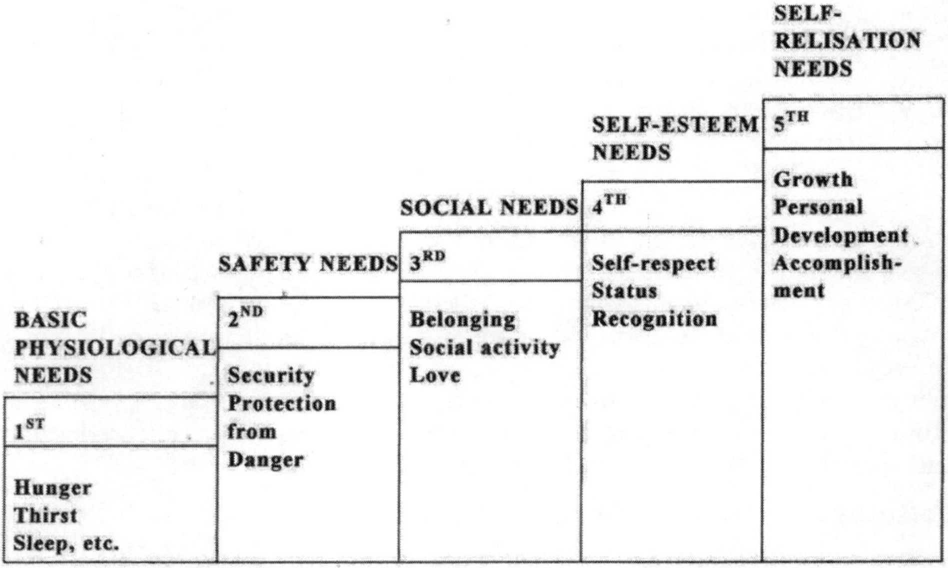

BASIC PHYSIOLOGICAL NEEDS	SAFETY NEEDS	SOCIAL NEEDS	SELF-ESTEEM NEEDS	SELF-RELISATION NEEDS
1ST	2ND	3RD	4TH	5TH
Hunger Thirst Sleep, etc.	Security Protection from Danger	Belonging Social activity Love	Self-respect Status Recognition	Growth Personal Development Accomplish- ment

Reference: A.H. Maslow in "MOTIVATION & PERSONALITY".

Group formations by mutual interactions lead
to a culture of open communication.

Managers and employees in an organisation form work -
teams for easy and fruitful communication with each other.

Group Characteristics

In general terms, group characteristics can be defined in eight catergories.

(1) ***'Insider' and 'outsider' attributes:*** In short, the identity of the person in the group. The member will be easily identifiable by fellow members and also by those who do not belong to the group. People outside the group may feel envious and like to be a part of the group as a desirable activity.

(2) ***Behavioral pattern:*** Each member may subscribe to common aims but have more than one objective in mind. The pattern of behavior will be guided by the individual member's thinking process. Nevertheless, the members of group will tend to conform to certain established norms of behavior in spite of differences in outlook.

(3) ***Aims and objectives:*** The group will have clearly understood, sometimes well- defined roles and objectives which are usually possible in organised and co-ordinated activities.

4) ***Unity of purpose:*** The group will set boundaries which, if crossed, will signal trouble, calling for review and corrective steps. The group must retain responsibility to achieve the group objectives. To reach a common understanding of goals or problems, the group evolves a common language in obvious terms.

(5) ***The leadership factor:*** A group should know at the outset that it must accept a formal or informal leadership which guides and controls its activity. At the same time, the leader must be capable of building the group based on goodwill and co-operation. Both are mutually interdependent.

(6) ***Individual uniqueness:*** In spite of a common identity communicators in a group activity must not forget that each person, in his own right, is a unique individual. Communi-cation, interestingly, is also a uniquely individual process. Each person, even in a group, has his or her own individual framework of understanding and needs.

Communication within an organisation, and both formal and informal systems supporting it, must make a perceptible adjustment between a person's individuality and organizational requirement of ensuring effective communication.

(7) ***Common Feelings:*** The members of the group are sensitive about their share of success or failure. In other words, they mostly hold sentiments in common and proudly proclaim their feelings. As a result, groups create measures that support their goals and everyone understands the goals in the same way.

(8) ***Basic features of a group member***: In the successful group functioning, it is essential to recognize that each member is an adult, rich with a wide range of experience but he may be unaccustomed to group atmosphere. Moreover, he has set trends of thought and behavior and may have resentful attitude to being advised or neglected by persons with superior feelings.

Why Form Groups

Many organizations have come to realize that truly functional teams can dramatically improve their levels of performance. In traditional systems, apathy and cynicism become an inseparable part of the working norms. One level blames the hierarchy in communication. A team based organization, on the other hand, where group activity is encouraged, can produce spectacular results. Here, everybody is treated as important components of the organizational system. As team-members they feel that they belong and their work makes a difference.

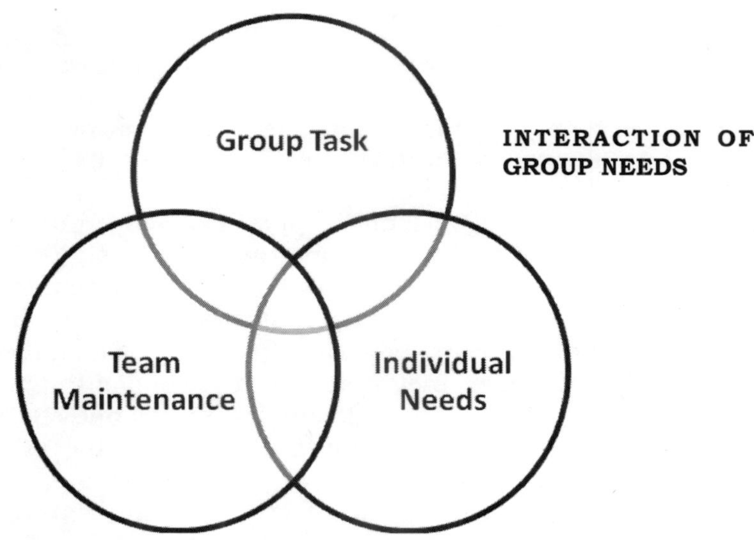

Reference: John Adair in "THE SKILLS OF LEADERSHIP"

Change Attitudes

For the management of the group of team-based organisations, a few attitudes changes are necessary. They are:

(1) Transition from a directive style to more interactive style is a primary need.

(2) Spread a culture of open communication. Managers must know that less communication to employees invariably results in grapevine being unusually active.

(3) Top management must provide training not only to managers but group members also in simple communication techniques. Professional communicators, in particular persons more involved in communication with the organsiation, have to be closely involved in this task.

(4) Managers and supervisors holding group activities are to be lauded. Incentives to them are a good idea. Group members also need similar encouragement.

(5) All employees in an organisation are to be organised into groups or work-teams for the purpose of easy communication and to achieve given results. However, these activities are to be more voluntary than a forced requirement.

(6) Encourage expression of different shades of opinion on various aspects of discussion topics. In other words, never impose one's own brand of discipline but maintain it by developing a sense of discipline among the group members.

Barriers in Group Activity

The barriers, in fact, are problems of transmission. What are these problems which create barriers in the process of good communication?

- The communicators themselves are not sure communicators.
- Communicators are not careful about possible distortions. Often they are misunderstood.
- Attitude of arrogance on the part of some members, which creates a feeling of dissatisfaction in other members.
- Communicators do not know how to put ideas into words.
- Physical facilities in a communication set-up are not adequate.
- Group members are not interested. But, truly, if the subject is not relevant to them they won't like to listen. If the message doesn't mean anything to the individual, how can one retain interest?
- The most difficult problem is the 'hostility barriers'. If the group members are hostile, they will not listen. And this is the most important road-block to effective communication. This kind of situation may discourage members or stimulate some of them to be in a combative mood.

Hostility Barrier

Seasoned communicators, anywhere in the world, say in one voice that 'hostility barrier' is the most difficult problem in group communications activity.

The first impediment, strangely, is the personal prejudices. It is not entirely about the person himself or herself. In fact, all persons carry a few prejudices about others as well. As long as the hostility exists, there indeed is a very serious communication problem.

Hostility in organisations, in the reality, is created by feuds. These feuds are always in departments versus departments. And managers themselves encourage such feuds. For example, there are endless fights between Production and Marketing, Purchasing versus Production, and

Accounting versus Engineering. These fights and feuds go on in every organisation.

As a first step, the groups and the organisation itself must define the problem and decide what corrective actions are necessary. It must be clear that the purpose of such actions is only aimed at solving problems and not to find fault.

The second step is to look at the transmission itself. If there are distractions or lack of interest, the communication environment calls for a radical change. It is important to realise that the problem of hostility does not come from outside. It comes from within as well as from the inside of the other person.

In many organisations the culture of toughness on the part of managers breed hostility. Such managers are mostly unskilled communicators, particularly where listening is involved. It is the duty of the top management to demand and reinforce good communication practices. The third step, again, is to establish a culture of open communication. Listening and two-way dialogues are essential components of free and frank communication.

The next move would be to conduct a lot of training for groups at all levels. In order to ensure that communication goes through, the barrier of hostility must be demolished. The effort is, to the dismay of many organisations, a never-ending process. Training and practice, obviously, are constant tools for people in organisations who care to communicate.

A simple but essential step is to work out informal procedures and ground rules for resolving 'In-group and Intergroup' differences within the organisation. Group members involved in hostilities or in conflicts are to the helped to find out areas which are common to all members and goals which they commonly share.

SEMINAR GROUPS

We may think of the seminar method as a discussion meeting in which groups or committees express their views on a particular subject. The original German word 'Seminary' refers to 'advanced class with limited attendance'. Admittedly, the word also means 'conference of specialists'.

However, the word 'seminar', as it is commonly understood today, refers to groups of any size, from five to five hundred, at different stages of performance. And the seminar, preceded by organised group activities, is conducted for several groups in a joint session for the participants who have a common need. This is more in terms of group discussions under the seminar.

The process generally goes by the following organised steps:

1. Organisers select a particular subject, preferably to the interest of the participants.
2. Working papers on the subject are carefully prepared.
3. Focus attention to different issues under the subject.

4. Selected participants are divided into small and manageable groups.
5. Groups may discuss identical working papers on the subject or different parts of the same working paper.
6. Each group will have a leader and a secretary for effective conduct of the group sessions.
7. After discussions in the groups, a report is made on behalf of each group which is to be presented in the joint session of the seminar.
8. A fresh opportunity is given for another spell of review and discussion of questions covered by the working paper.
9. The seminars will be chaired by the seminar leader (chairperson) and there will be a secretary or reporters for preparation of the final seminar report.
10. At the end of the joint discussion in the seminar, the chairperson sums up the proceedings as well as the decisions/recommendations of the plenary session.

Seminar can also be led by an expert in the topic area. In this form of group activity, a problem may be defined and then given to the participants to solve or rectify under the guidance of the seminar leader. The leader may present relevant research findings to enable the participants to come to correct solutions, based on those facts and information. Even though there will be scope for interpersonal communications, the seminar will usually follow more of a lecture format. The seminar may also begin with a presentation by an expert or a group of specialists before several groups together or just before one small, medium or a larger group of participants.

Again, while organising seminars one need not be too rigid on the procedural formalities. Some changes may be necessary to suit the interest, understanding and level of education of the participants. Be flexible and open minded for utilization of the seminar mode as a problem solving tool.

Checklist for success and good results

1. Do not criticize the participants for lapses or shortcomings. Offer guidance and counsel.
2. Encourage members to actively take part and to contribute as much as possible.
3. The working paper should be circulated among the members in advance to provide opportunities for preparation.
4. The working paper should be able to provoke the interest of the members on the subject. It should raise important questions without pre-determining the solution.
5. A list of selected reading on the subject may be given for the benefit of the participants.
6. Specialists may also be invited to speak briefly on the subject to all the group members together and to answer questions from them.

7. To ensure that the diverse nature of members is not so pronounced as to come in the way of unity of understanding during the discussion.
8. It should be a good idea to appoint a sub-committee to co-ordinate the final report of the seminar for adoption at the closing session.

Note: Any group of people can participate in a seminar for a considerably longer period without feeling tired than they could attend lectures.

Groupthink – A problem Region

We appreciate that group cohesiveness or inter-personal conformity is good for teamwork and allows smooth sailing in group process. Does this mean that a high level of cohesiveness among the group members would lead to wise or effective decisions? On closer examination, it may be seen that unanimity of views was reached because of a conscious effort to suppress dissent. Put simply, fear of harming good relationship or a desire to prevent conflict or confrontation induces a member to agree, as it is said, on the dotted line. Irving L. Janis, the social psychologist, termed this as "groupthink".

Janis defines groupthink as "A deterioration of mental efficiency, reality testing and moral judgment that result from in-group pressures".

The Causes

Groupthink is strengthened by a process of internal feedback from each person's thinking pattern. The feedback rings a kind of an alarm bell prompting a state of deliberate self-censorship. Members exercise self-censorship as they keep their opinions and oppositions about proposals to themselves and adopt themselves to group decisions. Here are some of the most common personalities that we come across in group performance. They can be easily identified as –

(1) The Indiscriminate Agreer.
(2) The Inarticulate talker.
(3) The Silent One.

To be precise, the indiscriminate agreer is a nice person who agrees wholeheartedly with any plan or suggestion, no matter how good or bad it may be. On the other hand, the inarticulate talker is one who has good ideas but is unable to express clearly and fully. The dominant members of the group will easily stifle such views and their effort to speak. The silent ones just refuse to talk. Mostly they remain silent because they fear that any opposition on their part might bring them some kind of rebuke from the group and labeled as "uncooperative". All these three sets of people constantly suffer from fear of reprisals and feel being warned by such things as "Don't make trouble for the group", "When everyone agrees, why you can't" or "you are either with us or against us".

In such situations, members are more concerned about retaining good relationships and rarely like to critically evaluate the opinions and recommendations of other persons. This creates barriers or obstacles to generating creative ideas and better solutions to problems from surfacing. One can find plenty of examples of consensus decisions and recommendations ending up as disastrous fiascos.

Experience tells us that groupthink occurs commonly in organsiational as well as in academic groups. Here are some of the telltale signs which can help us to identify the existence of groupthink in group activities.

- Evidence of direct pressure from the majority on other members and stereotyping of dissenting members "stupid", "incompetent" etc.
- Some members tend to adopt self-censorship, never disclosing their doubts and reservations.
- Any negative viewpoint or feedback goes unheeded while the dominant members provide strange reasoning to justify their actions and recommendations.
- Deliberate and visible effort to prevent members from examining the possible risks associated with their decisions.
- Careless or unmindful assessment of options to face problem situations.
- Silence on the part of a few members treated as total assent, leading to an illusion of unanimity.

Striving against Groupthink

Based on available evidence we may conclude that all groups are vulnerable to groupthink. Although a little of some traces of this phenomenon can be acceptable, a high degree of groupthink must be controlled for potentially adverse consequences.

Managing groupthink requires a series of systematic measures as below:

- The chairperson has to encourage members for critical evaluation and influence them to raise objections and doubts as part of group activity.
- One or more other people who are not members of the group may be inducted as observers. They should have a right to challenge views or recommendations labeled as common agreements but, in reality, are results of groupthink.
- The organisers of the group event, particularly on issue of utmost importance with wider consequences, should devote considerable energy for examining all aspects of such problems and not to be guided by constraints of time or sectarian compulsions.
- Inviting some members to assume the role of "devil's advocate", a very few of them asking searching questions challenging ideas and decisions.
- It's not a bad idea to encourage conflict and dissension whenever there is any possibility of groupthink during group discussions.

- Developing systematic approach for dispassionate analysis and evaluation of each suggestion and recommendation.

Unfortunately, many organisations in India are till now unaware of the existence of groupthink and thus all group activities are pervaded by a desire for consensus. As a result, what they get is neither consensus nor good judgment but a mix of "caucus mentality" in group functions. Earlier the folly is removed, the better for organisations and also the better for purposeful group activities.

SUMMARY

Group Dynamics and Group Communication is interdependent in organsiational environment. The concept of a group is largely abstract. Abraham Maslow's "Hierarchy of Needs" Theory applies to fulfillment of human desires and aspirarations while working in groups as well.

Group Characteristics are defined in eight categories which lead to a proper understanding of formation of groups. However, a few attitudinal changes are necessary for the management of the group in team-based organisations. Also necessary is to understand the problems which create barriers in the group process. The most difficult problem is the 'hostility barrier' in group communication activity. Therefore, corrective actions are necessary while working in groups. 'In-group and Intergroup' differences have to be resolved. Training and practice are known to be as constant tools for effective communication and successful group operations.

Organised group activities followed by the seminar methods is of great help in conducting joint sessions for several groups in order to find solutions to problems. A few organised steps have to be followed without being too rigid about procedural formalities. However, follow the checklist for success and good results in such activities.

A problem region is the existence of 'groupthink' and the organisers and the group members should understand the causes of its development and existence. By and large, all groups are vulnerable to groupthink. A little of it may be acceptable but a high degree of groupthink must be controlled for potentially adverse consequences.

KEY TERMS

1. ***Abstract*** : ***Not a concrete object.***
2. ***Apathy*** : ***Lack of interest; indifferent.***
3. ***Caucus Mentality*** : ***Adhering to an exclusive circle or clique.***
4. ***Cohesiveness*** : ***Be logical and consistent.***
5. ***Cynicism*** : ***Pessimistic view of human nature and motives.***
6. ***Fiasco*** : ***Ludicrous or humiliating failure.***
7. ***Grapevine*** : ***The means of transmission of rumour.***
8. ***Hierarchy*** : ***System of grades of status or authority ranked one above another.***
9. ***Holistic*** : ***Theory that certain wholes are greater than the sum of their parts, total and unbroken.***

10.	***Interpersonal***	: ***Between person and person.***
11.	***Mainspring***	: ***Chief motivating force.***
12.	***Sectarian***	: ***Narrow mindedness, sticking to own sect or belief.***
13.	***Self – esteem***	: ***Good opinion of oneself.***
14.	***Self – realization***	: ***Fulfillment of one's dreams and ambitions.***
15.	***Stereotyping***	: ***Conforming to a type, idea or attitude.***

Concept Review Questions

1. Discuss how Abraham Maslow's theory of Hierarchy of Needs should be applicable to group identity and in the fulfillment of the needs and aspirations of group members.
2. What are the essential characteristics of groups in organisations? Why groups are required to be formed particularly in team-based organisations?
3. How certain barriers in group activity create obstacles in the process of good communication? What are your suggestions to overcome such difficulties?
4. Do you feel that organising seminars are helpful methods to identify problems and to find solutions? Provide a checklist for success and failure in these activities.
5. Explain the term 'groupthink'. Do you feel that groupthink is an impediment towards successful group functioning? Why? How you propose to come out of such situation to ensure purposeful group activity?

REFERENCES

Adair, John **The Skills of Leadership: The Effective Communicator** *Jaico, Mumbai 2002.*

Cole, Kris **Crystal Clear Communication** *Easter West Book 2011.*

Eyer, EC **Effective Communication Made Simple**, *Rupa (New Delhi).*

Maslow, Abraham **Motivation and Personality** *Harper & Row, New York, (1985).*

Peters, Tom and Robert H. Waterman, **In Search of Excellence** *Warner Books, New York, (1982).*

Schram, Wilbur and William E. Porter, **Men, Women, Messages and Media Understanding Human Communication** *Harper & Row, New York (1982).*

Sengupta, Sailesh **Business and Managerial Communication** *PHI Learning Private Ltd, New Delhi (2011).*

Janis, I.L, **Groupthink, Psychology, Today** *Goodyear, California (1977).*

Janis, I.L., **Victims of Groupthink**, *Houghton – Mifflin, Boston (1972).*

Xander, Alvin, **Making Groups Effective** *Jossey-Bass, San Francisco (1982).*

Economic Times, *Best Companies to work for 2009, Study by the Economic Times, Mumbai / New Delhi.*

II

The Skilled Helper Communicating and Finding Solutions to Problems

LEARNING OBJECTIVES

This chapter enables the reader to know more about the scope or range of communication ideas in following areas:

1. How communication extends useful insight into problem situations.
2. The 'Communicating Star' by John Adair defines the aims fulfillment process.
3. Control Cycle of Effective Communication together with full knowledge of skill areas are useful tools for achieving success.
4. How to analyse problem situations with explanations for information and guidance.
5. Improving communication skills with suggestions for improvement.

Communication in case studies

Communication, either interactional or transactional or both, is a powerful instrument to influence human behavior. Interaction is the exchanging of messages that occurs among people involved in the communication process. Transaction, on the other hand, views communication between people as a sharing event. In simple words, communication is a state of common understanding and the art of being understood.

Communication, however, particularly in problem situations is not just instructing people about what to do and how to do it. They have to determine the goals and rationale of activities jointly and in unison. Simply put, make it entirely participative. Involvement and participation in the decision making process leads to commitment to full effort and that is what effective communication is all about.

The Communicating Star

We may recall John Adair's well known principles of the communicating star in any case process.

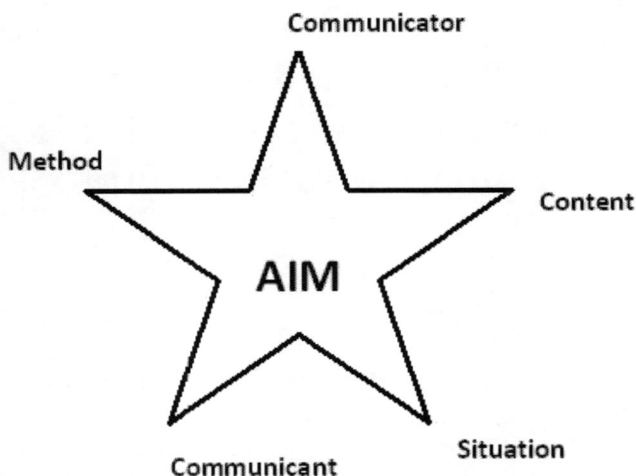

Communicating Star by John Adair

The core point in the graphical presentation is the "AIM" of the communicator. In fact, problems arise when communicators face obstruction in reaching the desired solution. We may, therefore, assume –

AIM	=	**Something we need to achieve**
OBSTRUCTION	=	**Anything that comes in the way of achieving the goals.**
AIM + OBSTRUCTION	=	**PROBLEM**

In this process, we need to know the various stages of problem solving and how the method of case studies is appropriate as a tool.

Problems and Pitfalls

In human society communication is spontaneous, simple everyday phenomenon. In case sessions it is purposeful and organised system intended to achieve specific objectives.

Communicating with each other for finding solutions to problem.

Analysing problem situations and guidance help learners in academic areas.

Organisers and the group members, jointly and severally, will seek to bring about a change in attitudes that will result in the development of favourable or realistic opinion towards the issues of common concern.

The purpose of such communication is to motivate people to –

ACT
CHANGE
ADAPT (adjust, fit)
ACHIEVE (desired results)

Note:

(1) On many occasions communication takes place but not effective communication.
(2) In case studies use of communication is to inform and persuade.
(3) Through right kind of information case discussions will remove misconceptions and achieve better understanding.

The control cycle of "Person to Person Effective Communication" is eminently suitable and applicable.

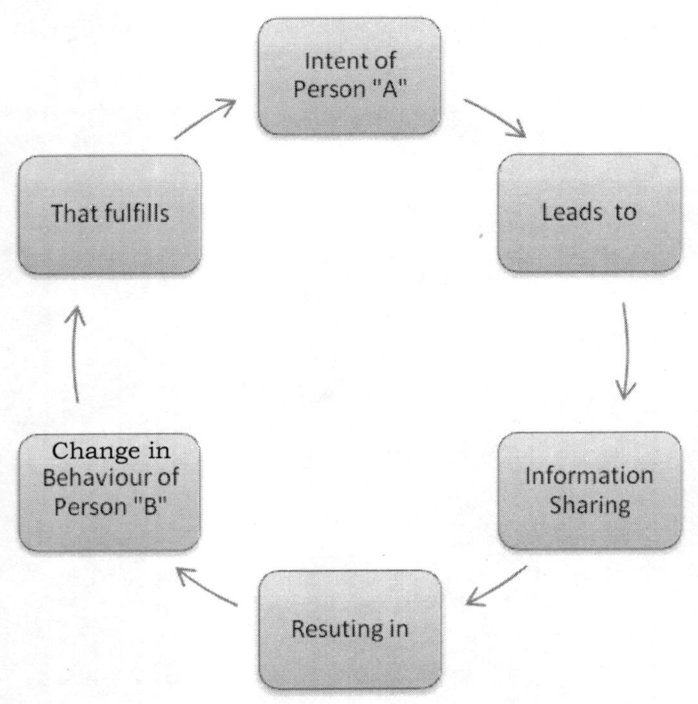

Causing influence attempt
(Change by stimulus)

Control Cycle Of Effective Communication

Peter Drucker felt that the "Recipient is more important" in any communication situation. He had added, "People with more information or with better access to information are accumulating more power, which is reflected in economic power".

On the other hand, Marshall McLuchan, the Canadian Communication Scholar, was of the firm belief that, in the last count, "medium is the message". In case situations, a case is the medium through which, step by step, we are able to perform the problem solving functions. And, eventually, the group achieves decision making abilities.

Five Styles Of Communication

In group activities for case deliberations, five specific styles of communication are noticeable. These are –

1. Instructional	:	One way communication.
2. Informative	:	One way.
3. Consultative	:	Two way (both upward and downward) but blind and hidden obstructions in the mind of the communicator.
4. Involving	:	Both bottom up and two way with mild appreciation but without firm commitment towards effective action.
5. Participative	:	Two way with the guarantee that the voice of everyone is heard and acted upon.

The participative process is the skilled helper and friend having a vision to reap the benefits of the team spirit. In management situations experts have cited examples of how building a team spirit leads to improved production, higher productivity, employee motivation, customer satisfaction and business reputation.

Every case session, whether in organisations or as a part of an academic activity, has to have a vision. Sharing of a common vision enables the participants to learn, self–regulate and run its activities successfully, instead of being dominated by one voice at the top.

Becoming Proficient

Communication skills are not special skills particular to case studies. They are extensions of the kind of skills we all use in our everyday interpersonal functions. Essentially, communication skills are not ends in themselves. In case-situations these are means or tools to be used in achieving desired results.

Skill Areas

At least five important skill areas can be developed through case studies.

1. **Analytical Thinking**
   Effective problem solving requires a high degree of ability for analytical thinking. One learns to classify, organise and evaluate all the information relating to the case. As is widely known, left-brain thinking is logical and analytical whereas right brain is concerned with emotional feelings. To be a good problem solver a person has to be able to switch from one side of the brain to the other side as well as back again.
2. **Creative Thinking**
   This skill is more useful as a decision making process. A creative approach leads one to apply intuition and imagination in preference to analytical approach. A good problem solver must however know how and when to apply creative and analytical skills. Thus effective case discussions require a judicious mixture of analytical and creative thinking.
3. **Communication Skills**
   Case studies provide unique opportunities to develop written, verbal and non-verbal communication skills. By writing well constructed reports, analyses and by face-to-face discussions these skills are developed and matured.
4. **Social processes**
   Case studies are an essential component of social and inter-personal processes. One gets to learn social skills, listen, support, argue, and control oneself as a part of an organised activity. Not just a problem solving function, cases train people more about human behavior in social, organsiational and academic situations,
5. **Self– assessment Skills**
   A case is an excellent step towards self-improvement. One is able to project oneself into particular situations and analyse the situation with reference to self. One must be entirely committed to the task and should be able to impartially assess own thinking, action and decisions.

Analysing Case Situation

Case analysis offers unique learning situations. Such activities provide excellent opportunities. For the learners and participants to consider, discuss and perform. Apart from wide exposures, case analyses are useful in illustrating theoretical concepts. They offer experience and exposure to tackling issues applied to a good variety of "live situations".

We may consider a twelve-step process for analyzing case situations. There is no uniquely right formula for such steps, some steps may be ignored or rejected and some new may be applied according to particular exigencies or situations. But overall objectives and approaches remain more or less constant.

The twelve –step process for analysis:-

1. Study the case. Highlight the issues.
2. Study the tables and figures.
3. Pinpoint the challenges & Recommendations needed.
4. Identify applicable tools.
5. Determine factors of the problem.
6. Reread the case. Do preliminary analysis.
7. Gather more information. Make deep analysis.
8. Prepare notes. Maintain record. Write report.
9. Consult. Test interpretations.
10. Develop set of results. Present results.
11. Cultivate wise, prudent, reasonable approach.
12. Examine how to apply learning in future analysis.

Explanations

(1) Study the case thoroughly and get a quick feel for issues raised. Highlight the most noteworthy points.

(2) Never minimize the importance of case figures and tables. It's a grave mistake if you do so. Study the tables and figures together with the case details.

(3) Pinpoint the challenges faced and determine the nature of recommendations required.

(4) Identify the most useful and applicable tools for analysis and decision making purposes

(5) Determine factors of the problem. Factors may be subtopics of the hypotheses or supposition.

(6) Reread the case, examine the suitability of applying the tools and get into the process of initial analysis of the case.

(7) Focus on the issues highlighted. Make deep analysis of the problems of the case. Gather additional information relating to the case. Cultivate a critical point of view.

(8) Prepare notes. Maintain record, write crisp report and contribute to a lively case discussion.

(9) Maintain a judicial attitude. Consult with others. Testing interpretations is a vital part of the case analysis.

(10) Develop a set of results from the analysis made. Present your results in concise, effective and inter-active style.

(11) Wise, prudent and reasonable approach make case discussions interesting and arresting. Never allow any bias in interpretations. Keep an open mind all through the case stages.

(12) Examine how to apply your learning in subsequent analysis.

Improving Communication Skills

1. **Good knowledge and useful ideas**

   Note: Skill in communication has no use unless one has important ideas. Important ideas have no use unless communicated.

2. **Intellectual Honesty**
The content of the communication should be believable and trustworthy. Communicator has to establish credibility and confidence.
3. **Remove barriers to communication**
Barriers refer to all difficulties in transmission of information, organsiational barriers, unqualified assumption, personal barriers as well as language Imperfections.
4. **Never try to defend own ego** by defending what you have said. No shame in acknowledging ignorance or lack of knowledge. And, control natural ego-building tendencies.
5. Develop **listening skills.** Try to understand what the speaker intends to convey even beyond the words used. Understand non-verbal or non-word communication signs or symbols.
6. Do not **presume, ask questions** to clarify ideas or concepts.
7. **Concentrate on problems** rather than on personalities and their way of expressions.
8. **Recognize, in group functions, disagreements are quite normal.** Although the objective is to reach a consensus or unanimity of views, alternative ideas should be encouraged and dispassionately assessed.
9. **Make the other person feel more important, even better,**
10. When **talking pause more frequently and more often to think .**

Suggestion For More Improvement

1. All communication events must be related to socio-cultural and economic environment.
2. Make communication receiver centered.
3. Do not try to achieve too much in a hurry.
4. Learn patiently, and step by step, how to interact, improve relations and achieve effective communication.
5. Try to appreciate that the participants, employees or learners have problems, expectations and values which may not be compatible with the organiser's objectives.
6. Tone of voice will matter in face-to-face communication.
7. Message or information not to be distorted.
8. Respond to the feedback and review progress.
9. Be direct ———————— as if listeners are more important.

Golden Rule: Communicate as you would like to be communicated to.

Example:

Communication Relationship Satisfaction (CRS)

CRS is now known to be an umbrella concept to fulfill the employees' needs from an altogether different standpoint. The value of communication is well-recognised by both the management and the employees in any organisation. But how far such communication, whatever way it is pursued or practised, is able to achieve the relationship satisfaction among the employees.

In a survey conducted by the Indian Institute of Management, Ahmadabad among 292 executives in different organisations, it was found that the employees do have some different perspectives on the issue. The employees appeared to give more importance to communication from the top management and their immediate supervisors than just general kind of communication from the organisation in the form of circulars, notice, instructions etc. Such communication was found to be like un-motivating information which could never create any kind of Communication Relationship Satisfaction (CRS).

A number of IIM studies have verified the importance of communication and its effects on job performance, job satisfaction and organsiational commitment. Moreover, effective communication within the organisations is also considered a source of strategic competitive advantage. Employees strongly feel that a healthy environment of communication is also characterized by open discussions, group exercises and also debates on issues related to work and workplaces. Employees also believe that rather than outside sources, the organisations management, supervisors and their own colleagues are much more trustworthy factors for ensuring communication satisfaction.

Finally, it emerges that employees assess their satisfaction level for communication on four different forms. These are

1. With supervisors
2. With colleagues
3. With top management
4. With the organisation as a whole.

(*Source: IIM* (*Ahmedabad*) *Survey*)

Concept Development Questions

1. Do you feel that communication is the most primary factor in case situations? Discuss how communication plays its part in analysing cases and finding solutions to problems.
2. Make a graphical presentation of control cycle of communication explaining all its components. Specify the five styles of communication and explain their role.
3. How at least five skill areas can be developed through case study processes? Do you feel one's thinking, actions and decisions can be largely influenced by owing these skills? Explain how.
4. List out the twelve steps that are usually put to use for analysing case situations. How these are useful for finding solutions to problems and for gaining benefits?

5. Provide some of the ways to improve communication skills and what are your suggestions for improvement?

Summary

Communication, interactional and transactional, separately or together, is a powerful instrument to influence behavior of group members. It's not an instructional tool but members must work together jointly and in unison. The "communicating star" by John Adair leads them to problem solving process more convincingly.

There are problems and pitfalls no doubt, but for case solving and for finding solutions they must continue to communicate and persuade others. The control cycle, of 'Person to Person Effective Communication' system is eminently suitable and highly applicable. One must, however, know about the five styles of communication in all case deliberations. Based on such styles, the participants have to learn, self-regulate and conduct their activities in achieving desired results.

It has been proved that at least five important skill areas can be developed through the process of case studies. Case analysis provides unique opportunities for learning as well as practising. This way theoretical concepts get into practical exposures. There are at least twelve steps for appropriate case situations. While in the process, some steps may be applied and some may be ignored according to needs and requirements. But overall objectives remain constant and unchangeable. Quite a few explanations relating to all steps are provided which should be studied for effective use and good results.

Another area of concern is guiding group members to improve their communication skills. The checklists of such skills are provided with explanations but all these need constant practice and careful application. Additionally, a set of suggestions are given for more improvement in skill development. The golden rule for all communicators, irrespective of status and knowledge should be: Communicate as you would like to be communicated to.

Key Terms

Analytical : *Detailed Examination of elements or structure of particular case situations.*

Compatible : *Consistent and able to co-exist.*

Consultative : *Provide professional guidance or fruitful advice.*

Credibility : *Believable or worthy of belief.*

Crisp : *Lively, brisk and decisive.*

Ego : *Part of the mind that has self-awareness and self-esteem.*

Hypothesis : *Proposition or supposition as the basis for reasoning or investigation.*

Imperfections : *State of being imperfect.*

Instructional	:	*Order and direction as to how something has to be done.*
Intuition	:	*Immediate insight or understanding without conscious reasoning.*
Judicious	:	*Sensible and prudent.*
Misconception	:	*Have a wrong idea or conception.*
Motivation	:	*Inducement or incentives that stimulate the interest.*
Participative	:	*Taking part or share as an equal partner.*
Productivity	:	*Capacity to produce, efficiency and also ratio between input and output.*
Proficient	:	*Adept and expert.*
Prudent	:	*Sound in judgment.*

References

Adair, John, ***Training for Communicators****, Jaico, Mumbai, 2002.*

Barker, Larry L, ***Communication*** *Prentice Hall, New Jersey, 1991.*

Drummond, H., ***Managing Difficult Staff: Effective Procedures and the Law****, Kogan Page, London 1990.*

Drucker, Peter, ***the Practice of Management****, Pan Books Ltd., London, 1975.*

Goldhaber, G.M., ***Organsiational Communication*** *Brown and Benchmark, CA, USA, 1991.*

Lane, L. Leroy, ***By All Means Communicate*** *Prentice Hall, New Jersey, 1991.*

Sengupta, Sailesh, ***Management of Public Relations and Communication****, Vikas Publishing House, New Delhi, 2007.*

Journal of Creative Communication, Vol 2 & No.3*, Sept-Dec 2007, Sage Publication, New Delhi.*

Vikalpa: The Journal For Decision Makers *Indian Institute of Management, Ahmedabad July – September 2010.*

III

Preparing for Brain Storming

LEARNING OBJECTIVES

Key areas of learning for this chapter are:

1. How planning and preparation can enhance the value of a group's performance.
2. The purpose and the process of a successful group activity are spelt out in detail through three sets of checklists.
3. The value of setting a standard agenda.
4. The format of a standard step-by-step agenda.
5. How application will involve proper simulation with real benefits of simulation to achieve good success.

Advance planning and preparation can do much to enhance the value of a group's performance. One of the oldest formulas for group problem-solving tasks is John Marston's R-A-C-E-formula, an acronym for Research, Action, Communication and Evaluation (John E. Marston in "The Nature of Public Relations"). The concept is also found in Scott M. Cutlip and Allen Center's "Effective Public Relations". It says: find the facts, establish a policy and / or plan a program, communicate the story, and get feedback from internal and external publics to help determine modifications or future planning.

At any rate, if participants in a group activity have the required knowledge and skills, they can very well achieve productive small-group communication. The aggregate views of such persons should however,

Planning and preparation enhance value of group's performance.

promote face-to-face interactions, based on shared values, expectations and rules, directed towards common goals.

Initial Checklist

While preparing for a case discussion, the organisers and the members must keep its purpose clearly in mind. Primarily these are:

1. Obtaining information and opinions about a subject of common interest, clarifying misunderstanding, sharing of ideas and getting an intended job done, thus ensuring participation in making decisions;
2. Conveying facts and information to members attending the meeting and purposefully to many others who are equally concerned with the subject;
3. Inducing change in behavior and attitudes and also providing opportunities for magnifying the personalities involved in the group activity;
4. Studying specific polices and problems, finding solutions, giving new insight and new experiences and determining ways of implementation of particular decisions.

Checklist Second

The organisers, most essentially, must never forget the basic needs that provide for a democratic forum for discussion which are:

1. Decide about the purpose and the objective of the meeting well in advance.
2. Ensure physical arrangements in accordance with the number of persons attending the meeting. The environment should be clean, attractive and appealing.
3. Decide about the size and composition of the group. In small groups, seating arrangements should preferably be U-shaped so that members are able to face each other. In joint sessions, when several groups meet together for presentations, the layout for the meeting should be planned carefully along with sound and acoustics.
4. Start meeting on time.
5. Ensure that time is not wasted on unneeded and unimportant items.
6. Meetings should not continue endlessly. It Is better to fix the duration of the meeting beforehand along with its time and date.
7. Look into the need for audio-visual aids and ensuring their effective presentation.
8. Be sure that the meeting runs smoothly because the chairperson knows for certain how to conduct a meeting.

Checklist Third

- As we say, a group without a leader is like a ship without a captain. Similarly, a meeting without a competent chairperson will land up in a whirlpool of stalemate and end up in confusion and conflict.

- It is of utmost importance that the chairperson, as the leader of the discussion group, makes constant check and double-checks on his own performance as well as about the performance of others.
- Have you or the organisers have given sufficient lead time for preparation to all persons concerned with the meeting?
- Are there a good agenda and supporting papers for the meeting prepared and distributed well in time.
- Do you understand fully the ingredients of an effective communication plan?
- In an organsiational situation, do you know the facts and figures about economics of the business and industry like wages, salary, profits, losses, grievances, investments, manhours, productivity, prices, competitions, social responsibilities and similar other vital topics of everyday interest?
- What steps have you taken or intend to initiate to curtail or to minimise the possible existence of communication barriers within the group?
  — Do you try to reach the level of the participants and talk in a language which is understandable to them?
  — Do you adopt action method of "learning by doing" and ensure smooth flow of two-way communication?
  — Do you throw up your hands in despair if there is no response from the group members? Isn't it your responsibility to create interest in them?
  — Do you know the intellectual level, the background and particular needs of individual members as well as of the group itself?
  — Do you mould the material, the agenda and the subject of discussion in such a way that they suit the knowledge, interests and the requirements of the group members?
- Do you summarise the points raised, discussed and decisions taken at appropriate times and at the end of the meeting?

  We may refer to the views of Cartwright and Zander about the traits of leaders which continue to hold good as always. "A 'new view' of leadership is emerging which stresses the performance of needed functions and adaptability to change situation .... Effective leaders are sensitive to the changing conditions of their groups and flexible in adapting their behavior to new requirements"

  — As a leader or as a chairperson do you identify the acts of leadership in the same way?

The Agenda

Good planning and preparation results in a workable agenda. An agenda establishes an orderly approach to the subject by breaking it down into a series of sub topics or steps that lead to conclusion. In simple terms, though, it is like a lesson plan which a good teacher prepares to facilitate perfect learning on the part of the students. The teacher has to plan in advance, methodically and logically, the whole teaching at a time. Unless there is an agenda for a meeting or a lesson plan for a teacher, the whole exercise is incomplete and ineffective.

Setting a Good Agenda

A good agenda, by form and content, is a plan or procedure the group agrees to follow. The speed and the quality of decision making can both be ensured and improved with the application of a planned agenda.

A few special steps towards preparing a useful agenda are offered below:

- Take the initiative before the meeting to plan an outline for the group to follow. But never be defensive or possessive about one plan. The agenda should be a group plan, not just one to be imposed on the group.
- An agenda will say clearly (i) what are the issues to be dealt with and why (ii) what contribution is expected from the members and (iii) exact objectives to be achieved through the process of discussion.
- A good agenda will ensure that no item is overlooked or left out in the process of discussion.
- Allows reasonable time to think about the items beforehand and gives confidence to organisers, chairperson and members.
- Delimits the field of discussions, keeps the discussion going ahead in easy steps and at the right speed.
- Motivates the participants to contribute and arouses their interest in the topics of discussion, familiar or unfamiliar whatever may be.
- Stimulates increased understanding and results in better decision-making.
- On the whole, however, a group meeting is a human activity and not a mechanical process. Therefore, it is rightly said that no agenda should ever be cast in concrete. Any adopted agenda should be periodically reviewed and strict rigidity about it may not help. The plan may have to be modified according to the trend of the discussion. Many related and unrelated questions may crop up while discussing an issue or a problem, and here the group as a whole must use its particular resourcefulness.

  Once the agenda is developed, the chairperson and the organisers (in company situations it's Co. Secretary) must make certain that all members receive copy of the agenda in time. This will allow reasonable time to think about the items beforehand and gives confidence to organisers, chairpersons and members.

Planning a Standard Agenda

Depending on particular circumstances, a wide range of standard forms of agenda can be used.

The three most known formats are —

(1) A problem – solving agenda

(2) A decision - making agenda

(3) A task agenda

Working with a clearly defined problem, a problem-solving agenda may be found appropriate. A decision-making agenda, among other things, will evaluate alternative decisions in terms of criteria and for taking actions designated by the group. A task agenda involves decisions that pertain to implementation of procedures, collecting inputs as well as analysing or interpreting information.

All the different kinds of agenda have distinct similarities and, therefore, a group can as well set its own agenda needed for the particular task or activity. Keeping in view the specific needs at different times, the format of a standard step-by-step agenda is given below.

(1) Defining the problem (Creating awareness, clarifies goal, establishes agenda and climate)

- Introduction by the chairperson who opens the discussion.
- Members become aware of the importance of the problem.
- Examine the nature and effects of the problem.
- What is the specific goal? Brainstorming.
- Ensuring participation by each member.
- What are the individual member attitudes towards the problem and individual as well as collective perception?

(2) Clear Statement of Problem (Understanding the Problem and Logical steps to state it clearly).

- **Stating the problem** in writing is good.
- **The problem statement:** May be (a) an infinitive statement (b) a question (c) a declarative statement or (d) a combination of all.
- **An infinitive statement:** "The purpose of the case discussion is to identify the causes of decline in demand for product X".
- **Question:** What are the exact reasons behind the declining sales of product X?
- **Declarative Statement:** Demand and sales of product are fast decreasing, and management wants to know why".
- **Review the present situation** related to the problem
  - — Current policies and strategies,
  - — Who are all involved or affected,
  - — Action so far taken to solve the problem,
- **How serious is the situation?**

(3) Analysing the problem (Look for the factors of the problem and applying the best logic to the problem).

- Why did the problem develop?
- What specific factors have prevented the solution?
- Seek possible explanations or solutions (hypotheses)
- Once hypotheses are determined, they are tested.
- Then they are related to the problem.
- Recognition of constraints in achieving success.

(4) Evaluating the proposed solutions (group suggests many possible solutions)

- Desirable features of each solution
- Strengths and weaknesses of the group solution.
- Identifying past events that contributed to the problem.
- Will the various alternatives work?
- Establish areas of agreement between members
- At least reach a mutual understanding and, if necessary, goals can be adjusted.

(5) Selecting the best possible solutions (Selecting the best and most acceptable solution – which does not create other problems).

- Think of possible explanations to the problem.
- Study, weigh, and select.
- Test each hypothesis.
- Advance additional hypotheses for further evaluation.
- Choose the best by means of resolving disagreements.
- Reach conclusions by unanimity of views.

(6) Implementing the Chosen Solution (deciding on steps for implementation)

- Are there obstacles to implementation?
- Can the obstacles be removed without causing any pains or disruption?
- How the solutions to the problem can be put into effect.
- What approaches to implementation should be the best.
- Who should be given responsibility for actions to the solutions?
- Examine the needs to meet after a specified period to determine the results of implementation.
  — How far the conclusions and recommendations were justified and to what extent simulation was instrumental raising the standard of performance.

Application

Simulation can be used in a variety of ways, rather than a simple case study or an organised group activity. A few of the uses can be in:

- **Leadership Development:**
  Leadership comes more in limelight in the event of an unexpected, untoward happening and much more in a chaotic situation. It is a test case as to how the leadership can turn the calamity into opportunity – a turning point for the better. Leadership training in

simulation roles can be varied as accidents, tragedy, and environment, industrial unrest to product or service launch, stock market crash, operational problems and so on. The list is endless.

- **Problem Solving:**
  May not be restricted to industry and business organisations as problems and crises are part of everyday process for individuals as well as groups. As it is said, every organisation, commercial or non-commercial, has the potential devil of a crisis and the situational role brings all risks into focus. The members will be asked to play and enact the role situations in each territory as well as in the territory of the opponents.
- **Skill Practice:**
  Can range from the most simple to the highly complex and can be connected to people and organisations to applied professional skills. The world of computer technology has worked wonders in a wide variety of analytical techniques. Indeed all of the inter-relationships between men, machine, money, material and information fall within given environmental constraints. In a few minutes of computer time, professionals can experiment with numerous changes in programmes, strategies, schedules and operations.

The Real Benefit

The great benefit of simulation in real situation is that the consequences of various courses of action may be examined before an actual decision is made.

Simulation is an extremely useful weapon in attacking problems whose elements are so vast and interactions so complex that they exceed the capabilities of normal human judgement

Correctly applied, although complex and difficult, successful simulations can produce learning rewards unobtainable by any other approach.

EXAMPLE:

How bad decisions by seniors got reversed by collective brainstorming.

How good leaders make bad decisions or how good companies turn into examples of dismal failures? These are endless issues and many an explanation can be offered. But the fact is that the brains of even the exceptionally intelligent people commit mistakes and blunders. Even though they possess strong logical side of the brain, which is known as the left brain. All of them, may be without exception, also do have exceptional right side qualities of the right brain, known as the emotional sides of the brain. Studies find that human brains jump to conclusions and are disinclined to consider alternative ideas. All of us are particularly prone to be obstinate and try to evade revisiting our original assessment of a situation. What are the ways to come out of such damaging behavior, keeping in mind the organsiational interest?

Let us take the example of Sumex Pharmaceuticals, a billion dollar strong turnover company with corporate headquarters in Mumbai. They have seven regional offices and several thousand executives and employees at factories and marketing offices all over India. The company takes pride in having an elaborate HR department at the HO. and small set ups in the Regional Offices. An internal dispute arose when the No.2 in the HR department left the Company and next person Ankita Bali, a young lady of just 30 years of age was expecting to fill up the position. The senior most HR Head was not agreeable. He started vacillating and consulted the CEO. There was no decision as both wanted to carry on as it was. Let the post remain vacant for some time.

The young lady who was No.3 now was not satisfied. She felt that the HR boss was against her because sometime she had the guts to raise questions or doubts about many an issue. The boss had to agree with her views at the end but he was not very pleased about her open disagreements. Ankita Bali felt that not only that she was eminently suitable but, on the HR hierarchy level others not getting promotion because of her stagnation would suffer.

Ankita Bali had a strong academic mind and she had made personal studies about leadership patterns in organsiational system. She listed out a checklist of blunders committed by bosses not only in her organsiation but elsewhere also. Ankita Bali's Checklist:-

1. Bosses think that they have all the answers to all the problems.
2. They eliminate all those who are not 100% with them.
3. They underestimate major grievances and ignore simmering discontent.
4. They fail to appreciate what rival companies could do to disrupt their operations when they come to know about their troubles.
5. They are unable to spot and safeguard against their own errors in judgment.
6. They do not see that all senior executives in the chain are highly qualified and fully competent in their jobs. Yet the HR head and the CEO are making decisions that are clearly wrong.
7. They must groom and continue to retain talented HR managers and other executives in many other departments. Otherwise they would be tempted to look for job satisfaction by leaving their present jobs.

Armed with her findings and study, Ankita Bali approached the CEO, mainly because her next juniors are going to suffer. CEO gave her a patient listening and agreed for a close group meeting in which the H.R. Head, Ankita herself and her next in line will take part in addition to CEO himself and two Executive Directors who also participate.

The six member team sat together for one hour and went on for a brainstorm collectively. Interestingly the HR Head was very accommodative and the group came to a unanimous decision to fill the No.2 position with Ankita Bali. They also decided that all positions downward would be filled up lifting up about half a dozen seniors and mid-level managers. The CEO felt happy and expressed joy by saying, "we all have done it together".

CONCEPT DEVELOPMENT QUESTIONS

1. Specify how the groups should plan and prepare to enhance the value of a group's performance. In this context, state the essential contents of the checklists for organising the group activity.
2. Why a good agenda is felt so very important for any useful group activity? What are the steps for working out a good agenda and spell out the different components of a good agenda.
3. How do you plan to set a standard agenda and discuss its usefulness? Discuss the format of a standard step-by-step agenda.
4. Discuss the application process of brainstorming in functioning of a group. What are the specific values of simulation activities and how such activities can produce learning rewards in group deliberations?

SUMMARY

Advance planning and preparation go a big way to enhance the value of a group's performance. The essential objective is to achieve a productive small-group communication.

While preparing for a case discussion the purpose of such an activity should be kept in mind. There should be three detailed checklists which are the guidelines for the intended task. These are (*i*) *initial checklist* (*ii*) *checklist second and* (*iii*) *checklist third. The initial checklist provides for obtaining information conveying facts and information to members, inducing change in behavior and attitude and finally finding solutions to problems. Second checklist provides for all details about advance steps towards making the group activity meaningful, smooth and purposeful. The third checklist looks into the aspects of the leadership process, the role and responsibilities of the chairperson and efforts towards minimising all communication barriers within the group.*

Good planning and preparation results in the framing of an effective agenda. The agenda ensures the outline for the group to follow. An agenda therefore must state clearly (*i*) *what are the issues to be discussed and why* (*ii*) *the expectations from the members and also* (*iii*) *the intended objectives to be fulfilled by the group efforts. An agenda therefore, motivates the group members to participate, arouse interest, contribute to collective brainstorming and finally arrive at a decision through problem solving process.*

The organisers of the group activity have to plan out a standard agenda as a step-by-step process to achieve the group objectives. It should contain:

(1) *Defining the exact problem*
(2) *Clear statement of the problem itself by explaining the problem*
(3) *Analyzing the problem*
(4) *Evaluating the range of solutions*
(5) *Selecting the best possible solution*
(6) *Implementing the chosen solution.*

Next comes the Application part for which simulation activities are recommended. It has been proved that simulation is very much useful for attacking the problem from all angles and consideration. Successful group functioning can show the way towards gains and learning rewards which may not be obtainable by any other approach.

KEYS TERMS

Acoustics	:	*Properties or qualities of a room in transmitting sound.*
Acronym	:	*Pronounceable word formed from the first or first few letters e.g. NATO, UNO etc.*
Chaotic	:	*Utter confusion.*
Constraints	:	*Restrict severely; being constrained.*
Declarative	:	*Assert emphatically; Acknowledging possession.*
Format	:	*Arrange or put into a shape.*
Grievance	:	*Cause for complaint.*
Hypothesis	:	*Proposition or suggestion as the basis for reasoning or investigation.*
Infinitive	:	*Causes which may be many or even endless.*
Instrumental	:	*Serving as an instrument or means in performing an action.*
Layout	:	*Way in which a printed matter, a land or building is arranged or set out.*
Mechanical	:	*Automatic, impersonal, unemotional.*
Mould	:	*Make a person or an object in a particular shape or character.*
Possessive	:	*Wanting to retain what one has; reluctance to share.*
Resolving	:	*Make up one's mind; firm decision.*
Simulation	:	*Pretend, imitate, creating imaginary situations.*
Stalemate	:	*Deadlock, no progress.*
Stimulate	:	*Act as a stimulus, animate or excite.*
Untoward	:	*Inconvenient, Awkward and Unseemly.*

REFERENCES

Beck, Robert C, ***Motivation Theories and Principles*** *Pearson Education Delhi (2000).*

Drummond, Helga ***Effective business Communication*** *Wheeler Publishing New Delhi (1993).*

Ludlow, Ron and Fergus Panton ***the Essence of Effective Communication***

Prentice- Hall of India New Delhi (2000).
Robbins, P. Stephen and Seema Sanghi ***Organizational Behaviour*** *Pearson Education New Delhi (2005).*
Scott, Cutlip M. Allen H. Center and Glen M. Broom
Effective Public Relations *Prentice-Hall International, Inc., USA (1985).*
Sengupta, Sailesh ***Business and Managerial Communication*** *PHI Learning Limited New Delhi (2011)*
Harvard Business Review *South Asia January 2010.*
Leadership Excellence *Magazine*
Manvi Publishing Faridabad (Sept 2009).
The Telegraph *Calcutta June 2010.*
Times Trend, Times of India *Jan 25, 2010*
Times Business, Times of India *New Delhi 1st Feb 2010.*

IV

Leadership in Groups Steering the Group Process

LEARNING OBJECTIVES

This Chapter intends to convey the value of good leadership through discussion on following issues:

1. How group meetings are to be organised and conducted.
2. The qualities of a good leader and group's expectations from the leader.
3. Approaches to leadership and pitfalls to avoid.
4. Key leadership functions.
5. The role of the chairperson in a group activity and qualities of leadership of the chairperson.
6. How a chairperson appreciates own responsibilities and the process of checking by the chairperson.

A group meeting, whether it is a small or a large group, should be an orderly process of joint deliberation. It is, therefore, extremely crucial to manage the proceedings in the appropriate manner and organisers should be able to sustain the interest o f the participants. Group discussions fail when objectives are not clear and meetings are dull, too long, and often uninspiring. Hence, organising a successful meeting is a skill in itself.

Meetings are the democratic method of group activity and are required to be organised in the most suitable manner. In practical terms, it is an organised dialogue in which members actively participate and exchange

Group's expectations from the leader are matters requiring brain - storming mutually among the participants.

ideas and views with a purpose. They examine a problem or a concept, raise questions, and make suggestions, present a different point of view, make plans and even determine policy matters. They must, however, finally arrive at a conclusion or at least find a common approach to the issues or the problems. In a good environment, members get encouragement to agree jointly and to shoulder responsibilities to implement the decisions. Thus from one step to another, from one step to the next, the members get opportunities to grow in ability and understanding for better and more harmonicons inter-relations. Here comes the role of leadership in achieving group purposes effectively? Wide agreement exists that leadership makes a difference in groups. But how to provide that leadership is not easily answered.

Group Leadership

In group performance, the most effective leader is one who can steer the group process with a minimum of direction and control. And that too without influencing the opinion of the members in any way. To quote an analogy suggested by Wilbur Schramm, the best groups become "local engines that run on their fuel, as it were, through that social pressure the members themselves generate by interpersonal communication within in the group setting".

Then what does the group leader do? Leadership is essentially an interaction between the leader, the group members, and the situation. Leaders not only influence group members, group members also influence leaders. For instance, a group may reject the leader's advice that it follows certain procedure and influence the leader to modify that suggestion. In autocratic style of leadership, the more dominant chairperson of a group activity might make own decisions and offer directives to inexperienced, unmotivated members. While working with an experienced, motivated group, the same chairperson, almost always, will use more democratic style of leadership.

Lau-Tzu's Oft-repeated quote about directing and manner of leadership attracts notice because of its excellence.

Directing And Manner Of Leadership

A leader is best when people barley know that he exists
Not so good when people obey and acclaim him
Worst when they despise him.
"Fail to honour people
They fail to honour you"
But of a good leader, who talk little,
When his work is done, his aim fulfilled
They will all say, "We did this ourselves"
BY Lao –Tzu
(Sixth Century B.C., Chinese Poet.

Approaches to Leadership

Group leader has to play the role of a facilitator. At the same time group members should also work as facilitators. This implies that the group members must have the ability to perform both the leadership and membership roles. Therefore, the functions of leadership are needed to be distributed throughout the group. It is neither feasible nor desirable that one person perform all the leadership functions. The most ideal leadership pattern is one that of "shared leadership".

A few cautions steps would be appropriate. Some of these are:

(1) Group composition must be balanced.
(2) Identify members with non-appropriate styles.
(3) Pinpoint (indirectly) members with superfluous strengths.
(4) Drop them (provided you are in a position to handle the task smoothly).
(5) Addition of members with adequate balancing profile may be made.

Leadership Process: Pitfalls to avoid.

We may refer to certain pitfalls given by Winston S. Churchill which are known as simple and commonplace axioms. These are:

(1) Don't look too far ahead: It is a mistake to look too far ahead. Exercise restraint in looking too far ahead.

(2) No excessive perfectionism: It breeds timidity. Churchill was fond of repeatedly saying, "Do not let the better be the enemy of the good".

(3) Never go for Decisions for Decision sake or Action for Action's sake: Many times a good leader has to be a fierce critic of perfectionism. Sometime decisions may have to be deferred. Fluid situations might present new facts. Sometimes it is wise to do nothing. Keep open to changing your mind in the presence of new facts.

Lessons to Learn

- We must learn from misfortune.
- Learning from disasters.
- Calmness under stress.
- Concentrate on the broad view.
- Know the art of independent judgment.
- Appreciate the value of self-criticism.
- Ability to face bad situation squarely.
- Above all, understand and make honest display of loyalty to the team, loyalty as a team leader.

Observations: Pains and Pleasures

Member satisfaction is the most important element in group decision making. Admittedly, a one-to-one relationship between leadership style and members' satisfaction may not exist, they are interrelated. Both in turn relate to the nature of the group task.

Many performing organisations have noted that member satisfaction is at its peak when members feel that:

(1) They have contributed handsomely to establishment and accomplishment of group tasks.

(2) They have good control over their own attitudes and behavior in achieving those tasks and objectives.

An extensive analysis of group member satisfaction in business and industry is given by Rensis Likert's in "The Human Organisation: Its Management and Value (McGraw-Hill)".Likert's research proves that good leadership and participative style of management, results in enhanced worker satisfaction as well as increased productivity. Understandably, increased productivity results from higher levels of satisfaction.

But, then, organisations are known to be systems of interlocking groups. No doubt, through these interlocking groups the goals of organisations are achieved. Experience shows us the presence of certain limitations even in democratic approach in group functions. These are –

- Groups are marked by a lot of power politics, attitude of indifference, hostility, non-task performance, in-group fighting.
- Evidence proves that most of the Indian managers are individually outstanding performers but collectively so many of them are dismal failures.
- Working in groups may not necessarily be a source of pleasure.
- Group efforts may not always be superior to individual efforts.

At the extreme, there may exist certain personal behavior which impede effective group functioning. Some of these are:

(a) Withdrawing: Members sitting tight-lip for the fear of being ridiculed or being non-cooperative.

(b) Competition: Trying to overdo all others, wanting to win.

(c) Win-Lose Struggle: Suppression of the timid and the weak by the stronger side.

(d) Scapegoating: Trying to find fault at every step, passing on the buck, putting on others or even clowning, disrupting.

Key Leadership Functions

The communication skills, naturally, occupy an important place in any kind of leadership functions. An effective leader not only helps group communication but also helps cross communication within the group. However, there are a host of administrative and specific leadership duties which a successful chairperson has to perform. These are broadly as under:

Key Leadership Functions:

- **Planning**
- **Initiating**
- **Controlling**

- **Supporting**
- **Informing**
- **Evaluating**

NOTE: Functional approach indicates interaction between leader, group members and the situation.

The broad-based leadership functions are briefly enumerated in tables as under:

PLANNING	INITIATING
• Thinking and Spade work • What do you want to achieve • Prepare an action plan • Analysis of gathered inputs • Allocating tasks	• Why need a group activity • Seek available information • Systematic approach to group response. • Briefing groups on the aims • Setting group standards
CONTROLLING	**INFORMING**
• Ensure satisfactory arrangements • Maintaining emphasis on issues • Blocking irrelevant digressions • Clarifying ideas, viewpoints • Restating useful ideas	• Proceed according to agenda • Preventing dominance by a few • Provide needed data, opinions • Offering examples and illustrations • Offering new perspective on a problem
SUPPORTING	**EVALUATING**
• Creating team spirit • Give credit where due • Reliving tension with humor • Examining implications of recommendations. • Checking for consensus	• Building status / confidence in group • Summarizing from time to time. • Assessing inferences and judgments • Assessing extent of cooperative participation • Evaluating use of role functions

The Chairperson as the Leader

The most effective chairperson of a group activity is one who can steer the meeting with a minimum of direction and control. The chairperson, as we noted earlier, goes about performing this task without influencing the opinion of the members in any way. The chairperson, who is a leader of such activities, controls and guides, clarifies misunderstanding, brings out hidden facts and implied meanings of issues and topics.

Qualities of a Chairperson

Whether as a designated chairperson or as a discussion leader, the chairperson needs to cultivate a few qualities of good leadership. Briefly, they are:

1. Be sympathetic, friendly, and tolerant without being submissive or meek.
2. Be able to influence good and respectable behavior from the members.

3. Be clear in thinking and lucid in expression.
4. Try to encourage unity of purpose and coherent thinking in the mind of everyone including the self.
5. Be free and frank ________________ no shame in admitting errors and even ignorance.
6. Be patient and understanding with excellent listening habits.
7. Encourage the members to respond and give credit whenever it is due.
8. Lastly, have faith in the value of participation by members in achieving success in the group activity.

On the whole, however, it is seen that the abilities required of all leaders are widely distributed among members as well.

Administrative Responsibilities

Admittedly, the communication skills must occupy a vital place of prominence in leadership functions. An effective chairperson not only helps group communication but also helps cross communication within the group. However, a successful chairperson has to perform a string of strictly administrative duties and broadly these are:

(1) To ensure satisfactory arrangements for the group meeting, that the meeting is constituted properly and that a quorum is present.
(2) To see that the proceedings of the meeting continue in terms of the agenda paper and that the discussion is confined to agenda.
(3) To initiate the discussion by outlining the problems or issues to the members.
(4) To keep the discussion moving as per time schedule and to elicit contribution from all members by providing opportunity to everyone present in the meeting.
(5) To ensure that motions and amendments are put in the formally appropriate manner.
(6) To assure freedom of expression to every member but with an eye to the achievement of results.
(7) To maintain order and decorum in the proceedings of the meeting.
(8) To conclude the discussions by ensuring that the decisions of the meeting are that of the group itself and not that of the chairperson or forced on others by one or two dominant members.

Furthermore, it will be useful to note that the traits of the leader or that of a chairperson which are necessary and effective in one group are not strictly universal in application. In fact, the requirements may turn out to be quite unlike those of another leader or of a chairperson in a different setting. Therefore, a more 'situational' approach to leadership is required rather than just providing people with a set of 'rule of leadership' (*Cartwright and Zander*).

Process of Checking by Chairperson

As we say, a group without a leader is like a ship without a captain. Similarly, a meeting without a competent chairperson will land up in a whirlpool of stalemate and end up in conflicts.

It is of utmost importance that the chairperson, as the leader of the discussion group, make constant check and double-check on own performance.

- Have you or the organisers given sufficient lead time for preparation to all persons concerned with the meeting?
- Are there a good agenda and supporting papers for the meeting prepared and distributed well in time?
- Do you understand fully the ingredients of an effective communication plan?
- In an industrial situation, do you know the facts and figures about economics of the industry like wages, grievances, profits, investments, man-hours, productivity, prices, competitions, social responsibilities and similar other vital topics of everyday interest?
- What steps have you taken or intend to initiate to curtail or to minimize the possible existence of communication barrier within the group?
  - — Do you try to reach the level of the participants and talk in a language which is understandable to them?
  - — Do you throw up your hands in despair if there is no response from the members? Isn't it your responsibility to create interest in them?
  - — Do you adopt action method of 'learning by doing' and ensure smooth flow of two-way communication?
  - — Do you know the intellectual level, the background and particular needs of individual members as well as of the group itself?
  - — Do you mould the material, the agenda and the subject of discussion in such a way that they suit the knowledge, interests and requirements of the group members?
  - — Do you summarize the points raised, discussed and decisions taken at appropriate times and at the end of the meeting?

Again, we may refer to the views of Cartwright and Zander about the traits of leaders which continue to hold good as always. "A 'new view' of leadership is emerging which stresses the performance of needed functions and adaptability to changing situations .... Effective leaders are sensitive to the changing conditions of their groups and flexible in adapting their behavior to new requirements."

- As a leader or as a chairperson do you identify the acts of leadership in the same way?

Leadership

"An accepted leader has only to be sure of what it is best to do or at least to have made up his mind about it". Winston's S. Churchill (1949)

In the case of Churchill, four essential aspects of character were the key to his leadership. The four aspects that set him apart were:

- Candor and plain speaking.
- Ability to balance and attention to details.
- Realistic view of the wide scene.
- Imagination and surroundings influencing judgment.

Churchill's maxim for practical leadership qualities apply to group situations very well.

- Provide clear direction
- Establish trust
- Back up your people through thick and thin
- Keep fully informed.
- Change your mind in the presence of new facts.

Example: **Leader and Non-Leader.**
Strengths and Weaknesses.

This is not a task. But one must identify the strengths and deficiencies of both. Who are they? What are the traits that clearly distinguish a leader from a non-leader? One thing, however, is certain in organsiational context. By virtue of rank or position both are leaders but one stands out whereas the other falls far behind. The identifiable features of each are many but some behavioral and attitudinal qualities or shortcomings are highly noticeable.

Leader	Non-Leader
1. Always available; never keeps any distance.	1. Difficult to reach from below.
2. Very humble and modest.	2. Arrogant.
3. Believes in 'WE' instead of 'I'	3. Always 'I' and 'I'.
4. Company is No. 1	4. Self is No. 1.
5. Invites and appreciates disagreement.	5. Doesn't tolerate disagreement.
6. Doesn't hesitate to take blames.	6. Puts the blame on others.
7. Gives credit to others.	7. Take all credit.
8. Patient listener.	8. Good talker.
9. Mostly goes for collective decision making by leading the team members.	9. Avoids decision making.
10. Delegates work to fellow employees.	10. For everything submit report and seek approval.
11. Believes in openness.	11. Nothing is open, everything is secret.
12. Straightforward approach.	12. Crafty and even deceitful.
13. Show respect and concern for everybody.	13. No concern, all just subordinates.
14. Treats mistakes of others as learning opportunities.	14. Mistakes are perishable under rules.
15. Allows risk taking and not a punishable offence.	15. Considers risk taking a matter of decision by the superiors.
16. Trusts people.	16. No one is believable and trustworthy.
17. Has a long term vision.	17. Looking for short term gains.

Concept Development Questions

1. Discuss how leadership can make a difference in group performance. In this context analyse Lau-Tzu's quote about directing and the manner of good leadership.
2. What are the pitfalls to be avoided in the leadership process? What are the lessons to be learnt by a good leader?
3. List out the primary facets of good leadership. Discuss the components of such functions in a tabular form.
4. Do you feel that the Chairperson of a group activity is essentially a leader of the entire group and what are the expected qualities of a good leader? What are the administrative responsibilities of a chairperson of a group activity?
5. Give an account of your views as to how a Chairperson can operate successfully to ensure effective participation by the group members. How does Winston Churchill's reference to leadership character and qualities apply to group performance?

SUMMARY

Organising a successful group meeting is a skill in itself. In practical terms, a group meeting is an organised dialogue in which members must actively participate and exchange ideas and views purposefully. They must finally arrive at a conclusion or at least find a common approach to the issues or the problems. This way they grow in ability and to eventual perfections. Here the leader has to extend full support and encouragement for success and benefits that accrue to individuals and the group as a whole.

It is found that the most effective leader is one who can steer the group process with minimum of direction and control. A few cautious steps, however, would be necessary for the group leader to play the role of a facilitator. The leader has also to avoid a series of pitfalls that may come in the way. It would be good to learn a few lessons in the process. These include, be calm and continue to learn, concentrate, do self-criticism and be loyal to the team in all situations.

All organisations are systems of interlocking groups. But there may be certain personal behaviors which impede group functioning. Key leadership functions include overseeing such possibilities and to take steps to promote interaction between leader, group members as well as apply situational judgements. The broad-based leadership functions provide for planning, initiating, controlling, supporting, informing and evaluating. There are number of essential elements in each step. The leader has to be adept and fully knowledgeable about all the components of each step of activity.

The leader must be an effective Chairperson of a group activity and steer the meeting with a minimum of direction and control. Therefore, again, the Chairperson as the leader has to cultivate the qualities of good leadership. Apart from communication skills, the Chairperson has to shoulder a set of administrative responsibilities. Check and double check at every step of group leadership process. Nothing should go wrong and see that you are fully prepared before, during and after as well.

KEY TERMS

Analogy	:	*Partial similarity; also reasoning from parallel cases.*
Autocratic	:	*Dictatorship, absolute ruler.*
Axiom	:	*Established or accepted principle, Self-evident truth.*
Candor	:	*Frankness, openness.*
Collaborative	:	*Work together, Cooperate.*
Consensus	:	*General agreement or opinion.*
Diagnosis	:	*Formal identification of problems.*
Harmonious	:	*Free from disagreement or dissent.*
Perfectionism	:	*Uncompromising pursuit of excellence.*
Pitfalls	:	*Unsuspected danger or draw back.*
Quorum	:	*Minimum number of members that must be present to constitute a valid meeting.*
Scape-goating	:	*Persons blamed for others' shortcomings.*
Software	:	*Programmer for a computer.*
Stalemate	:	*Deadlock, no progress.*
Uninspiring	:	*Not inspired, pedestrian, commonplace.*
Unmotivated	:	*No stimulation to perform better.*
Whirlpool	:	*Powerful Circle of Water.*

REFERENCES

Andal, N, ***Communication Theories and Models*** *Himalaya Publishing House Mumbai, 1998.*

Adair, John, ***The Effective Communicator*** *Jaico Mumbai, 2002.*

Drucker, Peter, ***The Practice of Management*** *Pan Books Ltd, London, 1975.*

Likert, Rensis, ***The Human Organisation: Its Management and Value*** *McGraw Hill, 1980.*

Robbins, SP and M. Coulter, ***Management*** *Prentice Hall Delhi 1996.*

Schramm, Wilbur & William E. Porter ***Men, Women, Messages and Media*** *Harper & Row New York, 1973.*

T +D, Training + Development *Journal Alexandria (Virginia, USA) August, 2011.*

V

Problems and Problem Solving How Case Studies Help

Learning Objectives

This Chapter will be helpful for the readers to perceive the case study subject as a problem solving method. The coverage includes:

1. How the case concept came about.
2. Application of the case method as a step-by-step process in the shape of guided discovery.
3. Why cases are different from exercises and why the cases are a popular method of study in business and professional circles.
4. How case studies can be turned into productive group communication functions.
5. Role of strategic planning and the application of R-A-C-E formula and the decision – making process.
6. Applying the case methods by organisations to gain benefits.
7. Steps in problem situations and differences between real life and fictional cases.

Problems and Problem Solving Cases and Case Studies

A "problem" is a "case" and all case studies are "problem solving methods". This may appear to be a very simple statement. Actually, a problem refers to a difficult situation which requires hard thinking and studying. A case or a problem is not a single question in an examination paper. Essentially, the purpose of a case study is to develop judgment and knowhow and evolve possible solutions with a host of alternatives.

A case is often referred to as a doctor's diagnosis. The physician, for identification of the disease, attempts to locate the real problem and is never guided by symptoms alone. He goes for solutions on the basis of anatomical findings.

In organsiational situations, as also in the academics, in-depth studying of problem are all extensions of structured activities. These have particular applications in professional fields like advertising, public relations, personnel management and industrial relations, marketing, sales promotion and the entire field of management. The case study method helps the professionals, as well as learners in training and development, to develop skills in finding alternative ideas and decision making in problem areas.

All difficult matters, hypothetical or actual situations, call for investigations. They do not, however, confine to certain specific disciplines only. In reality and in actual applications, such situations may pertain to many other professional activities. From economics to sociology, from medicine to psychology, finance to human resource, from production to communication and thus the situation moves on in varying degrees and methods.

How the Case Concept Came About

The case study method was first developed at the Harvard Law School (USA) around 1870. The idea gained momentum with further development of the process in 1910. The initial legal approach, aiming primarily at just one solution to the problem, did not serve the purpose of management. In the later period, Harvard's Graduate School of Business Administration adopted the case method as one of its fundamental mode of teaching. The approach now turned, from legal to management, towards greater appreciation of the managerial need to explore many ways to deal with a situation. It is another matter that the legal profession subsequently found the management angle of case studies as equally useful for achieving professional success. The case study idea is being propagated vigorously for the last few decades or so. Since then there has been no looking back for Business Schools and in other professional studies all over the world as regards production and utilization of cases. As was applied then and being appreciated anywhere now, cases may describe problems and recommend solutions relating to individuals, groups, institutions, or even nations.

The Applications

Cases are often structured like a play that opens in the middle of a story and uses flashbacks to describe the action that led up to the opening

Participants of different groups gather together to listen to group presentations to gain benefits.

Discussing how case studies can be turned into productive group communication functions.

scene, where an employee or an executive has just made a key decision. Questions are posed at the end of the case that asks the participants to analyse the situation and recommend a solution. For example, they may be asked to state the nature of the problem, identify the events that led to the problem and indicate what the individual should do to resolve the problem.

The step-by-step process in the case method is termed as "guided discovery" leading to acceptable solutions. The role of leader, the organisers and also some members as "facilitators" is crucial to achieving success. It may not be the 'right' or 'wrong' answers, but helps to teach the learners to identify existing or potential problems and recommend realistic solutions.

To make the method more and more useful, analysis of the case should involve studying actual situations, written as an in-depth presentation of a company, its market and its strategic decisions. The intended objective could be as varied as to improve a merger, an acquisition or a student's problem-solving ability. Cases typically investigate a contemporary issue in a real-life context. There will be multiple issues to consider and many 'correct' or viable alternatives to solve the case issues are presented.

In classroom or executive training sessions, cases allow students to explore actual decisions made by organisations. Cases, however, rely almost exclusively upon discussions to bring out different ideas, experiences and views about the case materials. Cases refer to the events that managers or executives had to deal with and charts various responses to these decisions.

"Case and Exercise"

Cases are different from "exercises". An exercise is to learn and apply a particular concept, technique or principle. A case can be used to learn a broad range of skills. It provides many choices. An exercise, on the other hand, has only one situation and just one way of finding a solution. Case studies are to practise and attain analytical and communication skills. These are tasks that provide examples of a task-subject to consider, discuss and perform.

In other words, the most significant difference between a case study and other structured group activities is in respect of process and application. Obviously, the latter are process based, the actual task being less important than how it is carried out, whereas case studies are firmly content and task based.

A case, as defined by so many experts, is a short description in words (and numbers) of an actual problem situation. It states the present and past position of the situation and the problem that is posed. It must be ensured that all the relevant data are provided. Even then, all the available information may not be quite adequate. Therefore, at the time of analysing a case much more information may have to be made available.

In organsiational situations, a complete historical background of the organisation included in the study is provided. The range of data given can be completely imaginary or, preferably, based on a real situation. In fact, the closer to the reality, the more acceptable will be the study, with errors and omissions less likely.

A case study, in spite of all its avowed realistic nature, cannot be all-inclusive or unique. It can portray a picture of a problem, an issue or a challenge confronting an organisation – commercial or non-commercial, which has some applicability in identical situations. Case discussions are mostly like an autopsy. A case is therefore, a form of qualitative and quantitative analysis of a situation as a whole. It must use all available and factual data to examine issues, happenings and realities of the environment systematically. In addition, field studies and detailed reports of personal experiences and actions are usefully applied. Another extremely valuable input comes in the form of 'historiography'. Newsom, Turk and Kruckeberg explain "historiography" as "reconstructing the past in a systematic and orderly manner. It involves recording, analysing, coordinating and explaining past event".

To-day, cases are a popular method of study in business and professional schools and are used heavily in training and educational programmes. Cases include actual information of a company's decisions and may include interviews, observations, or data from business or industry records. Additionally, there can be database record and published historical facts on the organsiation, business, and industry.

Planning and Managing Cases

Case studies often appear difficult to plan and manage because of high expectations, uneven levels of group and individual demand and the creative element. It is easy to become cynical about the potential of case discussions to accomplish anything. Yet, if participants in a case study have the requisite information, knowledge and skills, they can achieve productive group communication functions. The resulting success can be defined as an aggregate of views of members in face-to-face communication, based on shared goals, expectations and aspirations, all directed toward common objectives, aims and goals.

Many groups waste time weeding out irrelevancies because there was no planning. Planning establishes an orderly approach to the problem or the subject that lead to a solution or a set of solutions. A small group of organisers may even arrange a preliminary planning session to fulfill a number of important objectives.

The objectives can be a varied as:

(1) Building a team spirit
(2) Motivating the members to develop an effective group process.
(3) Defining the problem and contributory factors.
(4) Breaking the subject into a series of subtopics.
(5) Arranging place and time for group meeting and overseeing facilities.
(6) Finding out research and information sources.

(7) Planning a problem-solving agenda.
(8) Planning a problem-resolution pattern.
(9) Decide about group leadership as a source.
(10) Assign the task to a responsible person for recording the main ideas, suggestions, findings, and conclusions of the group.

Role of Strategic Planning

A very old formula for problem-solving is John Marston's R-A-C-E – an acronym standing for Research. Action, Communication and Evaluation. The problem-solving procedure has been offered in many ways by many more experts – sometime much more in detail and sometime in modified forms.

In the context of fast changing environment, Peter Drucker, the management thinker and one of the foremost guru of modern management, had to say a few words in favour of strategic planning over the traditional planning process. He says:

"Planning as a rule starts with the trends of yesterday and projects them to the future – using a different 'mix' perhaps, but with very much the same configuration. This is no longer going to work. The most probable assumption in a period of turbulence is the unique event which changes the configuration. Unique events cannot, by definition, be 'planned'. But they can be foreseen. This requires strategies for tomorrow, strategies that anticipate where the greatest changes are likely to be, strategies that enable a business – or a hospital, school or university – to take advantage of new realities and to convert turbulence into opportunity"

In the organsiational setup, solving the problem means recognizing the resources of the organisation, the power structure, existing decision-making process in the organisation, and the corporate culture.

A DECISION-MAKING PROCESS

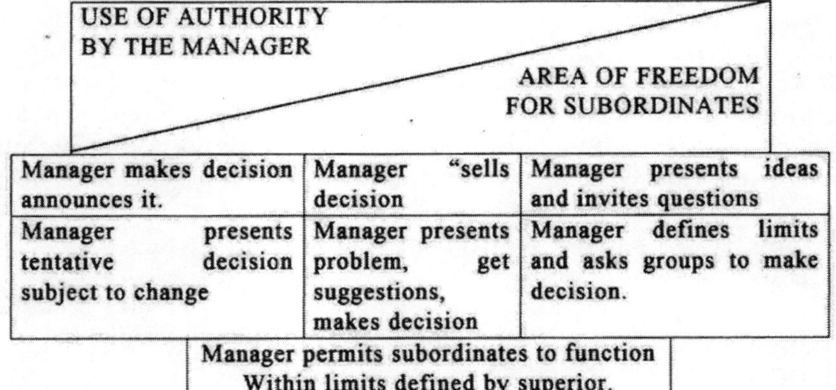

Ref: "How to choose a leadership pattern" – Harvard Business Review.

All these lead to a situation that compels deliberation, a need to solve a problem, the collective desire to create something new or a drive to develop new relationships.

The situation is well-applicable to a proper decision-making process in which the manager and the subordinates are equal players. The roles are pre-defined and the course of decision-making moves in a systematic process as shown below:

The Case Method for Organisations

Through the narration of events and conditions of an organisation, the reader of the case gets a first – hand impression about the situation. Organisations facing problem situations form the starting point of the case situations. The aim and the objective should be directed to:

(1) Identify problems, opportunities and possible solutions.
(2) Set realistic goals.
(3) Actively pursue the goals.
(4) Achieve results.

Problem Situations

Why organisations need to refer to case studies? Because organisations, like human beings, also have difficulties, crises, doubts, troubles, frustrations, threats, challenges, worries and anxieties. Cases provide opportunities to get exposed to such situations, understand and analyse them and work practical situations. In this process, people in organisations develop introspective abilities to judge and appreciate the complexities of managing and to think the ways of solving problems.

Steps in Problem Solving

We need to know the various stages of problem solving and how the method of case studies can be applied as the right tool.

- **The Problem**
  What exactly is the nature of the problem? Try to find out how difficult is the problem and how soon does it require a solution.
- **Group Problem–Solving**
  Can a group activity be the ideal method to identify the issues and find out solutions? What should be the composition of the group? Will it be able to recognize and define problems?
  In group exercise, try to generate fresh ideas and evaluate each solution impartially.
- **Malfunctions and Barriers**
  Be particularly conscious about malfunctions and barriers to communication. There may be many reasons for barriers and malfunctions. Whether organsiational, personal or even psychological, any distortions or threats may prevent progress.

Groups should be effectively led to overcome barriers and helped to find good solutions to the problem.

Developing the Case Concept

What are the basic tasks involved in creating, producing and presenting a good case study? Let us present a simplied model of the systematic process.

Systematic Approach to Concept Generation

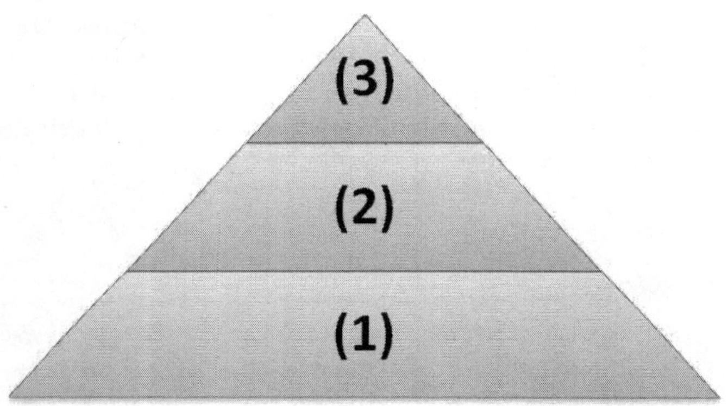

The concept of a case preparation is divided into three parts.

Phase 1: (i) Takes off from a Base.
(ii) Systematic accumulation of Facts.

Phase 2: Processing and Analysis of accumulated Facts.

Phase 3: Ideation which is the culmination of concept-making.

The creative process begins with fact finding exercise. This involves picking out and identifying the problem and gathering and analysing relevant data. The essential input for ideas is gathering of information from all sources. Leo Burnett, one of the greatest in creative output said, "Curiosity about life in all its aspects, I think, is still the secret of a great creative people". In particular, the involved individual or the team should get immersed in collecting as much factual information as possible. In an organsiational or academic setup, focus group interviewing is a good approach to generate useful ideas. Fact finding should include a digestive and incubation phase. Usually, the best ideas emerge only a short period of digestion and incubation.

The key factor in the process is to generate a range of ideas. Evaluation of a set of alternatives will not pose a problem. A good suggestion is to combine various concepts. Many fell that idea generation comes easier in a group. Here much more information and collective thinking are available. However, it has to be ensured that no inhibiting aspects of group behavior come to play. The participants have to be encouraged to build on ideas, combining and improving them. The objective should be both quantity as well as quality. Finally, whatever the mode, keep in view that the concept is one of central points of a case preparation as well as presentation. In fact, a case will stand or fall, work or fail by the strengths or weaknesses of the basic concept.

Real or Fictional Cases?

An important part of the planning requirement is to decide whether to use an artificial or a real problem. Indeed, cases may be based on real or fictional situations. The stages, as is the normal process, will include:

- Analysing
- Influencing
- Presenting
- Decision making
- Problem solving
- Evaluation of success or otherwise

The concentration should be on both the content or task bases of the activity and the processes involved. Although it is possible to provide cases for individual analysis, it is more useful to be analysed in small groups.

Cases, real or artificial, provide only the raw material for the participants to analyse and discover problems, so that they may work out practical plans and solutions for dealing with them. In the process, the participants assume various roles in the actual organsiational situations. However, real life cases enjoy certain distinct advantages owing to their truthful nature.

Real-Life Cases

- Cases are more believable and credible
- Much easier to produce than invented material.
- Can be followed by "what actually happened" input.
- Solutions to problems easily found.

From the case-writer's point of view, cases which are based on own or other people experiences are more acceptable and appealing in content.

Fictional Cases

- Case writer can control developments which might go against personal or orgnaisation's interest.
- Although created from own imagination should not lose the touch of reality.
- The task is creative.
- Case moves according to perception and attitude of the case writer.

For preparing a good and acceptable case, though artificially created, should pass through certain essential steps of the creative process. These are:

- Personal as well as group effort.
- Brainstorming to accept or reject sensitive or unneeded elements of the case matter.
- Actual preparation of the case.
- Incubation period to get the case mentally reviewed during a short period.
- Apply insight into the case once again before introducing the case.
- Final evaluation of the strengths and weaknesses of the case.

The task of constructing an imaginary case study is indeed easier. More so, if it is based on actual organsiational situations, which will make the study more acceptable to the participants. Irrespective of whether it is imaginary or real, the study and preparation should be complete and honest in all respects. Both types of cases, extensive or small, must contain a lot of background as well as problem detail for decision-making and implementation.

Motivating the Sales Force.

A different kind of example.

Realty Business Corporation is known particularly in Delhi and Mumbai as one of the most successful realty organisation. They build high value apartment blocks with the best kind of facilities in sprawling real estate properties in both Delhi and Mumbai. The company enjoys the maximum possible reputation in terms of external display of superiority with one of the highest business results in the real estate sector.

In spite of all the best things going around with the identity and image of the company, certain internal factors have started to disturb the highest management of late. The turnover of their efficient and effective sale persons have started to indicate that all were not as good as the external images. The CEO of the company together with about a dozen senior management people sat together in a group. They started to brainstorm collectively to pinpoint the reasons behind this sudden spurt in sales people separations.

A lot of reasons came to surface and a lot more were suggested to overcome the crisis. The CEO was not satisfied. He asked them straightway just two questions.

These are:

(1) How frequently do you sit together with your sales team to get to the pulse of your team?

(2) Do you feel you are able to motivate them towards increasing loyalties to the company?

The answers were defensive and unclear. The CEO closed the meeting with the decision to hire outside help for a study of the problem. However, with consultations of his senior team members, he decided that the outside consultants have to work together with three senior executives of the company for the proposed study, and subsequent recommendations.

The fact finding team, comprising senior management professionals and outside consultants, got into examining all the pros and cons of the situation quite earnestly. Eventually, although it took around six months, came out with a host of deficiencies in the organisation itself. They identified some of the major deficiencies in the organisation as under:

1. Poor recruiting system.
2. Improper selection and placements.
3. Deficiencies in training methods.
4. Inadequate supervision, guidance and counseling.
5. Lack of motivation.
6. No group communication from time to time and frequent breakdown in communication.
7. Unsatisfactory performance resulting in customer complaints.
8. Dissatisfaction leading to increasing turnover or finding better job environment elsewhere.

The final recommendations to overcome the crisis were quite startling for the top management. They came to appreciate the recommendations particularly because the team was having substantial representations from the company itself. Right from the CEO to senior most professionals they took up the recommendations quite seriously after group exercises amongst themselves. Briefly, the recommendations are:

1. Senior most sales executives first of all have to appreciate that their own job's existence is to contribute to the effectiveness of the sales force.
2. There has to be more and more interactions between the seniors and the junior executives and group communication should be held at regular intervals.
3. Motivation is important and optimum level of motivation for each job has to be encouraged.
4. Recruiting, selecting and training of the sales personnel will be an important part of productivity plans.
5. Cases and case studies, both real as well as fictional, to be taken up for discussions as well as for presentation by the sales personnel.
6. CEO should not be just a watch dog but must take part in all deliberations relating to group exercises held by senior managers.
7. CEO should himself call for group exercises for mutual interactions between himself and the junior executives.
8. It should be essential for each sale executive to maintain a feeling of group identity. The sales management at the higher level has to strive for developing and maintaining team spirit. This should be possible through providing added motivation with an eye towards achieving group performance standards.
9. Management must determine the amount of compensation a salesperson should receive on the average. The management must

consider that the compensation patterns are related to external supply-and-demand factors.

10. It is important that good and effective communications exist between each salesperson and his or her superior on a sustained basis. Otherwise, there is depressed morale and low productivity. Good communications will allow for free discussion of problems related to the sales person's job and of any personal problem that, left unsolved, hurt job performance.

Short and Long term gains for the Company

The implementation of the team recommendations took quite some time but subsequently these were fully accepted by the CEO and the top management of the company. But once they accepted the team recommendations there was no looking back and the company with utmost sincerity started to put all the recommendations into complete execution. In the short term there were visible gains but in the long run the company was able to achieve miraculous results. In the process, they were able to surpass most of their competitors and there was noticeable sense of pride and belongingness among the sales persons.

Concept Review Questions

1. Trace the origin of the case study concept and identify the distinctions between a case and an exercise.
2. Discuss the role of strategic planning in the case method and specify the objectives of case studies for problem solving activities.
3. Describe the usefulness of case method for organisations and draw out a chart indicating the Decision –making process for this purpose.
4. How you propose to develop the case concept in several stages and also specify the steps in the problem solving method.
5. For the purpose of a case study discussion and presentation in your organisation do you like to take up a real case or a fictional one? Explain the reason for a particular choice. In this context write a short fictional case for group discussion and subsequent presentation.

SUMMARY

A case refers to a problem situation for individuals, groups and primarily the organisations. Cases pertain to all professional activities including sociology, medicine, psychology, finance, production, human resource and communications.

Originating at the Harvard Law School, cases typically investigate a contemporary issue in a real-life context. There will be multiple issues to consider and many correct or viable alternatives will emerge to solve the problem. Today, therefore, case studies are a popular method of study in business and professional institutes and used extensively in training and educational programmes.

An age-old way of problem-solving is applying the R-A-C-E formula standing for Research, Action, Communication and Evaluation. The roles are pre-defined and the course of decision –making moves in systematic manner.

The aim and objective in case method should be directed to –

(1) *Identifying problems, opportunities and possible solutions.*
(2) *Setting realistic goals.*
(3) *Actively pursuing the goal and, finally,*
(4) *Achieve results.*

People in organisations must develop introspective abilities to reach the right path to problem solving situations. They have to understand the nature of the problem, go for group problem solving process and remove all kinds of malfunctions and barriers to communication.

The primary task involved is creating, producing and presenting a good case study. Try to develop a range of ideas rather than just one single idea. In academics, in particular, decide whether to use an artificial or a real problem. Even the organisations may initiate such studies for training and learning exercises. In both real and fictional cases, they must work out a lot of background material for decision-making and implementation.

KEY TERMS

Accumulation	:	*Amass, collect facts and information.*
Aggregate	:	*Combined total.*
Alternative	:	*Finding out availability of more choices.*
Anatomy	:	*Analysis of facts and details.*
Autopsy	:	*Post-mortem for final evaluation.*
Avowed	:	*Declared purpose or objective.*
Barriers	:	*Obstacle that bars advance or access.*
Brainstorming	:	*Single person or group trying to find ingenious idea or inspiration.*
Configuration	:	*Arrangement in a particular form.*
Contemporary	:	*Living or occurring at the same time which is modern or current.*
Credible	:	*Believable which is worthy of belief.*
Culmination	:	*Reach its highest or final point.*
Cynical	:	*Person who believes the worst about people's motives and with a pessimistic view of everything.*
Evaluation	:	*Assess or appraise the results and performance at the end.*
Fictional	:	*Non-factual or imaginative ideas.*
Flashback	:	*Scene or happening set in a time earlier than the main action.*
Ideation	:	*Conception or plan formed by mental efforts.*

Inhibition : *Restraint or resistance to a thought and action.*
Malfunction : *Failure to function normally.*
Turbulence : *Disturbance or Commotion.*
Weeding out : *Getting rid of unwanted materials by sorting out.*

REFERENCES

Adler Ronald B. and Elmhorst JM. ***Communicating at work*** *Seventh Edition.*
McGraw Hill Higher Education, New York, 2002.
Drucker, F. Peter, ***The Practice of Management***
Pan Books Ltd. London, 1975.
Lane, L. Leroy. ***By All Means Communicate*** *Prentice Hall,*
New Jersey, 1991.
Still, Cundiff, Govoni. ***Sales Management***
Prentice Hall of India, New Delhi, 1995.
Schramm, Wilbur, ***How Communication Works*** *Urbana,*
University of Illinois Press, 1973.
Sengupta, Sailesh ***Management of Public Relations and Communication***
Vikas publishing 5th Reprint, 2009.
Sengupta, Sailesh . ***Business and Managerial Communication***
PHI Learning Private Ltd. New Delhi, 2011.
Harvard Business Review*, South Asia, September 2011.*
Fortune Journal*, Asia. Pacific Edition July 5, 2010.*
T+D Training + Development *Journal ASTD, Alexandra, VA April 2011.*

VI

How Good are You at Group Communication?

LEARNING OBJECTIVES

This chapter provides essential information with following inputs:

1. The basic forms of communication.
2. How to write the case study and relevant guidelines.
3. The value of the spoken word in group sessions.
4. The roadblocks to effective speaking.
5. Knowing the fundamentals of speaking
6. Effective listening and improving listening abilities.
7. Guidelines for creative listening.

For some people, communication is a breeze. For many others, it's real struggle. They may even get stuck so often that they develop a mental block. Are you one of those people? Are you one of those persons who think that 'communication' and 'good communication' is the same thing? At any level of work, strong positive communication skills can improve job performance and productivity as well as one's chances of either a promotion or a new career move. In a group activity, whether a work or academic group, effective communication skills are a positive asset. The American poet and Pulitzer-prize winner, Robert Frost once wrote:

> ***"Half the world is composed of people***
> ***who have something to say and can't,***
> ***and the other half who have nothing to say***
> ***and keep saying it".***

What is so important about communication that organisation leaders, executives and employees get so frustrated and nervous about? So is true about the participants in a group function in academics as well as in business or industry case sessions. Why do we need effective communication as an essential ingredient for a group performance? At a personal level, why do you need to be an effective communicator?

Here, we will be searching for answers to these questions. We will also be giving some hints and suggestions on developing your own communication skills.

The Basic forms of Communication

Developing communication skills is like learning to play the game of cricket or football or hockey. You need to learn the rules, conventions and the skills. You also need partners to practice with and you need to know how well you are doing. You need to improve on your areas of weakness in playing and tactics. And it is only with practice and feedback that you will develop into a good player or an effective communicator. This is entirely an acquired skill.

So the emphasis must not be on theory but on observing and experience ____________ learning by doing ______________ and on receiving feedback.

For gaining proficiency in communication, one has to consider different aspects. It's true we have been communicating all our life but, perhaps, we have not given a serious thought or attention to the communication process. The process invariably needs a conscious involvement of the transmitter as well as the receiver of the message. One has to take it as a really serious exercise and improve on one's strengths. Improving the communication skills would involve trying out new approaches in communicating.

Communicating occurs in many forms. The process indeed is very much fluid, the form in which a message is communicated changes constantly. Communication can be informal or formal, written or spoken, and internal or external. In point of fact, it can just be a smile or an eye contact. Here we should be discussing communication in relation to any group activity.

Writing the Case Study

Even though oral communication is the preferred medium, there is the precise need for written communication in group discussions. This relates to preparing the case situations in the most appropriate manner and also when a permanent record is needed for future reference.

But, then, the main purpose of communication be it oral or written, is to get a message across from a sender to receiver.

In case discussions, written beforehand, of a case problem can be analytic, concrete, and sometime even abstract. Such expressions are

Self-assessment to find out in advance about one's capability for effective group participation at a later stage.

important for academic, technical and for dealing with organsiational problems. As a mode of communication, the written texts for case problems and situations must contain all the contextual and supportive details to convey the meanings. In other words, the written matter should be clear, complete, correct and to be fully intelligible.

The writer of the case study, or the group of people involved in its preparation, must keep in view the ten essential commandments of the writing process.

(1) Before writing – THINK. This is known as "pre-writing". One way is research – as concentrated search for relevant facts by reading, interviewing and scanning. Another way is brainstorming ________ a small-group activity in which a string of useful ideas are generated. These are put into the case for organised group consideration.

(2) Organise your text in the right way. Ensure that subject, purpose and the problems are clearly presented. Information provided has to be directly related to subject and purpose. Ideas are to be grouped and presented logically.

(3) Written communication has to be orderly and precise in its content and approach.

(4) It should pass on correct and accurate information.

(5) Written cases must not become instruments of excessive legalism and formality which cause disputes and arguments.

(6) Words may not contain different meanings and interpreted differently by different persons.

(7) Text should be concise to the point: refrain from using roundabout ways of expression.

(8) Visualize the readers. Picture their interests, backgrounds, knowledge of the subject, and vocabulary they are familiar with.

(9) Limit the scope of the case within four or five major points. Text the draft against length limitations and time availability for a group exercise. However, building consensus about a complex and controversial subject takes longer and more explaining, particularly if the group is composed of skeptical or a few hostile members.

(10) Finally, once again, be brief, be clear, be natural.

Remember:

(a) These are no strict rules.
They are just some general guides.
Never overdo them.
Apply your better judgement!

(b) A quote from Francis Bacon (English philosopher and writer 1561 – 1626) can be relevant:
"Reading maketh a "Full Man"
Conference a "Ready Man"
Writing an "Exact Man".

Spoken word in group Sessions

The ability to communicate effectively in group activities is becoming increasingly important. One obvious reason is organisation leaders are spending more and more time doing group activities. One study says that the managers spend 60 to 80 per cent of their time working with small groups of people. Yet each person in any group has a different personality and unique strengths and weaknesses. A good communicator has to realise that they are different and cannot be treated the same way like any other.

Small group communication builds on one-on-one communication, but it has a different dynamic. It is often said that a small group meeting is a place where everybody talks, nobody listens, and everyone discusses afterward. Moreover, when a person speaks the possibility of misunderstanding is tremendous. It is peculiar but the hearer is also sending verbal and non-verbal messages back to the speaker and others present at the same time. In turn these can be understood correctly, misunderstood, or ignored. It can be a very complicated process.

The Value of Speaking

Speaking is essentially a mode of communication. For that matter, any good talker, whether in a formal or informal situation, is always a hot subject of notice and attention. Speaking for these persons is primarily interacting through use of words. They also use non-verbal signals like gestures, postures, eye contact and similar signs very effectively.

The importance of speaking as a vehicle for dissemination of ideas and information becomes even more critical while working with people. Speaking for them is with the clear intent and purpose of getting desired results as a part of planned programme of action.

Of all human urges, indeed, speaking is one of the strongest but very few can ultimately excel in its useful and artistic application. It also satisfies the basic human need for recognition which, in turn, strengthens the speaker's self-esteem and morale. At work or at an informal or formal group activity, the ability to communicate or speak well helps one to get on well with people who are equally concerned with the problems and the issues. Nevertheless, whatever gift of the gab one may possess, the crux of communication is the earnestness of the person speaking every time. The vigor of continuity, sense of purpose and conviction of communication is that determines success and its consequent impact on the listeners, individually as well as collectively.

Roadblocks

Speaking confidently, interestingly and effectively is not an easy task. Indeed, careful preparation and practice are the hallmarks of good speaking. It could be wise for any unwilling speaker to keep in mind:

> ***"It is better to keep quiet even if others think that you are a fool rather than open your month and remove all doubts".***

No doubt, words are the major currency for group interactions but, without a purpose all words are empty sounds. And thoughts provide us with the words in which to express them. Success of a good oral communicator is dependent upon one's ability to say what he or she means.

What are the roadblocks or barriers to good verbal communication? While there may be many, many more possible shortcomings, a few are listed here:

(1) The fear of speaking.
(2) The fear of confrontation with other team members.
(3) Lack of attention from those who are expected to listen.
(4) Lack of knowledge about the subject of discussion.
(5) Sometime the overbearing attitude of the speaker _________ rather than speaking to them, the speaker talks down on the listeners.
(6) Getting tongue-tied owing to nervousness.
(7) Talking in a ponderous manner, trying to impress others.
(8) Venturing into a long speech.
(9) Trying to communicate while one is angry.
(10) Internal and external distractions while speaking.

The Fundamentals

For a group member success in group deliberations is dependent upon one's ability to say what is in one's mind. You need to master a few fundamentals, and then keep practising.

Whenever any group of individuals comes together, the individuals bring with them a wide range of tacit, unexpressed differences in perspectives. A few guidelines in the context of the common threats should be worthwhile:

(1) Try to outgrow the fear of speaking or the haunting fear of confrontation. If speaking is unavoidable _______ speak out. Remember, you have to walk a little to go a long way.
(2) Develop the art and practice of conversation. As a group member, use conversational style of talking even on very serious matters.
(3) Be prepared but most know there is a difference between the written and the spoken word. At the same time, be assertive and never be overbearing.
(4) Compose yourself and do some deep breathing before you speak. Say clearly and slowly, maintain eye contact and good posture.
(5) You have to cope with your nerves. Never let your nerves control you. Isn't it true that everyone suffers from nerves? Your motive should be to turn negative nerves into positive power.
(6) Consider the group activity as a forum to express your opinion or an opportunity for exchange of ideas. Therefore, present your case firmly and convincingly.
(7) Identify goals ___________ what you want to achieve by saying something otherwise your words will sound empty without purpose.

(8) Handle questions and comments politely and calmly. Resist the temptation to jump in with an evaluative, critical or disparaging reaction at the moment a remark is uttered by any listener.

(9) Maintain focus .... Stay on track. Do not try to achieve too much at a time. Fewer your objective, sharper is the focus, and greater will be your chances of success.

(10) Reflect on your performance, after each activity. You will be successful!

(11) Profile of a good Speaker

(a) BE PREAPRED	:	Collecting, surveying and arranging material.
(b) BE CLEAR	:	Easy to understand.
(c) BE SIMPLE	:	First cousin to clarity.
(d) BE VIVID	:	Interesting, arresting, attractive.
(e) BE NATURAL	:	Manner of speaking-ability to motivate.

On Listening

If the communication process is to function effectively, both the listener and the speaker must do their part. As a speaker, you need to do what you can to help listeners comprehend your message. On the other hand, recent studies show that the listener's respect for listening as a method of learning increases listener comprehension. In addition, speaker has to be responsive to feedback. In group activities, feedback serves to control and correct the messages that we transmit to others.

Inefficiency of Listening

Just how inefficient people are as listeners is difficult to say. Expert opinions show that we miss much that is said and forget much that we hear. Organisers of group communication activities complain that the participants don't listen and ignore much of what is said. Worse still, as authorities tell us, that we retain only about a fourth of what we hear just after two days. They also tell us that listening is the weakest link in oral communication.

Communication experts have always called listening as the most important of all the communication skills. If that was not enough, experts have also found that it is the most neglected area in communication. Although most of us think we know how to listen, in reality most of us are poor listeners. We all let our minds wander now and then, plus we are specially likely to drift off when we listen to information that is sometime difficult to understand. Thus, poor listening is a major cause of miscommunication, particularly in group activities.

Why is it so? What is listening? Why is it so difficult? And how can we improve our listening skills?

Improving Listening Ability

Listening is a four part activity. It involves hearing, interpreting, understanding and appraising. Improving your ability to listen is largely a matter of mental urge-that is, you must "want" to do it. It is a determined choice, a willful act.

Work situation and group functions call for active listening. Here one has to use eyes, ears and mind. One has to look for both verbal and non-verbal cues. All this requires disciplining the mind. To understand the message, the listener must be fully alert. You must force yourself to pay attention to the words spoken. You should ask questions to test the reliability of what you hear and try to make a distinction between the wheat and the chaff. Carl Rogers and Richard Farren, pioneers in this field, explained the concept of active listening this way:

"To be effective, active listening must be firmly grounded in the basic attitudes of users". They felt that "active listening cannot be employed as a technique if our fundamental attitudes are in conflict with its basic concepts".

As we said, listening demands a lot of conscious effort. One has to really use restraint and control when someone else is talking. One has to wait for one's turn. In groups, therefore, active listening involves 'switching on' and staying 'tuned in' to others speaking. At the same time, the listener has to pass through intra-personal communication and internal processing of information received.

An example of the process can be like:

What the speaker is saying?
What are his main ideas?
What does he really mean?
What exactly is the problem?
What is there in it for me?
Am I a part of the problem situation?
How can I help solving the problem?
What can be my suggestions?
What am I going to say?
Guidelines for Creative Listening

The following "Ten Commandments of listening" should serve as a useful guide to listen fruitfully in skillful discussions. The credit for these often-quoted comments about listening goes to some anonymous author who had created these classic commands.

1. **Stop talking:**
   To yourself and to others. Learn to still the voice within. Say to yourself "you can't listen if you are talking" Wait for your turn to speak.
2. **Make the talkers feel good:**
   Help them feel free to talk. Play your role as a sincere group member and be interested in the proceedings.

3. **Show convincingly that you want to listen:**
They will reciprocate the way you behave with them. Try to create a climate for free, frank, and purposeful exchange of information.
4. **Remove Distraction:**
Don't doodle, tap, or shuffle papers or the like. Don't get involved in side conversation.
5. **Observe Non-verbal behavior:**
Note the body language, gestures, postures, eye glances to glean meanings beyond what is said.
6. **Listen empathetically:**
Imagine yourself in other person's place and try to walk in his shoes. Seek to understand other people's perceptions, desires, hopes and limitations as well.
7. **Listen between the lines:**
Everybody may not have a perfect communication skill. Try to understand implicit as well as explicit meanings. Is there a gap between what one says and what one really means?
8. **Be Patient:**
Don't interrupt. Sit still past your tolerance level. Don't be angry either. Realise that angry minds can never contribute to group communication activities.
9. **Ask Questions:**
That's sure way to prove that you are listening. But go easy on argument and criticism. These are roads to nowhere and nobody is a winner in a senseless controversy. Group exercise should aim exclusively towards building shared understanding.
10. **Stop Talking:**
This is the first as well as the last. All other techniques of listening depend on it. Take a determined vow of silence once in a while.

Golden Rule:

"Give every man thine ear
Few thy voice"
(Shakespeare in Hamlet)

Group Communication Questionnaire: Try this Test

Scale of Performance

1 = Never 2 = Rarely 3 = sometimes 4 =Usually 5 = Always. Mark your preference at the right.

1.	As a leader in group discussions I always listen seriously and show it.	1, 2, 3, 4, 5
2.	I try to be modest and don't try to have all the answers.	1, 2, 3, 4, 5
3.	I believe that leading is about allowing other persons to speak up freely.	1, 2, 3, 4, 5

4. While conducting a meeting on new company strategies, some employees keep interrupting with questions not relevant to the subject. Although I try to be patient, I find an amicable way to back them down. 1, 2, 3, 4, 5

5. I don't start or allow myself to be drawn into arguments. 1, 2, 3, 4, 5

6. When I sense that the other person disagrees, I stop talking, ask for the other person's opinion, allow him to present his points of view before I address his objections. 1, 2, 3, 4, 5

7. I repeat, rephrase, and summarise when I'm trying to communicate when my listener doesn't appear to understand. 1, 2, 3, 4, 5

8. I do not try to win arguments by dominating the discussion. 1, 2, 3, 4, 5

9. I invite disagreement but don't criticise others, even when I must correct them. I do my job at the right time. 1, 2, 3, 4, 5

10. I try to come to terms with my disappointments sometimes at the group proceedings but express my disapproval when needed. 1, 2,3,4, 5

11. I try not to be influenced by pessimists but do have faith in myself and the team's abilities. 1, 2, 3, 4, 5

12. Before and after a group exercise I evaluate my participation to create self –awareness. 1, 2, 3, 4, 5

(Answers at the end of the chapter)

CONCEPT REVIEW QUESTIONS

1. Discuss how basic forms of communication are applicable and useful in group communication activities.
2. Do you think that writing the case study for group discussion in advance is necessary for effective discussions and finding solutions? Give your views with reference to some of the essential commandments of the writing process.
3. Identify the value of speaking as a vehicle for dissemination of ideas and useful information in group functions and in many other forums. What are the fundamentals of effective speaking?
4. Do you feel that inefficiency in listening is a major obstacle to good performance as a group member? How can you enhance your listening skills?

SUMMARY

The subject of communication has been a matter of concern for all professionals in organisation as well for the organisation leaders. So is true about the participants in a group function everywhere, whether in academics or business, and industry case session. Communication is an acquired skill but one must painstakingly learn the basic forms of communication.

First of all, there is the precise need for written communication in group exercises. The case situation has to be prepared, whether academic, technical or for dealing with organsiational problems. The written text of a particular case has to be clear, complete, correct and to be fully understandable. It has to be systematic and precise in its content and approach. There could be so many rules but never overdo them.

The value of spoken words in group sessions is becoming increasingly important. The importance of speaking as a vehicle of transmission of ideas and information gets to be more critical while working with others in groups. If one does the job successfully, it strengthens the speaker's self –esteem and morale.

No doubt, there are roadblocks to perfection but one must overcome the barriers by constant practice and sincere efforts. One must be aware about a few fundamentals which should be helpful in mastering the art and science of speaking in group deliberations. One vital lesson to remember: fewer your objective, sharper is the focus, and far greater will be the chances of success.

No less important is the listening abilities of the group members. Indeed, communication experts called listening as the most important of all the communication skills. Listening is a four part activity. It involves hearing, interpreting, understanding and appraising. One must force oneself to pay attention to all the spoken words. A comprehensive ten-point guideline should be useful to enhance the listening ability of each person, whether in groups or in every day work environment. The golden rule given by Shakespeare said it so very convincingly: "Give every man thine ear, few thy voice!"

Answers to the Test: Group Communication Questionnaire

The model situation will be when one prefers the "Always" answer and marks (5) as the choice. However, there may be disputes on a few issues but better and the right preference should be "Always" and (5).

KEY TERMS

Abstract	:	*Not concrete, not specific.*
Appraising	:	*Estimating the value or quality.*
Assertive	:	*Tending to be forthright.*
Breeze	:	*Gentle wind.*
Chaff	:	*Corn husks, worthless things.*
Cues	:	*Stimulus to perception.*
Concrete	:	*Specific and definite.*
Disparaging	:	*Bringing discredit.*

Distractions	:	*Draw away the attention.*
Doodle	:	*Absent-mindedness, also scribbling something.*
Empathetically	:	*Capacity to identify with a person or object.*
Explicit	:	*Expressly stated, outspoken.*
Fluid	:	*Constantly changing.*
Glean	:	*Acquire and gather facts.*
Haunting	:	*Tending to linger in the mind.*
Implicit	:	*Implied though not plainly expressed.*
Ingredient	:	*Component.*
Legalism	:	*Adhering excessively to a law or formula.*
Overbearing	:	*Domineering and bullying attitude.*
Pessimist	:	*Tendency to be gloomy or expect the worst.*
Ponderous	:	*Slow and awkward, also laborious.*
Postures	:	*Assume a mental or physical attitude.*
Proficiency	:	*Adept and expert.*
Roadblocks	:	*Obstacles to progress.*
Scanning	:	*Examining analytically.*
Skeptical	:	*Person inclined to doubt accepted opinions, ideas etc.*
Tacit	:	*Understood or implied without being stated.*
Tongue-tied	:	*Too shy or embarrassed to speak.*
Vivid	:	*Clear, lively and graphic.*
Vow	:	*Promise or declare solemnly.*

REFERENCES

Adair, John. ***Training for Communicators***
Jaico Publishing House, Mumbai, 2002.

Lesikar and Pettit. ***Business Communication: Theory and Application*** *AITBS, New Delhi, 2000.*

Ludlow, Ron and Fergus Panton. ***The Essence of Effective Communication***
Prentice Hall of India, New Delhi, 2000.

Osborn, Michael and Suzanne Osborn.
Public Speaking *AITBS, Delhi, 1998.*

Stuart, Christina, ***Effective Speaking***.
Pan Books Ltd. London, 2002.

T+D. Training + Development Journal
Jan, Feb, March, Alexandria, VA 2011.

VII

Way to Success and Gaining Benefits

LEARNING OBJECTIVES

Essential elements of learning in this chapter are:

1. Leaders, organisers, and group members have to be result-driven rather than just be format –driven.
2. The steps involved to add value to the whole process.
3. The range of tasks and the conditions for success are spelt out clearly in detail.
4. The importance of listening for each participant will be involved and its applications.
5. Use of empathy as an effective way of communication.
6. How one should be a conscious and alert communicator.
7. A suggestion for improvement is provided in detail.
8. How the individuals, the organisers and the organisation can reap benefit out of the whole process

Success in group methods for case situations calls for a series of necessary norms. This applies not only to the leader and the organisers but more essentially to group members. These are areas which are to be attended to, but never lose sight of adding value to the whole process. The case model may not be applied too rigidly and leaders must not try to overcontrol the whole exercise.

Cases are no doubt powerful tools but the study should be result-driven rather than format-driven. The question is about core competence which by itself is value enhancing. Instances are plenty that many group leaders and organisers are, as researchers say, "unconsciously incompetent".

On the other hand, many of the less educated or newly inducted member- participants are "Consciously incompetent".

Adding Value

To add value to shadow-side pitfalls, the following steps should provide positive directions:

(1) Become good at all stages:

Try to be good at everything and at every stage. Shape up more in tune with the situation.

Becoming good goes beyond understanding the problem and its focus is much, much more result oriented. Make self-assessment at each step to develop an intellectual perception, helping real life situations.

Becoming good is an acquired skill. But the best way to success is persistent practice. It's learning and practising process. It's also a changing, adjusting and continuous process.

(2) Practise as you preach:

Demonstrate your competence by modeling the kinds of things you want others to do. If you want them to be free, frank and open, you have to be so.

Share your own experience with others as a way of modeling self-disclosure. Help them move beyond blind spots.

(3) Be polite, but firm. Be assertive:

Be friendly without being submissive. Be firm but never be rude. Be assertive and do not be afraid to claim your due rights. As a leader, you may not like to settle for a caricature of nondirective counselor. As a member, would you like to be one who "just sits there and nods".

Effective leaders, organisers and participants in a group session use their tools of trade on problems and solutions.

(4) Develop a state of advanced empathy:

Sharing with all about their experience, behaviours, and feelings to help them move beyond weak spots and create new perspectives.

(5) Competence in behaviour and in Outcomes:

Competence does not lie just in behaviours but primarily in the accomplishments toward which these behaviours are directed. Now comes the process of decision making which, in its broadest sense, is the same as problem solving.

Range of Tasks

Harvard's Argyris outlined a range of tasks to be accomplished in almost similar situation. Many of them require, directly or indirectly, a tilt toward action. Some of them are:

The importance of listening for each participant to add value to group exercises.

- Assume an active rather than a passive role in case situations.
- Widen your range of behaviours. Act in many rather than few ways.
- Develop a wider range of interests _____ moving from erratic, shallow, and casual interests to mature, strong, and enduring interests.
- Move towards relationships with others as equals or superiors.

Here, we may also quote Tom Gilbert who aptly noted, "Human competence is not found in human behaviour, rather it is found in human accomplishments." To fulfill the needs of problems-managing or opportunity-developing case action, actions must lead to productive outcomes.

Conditions for Success

Both the organisers and the participants of the case study sessions need a range of skills to make the exercises successful. These include:

(1) Basic and advanced communication skills.
(2) Creative judgement.
(3) Skills in problem clarification.
(4) Ability to reduce fear and anxiety.
(5) Appropriate goal setting.
(6) Development of a realistic action plan.
(7) Suggest implementation process.
(8) Evaluation at every stage of progress.

In practical life, the only way to acquire these skills is by learning them experientially, practising them, and using them until they become second nature.

Importance of Listening:

Proficiency in communication involves listening carefully to what everyone is saying both verbally and non-verbally. Complete listening involves listening to and understanding non-verbal behaviour.

We may refer to A. Mehravian's research to know what cues people use to judge whether another person likes them or not. He has discovered that the other person's actual words contributed only 7% to the impression of liked or disliked, voice cues contributed 38%, and facial cues 55%. It was also found out that when facial expressions were inconsistent with spoken words, facial expressions were believed more than words.

The above findings signify that not the exact percentages but rather the non-verbal behaviour is much more important in the communication process. Therefore, good and effective listeners learn how to listen and act systematically.

Obstacles and distractions abound in the silent process of communication. It is not as easy as it sounds. The following kinds of ineffective listening overlap with one another.

1. **Half-hearted listening:**
   Listeners often get distracted from what others are saying. They get involved in their own thoughts or begin to think about what they are going to say in reply.
2. **Listening Evaluatively:**
   Many people though may be listening attentively, listen and evaluate simultaneously. They try to judge the merits and demerits of what the other person is saying in terms of good-bad, right-wrong, like-dislike, acceptable-unacceptable, relevant-irrelevant and so on. This is indeed a very common tendency and not entirely dispensable. There are, indeed, brighter aspects of evaluative listening. No one can postpone judgement completely while listening. Nevertheless, it is possible to set one's judgement aside for the time being so as to ensure accurate perception and understanding of other's points of view.
3. **Filtering Listening Process:**
   We use a range of filters to listen to ourselves, others and the world around us. In communication there is a familiar dictum.

   "We see what we want to see,
   We communicate what we perceive,
   We perceive what we filter".

   The filters vary from situation to situation and have a social and cultural bias.

   Similarly, prejudices, gender, race, income pattern, lifestyle-whether conscious or not- distort understanding owing to use of filter at each step.
4. **Sympathy and person-centered Listening:**
   In case related and problem solving discussion it should be a combination of both fact-centered and person-centered listening. It's entirely a good idea to collect facts but never miss the person. Listen to everybody contextually, try to focus on themes and pin down the key messages.

   In human communication, sympathy has an unmistakable role and more so in case situations. But, truly speaking, its place in group activity is highly limited. No one must, directly or indirectly, become an accomplice to drive out problem-managing initiative of the group. This happens on account of over display of sympathy leading to inaction or inertia.

EMPATHY AS A WAY OF COMMUNICATION

Empathy, as a way of being or as a communication skill, sometimes creates confusion in the mind. C.R. Rogers in his treatise "A way of being" talks about basic empathic listening and gives us his description of the same.

"It means entering the private perceptual world of the other and becoming thoroughly at home in it .... It means temporarily living in the other's life, moving about in it delicately without making judgements".

Empathy as a form of human communication demands listening to everyone involved in the group process and understanding them to the extent that is realistically possible. In turn, it also involves communicating this understanding to them so that they might understand themselves more accurately and act purposefully on their understanding. H Kohut ("The Search for Self") says it so searchingly and almost lyrically about empathy.

"Empathy, the accepting, confirming, and understanding human echo evoked by the self, is a psychological nutrient without which human life, as we know and cherish it, could not be sustained".

All these lead us to believe that empathic communication is one of the supreme habits of highly effective people. It provides a psychological air and helps us breathe more freely in our relationships.

Gerard Egan ("The Skilled Helper"), an avowed protagonist of the "Art of Empathy", however issues a caution. He says, "Care must be taken not to make a cult out of empathy". "However important empathy is", he adds, "it is not the only mode of being in the helping relationship".

Empathy is certainly not a miracle pill. It can, however, contribute to the success of any communication programme in a variety of ways. Empathy acts as a kind of communication lubricant, it encourages and facilitates dialogue. It thus encourages collaboration in the group process.

Golden Rules for the use of Empathy

- Develop sensitivity to the feelings of others and fire an urge to be of help to someone.
- Try to imagine how another person feels and act supportively in response.
- Set your judgements and prejudices aside and walk in the shoes of the other person.
- Listen to both verbal and non-verbal messages and their meanings and context.
- Keep in mind that the skill of empathy, though important, is a tool to help the group members see themselves and their problem situations more clearly. Their ability to perceive correctly will lead them to managing their problems more effectively.

Point to Note: Many people confuse empathy with sympathy. Being sympathetic denotes experiencing compassion in observing the other person's pains or problems. But, then, whereas a sympathetic person looks into the other person's eyes and tries to understand, the empathetic person looks through the eyes of the other person and feels what he or she feels.

Be a conscious and alert communicator

Be conscious about malfunctions and barriers to communication. Although the objective is clearly defined, distortions and malfunctions may impede progress. Groups should be effectively led to find good solutions to the problem.

A detailed analysis of communication barriers can be helpful in this process.

CAUSES	MALFUNCTIONS
1. **Own assumptions**	1. **Language Imperfections** Awareness of the problem and using words precisely.
2. **Attitudes**	2. **Incorrect Thinking Process** Not to go by 'yes' or 'no' decision. Other solutions exist.
3. **Anxieties**	3. **Fact – Inference Confusion**Confusing inferences with facts creates miscommunication.
4. **Status Differences**	4. **The Blocked Mind**A blocked mind is closed to reality. Tendency to reject ideas that oppose our viewpoints.
5. **Stereotyping** Not to form stereotypes – Never make judgements by limited observation and emotional response	5. **The Static Viewpoint**Not to hold a static view of anything. Because reality is always changing.

Evaluate and Implement

Evaluate solutions and get recommendations accepted. In this task evaluate against results expected. Assess risks involved. Apply strategies of persuasive communication.

Create action plans to formulate cases that pertain to actual work situations. Keep in view that each problem is unique by its nature and occurrence. A realistic blend of ideas and imagination will be needed in each case activity.

In business and organsiational situations implement solutions without the least hesitation. In fact, participation process of group activity will have a positive response and a ready acceptance.

Suggestions for Improvement

(1) All communication events must be related to socio-cultural environment.
(2) To be objective oriented.
(3) Make communication receiver centered.
(4) Keep in touch with reality while communicating.
(5) Check your communications with the real world situations.
(6) Seek to clarify your ideas before communicating.
(7) Consult with others, whenever necessary, while communicating.
(8) Seek not only to be understood but also to understand.

(9) Consider the other person's needs and interests.
(10) Communicate for today as well as for tomorrow-must be consistent with long-range interests and goals.

Golden Rule: Communicate as you would like to be communicated to.

Benefits of the Case Method

As we have discussed, case study is essentially a behavioural process which facilitates group members to learn the skill of functioning in new ways. The process helps in logical deduction and realistic analysis. The method, therefore, is best suited to develop the right kind of attitude as well as perception. In an organised group discussion, a participant can form a more objective view of one's role and functions. Another significant benefit is that the views expressed are reasoned out in the presence of other group members.

Some of the key benefits of case study method that apply to individual participants as well as to the organisers are:

Gains for individual participants

- One learns to develop both written and verbal communication skills as one is supposed to present, analyze and, when necessary, defend the results of findings. Each member learns to recommend solutions and steps for implementation through case discussions as well as through written reports. One develops improved thinking and even complex thinking abilities involved in analysis and judgement. One also learns to put the right questions at the right time.
- A good case can stretch the skills of the participants in separating the wheat from the chaff, getting to the root of the problem quickly and decisively.
- The process can contribute to development of personality, sense of confidence, initiative, skills of interpersonal relations, and understand problems of human affairs.
- Everyone comes to appreciate the need to contain conflicts, if any, and find solutions to the problems eventually.
- Finally, the case method, practised in case after case, develops mind which is oriented towards getting things done. This allows each participant to tailor what he or she learns in particular situations.

Gains for Organisers and Organisations

- A case may be used for arriving at general conclusions on challenging organsiational and management tasks and principles from specific examples.

- In academic exercises, cases provide extended experience by role-playing various parts which often cannot be done in other activities.
- In the organsiational framework, the case study method throws open the problems of management and problems which require judgement; many dimensions are to be seen can be weighed with reference to various constraints.
- Essentially, cases teach the skills of diagnosis, action planning, direction, monitoring, implementation, appreciating other people's points of view and realising that for any problem situation there are many possible ways to deal with it.
- Briefing, clarifying, conveying facts and information at the very beginning is highly useful. This helps members to understand the tasks clearly and adequately.
- The technique of "brainstorming" helps everyone to contribute ideas as also the group leader who is also a member of the group.
- The entire activity, if appropriately handled, can promote an internal standard of performance and fire an intense urge to excel in the functioning of the group. Moreover, the process can stimulate creative as well as logical thinking which finally merge into the collective thinking of the group.

An example: Steps to High Impact Group Meetings

One frequently hears about marathon group meetings, some of which last for quite a few hours. Many such meetings quickly lose focus and end up being a waste of everyone's time. One reason could be that many leaders are not properly trained and results in poor team management. Just a few steps, however, can help team leaders successfully facilitate higher team performance. These are the findings by universal surveys on successful team management in many leading organisations. Here are a few guidelines to help leaders get the maximum out of the team members.

1. **Build an effective agenda**

   Meetings must not be conducted without agenda or clear objectives. Decide about the participants and give them as much prior notice as possible. Send meeting reminder after a reasonable time along with the agenda papers. Give the members sufficient time for preparing themselves. And the leader must also prepare him or her adequately well.
2. **Choose the right medium**

   Remember that face-to-face interactions are the best and the richest medium. There may also be video conferencing when participants are distantly located or they are not to be called personally to save their precious time. When team members are required to solve difficult problems or make decisions, better to use collaborative software tools. Go for brainstorming the team's ideas and polling questions that can be used subsequently to get feedback and also to engage team members effectively.

3. **Emphasize shared responsibilities**
   To reinforce shared responsibility, let different persons to lead different sessions or parts of the session. When necessary, rotate the Chairperson's role among team members.
4. **Minimise diversion or "side trips" during meetings.**
   Purpose is to keep everyone on track during group deliberations. Ensure that all are well-prepared to make the meeting more efficient. If necessary, interrupt a discussion to re-focus the participants or re-balance group interactions.
   Three key practices help the leader determining the time and ways of intervention. These are: (1) Observation (2) Diagnosis and (3) Actual intervention.
   Observation is paying close attention to the flow of discussion. Focus on behaviour and body language of the members. Listen carefully and decide about appropriate steps to infuse life into the deliberations.
   Diagnosis indicates your decision when there is a 'side-trip' or members stray away from the agenda. In situations when the team productivity suffers you just cannot be a silent observer but must act without being rude.
   Finally, based on observation and diagnosis, choose the right kind of intervention technique that helps the team. Sometime ask a question and bring back the members toward a goal. Even summarizing just a point helps the members to find a new meaning as well as fulfillment of objectives.

(Based on an article by Darleen De. Rosa in T.D. (Training & Development Magazine)

CONCEPT DEVELOPMENT QUESTIONS

1. Elucidate your views about ways to add value to group methods for case situation within the organsiational framework. Work out your suggestions to ensure positive directions.
2. Do you think that participants in the case study situations have to acquire a range of skills to achieve success in their efforts? Give your views with a checklist of conditions for success.
3. How much importance do you attach to the factor of listening in group activities? Discuss the process together with reference to modes of listening.
4. Explain "Empathy" from your own standpoint. In this context specify various communication factors involved with suggestions for further improvement.

5. Discuss how the individual participants, organisers, leaders and the organisation as a whole stand to gain benefits out of the case study method.

SUMMARY

Success in group methods depends on collective efforts. This involves the leader, the organisers and more essentially the group members. The case study discussions should not be just format -driven but should be more and more result-driven.

The objective is to add value to the whole process. This requires all involved to be conscious about (i) becoming good at all stages (ii) practise and preach together (iii) to be polite as well as assertive (iv) devotion and empathy (v) competent behaviour and getting the right outcome.

The range of tasks include active roles for all, widening of behavioural aspects, developing wider interests and moving towards relationships with equals as well as supervisors. Both the organisers and the participants need a higher range of skills which are clearly specified. Similarly, the importance of listening needs total understanding and assimilation of the requirements. Never listen half-heartedly and go for good evaluation and filtration of the process. If should be entirely person-centered listening.

One has to fully appreciate the truth that empathy is a positive way of communication. Empathy as a form of human communication demands listening to everyone in the group process. As a result, everyone in the group is able to understand and act purposefully, thus fulfilling the group requirements. However, experts caution out that empathy should not be overstressed and other modes must be fully used to promote understanding and relationship. The golden rules of empathy have to be followed and put to use in group deliberations.

Another call is to be a conscious and alert communicator. The participants also need to be alert about the malfunctions and barriers of communication. At all stages they should evaluate and implement. Suggestions for improvement are provided and need to be studied and adhered to.

There are immense benefits for the case method and there should be specific benefits for individual participants as well for the organisers and the organisation as a whole. The entire activity can indeed promote an internal standard of performance and groups can excel in its own functioning. The process also stimulates creative and logical thinking which finally merge into the collective thinking of the group itself.

KEY TERMS

Accomplice : *Partner in activities.*
Assertive : *Enforce claim to one's rights.*
Caricature : *Ridiculously poor imitation.*
Chaff : *Worthless things.*
Compassion : *Be sympathetic to help or be merciful.*

Contextually	:	*Relevant circumstances.*
Cues	:	*Stimulus to perception, signal for action.*
Dimensions	:	*Measurable extent.*
Distractions	:	*Draw away the attention, diversion from the main theme or activity*
Experientially	:	*Getting skilled from experience.*
Impede	:	*Obstruct or hinder.*
Lubricant	:	*Efforts made to reduce friction and inject life into an activity.*
Norms	:	*Standard or pattern of behaviour and performance.*
Shallow	:	*Not deep, superficial in knowledge.*

REFERENCES

Adair, John ***The Effective Communicator***
Jaico Publishing Mumbai (2002).
De, Nitish ***Organsiational Scanning***
Prentice Hall of India New Delhi (1991)
Lane, Leroy L. ***By All Means Communicate***
Prentice Hall, New Jersey (1991).
Lesikar, R.V. and M.E. Flatley ***Basic Business Communication***
Tata Mc Graw Hill (Tenth Edition) New Delhi, 2005.
Ludlow, Ron and Fergus Panton ***The Essence of Effective Communication.***
Prentice Hall of India New Delhi (2000).
Mehravian, Albert ***Silent Messages***
Belmont, California Wordsworth Publishing Co. (1971).
Sengupta, Sailesh ***Business and Managerial Communication***
PHI Learning Private Ltd. (New Delhi 2011).
Zander, M. ***Making Groups Effective***
Jassy Bass, San Francisco (1982).

VIII

Presentations and Role Play

LEARNING OBJECTIVES

This chapter attempts to enhance individual as well as group perception of communication in the following key concept areas -

1. Value of presentation in the organsiational context and the essential components of perfect presentation.
2. The need for persuasive skills and how the objectives can be achieved by skillful techniques and effective communication.
3. Preparing for presentation with an eye to the purpose of the presenter.
4. The role of planning and designing the presentation together with researching the audience.
5. How role plays can be used as a method of learning and creating role playing situations.
6. Stages of role playing in groups and solving role playing problems.
7. Benefits and gains of role playing and the right methods of handling the questions and answers in group discussions.

Presentation is a communication process. It is both an opportunity and a challenge. The opportunity lies in the interaction that is possible between the presenter and the audience. When you make a planned presentation before a group, as a part of the communication process, you can receive information and can transmit information. You can adjust both the content and the delivery of your message as you proceed with your task. Not just that, you can make your message clearer and more compelling, by instantaneous editing of your oral presentation which only you would be aware about. Instead of simply stating your ideas, you can draw out the audience's ideas and use them to reach a mutually acceptable conclusion.

The challenge comes in the form of (i) having less control of content and (ii) enabling the audience to stay on track. How these happen? Curiously, the more you try to interact with the audience, the less control you'll have on their reactions and responses. Again, in the midst of your presentation a comment or an unexpected query from anyone in the audience might distract you or even force you to shift from intended topics. Better would be to anticipate such interruptions or shifts and prepare for them as you develop your oral presentations. Take care of the four most essential components of any material for "perfect presentations".

(1) The introduction
(2) The body
(3) The summary or the close

In essence, and just in one sentence, the first three ingredients mean to say: "tell them what you are going to tell them, then tell them, and then tell them what you have told them". And the fourth component should be

(4) The question – and – answer session.

For a perfect presentation, as well as to carry confidence and conviction, simple visual or audio-visual applications will be sources of positive enhancements.

Persuasive skills

Presentation skills apply to an endless and a wide variety of subjects and situations. In every case, however, the purpose of making a presentation is to persuade the audience towards making a decision. And the decision, by and large, should go in favour of the presenter's ideas or propositions. That is, ultimately and putting it too simply, the aim of all presenters and their presentations.

By means of skillful techniques and effective communication, trained, knowledgeable, and expert presenters try to persuade people:

- To buy a product or use a service.
- To adopt an idea or a concept.
- To lend support to an issue or a campaign.
- To donate funds for a good cause.
- To learn and apply the information presented.
- To move to a desired attitude, behaviour or action.
- To appreciate an image or a strategy.
- To accept change and to reduce or eliminate the resistance.
- To dissuade from certain detrimental activities.
- To approve suggested solutions to certain problems.

Preparing for presentation in the organsiational and academic context is an essential component of perfect presentation.

- To follow a new work procedure.
- To vote for a candidate or to select a leader.
- To participate in a group or a community activity.
- To give consent or views about the budget allocations.
- To respond favourably to the presenter's viewpoints and recommendations.

Let us agree that the list above does not provide a uniform model for all situations. But the list, as it is, and with necessary modifications, partly or wholly, can be made applicable to a range of professional fields. The occasion may vary from classroom to non-classroom activities and wide-ranging functions from advertising and public relations to marketing, human resource management, general management and all.

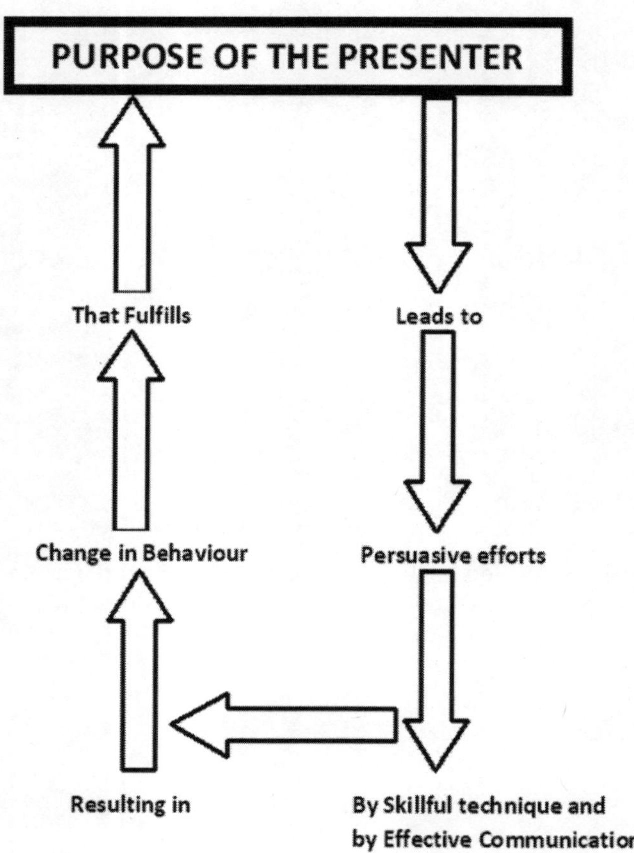

Preparing for Presentation

Decidedly, an effective presentation is one which produces the desired results. It is almost like a successful military campaign. The original Latin word campaign means battle maneuvers in warfare. In other words, it meant a series of operations and skillful movements for a complete assault on the enemy position. Now, in our context, presentation is a campaign process which makes highly systematic efforts. It is a unit of effort to accomplish a set of objectives. The presentation, therefore, has to be uni-focus, a short term programme with set of communication aims.

The scope and objectives of any planned presentation may be framed almost on the lines of a good advertising campaign. But, then, planning is the essential first step while preparing for a good presentation. Planning focuses on the primary factors that govern the outcome of a presentation. One useful approach- systematically, thoroughly, and creatively- is to ask a few questions. These questions relate to universal five Ws and One H, which go to define the scope and objectives of the presentation. And there we find the clues to planning and preparation.

Five Ws and One H

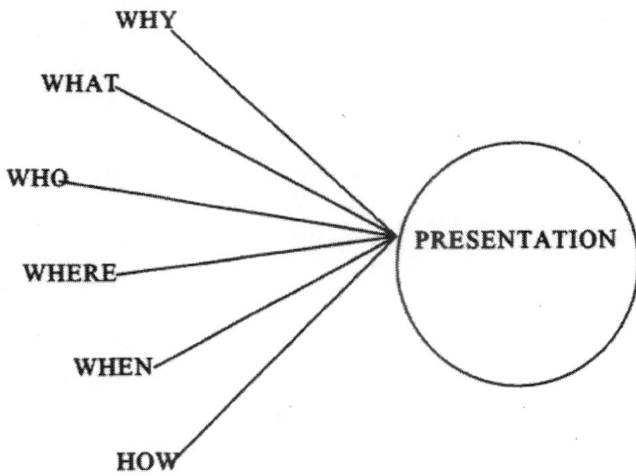

As Rudyard Kipling said in another context:

"I keep six honest-serving men,
They taught me all I know,
Their names are what, why and when,
And how, where and who!"

Let us get into the nature and content of the reflective questions.

- **WHY** need the presentation? (purpose)
- **WHAT** needs to be said to elicit the desired response? (Outcome)

- **WHO** needs to be reached? (Target group)
- **WHERE** to locate the ideal material for the message?(Information)
- **WHEN** to start and finish the presentation? (Time table)
- **HOW** to persuade the listeners (Art and Science)

Planning and Designing

Stages to consider for a successful case study include:

- Set objectives in clear terms.
- Decide whether to use an artificial or a real problem.
- The extent of coverage of the case situation e.g. a complete organsiational problem, specific managerial problems or personal value situations.
- The resource requirements are a written case, visual aids, role playing, video clips, computer application and so on.
- Allowing sufficient or reasonable time for preparation, discussions, brainstorming and final presentations.
- Follow a logical sequence with a good balance between arguments and facts.
- Objectives again.................go for realistic evaluations of achievement of objectives.................how far in real sense and term.

Effective Presentations

In a case study or in a direct business presentation, the real challenge is in the matter of capturing attention. It is the challenge of finding the means to command attention as the competition for people's time and attention is greater to-day than it has ever been. To succeed, a person has to develop ways to have a highly positive and lasting impact on the people with whom they deal.

Reports clearly indicate that people in an audience want a relevant, focused, well-organised message delivered by a presenter who is well-prepared.

Presentations today are not just restricted to group members as direct audiences. Portal presentations have come up in a big way by applying innovative ideas in money market operations around the globe.

(See example).

Researching the Audience

From an objective point, we should try to consider the audience or the group composition in a number of ways:

- Who are these people?
- How many of them are known to you?
- How much do they know about the topic?
- What will make the message meaningful to them?
- What will move them to act on the message as intended?
- What will provide balance among possible differences of opinion?

- What are the objectives of this people in the audience?
- What information and techniques would gain attention and promote a favourable response?

All these are part of the planning and adapting process. The idea is to concentrate wholly on the nature and needs of the participants. Knowing the composition of the group is a part of the "demographics" which provide a presenter with a "picture of people". For identical group compositions, it should be sufficient to identify just a few demographic specifics. All such information should be available relatively quickly and easily. Some of these are:

1. Age
2. Education
3. Gender
4. Occupation
5. Income pattern and status
6. Special interests

All such factors provide a presenter with insight into participants' needs, interests, concerns, and factors that are likely to influence their demands

In academic or in the same organisation circles, the advantage of knowing the audience is immediately noticeable. The more one knows the audience, the more powerful one's impact on the audience will be.

The techniques which can help to ensure a successful presentation are concerned with a lot of abilities and arrangements. They are:

Spoken word communication,

The use of voice,

Persuasive skills,

Non-verbal skills including Body Language,

Visual aids

Answering questions.

Role Play

Role playing, as a method of learning, was introduced by Moreno, a Vatican psychiatrist. It is now universally recognised as a learning by doing or training through action. Role playing is one the oldest techniques devised to assist learners by direct experience in a simulated setting. It should be a simple and informal drama in which some of the participants act a problem or a situation.

A group exercise based on a role play can help the members to perceive and interpret key elements in a situation. The method therefore has some members acting out parts in contrived problem situations. A role play, therefore, represents graphic illustrations of effective or ineffective behaviour which the participants have generated for themselves. As a result, we can learn how these behaviours affect other people.

An international hostel and restaurant chain regularly uses role playing to teach managers and employees how to communicate with fellow workers and customers.

After the role play, both group members and observers should analyse and discuss the whole process. The role players by acting the situation and the audience by seeing it can analyse and interpret the issues properly. In fact, they can examine different points of view arising out of the role play. They can also appraise each player's effectiveness and suggest how the performance of each might have been improved.

Role-playing Situations

The specific situations, which are suitable for practising role plays are those which need analysis, preparation to meet future situations and brainstorming in a creative mode. Role playing acts as a stimulant for participation and involvement. While the method is more and more being applied to academic learning, it has its practical utility in organisations as well. Role playing is indeed one of the best and spontaneous devices of problem analysis. It can help teach useful techniques which are concerned with day-to-day work and interpersonal relations. There cannot be any uniform model of application but may cover situation like:

(1) Negotiation of a collective agreement.
(2) Meeting of workers and management on some vital issues.
(3) Board of Directors meeting or an Annual General Meeting (AGM).
(4) Any "Sweat Session" relating to business, advertising, marketing or sales promotion.
(5) Customer Relationship ________________________ challenges and management.
(6) Media presentations.
(7) Organsiational communication problems ____________ relations between equals, relations between subordinates and superiors.
(8) Crisis Management and Crisis Communication.

Therefore, role playing may be used to develop skill in any area that involves interaction between people. It can also be most ideally used for teaching human relations and sales techniques. So, case method and role plays are often used in conjunction with one another. The method is applied either in class-room or in non-class room activities or both.

Stages of Role Playing

The roles people play in groups can fall into several stages. While many of the functions are stated in the chart given here, some steps would require careful planning and execution. For example, after the play starts conversation follows spontaneously among the members. Here the leader has to remain alert. He has to keep the play on the track. He has to keep an eye that the play does not become embarrassing or motionless.

The discussion after role playing is to be conducted while the interest of the group is still intense. This is the final stage of translating into action what has been seen and talked about. The aim is to develop the role playing into a rehearsal for a real life situation.

STAGES OF ROLE PLAYING IN GROUPS

Problem Solving	Defining Roles	Actual Play	Post Play Discussion
1. Choosing the problem	1. General guidance given.	1. Play Starts	1. Discussion follows
2. Provide needed Props.	2. Make realistic through experience.	2. Dialogue follows spontaneously.	2. Gather reactions
3. Provide bases for Roles.	3. Allocation of roles	3. Leader keeps on track. Regulate.	3. Suggestions Comments
4. Draw Attention & Recognition.	4. Give time to think.	4. Not to turn into motionless or embarrassing	4. Remove misunderstand-ing
5. Warm up Sentiments.	5. Practise Human Relations Skills.	5. Appraisal of each role.	5. Eliminate conflicts
6. Readiness to find Solution.	6. Role of Non-active members Defined.	6. Put on end at the right moment.	6. Develop Actions
7. Feeling of partici-pation	7. Plan sequence of Events		7. Final Conclusion.

Role Playing Problems

Role playing presents few problems, but there are some. Role playing is more difficult to use effectively than other problems. If inappropriately used it spoils the whole purpose. Such situations arise when more emphasis is placed on action than the problem or when the group is so involved that the subject-matter, the content and the purpose are forgotten or neglected.

A few other specific problem areas can be as under:

1. Those playing roles must become actively and emotionally identified with the characters they portray.
2. Audience interest must be maintained throughout.
3. If unimaginatively introduced, the group may take it as a childish approach to a serious problem and the attempt may backfire.
4. Lack of planning. If the role play is not very carefully planned and carried out, it becomes ridiculous, unreal and ineffective.

One very important aspect of the role playing activity is that role play alone does not deal fully with the subject. It can illustrate the theme, underlines key ideas. Any role playing must be followed by discussion to bring out a moral. A role play has a lasting effect on the personality of the actors and the participants. We need greater caution in using it as a tool of learning.

Benefits and Gains

Role playing lends itself to training and education of new or experienced people, mixed group situations or realistic experience in applying to any professional activities. The benefits and gains in real terms are immense and include:

- It can liven up a group activity.
- It demonstrates how to handle similar situations and put feelings and attitudes in practice.
- It develops among participants the ability to put forward logical and relevant arguments.
- Role players practice introspection through participating in the appraisal of their own performances. Videotaping makes self-criticism even more beneficial and objective.
- Role players, by the free-wheeling nature of role playing, gain new ideas and approaches. Defects inherent in stereotyped solutions become apparent.
- Role players learn to accept criticism from others, and the group soon comes to realise that sound suggestions benefits everyone.
- Role players gain acting experience, which may help them later in handling difficult situations.
- Role playing develops sensitivity and mutual understanding among participants which is quite helpful in maintaining better human relations.

Handling Questions and Answers and Queries

Be sure to plan for an opportunity for questions and answers. There may be certain comments as well, which should invite clarifications of issues being discussed. Q&A as well as comments occur primarily in the inter-active mode. If the organisers do not expect to interact with the participants, they are wasting the real advantages of a group effort.

If the case situation is unpopular in the organsiational framework, there may be a series of hostile questions. Treat them as genuine requests for information. Organisers, leaders and presenters should maintain professionalism and thus improve credibility. Give as many members as possible a chance to participate in a quick time frame. But never lose sight as well as vision to find solutions to the problems, which should finally take the shape of recommendations by the whole group.

A few suggestions towards "How to Handle Questions Effectively" and "How to encourage Members for continued Participation" are given below:

1. Communicators themselves have to be sure communicators. They need to be broadminded, humble and diligent persons.
2. Be careful about distortions by members. This may happen if the issues at discussion are not clearly and lucidly explained.
3. Encourage freedom of expression to every member but with controlling authority and with an eye to the achievement of results.
4. Listen actively. When required paraphrase the question is simpler terms. But must do it to the full satisfaction of the speaker himself or herself.
5. Extend particular support to junior team members and tell them to ask questions first.

6. Members may disagree. Try to understand why they disagree. There may be lots of arguments over something or even everything. An example:

An employee in a group meeting raises a question about his collegues not getting a moment of respite. He demands more persons in the department.

Stage I of handling the question

1. Make clear that you understand and appreciate their work.
2. Ask questions about time taken by them to complete their jobs.
3. Summarise the key points back to the questioner.

Stage II

4. After this, use the error correction process. Explain they are working on piece basis and paid accordingly.
5. If more people employed, their earnings will decline making them unhappy.
6. Emphasise the goal, provide positive incentive and reinforce the goal.

Stage III

Employees now say, don't worry, Sir, we can handle the situation!

7. Be mindful of your body language. Give approving, encouraging gestures and refrain from "negative feedback".
8. Need to have the attitude to view the question and the problem objectively without being judgmental. Never get emotionally involved even if your stand and opinion get challenged.
9. Give credit wherever is due. Involve everyone in the role-playing episodes. Next time make it a rotational event so that no one is left out from playing different roles at different situations. This applies both in academic activities as also for employees and executives as a learning process in business and industries.
10. Some queries are in the self-glorifying nature. A questioner makes a query from another participant. You have some suspicion in your mind. You may ask him "do you know the answer? The person replies, "yes I know, but I wanted to find out if he/she knows the answer."Tackle such situation in a way that no one feels offended.
11. Even if you believe what the person is asking is wrong or irrelevant, give the speaker a chance at self-expression. You're listening with interest and understanding is a good motivating factor. Correct the person later in a cool environment.
12. Develop empathy and rapport with the questioners and the listeners. Develop infinite capacity to remain calm under most provocative situations.

An Example

Portal Presentations
Innovative Ideas in Money Market Operations

Money market funds have been a popular investment vehicle for businesses around the world. New technology and a renewed focus on transparency is further increasing its appeal for investors seeking safe and liquid investment vehicles for their organsiational cash reserves. Although money market fund offerings are currently in their infancy in the markets, this is likely to change in the near future, with many more countries like India and China taking the lead. The apparent clarity and common understanding will ensure that money market funds remain a consistent and viable contributor to a healthy global financial system. No doubt this has already become a major global industry.

A clear indication came from Sanjay Dalmia, CEO of India-based financial software maker Fundtech, which enjoys a global reputation. He said Europe and USA are more advanced than Asia but now this is being exported to other countries like Asia (as reported by Global Finance). Countries like India and China are taking measured, but firm steps in quick succession to initiate liquid management techniques.

Portal Power

In came the online portal technology, a new form of presentation to clients, which is now driving the growing popularity of money market funds globally. Portals facilitate centralized management of short-term investments on a global basis. For example, Citi Bank's Portal, Citi Bank Online Investments, integrates investments in dozens of countries and currencies. Clients can now access more than 175 institutional funds. This has made liquidity management much easier and more efficient.

The portal also makes systematic presentation to the users to view rates, initiate trades and get immediate confirmations through a secure infrastructure. In addition, the portal incorporates a solid entitlement and presenter/checker process to maintain control over the investment process.

The future holds promises to increase demand for money market funds globally.

After all, liquidity is the lifeblood of an organisation, and the companies need to ensure they are satisfied how they use their portals with powerful presentations to offer innovative solutions for companies looking to optimise the interest they earn on excess cash balances. Indian Banks are not falling behind and have started to join the international trends in the banking sector.

Selecting an online investment portal

Investors evaluate the portals in several key areas. The abilities to make faultless presentations which attract them are:

- **How to Choose:** Does it offer products in multiple currencies?
- **Suitability:** Does it offer an automatic process without interruptions?
- **Complete:** Does it integrate global investing with appropriate policy management?
- **Reliable and Trouble free:** Does it offer total security of all transactions?
- **Centralised Viewing:** Does it offer centralised visibility and full reporting capability?

An effective and informative presentation must look into all such aspects and more to provide perfect presentations in newly developing areas in the financial sector.

(*with inputs from "Global Finance"*).

CONCEPT DEVELOPMENT QUESTIONS.

1. Elucidate the value of presentation as a group communication process in organisations as well as in classroom deliberations. Provide examples of situations where presentation could be purposeful to persuade people.
2. How you intend to prepare yourself for successful campaign purposes? Explain five Ws and One H in terms of planning and designing for a successful presentation.
3. Do you think that researching the audience is a needful activity before you make a presentation? How you propose to go about it and what are the essential features of audience researching?
4. As a business professional or as an academic learner how far the concept of role playing is useful and applicable to fulfil your presentation objectives? Prepare a chart of the role playing stages in groups. Also explain the benefits and gains of role playing as part of presentations.
5. Do you agree that handing questions, answers and queries during and at the end of the presentations will be a major part of the presentation requirements? Provide a check list as to how these are to be handled to achieve objectives?

SUMMARY

Presentation is both an opportunity and a challenge. A planned presentation before a group is a part of the communication process. The presenter, in addition to stating own ideas, can draw out the audience's ideas and use them to reach a mutually acceptable conclusion.

As a presenter you have to take care of the four most vital components of any material for perfect presentations. These are (i) the introduction to the subject (ii) the body (iii) the summary and (iv) the question-answer session. Remember, to carry conviction and confidence, visual as well as audio-visual applications will be sources of positive enhancements.

The presenter needs to have the right measure of persuasive skills. The trained, knowledgeable and expert presenters try to persuade people by means of skillful techniques and by effective communication. A range of situations can be usefully handled by presentations in academic, business and industry environments.

While preparing for presentations, to produce the intended results, the presenter needs to be aware about the application of Five Ws and one H. These are why, what, who, where, when and How. This concept was originally created by the celebrated poet Rudyard Kipling in another context but the professionals have now started to use the concept at work-related solutions.

One has to be mindful about the stages of presentation to achieve success and perfection. Even poral presentations have come up today by applying innovative ideas in money market presentations.

Go for researching the audience or the group composition beforehand. These are part of the planning and adapting process. Take care of the demographic specifics which should provide a right picture of the people in the audience. Such factors also provide a presenter with insight into participants' needs, interests, concerns and factors that are likely to influence their demands and aspirations.

Role play is another valuable idea which is globally recognised today as a learning by doing or training through role actions. Role playing can cover a large area of situations in organsiational as well as class-room training and learning method. The aim is to develop the role playing into a rehearsal for a real life situation.

Role playing can face certain problems which have to be particularly noted. At the same time, role playing offers handsome benefits and gains to the group members and they learn how to handle similar situations and enable them to put feelings and attitudes in practice. However, in presentations and role playing one must know how to handle questions, answers and queries from participants to make such events useful and rewarding. A twelve-point checklist is provided in the text to prepare the presenters and the role players to do their jobs successfully and effectively.

KEY TERMS.

Adapting	:	*Adjust oneself to new conditions.*
Backfire	:	*Fail a plan adversely.*
Campaign	:	*Organised cause of action as in military operations.*
Credibility	:	*Believability of message, reputation or status.*
Demographics	:	*Study of details of person's background, education, earnings, residence etc.*
Detrimental	:	*Harm or damage and causes of such occurrences.*
Diligent	:	*Hardworking as also showing care and effort.*
Free-wheeling	:	*Free and frank expressions and activities.*

Graphics	:	*Of or relating to the visual or descriptive arts; vividly realistic.*
Infrastructure	:	*Basic foundations.*
Introspection	:	*Examination of one's own thoughts.*
Judgemental	:	*Making judgements specially critical or subjective thoughts.*
Lifeblood	:	*Vital factor, as being necessary for liveliness.*
Liquid fund	:	*Assets, which can be easily converted into cash.*
Lucid	:	*Simple and clear expression.*
Optimise	:	*Obtaining the fullest benefit; most favourable conditions.*
Paraphrase	:	*Explaining the meaning of a statement; summary of expression in simple words.*
Portal	:	*Access points (or front doors) through which a business partner access secured, proprietary information from an organisation.*
Props	:	*Person or thing that supports; support with or as if with a prop.*
Stereotyped	:	*A Person or thing seeming to conform to a widely known type.*
Strategy	:	*Long term plan, policy or management.*
Sweat Session	:	*A work or discussion strenuously carried through; sweat it out for finding solutions to problems.*
Unifocus	:	*Single minded attention to an idea or a subject of discussion.*
Viable	:	*Feasible, capability of survival in difficult circumstances.*

REFERENCES

Adair, John, ***The Effective Communicator*** *Jaico, Mumbai, 2002.*

Drucker, Peter, ***The Practice of Management*** *Pan Books Ltd. London 1975.*

Forsyth, Patrick ***Powerful Reports and Proposals Kogan*** *Page India Pvt. Ltd New Delhi 110002.*

Lane, Leroy L, ***By All Means Communicate*** *Prentice Hall Englewood Cliffs, New Jersey 1991.*

Lesikar R.V. and M.E. Flatley ***Basic Business Communication*** *Tenth Edition. Tata McGraw Hill New Delhi, 2005.*

Ludlow, Ron and Panton Fergus ***The Essence of Effective Communication*** *Hall New Jersey, 1999.*

Robbins, SP and M, Coulter ***Management*** *Prentice Hall New Delhi 1996.*

Scot, Ober ***Contemporary Business Communication***
Houghton, Mifflin, Boston 1995.
Sengupta, Sailesh ***Business and Managerial Communication***
PHI Learning New Delhi 2011.
Times of India *New Delhi February 2, 2010.*
Global Finance*, New York, April 2011.*

IX

Intergroup Problems and Competitions How to Acieve Group Compatibility

LEARNING OBJECTIVES

This chapter provides close insights into the aspects of learning and development together with strategies for winning the challenges. The coverage further includes:

1. First of all, this is an educative process and knowing how to go about it.
2. Right approach to intergroup problems and competitions.
3. Achieving group compatibility.
4. What and how of quality circles.
5. Brainstorming process and its value and usefulness.
6. Simulations or empathy as a unique training and learning opportunity.
7. The golden rules for questions and answers and how to go for an extensive review at the end.

Organisations universally claim that they work extensively towards creating a healthy environment among all the employees, executives and the senior management persons. Even so, feelings of dissatisfaction are bound to creep in every now and then. It is true when groups of people are working together, disputes and disagreement, disbelief and discontent are bound to occur. There can be lots of reasons giving rise to problems and conflicts within a team. And when there are numbers of groups or teams in the organisation for supposedly better results, the extent of mutual conflicts might further escalate.

Competitions many times generate spectacular results in terms of performance, innovation and unforeseen growth. But unhealthy competition between teams is an indicator of poor team work. While one must agree that competition is the life – blood of an organisation there is wide difference between two extremes. Unhealthy nature of intergroup problems and competitions keep spreading to rivalry and tussles between and among departments. At the same time, we have to appreciate that many organisations involved either in productive or creative tasks, profit or non – profit jobs own their success to their natural competitive spirit. All successful organisations today accept universally that openness and honesty are the primary indicators of organsiational health. There will be no space for dirty tricks, back – biting or reckless rivalry among the employees as well as their managers.

What are the most common results of intergroup conflicts? This refers to small groups of individuals in the same group or between two or more groups. A short list of such situations is given here:

(1) More and more tension and anxiety among all group members.
(2) Task motivation goes down significantly.
(3) Feeling of acute resentment among the members.
(4) Pattern of behaviour changes and feeling of frustration in the work environment.
(5) Sense of identity, feeling of unity and urge to excel disappear from work areas.
(6) Crucial decisions or action by the managerial teams are delayed or altogether avoided.
(7) Negative aspects always lead to confrontation and hostility among the group members.
(8) Results of all the above create a feeling of apathy in the mind of group members and also their leaders

However, healthy competition among individual group members or between groups will result in quite a few benefits to groups as well as to orgnaisations. Instances are:

(1) Cohesiveness among groups tends to increase.
(2) Groups and members become more task oriented.
(3) Group norms become noticeably stronger.
(4) In most cases group conformity increases loyalty to the organisation.
(5) The form and structure of groups get clearly defined. And duties and responsibilities of the members are spelt out to their advantages and for the good of the organisation.

Moreover, there can be a host of other positive outcomes as a result of sorting out intergroup problems and conflicts. A few of these benefits are:

(1) Intergroup compatibility is seen to be actually feasible and members feel satisfied about their tasks and standards of performance.

Getting together to achieve group compatibility.

Another group interaction to promote understanding with each other.

(2) Sense of fulfillment and attachment to the organisation goes on increasing.
(3) Better ideas, sometimes even innovative ideas, are generated by the groups to the benefit of the organisation as a whole.
(4) Longstanding problems get easily sorted out.
(5) Willingness to cooperate and finding new approaches to solution to problems are found.
(6) Enhanced interest in work and degree of motivation shows significant upward trend.

The case study is universally acknowledged as an excellent education process. It is essentially a learning activity. A case provides opportunities to both the teacher and the taught to analyze, understand, and develop a high skill of conscious competence. Howell (1982) gave us a good description of learning as he said, "learning is incorporated into living to the extent that viable options are increased".

Conventional wisdom tells us that experience is the best teacher in life. But, as case studies have shown, self-enhancing options provide greater opportunities to learn. Experience will be an additional input into the process. A serious learner will find a model, a theory or a framework to use as a tool to extract learning that experience can offer.

An Educative Process

Imparting, instructions in professional subjects like public relations, marketing, advertising, management etc. need a high degree and varied form of skills. A combination of both lectures and cases, in addition to other media of communication, has proved to be ideal and appropriate. The case method, however, goes much beyond.

The purpose of teaching or training through the use of case studies is to provide a different kind of learning experience. It helps the learner to develop habits and skills of analysis, clear reasoning, use of imagination and good judgment. Active case study methods have proved to be far superior, in form, content and application, to various other passive inputs such as traditional lectures. Case presentations, sometimes in conjunction with role playing, of true or imaginary situations develop **judgment** or knowhow in learners, who, individually or as group, evolve possible solutions.

In its elementary form, a case must set the situation truthfully. It has to give all the relevant facts, data, even feelings, emotions, opinions, attitudes and grapevine surrounding the particular situation. A real-life situation is to be created so as to give the participants a feel of the circumstances in which one has to take the right kind of decisions. The case should thus throw open different interpretations of the problem, leading to more than one solution to the task given. Interestingly, if just one correct solution is available, as in mathematical or accounting studies, there would be much less scope for decision making. Many experts feel that such a situation may at best be treated as an exercise and do not qualify as a case.

Preparing for Case Discussions

Whether in the academic or in an organsiational situation, a case calls for a systematic approach. There can be several approaches to case analysis. Primarily among them are:

(1) Individual analysis and presentation.
(2) Group discussion and group recommendation
(3) Group discussion followed by group presentation in a joint session of all groups together and final recommendations. Case analysis has to be a highly effective experimental exercise in all mode of approaches, individual or group.

Developing the Right Approach

Let us once again try to recall the most obvious difference between a case study and many other structured activities. While any other activity is process based, case studies are firmly content or task based.

Preparing for a case discussion needs a well-organised and systematic approach. The essential ingredients, among many others, are –

(1) A complete background, sometime even history of the organisation is included in the case study. If the situation is imaginary, it should be realistic, based on a truthful organsiational scenario. Remember, the nearer to the real event, the more acceptable will be the study, errors and omissions will be less likely.
(2) The learners are presented with a problem to be solved. If necessary, additional data and factual inputs are to be made available.
(3) Read the case thoroughly, be familiar with the situation. Read again for grasping the facts. Identify important issues and make relevant notes.
(4) Make objective evaluation of the given situation. Try to gain an understanding of the purpose, strategies, policies and the problem at hand. Analyse the roles of key individuals in the case situation.
(5) Now is the time to prepare the threats and opportunities in the case profile.
(6) Consider the strategic alternatives, suggest the best acceptable solutions, and make recommendations with facts, arguments and justifications.
(7) Prepare an action plan for actual implementation of suggested strategies and recommendations.
(8) Evaluate your particular stand and recommendations. You may even suggest contingency plan to handle post-decision threats and difficulties.

(9) A very detailed and careful planning and preparation will be needed for oral and written presentation subsequent to group discussions. This should be a challenging task since many doubts and queries will come up at the presentation stage.

(10) All the stages noted above are not to be rigidly followed. Remember, all rules are general rules. One has to apply own judgment, understand the realities of the case situation and communicate with persuasive skills.

Building Winning Teams

The problem-solving possibilities through group communication are not restricted to industrial and commercial organisations. The practice of co-working can be ideally modeled to give learners and trainees the opportunity to learn many of the skills and techniques of problem-solving activities. They can practise these to a great extent in case studies combined with role plays and instructed group programmes. But, at the same time, a group problem- solving method is a highly skilful operation.

In general, the essential purposes for such exercises are –

(1) To learn about a subject.

(2) To decide about a course of action.

(3) To find solution to a problem.

To repeat, a well-planned group activity, thereof and are, is itself both a social action and training ground for further action. A prerequisite for successful action is skills in human relations, public relations and communication techniques. In practice, free and frank exchange of views in a purposeful discussion can foster these skills very rapidly.

In academic or training, social or organsiational, a group communication activity can be applied for:

(1) Obtaining information and opinions about a subject of common interest, clarifying misunderstanding, sharing of ideas and getting an intended job done, thus ensuring participation in making decisions.

(2) Conveying facts and information to participants attending the group activity purposefully to many others who are equally concerned with the subject;

(3) Inducing change in behavior and attitudes and also providing opportunities for magnifying the personal and group attributes;

(4) Studying specific policies and problems, finding solutions, giving new insights and new experiences and determining ways of implementation of particular decisions.

No denying there may be many pitfalls, noises, barriers in the system. Each team member, owing allegiance to the group has to contribute in the buildup of a winning team. The role of an effective teamster can be indentified in a moving cycle as below:

How to Build a Winning Team And How to be an Effective Teamster

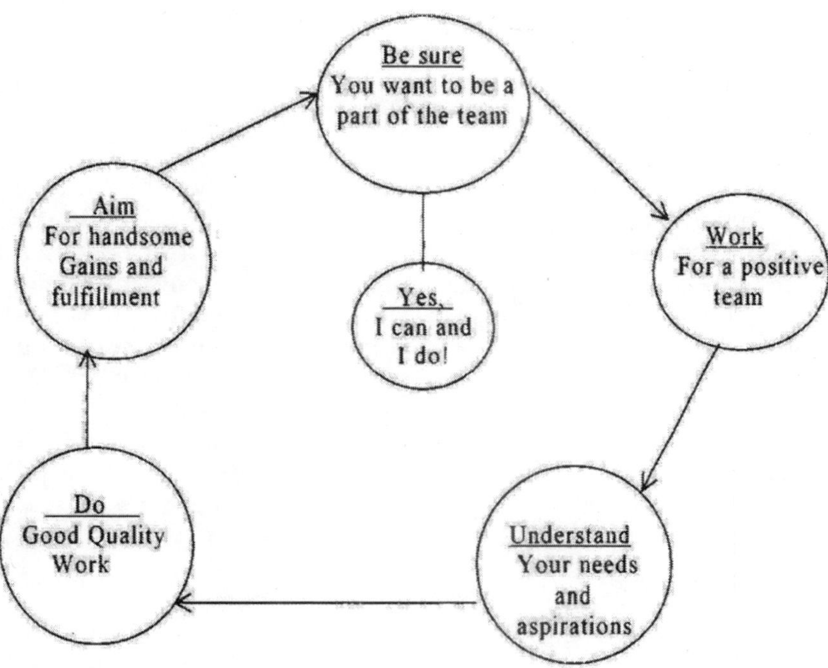

DEVELOP : A positive role and team spirit.
REACH : Personal goals and objectives.
HELP : Individual creativity to merge with the creative output of the team as a whole.

Quality Circles

A quality circle is primarily a group of employees who meet voluntarily at frequent and regular intervals to solve their work-related issues. The circles have around 5-15 people usually drawn from the same work area. Circles meet in working time with management support. The circles are primarily concerned with problem solving but serve additional, broader functions.

It is known that quality circles were first put to use in Japan in the 1960s. The sole purpose was toward improving the quality of Japanese products. At later stages, in many countries, circles were introduced as productivity techniques aimed at not only improving quality and services but also reducing the costs as well.

Rewarding Quality Efforts

In this context let us refer to what Tom Peters, the noted management expert, had to say about the "Quality Circle" movement. In his celebrated book "A Passion for Excellence", Tom Peters observed:

- Quality is not a technique.
- It is a commitment by management to its people and product.
- Quality is about passion and pride.
- Quality is about people.
- There has to be teamwork.
- So measure it, by all means. Reward it. Celebrate it.

Quality circles, therefore, are a learning and action mode – as effective tool for encouraging people to contribute to the success of their assigned functions. In an organisation, management has to provide information input and facilitate use of a range of visuals aids. Apart from solving issues and problems, a group can take idea generation or innovative tasks. For instance, a marketing group can generate brand names for a new product. A two-hour session may generate hundreds of brand names or can evolve fresh techniques in the face of fierce competition in the market. Display all the ideas to stimulate more and more ideas.

Many companies now treat the recommendations as part of the "Suggestion Schemes" and offer handsome rewards to encourage such activities. In real good terms, quality circles can produce the inducement to achieve improvement and excellence at any level.

Social and Technical Aspects

As in organised group activity, quality circles, through discussions and brainstorming, provide the motivation of allowing people to take part in their own actions and decisions. Total Quality Management (TQM) is one more process to remove wastes and errors, by involving everyone in improving the way things are done. Once again, the primary need is to promote good teamwork and a keen urge in everybody to excel. The process of teamwork in the functional chain can be as under:

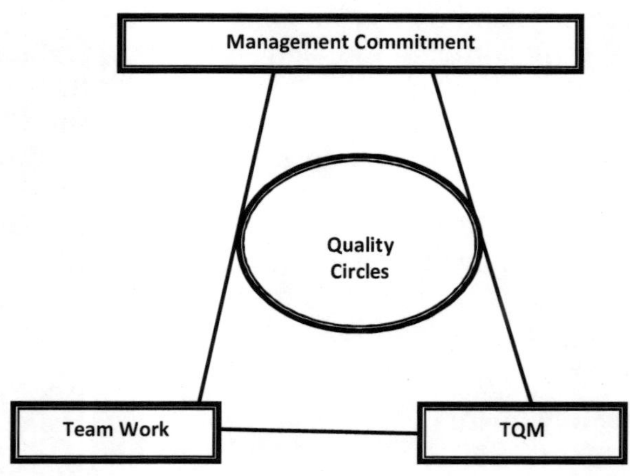

TQM is a matter of total commitment and must be applied throughout the organisation. it's teamwork, teamwork and teamwork- which thrives in a culture of free, frank and open communication.

Brainstorming

Brainstorming is a useful technique to generate a large number of ideas for solving problems. It's a group decision making process in which members adopt fresh approaches to problems.

Prior to brainstorming, the group has to determine the nature and extent of the problem and then again generating solutions through brainstorming. Here members agree to offer ideas without criticism. Brainstorming, moreover, thus is a source of enhancing creativity to secure all possible ideas relevant to the problem.

Although four basic principle of brainstorming are normally applicable, group may adhere to a set of norms as under:

- There must not be any opposition or criticism at the idea-generation stage.
- In small group activities, better would be to invite and encourage members in the production of ideas.
- At this time, verbal rejection or body motions must not communicate negative reactions to ideas.
- Emphasize quality of ideas and not to make any reference to qualitative value. The purpose is simple. The more ideas, the more creativity and greater would be the chances of hitting upon brilliant ideas.
- Members are allowed to give free rein to their imagination.
- Ideas should be allowed to be combined or improved. In essence, brainstorming has to enhance creativity and not inhibit the process of creative output.
- Ideal situations is when the group members find one idea generating another and discover their capability of joining two or more ideas to form a new entity or a fresh, unknown concept.

Members of a brainstorming group may preferably work through the following steps (chart given):

1. The group leader explains the process and the purpose of the brainstorming session.
2. Each member contributes at least one idea. Members not having any idea may pass on to the next member.
3. Record all ideas on a flip-chart or on the board. This avoids repetition and ensures instant visibility.
4. List all possible solutions to the problem or the difficult situation.
5. Review for appreciation of the situation. Allow additional options on a rethinking process.
6. Identify the most acceptable solutions instantly. But do not reject the other options.

7. All ideas are recorded. These may be practical, imaginative or scientific.
8. Evaluate all the ideas. Each idea receives attention, none gets lost.

BRAINSTORMING STEPS

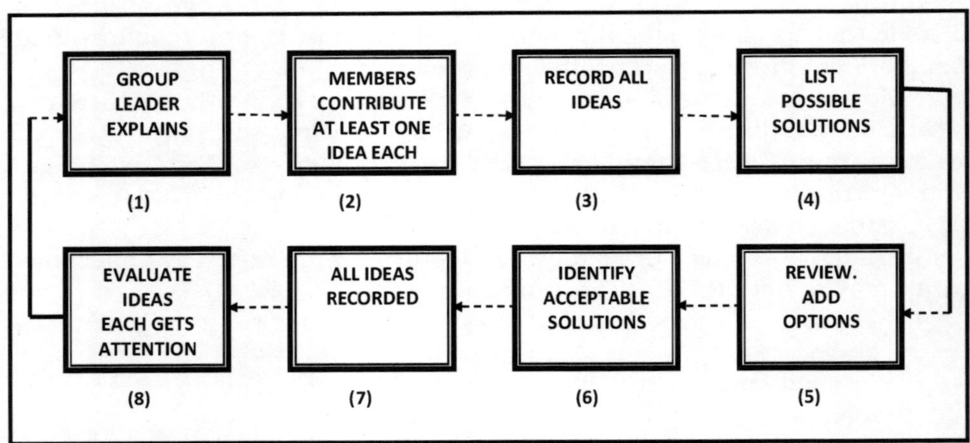

Some analysts have raised doubts about the value of brainstorming. Some go to the extent of calling it a process of brainwashing, as it occurs in groupthink. Yet, practical evidences go to prove that the technique is highly useful in business and industry, trade and commerce, the government and military functions and, decidedly, in education. Both as a creative and a psychographic booster, brainstorming provides increasing self-confidence to members of a group as a result of having their ideas treated with respect and confidence.

In appreciation of the existing process, "electronic brainstorming" as a new tool has now been put to use for faster generation of more ideas. Using this technique, participants generate their thoughts and ideas on computers and come prepared for face-to face group communication activities

Simulations

This is a method of initiating or pretending, as if one is in the same situation. Interestingly, simulation resembles "empathy" in-as-much as it points to the capacity of identifying oneself with a person or object. In simulations, the members or the learners take on roles, but much more real than on role playing occasions.

In education or in organisation, stimulation is a highly active as well as interactive activity that covers almost every real role or organsiational process. The members can discuss, interpret, review, evaluate, and prepare action steps, actually act, correct and adjust in a way certainly not possible is any other learning process.

In a simulation, by some means or other, each and every participant gets involved and has a precise role to play. The realities of the stimulation provide a unique training and learning opportunity for all the participants.

Another benefit comes as a result of the extensive review at the end which is performed by members themselves.

Some of the requirements for a successful simulation are as follows:

- It requires adequate, more extra time of preparation of materials and details of an extensive simulation programme.
- Go for fact finding, planning, research, analysis and evaluation as essential ingredients of systematic simulation. Provide entire case material–including detailed data base of the organisations, its activities, its functional challenges.
- Involve people who have practical experience of the situations modeled in the simulation and may have been involved in the problems being focused.
- The experienced persons inducted as Guides may be advised not to solve the problems for the learners
- With the advent of computer technology and with the availability of multi-media, simulation can be speeded up, data amended and updated for the benefit of the participants.
- Must have an extensive review at the end to consider mainly
  - Whether the aims were fulfilled;
  - Who and what were the contributing factors of success;
  - Who and what were the obstacles to success;
  - What the role players felt about themselves, their successes and deficiencies and in the same way about their fellow role players,
- Emphasize the point that a group activity is aiming for finding solutions to certain problems ________ not for answering series of questions from the participants.
- Questions and comments should focus on clarifying situations which might need elaboration for good participation.
- If members try to turn a question into an opportunity to mount their own personal interests or complaints, you have to stay in full control. Avoid a lengthly debate or additional questions.
- As a preparatory step, it should be good to write out answers to anticipated questions and comments.
- Listening skills are equally important. Make focused, meaningful eye contact with the person who is talking or asking questions. Make facial expression to visually convey interest.

Golden Rules for Questions and Answers

- Questions and Comments signal interest.
- Silence suggests inattentiveness.
- Silent audience is unresponsive.

- Silent audience is reluctant to interact.
- Questions provide opportunities to correct misunderstandings.
- Questions can clarify and reiterate key points.
- Questions and answers signal a participative process.

THEREFORE: LISTEN, DISCERN, AFFIRM, AND ANSWER.

An Example

How Maruti Workers performed Successfully as a Team without leaders from Trade Unions

Strike by Maruti Suzuki workers at Manesar in Haryana had drawn wide concern and also interest, particularly of the corporate circles in India in the year 2011. The strike took place in October and continued for 14 days.

There was no recognised union at the Manesar plant in contrast with the not so far Gurgaon plant of the company. The workers strike caused Maruti Suzuki to have lost around Rs. 1500 Crore. Why the unrest attracted particular notice was that the Manesar unit, not having any recognised union as such, could have organised such work disruption as a united force of workers. Not so much earlier, strikes had taken place in such reputed organisations like Bosch's Bangalore unit, Moser Baer's Noida plant and Chennai units of Hyundai and Nokia. But in all such units there were well organised trade unions which had spearheaded the work stoppages. Maruti Manesar unit is however an exception. Neither the management nor the State Labour Department could even think there could be such strike for 14 days without any major trade union leadership.

The Maruti workers, to the surprise of everybody, created a total strike by their united stand to press for their demands. The company took police help for evicting more than 1500 workers from the factory. This is the factory which rolls out some of the largest selling and prestigious cars life Swift, Dzire and SX4.

Disputes truly, between worker-management are nothing new anywhere in the world but Maruti workers here had proved their united strength, teamwork, own leadership qualities hitherto mostly unknown elsewhere. The non-existence of any recognised union couldn't deter them, nor could dampen their spirit of unity and absolute faith in themselves.

After 14 days the management gave in, sat across the table for negotiation and came to an amicable settlement. There was no need for a recognised union but both the parties together agreed for formation of a Grievance Redressal Committee with the representations from both sides along with a labour officer from the state government. They also agreed to set up a Labour Welfare Committee to promote good relations between the management and the workers. There were quite a few more issues which could not be immediately sorted out but they agreed to settle all the problems without any kind of work disruption.

The Maruti workers proved that they could efficiently function as a well-coordinated team without the guidance of a union leader. They have been able to generate a harmonious and conducive work environment by avoiding a major part of the work-related stress. These factors are amply proved by the subsequent constructive and collaborative team effort of the Maruti workers at the Manesar plant.

CONCEPT REVIEW QUESTIONS

1. How far do you agree that learning and developing through case exercises is an educative process? Explain your views.
2. Specify the right approaches for useful case discussions. How you propose to build your winning team in a group communication activity?
3. What are Quality Circles? How does the quality circle resemble the suggestion schemes and what are the benefits of both?
4. As an organsiational professional describe your ideas about the usefulness of brainstorming process for problem solving requirements. Identify some of the norms that apply to brainstorming sessions.
5. Write a brief article specifying the brainstorming steps and simulation system as a different kind of training and learning opportunity for the participants in group activities.

SUMMARY

Case study is one of the most or even the foremost learning activity. A case, particularly in business organisations as well as in the academics, provide opportunities to all the participants to analyse, understand and develop a superior skill of perception and capability. It is indeed an educative process which provides a different kind of learning experience. Active case study methods together with good presentations enable the group members to evolve solutions to problems they face.

Any case will call for a set of systematic approaches. But these are not rigid rules. But at least a detailed careful planning and preparation will be needed for group deliberations as well as for oral and written presentations subsequently. Each team member, owing loyalty to the group has to contribute in the buildup of a winning team. The team members have to develop a positive role and right team spirit with personal goals and objectives which at the end should help to merge individual creatively with the creativity of the team as a whole.

In the same way, organisations today attach tremendous values to quality circles of 5 to 15 people to solve many work-related issues. Quality circles are a learning and action effort to encourage employees to contribute to the success of their assigned functions. Apart from solving many a problem, quality groups can also handle generation of new ideas and provide innovative solutions.

Individual and collective brain storming is another useful technique for enhancing creative ideas. A set of norms are suggested for effective brainstorming sessions. A number of steps are also recommended. Interestingly, in addition to the existing process, "electronic brainstorming" has now been put to use for faster generation of more ideas.

Simulations, resembling empathy, is an interactive process that covers almost every individual in organsiational functions. Participants have a precise role to play that covers almost every real role or any organsiational situation. The activity aims towards successful fulfillment of individual, group as well as organsiational needs.

KEY TERMS

Allegiance	:	*Loyalty for a person, group or cause.*
Brainstorming	:	*Finding an idea or inspiration by brain exercises, individuals or by a group.*
Conventional	:	*Bound by social conventions which are mostly usual or commonplace.*
Discern	:	*Perceive clearly with the mind or senses.*
Empathy	:	*Capacity to identify with a person or object.*
Experimental	:	*Based on or making use of experiment.*
Flip chart	:	*Educative chart which can be turned over page after page.*
Groupthink	:	*An unthinking conformity in which members suppress their critical appraisal of ideas and suggestions that leaders and majorities support.*
Inhibit	:	*Resistance to a thought or action.*
Passive	:	*Showing no interest or initiative.*
Prerequisite	:	*Required as a precondition.*
Psychographic	:	*Psychology of the soul, spirit or mind.*
Simulation	:	*Pretend or imitate a situation, event.*
Teamster	:	*Main driving force in team work as the driver of a truck.*
Thrive	:	*Prosper and flourish, being successful.*

REFERENCES

Adair, J. ***Great Leaders*** *Talbot Adair Press*
Guildford, UK (1989).
Brilhart, John K. ***Effective Group Discussion***
WM. C. Brown Dubuque (1985).
Leondard, D & Swap, W. ***When Sparks Fly: Igniting Creativity in Groups*** *Harvard*
Business Press, Cambridge, MA. (1999).
Michael, Dr. VP. ***Communication in Research for Management****,*
Himalaya Publishing New Delhi (1998).

Peters, Tom ***A Passion for Excellence****.*
Sengupta, Sailesh ***Business and Managerial Communication*** *PHI Learning Delhi (2011).*
Harvard Business Review *Managing yourself, September, 2011.*
The Economist *January 30th, 2010.*
Times of India *New Delhi October 22, and October 25, 2011.*
Times of India *New Delhi October 29, 2011.*

X

Decision Making in Groups Win–Win Strategies

Learning Objectives

This chapter deals with steps towards managing problem situations and refers to following major components:

1. Different kinds of problem situations.
2. CSPs or common starting points of problem situations.
3. Knowing about the right approaches to all problems.
4. Decisions and post-decision phases.
5. Role of Analytical and Critical Thinking.
6. Four stages of managing a problem.
7. Implementation and Action Plans.

Organsiation refer to case studies because they have problems and no organisation for that matter is immune to problems. They have crises, difficulties, doubts, frustrations, concerns or anxieties. In the field of education, a case is a very special type of instructional material that constitutes the basis for in-group discussion and debate required by the case method. In this sense, a case is a description of a situation involving problems to be solved.

The objectives can be achieved by an effective combination of the following gains:

- Introduction of realism into formal instruction or discussion.
- Development of independent thinking.
- Development of cooperative approach to work in team situations.

Analytical and critical thinking help in decision making for group members.

Win -Win situation creates happiness and jubilation among members.

Problem Solving Situations

In a difficult situation, the major question is not what is going wrong, but to find out what could be better. A crisis or a difficulty can as well be viewed as "a turning point for something still better". Instances show that orgnaisations grapple with difficulties but fail to take advantages of opportunities and unused potential. An industry which falls "sick" will create a situation of overall crisis for the management, employees, shareholders, suppliers, distributors, financial circles and many more publics with whom the organisation has to interact. The other side of this gloomy picture is that some persons will consider it as an opportunity to turn the organisation into a viable unit. Calamity and opportunity are indeed two sides of the same coin because people involved in the business are ready to clutch at a straw.

The problem, as the case must reveal, can thus lead to an opportunity and nurture, for example, a sick unit back to health. Provided, of course, all aspects of the crisis are handled with understanding, efficiency as well as business acumen.

The operations of a business, industry or an organisation may get disturbed by accidents, environmental pollution, product defect or failure, hostile take-over, strike, lock-out or closure, stock – market crashes, explosions and fires and many more circumstances. A crisis or an untoward situation may occur owing to flood, earthquake, drought or civil riots. Internally major corporate problems are characterized by low productivity and operational inefficiency that tend to threaten the basic goals of an organisation.

Common Starting Points

Organisations facing difficulty or requiring managing problem situations constitute the starting point of the case situations. The purpose of such exercise should be to:

- Explore problems and opportunities.
- Set goals in real terms.
- Pursue the goals actively and with determination.
- Achieve results.
- Evaluate results and decisions.

Learning through case method involves analysis of the case to identify the problems involved, finding out solutions to the problems, identifying alternative solutions, and arrive at a decision to solve the problems. Case discussions in groups must allow each member to put one's viewpoints, appreciate others' opinions or judgments and produce a written report to focus more sharply on what has been discussed.

Problems with Problems

Knowing about various stages of the right approaches to a problem are pertinent as well as significant. This means stepping into and finding out "how to manage a problem situation". In practical terms, handling a problem in the work area and searching for solutions through the case method have good similarities.

Interestingly, the Greek word, "problema" very ably explains the situation as "something hard to understand or accomplish". In reality, the situation may be one or a combination of the following:

- The organisation may be unaware that a problem exists.
- The problem is not correctly defined.
- The problem, owing to being ignored persistently, turns eventually into a major crisis,

Problem recognition depends upon two key factors, namely:

- Information, and
- Interpretation.

A brief checklist at this stage is quite useful:

- What are the likely problem areas?
- Identify the problem.
- Recognise the significance of the problem.
- Nature and extent of the seriousness of the problem.
- Search for relevant information.
- Go for environmental scanning for right interpretation of the problem.

Decisions Post – Decision Phases

Information and interpretation are vital input for the decision-making phase. Information collected may be partial and, as a result, mistakes are often made. The importance of correctly defining the problem cannot be obveremphaised. Problem definition is the most critical part in the decision process.

What happens if the problem is misdefined or misinterpreted?

- The real problem continues to exist and
- Misdirected action may create another problem or a set of fresh problems.

Never to ignore post-decisional consequences of the decisions made. At the case discussions or at intensive brainstorming sessions these are to be taken up seriously. While generating alternative solutions to a problem, evaluate the alternatives and select the alternatives. The check lists for post decision phase are:

- Anticipate post-decisional consequences.
- Not to concentrate on just one or too few options.
- Do not ignore a problem or an issue if the solution appears to be difficult.
- Strategies are to be carefully evolved.
- Formulate action plans.

PROBLEM SOLVING
&
DECISION MAKING

- SOLVING PROBLEMS
- GENERATING NEW IDEAS
- MAKING RIGHT DECISIONS

STAGE 1

Thinking	Analysing	Sifting
Synthesising	Valuing	Conclusion

STAGE2

Specify Aim	Review Factors	Courses Open
Making the Decision	Implementing	Evaluate the Decision

Problem Solving: Analytical and Creative Thinking

Effective problem solving requires a high degree of ability for analytical and creative thinking. In reality, these two abilities can be used separately as well as in an innovative blend.

Analytical Thinking

May be, a little conceptual diversion into the thinking process will not be out-of-place. As is known Left-brain thinking is logical and analytical whereas right-brain is more holistic and is concerned with emotions and impressionistic relationships.

To be a good problem solver one needs to be able to switch from one side of the brain to the other side as well as back again.

An analytical approach means one prefers logical analysis, investigates problems carefully and tries to find all the facts of the case. One weakness in this process is that you may ignore certain novel ideas which could lead to good solutions, here the logic suggests you may apply creative thinking skills as a problem-solving tool.

On the other hand, creative approach leads one to use intuition and imagination in preference to analytical approach. Here again, to find true nature of the problem and all relevant information it should be advisable to resort to analytical at the appropriate time.

Thus, effective case discussions require a judicious mixture of analytical and creative thinking. A good problem solver must know how and when to apply creative and analytical skills. Interestingly, analytical thinking requires concentration on various facts of the problem, while creative thinking mostly requires a much more relaxed, free-ranging environment.

Analytical and Creative Output

Analytical Thinking	Few SOLUTIONS	Creative Thinking	Many SOLUTIONS
Logic		Imaginative	
Unique		Inventive	
Having no Parallel		Make-believe	
Few Answers		Many Answers	

Systematic Approach to Blending Analytical and Creative Thinking
The approach is divided into three parts.

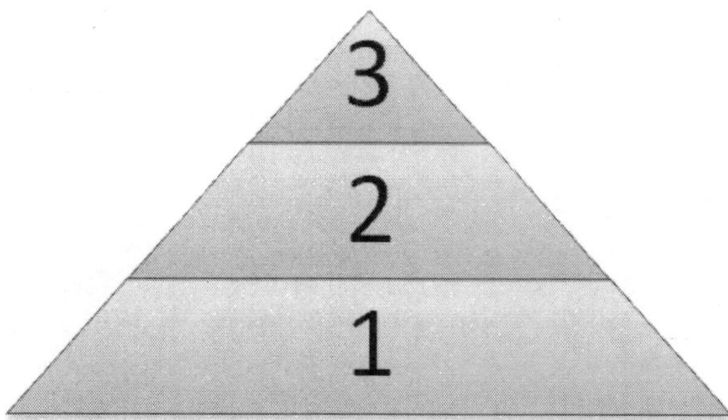

Phase 1: Takes off from a base. Refers to systematic accumulation of facts and information.

Phase 2: Processing and practical analysis of accumulated facts and details.

Phase 3: Ideation or conception by mental effort. This is the culmination of creative efforts.

How to Regulate a Problem

There are at least four stages in the process of managing a problem situation. As we know, the stages might overlap and interact with one another in the natural flow of case solving process.

Step I – Reviewing the Problem and the Situation

Pinpoint, interpret, and appraise the problem and the circumstances that gave rise to the difficult situation. Explore the unused opportunities.

Step 1 – makes systematic effort to understand the ongoing scenario. Take careful stock of the opportunities not being utilized.

Are there some blind spots that stop seeing problems and prevent favourable chances of solving them effectively?

Therefore, the main elements of the process are –

- Clearly and completely identify the problem and its extent.
- List of the facts relevant to the problem situation.
- Pinpoint the unused opportunities.
- Identify the kind of problem you face while approaching the problem-solving, solution-generating task.

Step II – Developing the Proper Approach

Identify the aims and objectives which should be based on the right appreciation of the current problem situation. Understandably, the step has to make realistic assessment of the expected benefits, outcomes, results.

At this stage, it is also necessary to develop new, more useful perspectives on both problem situations and unutilized opportunities.

Remember, these are very difficult and challenging tasks. Never be stubborn in thinking or insisting that only your ideas are good. At the same time, do not also be sheepish when it comes to defending your ideas.

Obviously, the goals and objectives at this stage are largely based on the current situation. The essential areas are –

- Analyse additional information.
- Indentify correctly the impact produced by the information.
- Work together as a problem-solving group and effectively interact with each other.
- List the alternative course of action and pinpoint the advantages.
- Recommend the most favored option in the string of alternatives taking into account cost, time, resources as well as possible threats and difficulties.

Step III – Reaching the Desired Goal

Recognise that you are involved in a problem or a conflict or a dilemma or a difficult situation. Be certain that it is a problem you really want to solve, and you have not found a satisfactory solution for it.

Once you have made the commitment, you have empowered yourself to examine all sides of the issues involved. You have thus taken the ownership of the problem. You can now set the goals to be reached. This involves developing action strategies for accomplishing goals. One must not rush into "where to go" usual syndrome. More important would be "how to go there".

Presumably, therefore, this step refers to developing action strategies for achieving desired results. Actions are –

- Understand where you need to go and how to go there.

- Recommend how the solution and implementation can be monitored and success evaluated.
- Present action and recommendations on display board or use the audio-visual medium to enable everyone grasp own viewpoints and suggestions.
- Although unanimous recommendations will be preferable, dissenting views can also be presented.

Step IV – Achieving Results

There will only be frustrations if the case study session bears no visible fruits at the end. It just makes no sense to say, "We had a good session today". The session-effectiveness can be judged only by the expression of happiness supported by statement, "we did these ourselves"!

Help participants evolves a plan, a step-by-step procedure for achieving the desired goal of each scenario. Give direction to problem – managing and opportunity –developing action.

At this stage, the checklist provides guidelines for translating strategies into goal- accomplishing actions-

- Make sure that the case-session bears fruits at the end in terms of gains, outcomes, results.
- Be careful, be cautious. Do not choose strategies that may eventually lead to failures.
- Planning, organising and designing the sessions and tasks allotted must give strength and sense of judgment to each member at every step.
- Give direction to problem-solving, solution-searching and opportunity-grapping action.
- The recommending groups should be encouraged to present and argue their actions and recommendations clearly and convincingly. The obvious objective is to reach a stage of final agreement, mostly unanimous, and acceptance.

Matter of Implementation

In organsiational framework, the process must not terminate when a choice or a range of choices are made. As it comes to managerial situations, implement solutions unhesitatingly. The motivating style of participation can easily achieve involvement and encouragement in the implementation process.

The purpose is to give new insight and new experiences and determine ways of implementation of specific decisions.

Action Plans

Create planned programme of actions that pertain to actual work situations.

Remember, each problem is unique by its nature and particular occurrence. A creative blend of ideas and imagination will be suitable in each situation.

The buzzwords are: "Nothing is more dangerous than an idea, when it is the only idea we have" (Alain, 1908).

Example:

How Nestle Became World's No. One Food Giant

Nestle is recognised universally as one of the most admired companies of the world. The company is having almost 3, 00,000 employees and deals with more than 6000 brands with more than 100 billion dollars of turnover. They sell their products in more than 140 countries. Nestle proudly claims that they have 450 factories around the world. The company empowers its people to make consumer relevant decisions as close as possible to the markets.

As we know, the company had its origin in Switzerland and they maintain their Swiss identity sincerely and quite strongly. Interestingly the word Nestle in English has a sweet connotation. It means "Selling oneself comfortably." And they have achieved this purpose internally and externally quite decisively. How have they been able to do a series of astounding accomplishments?

One explanation is that, even during downturn, Nestle developed a distinctive business model which everyone faithfully continued to execute. Each employee, under constant encouragement of the seniors, was very, very focused. All around the world, in spite of wide differences in culture of work patterns, and ethical values, they built up total commitments and capabilities to achieve one particular vision. All the employees together developed the organisation into a community of shared purpose, specially marked by high levels of emotional connection, trust and mutual respect.

In Nestle, the managers are trained to see themselves more as catalysts for problem solving rather than as problem solvers. The company never encourages managers to feel themselves as leaders who seem to have all the answers. Nestle appreciates those managers who have the willingness to admit,

"We are not sure about the answer or what the correct solution should be. Let our team work out their ideas and we are with them". The best solution comes out this way to the satisfaction of the employees and their managers.

Nestle reaps huge rewards by very simple appreciation that problem solving, decision making and implementation processes are not just instructing employees to carry out orders. Instead, they prefer their mangers and senior leaders to engage, empower and motivate the employees to contribute their knowledge and experience to a consensus approach.

SUMMARY

No organisation is exempt from problem situations. They have to face untoward situations, crisis, difficulties, threats, and challenges and so many other kinds of problems almost every day. The operations of a business, industry and even non-profit organisation get disturbed owing to serious confrontations. It is being increasingly realised today that calamity and opportunity are indeed two sides of the same coin and can be used many a time to the advantage of the organisation itself.

The organisations have to be knowledgeable about the Common Starting Points (CSPs) to manage problem situations. They have to be conscious about the right approaches which include problem recognition, searching for relevant information, going for interpretation of the problem and finding solutions collectively. Similarly, decisions and post-decision phases are to be taken up quite seriously.

Similarly, in any case situation or in academic discussions these issues are to be taken up for intensive brainstorming sessions.

In problem solving, both analytical and creative thinking can be used separately or in an innovative blend. Analytical approach denotes logical analysis whereas a creative approach leads to use of imagination and intuition. Both have their uses but sometime the problem situation or case study exercise may require a sensible mix of analytical and creative thinking. What will be needed is to go for a systematic approach for blending of analytical and creative thinking.

Briefly, for the purpose of regulating a problem the four stages come to work one after another. Next will came the matter of implementation and action plans preceded by a number of ideas rather than having just one idea.

(1) *Reviewing the problem and the situation.*
(2) *Developing the proper approach.*
(3) *Reaching the desired goal and.*
(4) *Achieving results.*

KEY TERMS

Accomplishment	:	*Completion of a task, thing achieved.*
Acumen	:	*Sharpness, having good judgment.*
Blend	:	*Harmonise, mix together as required.*
Buzzword	:	*Catchword, specialist word.*
Calamity	:	*Disaster, great misfortune.*
Catalyst	:	*Person or thing that precipitates change.*
Clutch	:	*Grasp Tightly.*
Connotation	:	*Implying in addition to the literal or primary meaning.*
Compatibility	:	*Able to coexist and reach understanding.*
Downturn	:	*Decline, specially economically.*
Grapple	:	*Try to mange a difficult problem.*

Holistic	:	*Treating the whole problem rather than the parts.*
Immune	:	*Exempt from influence or problems.*
Judicious	:	*Sensible, prudent.*
Perspective	:	*Ability or mental view to discern the relative importance of things.*
Pertinent	:	*Relevant.*
Reap	:	*Receive benefits as a result of one's own actions.*
Realism	:	*Practice of regarding things as they are and dealing with them in the right way.*
Sifting	:	*Putting through a sift, separating finer or coarser parts from materials.*
Stubborn	:	*Obstinate, inflexible.*
Synthesizing	:	*Combining of elements into a whole.*
Syndrome	:	*Characteristic combination, group of characteristic combination.*
Untoward	:	*Inconvenient, awkward, difficult situation.*

REFERENCES

Drucker, Peter. ***The Practice of Management****, Pan Books Ltd, London, 1975*

Etzioni, A, ***Modern Organisation*** *Prentice Hall, New Jersey. 1964.*

Putnam, L.L. and Pacanowsky, M.E. ***Communication and Organisations: An Interpreteve Approach****, Beverly Hills, CA, 1983.*

Sengupta, Sailesh **.** ***Business and Managerial Communication****, PHI Learning Private Ltd, New Delhi, 2011.*

Peters, Tom and Robert H. Waterman. ***In Search of Excellence****, Warner Books New York 1982.*

Fortune Journal*, World's Most Admired Companies, Fortune Journal, Asia Pacific Edition, July 5, 2010.*

Harvard Business Review*, South Asia, September, 2011.*

XI

Management of Conflict

LEARNING OBJECTIVES

This chapter aims to enable the reader to understand the many facets of the management of conflict and associated issues and problems and to find solutions to them. The following related areas have been fully covered:

1. What is a conflict and how they come to play in the organsiational environment.
2. The interactions of group team work and how they can help to resolve conflicts.
3. How to manage inter – personal and intra – personal conflicts amidst members themselves in groups.
4. Knowing the types and styles of conflicts with examples.
5. Guidelines for managing conflicts.
6. Role of Negotiation in resolving conflict and the specifics of Negotiation.
7. A series of case studies and examples of conflicts and negotiation in organisations.

MANAGEMENT OF CONFLICT

What and Why of Conflict

Conflict denotes a state of opposition, a fight or a struggle between person and person, between one group and another or a situation of incompatibility between one and the other. Truthfully, conflict is a part of life and cannot be totally eliminated. All organisations, commercial or non – commercial, have to face it almost every day. They make the utmost effort to control it or just manage it in a way that serves their purpose.

There are instances that conflicts are suppressed from time to time or by just casting them aside but they raise their heads at their opportune moment. In the areas of industrial relations in companies, groups of employees or their unions face the management over conflicts whenever there are differences of interest. In smaller organisations, as in the small industries sector, conflicts may not be so very visible because the owners as a stronger group can easily suppress the weaker groups of workers. But where the relations are of almost equal strength, like a strong trade union and the management of a large organisation, there is bound to be conflict and clash of interest.

Although we normally think of conflict as a bad phenomenon, but it is not only real but also natural to human relationships. In realistic terms, it is only through conflict and its resolution that a just and humane society can emerge. A society without conflict would stagnate and decay. A disputable idea no doubt, but truthful in all human context, if we look at it from a perspective of the realities of the environment.

Defining Conflicts

We will find a variety of definitions by authorities on the subject. Only one to quote here:

"Conflict is a process that begins with one party perceives that another party has negatively affected, or is about to negatively affect, something that the first party cares about"

(*Stephen P. Robbins in Organsiational Be*haviour 2006).

Broadly, conflict is the experience between or among parties that their goals or interests, are in opposition with each other, giving rise to tension and disagreements all over.

Group Characteristics in Organisations

As we have already noted, individuals belonging to groups in organisations are directly different from any random collection of human beings. More the unity amongst themselves, the group activity becomes more and more planned and systematic process. Many a time, in such situations, conflict resolution turns to be more organised and methodical. After all, groups function for the purpose of fulfilling certain predetermined objectives. The purpose may be political, economic social, cultural, commercial, sporting or any other human activity.

Conflicts and Organsiational groups

By and large, organisations today have come to appreciate that cohesive groups can effectively contribute to the levels of performance in the

Interactions among group members can help to resolve conflicts.

organisation. So in the events of conflicts arising, such groups should also be able to resolve conflicts by mutual interactions with other groups and the organsiational management. A team – based organisation, therefore, encourages group activity as part of day – to – day survival and success. As team members, employees also feel that they belong and their work makes a difference.

Even so, there are quite a few barriers which come in the way of resolving conflicts and finding solutions to problems. A few are noted here together with suggestions for improvement:

(1) Many a management believes more in the directive style of working and they try to suppress conflict by hard and punitive action. Efforts are called for immediate transition from directive to interactive style of management. Moreover, managers and supervisors are to be encouraged to hold group communication activities as part of working system.

(2) Absence of culture of open communication in the organsiational environment. Many a top management do not understand that it does not pay to be secretive about decisions which affect the employees directly.

(3) Arrogant and hostile behaviour on the part of management as well as many group leaders representing the general employees. Hostility in organisations originates from a situation of conflict between two opposite groups of management and their employees. Immediate result is mutual distrust and unwillingness to sort out the conflict. Such situations do not help either parties and both suffer the aftermath of such conflicts. There has to be a readiness to solve the conflict for the ultimate benefit of all concerned. The conflicting groups have to sit across, exchange opinion and be ready to come out of prejudices of one against the other by systematic group exercises.

(4) Many managers bear in – born apathy towards the lower levels of employees and they are still ignorant about the changing environments. These sentiments do apply to both the groups. Even in very successful companies in business and industry such feuds are quite often. In downward communication from seniors to juniors and upward communication from lower to upper, distrust and suspicion are common, giving rise to more and more conflicts. Incidents of conflict do happen among seniors themselves mostly in horizontal levels of communication and functioning. It does not matter that they all belong to the same group of senior executives but they represent strongly about their own departmental belongings. For example, conflicts are rampant between production and marketing, all departments versus Human Resource Departments Production versus Purchase and Material Supply, Finance versus other departments and so on.

Until all departments come to appreciate and realise they all belong to just one team such frictions will continue to occur. Frequent group exercises and interactions at the behest of the senior most management is the only way out of such conflicts and mutual tussles.

(5) Do you have conflict management procedures? If you have it in your organisation well and good. But do check and recheck every now and then and go for revision whenever needed. Many times you don't get productive results out of the existing procedure but you leave it at that nonchalantly. Results could be disastrous as well as harmful to the organisation itself.

Here comes the crucial aspects of how organisation heads behave and what are their mental attitudes. As we try to draw examples we find that organisation leaders are quite distinctive with exemplary social and communication skills. We will not be interested in the non – exemplary and non – communication leaders who prefer to be in silent modes. As for managers, executives and various group members they have to start developing their Conflict–Management Skills by (i) Studying the roots of conflicts and their curtailment processes (ii) Eliminating the conflicts at a later stage by cooperation and collaboration and (iii) Designing well – structured conflict – management procedures.

Don't be afraid of mistakes. As a wise man had once said, "An error does not become a mistake until you refuse to correct it". Thus, one should never be afraid to reverse a decision if it was based on judgements and not based on realities of the group feelings. Bill Gates gave the warning by saying "Success is a lousy teacher. It seduces smart people into thinking they can't lose". As stated earlier, most of us hate and dread mistakes. But in group problem solving process never be afraid of mistakes but always be ready to correct the imperfection.

An Example: Watson Case

Today, almost everyone knows the name of Tom Watson Sr., the legendary founder of IBM. He had recruited an exceptionally bright and highly promising executive for IBM. The executive got involved in a risky venture for the company, lost or wasted more than 10 million dollars in the process. Not that he didn't consult anyone in the organisation. Several times he sat down with senior colleagues and spent time in discussions and brain – storming exercises. Ultimately, he applied his own judgement and mostly went forward boldly on his own.

Tom Watson called the nervous executive to his office. The young man was nervous and also angry with himself. He blurted out, "I can understand, you want my resignation or you want to do something more"?

Watson very mildly told him, "Young man, don't be so serious. I look at it this way. We have spent 10 million dollars to educate you."

The young man looked at his boss blindly not knowing what to say. Watson added, "Now sit down comfortably. I want to discuss future plans, programmes and projections with you."

Managing Interpersonal and Intra personal Conflicts

Let us now be clear about interpersonal and intrapersonal communication, both in human and organsiational context. Interpersonal communication happens whenever one person communicates directly with another or persons in a one – to – one situation or in smaller groups. Thus, interpersonal communication is interactions in which participants have a one – to – one relationship with one another. On the other hand, communication of a person with himself or herself and the processing of internal feedback should be known as intrapersonal situations. In both context, conflicts occur as frictions and disputes are most common in small group communications. In intrapersonal situations, the same person fights within himself/ herself about choice among more than one conflicting ideas.

Joseph P. Folger and Marshall Scott Poole, two known authorities on interpersonal conflict management identified conflict types as (i) Competitive (ii) Accommodative (iii) Avoiding (iv) Collaborative and (v) Compromising. They were of the opinion that one can make partial or altogether total changes in one's conflict style to achieve better results in conflict management. In group communication activities all these five factors dominate in the individual or in group behaviour as well as in group performance.

Explaining types and styles

The Competitive Style of conflict refers to state of aggressiveness without much of a trace of cooperativeness. Some of the group members or even all of them are hell – bent on winning the argument. They will not heed to opposite views even if such views are more sensible or even justified. This way conflicts get to be more and more troublesome and one blames the other for non – cooperation and destructive behaviour. An example of an intra personal conflict can be given here:

Your boss's immediate senior invites you to lunch. When you return to office after the lunch you sense your boss is curious. What do you do? Intrapersonally you toy with several ideas (i) Give your boss a detailed description? (ii) Avoid telling your boss anything (iii) Mention the lunch casually to your boss, as though it really had no significance.

Finally, after careful introspection you come out with this decision. Let me tell my boss the whole lunch episode because I cannot forget who really my boss is. I won't like to plant seeds of doubt or mistrust between the boss and myself. By all means, your effective intrapersonal communication has shown you the right way.

In Accommodative Style the group members are normally neither assertive nor aggressive. But this may not mean that they are timid or ignorant. On the contrary, they are more concerned about mutual cooperation and they extend their helpful hands for collective functioning. Sometime, though, it may appear that one party is comparatively weaker and thus ready to sacrifice their own views and interests for fear of aggression and reprisals. Not to be bogged down by a feeling of inferiority, the accommodative style of one – one or both the parties go a long way to resolution of conflicts.

The Avoiding Style is an easy way to escape or keeping away from a decision. In fact, avoidance signifies a kind of cowardice and refraining from involvement where decision making may spark off controversy or criticism. In group activity group members have to appreciate that their primary responsibility would be to find solutions to problems. That is why groups are formed. If they try to evade or keep away that will hit the very foundation of group communication system. At any cost, they have to come out with their opinions and recommendations, which will ultimately serve the interest of the groups and the organisations they represent.

The Collaborative Style is one of a spirit of working together with willingness and desire to cooperate. As such collaboration means cooperation even with enemy. In group activity, the groups may well be assertive in their behaviour and a sense of right and wrong prevails. But they make sincere efforts to reach an agreement that will benefit all of them. In this kind of effort, groups go much beyond and are able to find creative solutions to problems. Mostly, such solutions are distinctive and many times even outstanding.

In Compromising Style the parties agree to mutual settlement of disputes without hurting the sentiments of the other group. This way they find easy solutions to problems but many a time one group has to yield to the wishes of the other group and some members may feel to be let down by their own colleagues. It is true that sometimes there may be indiscretions creating further conflicts among themselves and other groups. However, we have to agree that in many situations one group has to give up something for greater good for one and all.

An Example: Barack Obama and the Young Blacks

American President Barack Obama in early 2013 made certain revelations about himself which were mostly unknown. He advised Young American Blacks that they should take responsibility for their lives and stop making excuses. He said *"I was from a broken family and I would have easily ended up behind bars. I might have been in prison. I might not have been able to support my family – and that motivated me. I wanted to be a better man, a better husband and a better father"*.

He did not stop just being himself. He started talking to his friends, other neighborhood black young people and they frequently formed groups to talk among themselves about their future. The change was immediately noticeable. Many times, Obama felt, they had the excuses why they were going wild and desperate. They were feeling that the entire world was trying to keep a black man down. In their mutual discussions and groups exercise all types of interpersonal conflict came up but Barack Obama had only one mission. They must come out of all such despondency or despair. It was their own personal and collective fight against the situational conflict and they must stop accusing others for thier own failure. Obama himself realised and made his friends to realise that there was no longer any room for excuses.

The world knows how Barack Obama came up in life as a bright star in the whole Universe. Almost all his friends were successful in life and they set examples which were hitherto unknown.

(***Source: Daily Mail*** (***London***) ***May 21, 2013, Time magazine July 2013***).

Some more Guidelines for Managing Conflicts

We need not subscribe to the usual feelings that all conflicts are bad and they can be eliminated from any organisation. Now there is increasing recognition that some kinds of conflict reveal a healthy organisation.

However, in cases where it is not possible to reduce or settle the conflicts or disputes on an interim basis, it may indicate that the nature of disputes are complex or caused by extremely opposite view points. In the event of problems like this, more time is needed to consider the intricacies of the case and to allow each party to prepare thoroughly.

Even so, the following guidelines are suggested for conflict resolution among various groups:

(1) ***Do you turn a blind eye to existence of conflict?*** Many managers have an easy – going answer to all problems relating to conflict. They feel “Time will heal the wound and eventually will disappear”. Recognize the signs of tension at an early stage and involve everyone to feel that they are important. Groups and all members join hands to eliminate problems and disputes by collective brainstorming and thus solve problems by mutual action.

(2) ***Putting heads together to exchange ideas .*** Opposite groups or persons with conflicting ideas must assemble together in organised group activity. Discuss all issues threadbare but take care of the expectations as well as the obligations of all groups and their members. Such group discussions should be designed to broaden horizons and promote understandings with each other. Leaders have to clarify the differences to reach an agreement which should be acceptable to all members.

(3) ***Concentrate on maximizing the performance of group members.***

It will also mean influencing groups of diverse individuals and even promoting internal competition. For example, IBM is the acknowledged master in fostering competition among its own people.

Tom Peters, the celebrated management authority, in his book. "In Search of Excellence" suggested many a steps to achieve people orientation in organisations. He said "Treat people as adults, treat them as partners, treat them with dignity; treat them with respect".

(4) *Managers have to play the role models of leaders.*

A manger has to constantly go for self – assessment in terms of optimism, persistence and more importantly, motivation. They must communicate persuasive messages that inspires the team members to be active in the right way and in the right direction. The motivation aspect applies to both managers and the followers.

The members need to be motivated to put their heart and soul into a task. They will not while away their precious time in conflicts and disputes. The manager, as true leaders, have to be fully aware of their needs and aspirations and constantly strive to satisfy them.

(5) ***In all communications give and receive feedback .***

In today's communication, if there is no feedback there is no communication. In person to person and more so in organsiational groups, every member wants to express feelings and reactions and they expect the seniors to express themselves openly. Such exercises will smoothen the way towards working out the conflict management procedures which should be acceptable to all groups and their managers.

Conflict resolution moves through the process of positive and negative feedback on both sides. Also, such feedbacks from all sides and everyone improves their communication abilities by pinpointing their strengths and weaknesses for future corrections.

WAY OUT–NEGOTIATION

Negotiation is primarily a process of mutual bargaining. In groups or between the management and the employees or between the manager and an individual employee, negotiation is an everyday process. In simple terms, negotiation stands for achieving a situation which should be acceptable to involved parties. In intergroup conflict or even in inner group deliberations negotiation is a suitable method to come out of a problem even before it takes the shape of a conflict. The renowned professional mediator, Tammy Lenski, had put it so simply by saying, "At work, every conversation is negotiation."

In group functioning, all negotiations, are interpersonal with good traces of intrapersonal operations at all stages of progress. Negotiation is the most dominating area in group exercises everywhere. The group members come to appreciate the role of negotiation as the quickest remedial measure to solve conflicts and disputes.

Defining Negotiation

In general terms, negotiation will mean "to discuss in order to reach an agreement." It is way to find solutions to problems whether in groups or in organisations or between organisation and organisation" Oxford Dictionary says negotiation refers to "Confer with another person with a view to compromise and to reach an agreement."

Hiltrop and Udall (1997) had simply but convincingly stated, "Negotiating is rather like taking a journey .... You cannot predict the outcome until you have undertaken it".

Gerard Nierenberg, President, Negotiation Institute USA and a contemporary expert on negotiation gave a useful definition. He said "Negotiation depends on communication .... An element of human behaviour .... dealt with by both the traditional and the new behavioural sciences" (*Nierenberg in The Fundamentals of Negotiating"*)

In other words, we may simply state that

"Conflict leads to negotiation,
Negotiation leads to problem solving,
And problem solving leads to survival and success".

Problem Solving Through Negotiation

It is said that negotiation skills are the highest in demand and shortest in supply. In negotiation you do not just strive to win but suggest superior logistics that will benefit all the members of the groups. A good leader in a group or an effective manager takes care of the details. Allow others to ask more questions in the negotiation process. The challenges are: " Who is a better listener? Who encourages harmony and agreement? Who's better in keeping in touch with others?" These are what we call multi tasking in the process of negotiation.

Decision making through Negotiation

In group communication, a kind of situational leadership is called for. That means the right person at the helm, the right style of negotiating, and the right situation. In doing so, such leaders motivate all group members and many others. And this creates a vision for the future – a vision of success and achievement of desired growth. Two management gurus, *Gary Hamel of London Business School and C.K. Prahalad of the University of Michigan had said that such leadership process creates the "Core Competences of any successful organisation."* In group activity, many believed that there have to be a winner and a loser. No more so. Through good negotiation methods we create multiple winners.

The process will imply application of creative thinking and involving all members to participate and purposeful brainstorming to find solutions to conflicts. This is also a part of the motivation programme for all group members. However, there has to be open communication through open house sessions. The final decision making by fruitful negotiation can be depicted by a chart as under:

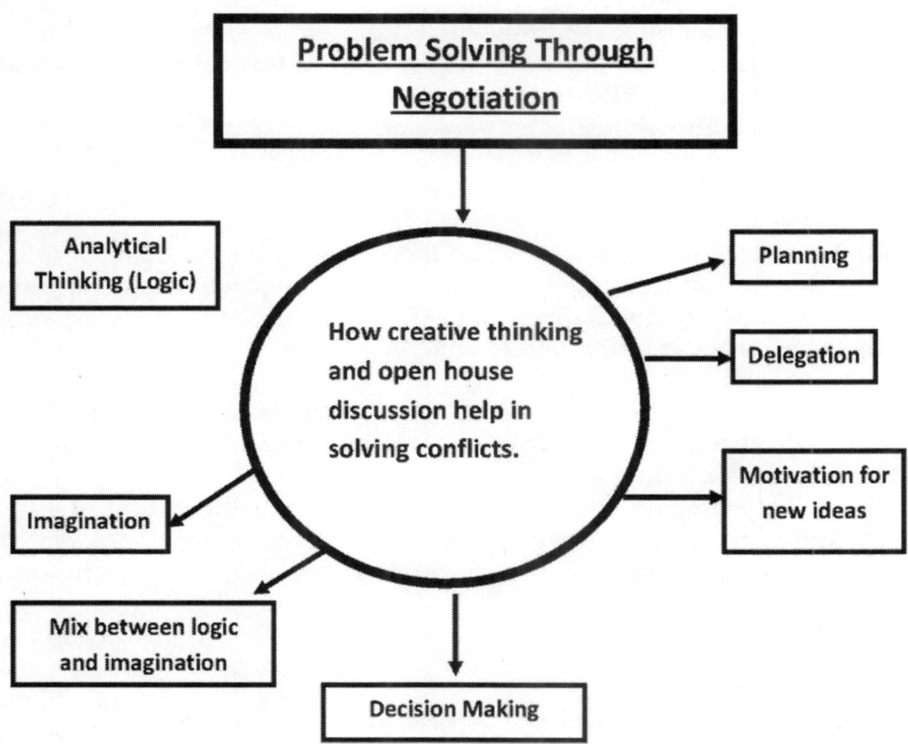

While logic and imagination as well as a mix between two have been discussed earlier, certain management aspects like Planning, Delegation and Motivation for ready acceptance of new ideas are needed to usher in the desired process of change.

Negotiation Specifics

Negotiation in group activities is founded on Collaborative behaviour from both sides. To achieve goals and objectives, conflicts and negotiations work simultaneously in the groups and in organisations. It has been observed that good public relations functions can provide the real healing touch in cementing relations as well as in encouraging change. Normally, what people disapprove of is not the idea of settling disputes through negotiation but methods of its implementation. The resistance to new ideas can be overcome by PR action and participative implementation.

Simply stated, the goals are not difficult to reach if the leaders and group members act together in the following areas:

(1) Identify the present culture of the organisation.
(2) Construct and deliver the new culture.
(3) Motivate groups and individuals towards accepting new ideas and pattern of change.
(4) Put together effective implementation teams.

At the same time, periodic review and interactive sessions are needed to study the following issues:

(1) How far the group members are trained and experienced in negotiations?
(2) Are they authorized to make decision without referring to seniors at every step?
(3) What type of approach will be more acceptable to them?
(4) The negotiating steps they have adopted so far and to what extent the steps are justifiable and useful?
(5) What are the usual questions they asked every time and their reactions?
(6) Their negotiating steps till now and changes required, if any.
(7) Their strengths and weakness and their own feelings about their success or failure.
(8) Do they prepare themselves well in advance and extent of advice and cooperation received by them from their seniors.
(9) What communication barriers they need to cross to increase chances of success?
(10) Leadership capabilities of groups leaders involved in negotiating process.

Negotiation Strategy and Behavioural Aspects

Never forget that you also belong to some group. You have your own group identity and sense of belonging as others do have. Some precautions for any group member go a long way to promote an environment of harmonious negotiation. Keep in mind "When there is conflict, there has to be cooperation".

A few suggestions are:

(1) Use open – ended questions to build understanding.
(2) Never put the other group in any kind of motives and intentions by your behavioural expressions.
(3) What are their expectations, their strengths and weaknesses?
(4) Never try to use their weaknesses in your favour.
(5) Use a sense of humour and make positive comments.

(6) Don't deliberately try to put them down. Better to find common grounds of openness and agreement.
(7) Train up and educate your own group members to develop positive perceptions and a sense of constructive cooperation.
(8) Try not to retaliate when abusive behaviour is used by some of the group members from either side. Sensible group members must control them, guide them and make them to see reason.
(9) Take frequent breaks to relieve tension.
(10) Collect all information pertaining to conflicting issues under discussion and share the information with members of both sides.

Study of organisations all over the world has convincingly proved that team – based organisations, where group activity is encouraged, can produce *spectacular* performance. Here, the employees are treated as essential components of the organsiational system. In the process, as team members, they feel that they belong and their work makes a difference.

Case Study: Marriott's Way to Conflict Management

The first Marriott Hotel was opened in January 1957 by J. Willard Marriott at Arlington, Virginia (USA). To –day, Marriott's got more than 2000 hotels worldwide, with over 15 billion dollar revenue earning multinational giant, under its CEO J.N. Marriott Jr. elder son of senior J. Willard Marriott.

All Marriott employees, including all their seniors are known as "Associates". At the very initial stage, Bill Jr. had introduced profit sharing programme. He used to term this step as a fitting reflection of their corporate culture's emphasis on teamwork. Many former junior executives used to claim that the genius of Marriott lies in treating all associates as if they were managers.

Now about some of the problems. In 1990, as a result of world – wide economic downturn the business shrank. The top management including Bill Jr. made decisions for layoff and retrenchment. Sadly, instead of hiring they had to resort firing. There were conflicts and confrontations but the Co. set up a helpful wing for finding alternate jobs for those who were forced to depart. Out of more than 1000 people, only 2 went for legal actions against the company but here also the disputes were amicably settled. Bill Jr. at that time, frequently quoted Winston Churchill by saying,

"Success is never final".

One thing that confronted Bill Jr. was the negative press. This happened when the company resorted to retrenchment and also its split into two companies. The media used to give favourable coverage till 1990 but was equally critical when the company suffered set back. But he knew that the real solution to such problems was not fighting against the press but to fall upon the support from its own associates. Marriott associates came together in exemplary team spirit and worked hard to bring back the company from disaster to revival and success. A long tradition of teamwork and a healthy track record of taking care of each other helped all of them from falling apart. Finally, there was general compassion for Marriott's problems, including that of the press, and the organsiation and its associates came out to be victorious.

Discussion Questions

(1) How far Marriott's successful "Associate" example can be followed by other companies to foster unity and teamwork to overcome conflicts and confrontations? Justify your comments and provide other such examples.

(2) In the face of an adverse press how organisation should behave and function in order to gain support provided the company is on the right path? Do you feel that good public relations with the media can help the company to put forth its rightful stand?

(3) We have seen that the Marriott's faced real problems in 1990s and had to resort to extreme action against their own associates. Do you agree to Marriott's steps or you have other suggestions to make? Please specify.

CONCEPT DEVELOPMENT QUESTIONS

(1) Discuss the group characteristics in organisations and explain how conflicts come to play a disturbing role in group functioning and group performance.

(2) How you propose to handle interpersonal and intrapersonal conflicts while being a member of an organsiational group? Provide an example.

(3) Provide details of the types and styles of conflicts in organised groups. Do you think all such types are noticeable in group activities and one must have full knowledge about these types and styles for drawing lessons and suitable applications? Explain your stand.

(4) Provide a list of guidelines for managing conflicts and discuss them in detail.

(5) Do you agree that Negotiation is a good way to come out of conflicts in organizational group functioning? How far decision making is justifiable through the process of negotiation? Provide your particular views.

(6) What are the specifics that apply to the system of negotiation? Is the implementation of agreement after negotiation is of more priority than negotiation itself? State your views with justifications.

SUMMARY

Conflicts are known to be a part of everyone's life and possibly cannot be totally eliminated. All organisations and all human beings make utmost effort to control and manage conflicts to serve their business or personal objectives. We have however to understand the nature and how and why of a variety of conflict. Today, in spite of being known as a bad phenomenon, it has been realised that it is only through conflicts that a just and humane society can emerge.

A team – based organisation encourages group exercises in large measures and they are adapting interactive styles rather than the most usual directive style of management. This way, by mutual cohesion and understanding, groups have also started substantial resolution of conflicts within the organisation. At the same time, all group members, team leaders and managers themselves have to handle interpersonal and intrapersonal conflicts in right way.

One must also have the knowledge about different types and styles of conflicts. These are primarily known as (i) Competitive style (ii) Accommodative style (iii) Avoiding style (iv) Collaborative style and the (v) Compromising style. There are plenty of useful examples which can be applied suitably by anyone adopting any such style or any mix of several styles.

A series of guidelines are in place for managing conflicts in organsiational group exercises. Primarily these are (i) Do not turn a blind eye to existence of conflict. Better to go for collective brainstorming and exchange ideas as soon as signs of tension are noticeable (ii) It is necessary to concentrate on maximizing the group potentials and their performances. Examples are many among the most successful organisations (iii) Managers are the role models and they should be able to motivate the group members towards common objectives. (iii) In all communications, feed back must be sought and given at all times.

Negotiation is an important step towards settling conflicts. Always go for creative thinking and all group members have to participate and contribute. Negotiation specifics are of crucial importance and the leaders as well as the team members have to work hand in hand together within these guidelines. Similarly, negotiation strategy and behavioural aspects apply as they belong to same groups within the organisation. At all costs, therefore, promote a culture of harmonious negotiation.

KEY TERMS

Aftermath	:	*Consequences mostly unpleasant.*
Apathy	:	*Lack of interest, indifference.*
Bargaining	:	*Discuss the terms of sale or any agreement.*
Barriers	:	*Obstacles, impediments.*
Compassion	:	*Inclination to help or be merciful.*
Core	:	*Central or most important part of anything.*
Deliberations	:	*Careful consideration, discussion.*
Directive	:	*Order or instruction from an authority.*
Disaster	:	*Catastrophe, complete failure.*
Fostering	:	*Promote the growth or development.*
Hell – bent	:	*Recklessly determined.*

Incompatibility	:	*Not able to live in harmony.*
Interpersonal	:	*Between persons.*
Intricacies	:	*Very complicated.*
Introspection	:	*Examination of one's own thoughts.*
Lay off	:	*Discharge unneeded employees temporarily.*
Logistics	:	*Organisation of services and supplies.*
Motivation	:	*Stimulate the interest.*
Nonchalantly	:	*Calm and Casual.*
Non-exemplary	:	*Not characteristic of its kind.*
Reprisals	:	*Act of retaliation.*
Strategy	:	*Long term plan, policy or management.*
Tussle	:	*Struggle or scuffle.*

REFERENCES

Johnson, David W. Reaching Out: Interpersonal Effectiveness and Self – actualization Englewood cliffs, New Jersey, Prentice Hall, 1986.

Hiltrop, J.M. and S. Vall, The essence of Negotiation Prentice – Hall of India, New Delhi (1997).

Marriot, J.W., Jr. and Kathi Ann Brown The Spirit to Serve, Marriott's Way, Harper Business New York (1997).

Nierenberg, G.L. The Art of Negotiating Pocket Books New York (1984).

Robbins, Stephen P. Organsiational Behaviour Prentice Hall of India

New Delhi (2005).

Daily Mail (London) May 21, 2013.

Harvard Business Review Jan – Feb 2013 and

HT Value March 07, 2013 and April, 2012.

Mint August17, 2013 The Notion of Team work by Sudin Vadakut

Times Ascent October 14, 2009.

Tugend, Alina, Better By Mistake, The Unexpected Benefits by being Wrong Riverhead Books, Penguin, New York (2011).

Sengupta Sailesh Business & Managerial Communication PHI Learning Private Ltd. New Delhi (2011).

XII

Achieving Group Teamwork and Leadership Matrix

LEARNING OBJECTIVES

This chapter aims to provide right steps towards achieving group teamwork and refers to following decisive actions.

1. The art and science of building great teams.
2. Failure factors and communication values.
3. Characteristics of great team building.
4. Role of human relations in team work.
5. Importance of group teamwork.
6. Matrix of good leadership.
7. Related examples and case studies.

ACHIVING GROUP TEAMWORK

Organisations are primarily about people working together to fulfil organsiational as well as individual objectives. Yet so very often they fail to capitalise on their mutual potentialities. An established truth today is that a team or a collection of several teams can accomplish much more than the sum of its individual members striving alone. Even so, feelings of dissatisfaction do occur while organisations may work relentlenly towards creating a healthy environment of collaboration and cooperation. The managerial team, however, has to share equal or even more blame for such a situation.

The art and science of building great teams is no easy matter. Harvard, Columbia, MIT and several Universities in the USA and a few more in other countries have been trying to identify the elusive group dynamics that characterise high – performing teams. Over the past many years we have seen a host of approaches aimed at increasing organsiational effectiveness in creating team based organisations. They started paying more attention to training and development, skill development and also, communication abilities. But mostly such programmes were aimed at managerial development programmes. The top management believed that, in turn, their managers would by themselves work as the change – agents for team building within the organisation. By and large, such efforts failed. We may try to identify the reasons of failure.

Failure Factors:

Apart from the above – noted causes, a few more are identifiable:

(1) One particular reason that has been identified by many experts is the absence of good leadership and lack of mutual faith.

(2) Symptoms of frustration. In many organisations opportunities for personal expression become less and thus elements of satisfaction are much less. Many employees feel frustrated because they find no clear way of meeting their own needs and aspirations.

(3) In a frustrating environment people lose inspiration and lack the commitment and motivation. These are essential ingredients of effective teamwork.

(4) No focus on employee issues, improper work – life balance and delay in redressal of grievances. There is little or no availability of frequent group exercises in the organisation, adding to the feeling of all-round discontent.

(5) The increasingly complex and vast structure of industry and their top leaders' growing remoteness from direct contact with their own people.

(6) Development of literacy and education in all third world countries. As a result, there is more and more expectations from the internal people for facts and information pertaining to themselves and even for the public.

(7) The lack of effective communication and the absence of such a system in the organsiation spell further problems.

(8) Many organisations and their managers, who encourage teamwork also spend quite some time on retaliations. They find excuses for finding faults and taking them to task even for small mistakes.

(9) So many hierarchical levels in both upward and downward communication spoil even the CEO's attempts to be in touch with the lower levels of employees. Many managers distort or change the messages from the top to the downward levels. This also happens when the lower level employees try to pass on messages

Achieving group team work is a matrix of good leadership.

Happy expression of success for members of a group.

of suggestions or feed back to the uppermost levels of the management.

(10) Sometimes poor teamwork results in a very poor relationship between the managers and those they manage. The employees continue to wear an exasperated expression on their faces that further destroys the possibility of a happy environment at the work places.

Communication Values:

Why do patterns of communication matter so much? MIT's Human Dynamics Laboratory conducted a study of patterns of communication in organisations. Their comment: "it seems almost absurd that how we communicate could be so much more important to success than what we communicate".

Researchers further added, "By comparing data gathered from all the individuals on a team with performance data, we can identify the communication patterns that make for successful teamwork".

Interestingly, these patterns vary little, irrespective of the type of a team and its goal. It is mostly immaterial be it a call centre, a FMCG production team, or a pharmaceutical company. In spite of so much progress in communication medium, the most valuable form of Communication is face – to – face interactions. E – Mail and texting are the least valuable.

An Example

At the higher level at teamwork it took 600 Apple engineers less than two years to develop and deploy a revolutionary change in the company's operating system. On the other hand, it took more than 10,000 engineers around five years to develop, deploy and retract Microsoft's Windows Vista. Both organisations had star teams and no team was in any way inferior to another. This is an exceptional comparison but attempts to prove that putting the best thinkers on a team together can spur extraordinary creativity.

Teamwork and creativity work in unison and flourish in the right conditions. Common sense tells us that the conditions are personal freedom and support from managers, leaders and other team members. Then, there are the factors of freedom to experiment, trying out new ideas and encouragements from those who listen, evaluate and offer help.

Characteristics of Effective Teamwork.

In many organisations the quality of relationship at all levels, including even among the members themselves is so low that effective team work cannot get off the ground. Even, with each passing day, the relationship gets to be worse. Just one dissatisfied team member can affect the morale of the entire team and cause a lot of damage. A few widely – tested solutions to such problems are:

(1) The enterprise managers make painstaking efforts to foster inter – group and intra – group relations. Each member values and respects the others including the leaders and seniors. This may be considered as the first step towards building effective teams.

(2) Ensure that group meetings are productive and stimulating with participation by all members. New ideas will abound and decision making will be mostly quick, appropriate, and mostly unanimous.

(3) Personal and individual development is to be highly rated, encouraged and constantly given support by everyone.

(4) Team members to express views and opinions honestly and openly. Be always open to ideas that may even look or sound absurd.

(5) Remember to discourage any kind of negative approach or outlook. Negativity begets negativity and it's most essential to have a positive environment within the organisation. Politicking, using abusive languages or any kind of harassment have to be dealt with immediately but tactfully and politely.

(6) The involved groups should be well aware of the aims and objectives of group exercises in which all ideas are listened to and encouraged. Criticisms are not to be rejected but these have to be positive and constructive. After all, group dynamism comes from an ability to appreciate, and share various conflicting ideas, find out the best and finally decide about practical implementation within the organisation.

(7) Suggestions and recommendations will be meant for execution and the benefits as a result must be shared between the organisation and the group members. Here comes the specific responsibility of the organisation leaders to ensure later day implementation and rewarding the group.

(8) Any inefficient and unproductive use of time has to be discouraged. Most such groups activities within the organisation are held during working hours and both sides have to be conscious about good time management.

(9) The value of assertive behaviour in group functioning reigns supreme. Assertiveness will signify your alertness about your own rights but at the same time you are equally conscious about the rights of others.

(10) In work groups, as well as in all informal groups, a family, club or a social group, the primary ingredients bind the members in the same way. Any participant can take up the role of one who is adept at challenges, manages conflict, smoothens out difficulties and paves the way towards group teamwork.

A Few Corporate Examples

(1) *Suggestion Schemes in India.* A large number of companies in India had introduced the suggestion scheme as the hottest advantage for them. Some succeeded and a few failed. The purpose was to develop a two – way communication process between the organised groups and the management of the enterprise. A few successful examples are Larsen and Toubro, TCS, Tata Steel, Procter & Gamble in the private sector and Steel Authority of India, Life Insurance Corporation (LIC) and Indian Oil Corporation in the public sector. All these Companies came to realise the benefits of group involvement through suggestion schemes.

The scheme provides simple rules and procedure for submitting fresh ideas in any field of operating and functioning process. These included production, employee relations, communication, information technology, marketing and sales, preventing wastages, work safety or any. These companies managed to trigger off idea generation through communication and organised teamwork. The group members giving the suggestions were entitled to a part of the benefits that resulted from implementation of the idea.

(2) *Tata Consultancy Service* (*TCS*) is a major example of effective teamwork. Many feel that TCS has been able to reach the highest position in IT Sector owing to its visionary ideas about group functioning in the organsiational framework. They created an open environment that allowed the formlised groups within the company to discuss issues and challenges confront both the management and the employees. They took pride in claiming, "In our organisation, everything is open and nothing is secret".

The top management was always ready to listen and go for brainstorming exercises off and on. Moreover the management ensured speedy implementation of acceptable ideas. The process became the cornerstone of the very existence of TCS and its operating system.

(3) *KPMG:* in KPMG, the organisation believes in resolving issues by interactive processes. They encourage teamwork, group discussions and they do not hesitate to identify when things are not fine in a team. They also pinpoint poor leadership among managers and shortcomings in people management which could be major factors for disgruntlement within the team as well as in the organisation. Whenever such situations occur KPMG top managers step in and through interactive sessions try to promote the feeling that it's all about working together and working in harmony. They never resort to interrogating manner of confrontation but with positive and problem solving mindset.

All these have proved to be effective and useful. KPMG conducts periodic Role Negotiation Techniques to engage the team members on a 360 degree basis to communicate and perform. All these have led to a common understanding as well as appreciation of their own success and performance in group teamwork.

Human Relations and Teamwork

Human Relations today has come to occupy the first place for the proper working of an industry for any profit or non – profit organisation. It is a subject of vital interest and prime importance when we refer to the subject from teamwork perspectives. Nothing happens or moves in business and industry except through people – how they behave, how they are treated and how they perform. In fact, management by definition is the art of getting things done through people. Several noted experts have defined Human Relations as the "Development of joint purpose and motivation in a group". We may apply the concept in industry, business or in any work environment. It is the integration of people in a work – situation and formulating teamwork to achieve collective objectives.

Is there a magic formula or Aladin's lamp to conjure up good human relations? The improvement of human relations in the organised society is one of the best means to achieve group teamwork for ultimate fulfillment of desired objectives . To do so the first requirement is to assure a state of free and frank opinion making and self – respect in mutual relationship with each other. Second, there should be realistic appreciation of each other's needs and interests, both management and team members. The existence of effective channels of communication and group interaction facilities go a long way to foster team spirit and teamwork. Third, an appropriate system to identify conflicts and dissatisfaction should be in place for instant steps to replace such situations by cooperation and control measures.

Handling Human Realtions Problems

Most common feeling among all human beings is to secure a friendly, humanistic and supporting relationship in work and even outside their non- working environment. They look forward to a sense of worth in face – to – face groups and feel his/her importance of equality and acceptance. The groups in organisations and the managerial teams must recognise basic individual needs. Primarily these are:

(1) Recognition as an individual and promote the feeling that every member counts in group deliberations.

(2) Each member has to carry a sense of self – respect and this has to be recognised and adhered to.

(3) Need for communication abilities for each member of the group. Those who are lacking in their capabilities have to be provided with training and development.

(4) Members attending the group deliberations may have a sense of pride but they must possess a good measure of self – confidence that individually and collectively they can deliver.
(5) Participation in group activity by itself is an opportunity and distinctive but they must understand the value of discipline in good teamwork.

For both sides a sense of belonging and appreciation of their roles and responsibilities will help them to overcome all possible obstacles and difficulties. Additionally, a few more steps and suggestions for group cohesion and decision making could be of help.

(a) Collect all information, facts and study materials that could help in the group sessions.
(b) Recognise that in spite of best efforts for unity of feelings there will be differences as all human beings are different.
(c) It would be advisable to keep informal notes of discussion for easy references later.
(d) Understand the difference between facts and opinions and handle them in the right frame of mind.
(e) Be willing to understand and to respond to the feelings and attitude of others which might not be entirely logical or justified.
(f) Many a time one has to appreciate the social structure or social system in which individual members are involved.

Most of the suggestions are applicable to each member of groups but primary responsibilities are on the group leaders and managers of the organisation.

Why Group Teamwork

The above issues prompt us to understand why group teamwork is so very vital in to-days organsiational framework. By constant trials, experiments and experiences, many management groups have come to appreciate that truly functional groups can dramatically improve levels of performance at all levels. In earlier work pattern, employees and frontline supervisors felt isolated and frustrated. A team – based organisation, on the other hand, can produce unique results and unity of performance. As members of teams they started failing that they really belonged and their work made a difference.

How to make an attitudinal changes in team based organisations? A few steps are:

(1) Transition from directive style to interactive style of communication is a primary need.
(2) The organisation managers, with the support and involvement of all employees have to promote a culture of free and frank expression of views and opinions. This is more required in all group forums.

(3) Tactless criticism from either side makes people so mad that it does more harm than good. At the same time, one has to be careful not to act as if your brain is superior to any other person.

(4) Communication barriers have to be removed for easy understanding and clearer perception. For example, attitude of arrogance on the part of some members creates dissatisfaction and resentment in other members.

(5) May also happen that group members are not interested. Take care that the message should be meaningful and relevant to members. They will listen.

(6) Encourage members to express openly thus relieving any kind of tension in their minds. It is necessary to accept emotions as being part of a person's very existence particularly in a work environment. It is not advisable to prevent emotional outbursts at times as this may give rise to serious personal and organsiational problems.

Harvard Researchers found out that emotion plays a positive role in decision making, creativity and relationship building.

Leadership Matrix

Who is a leader in an organsiational set up? All employees look up to their managers who will guide them, lead them and inspire them towards all things better and desirable. As for managers, they are told that they have to get more than adequate results out of available or even less than adequate resources. Whatever way we look at the functional managers they have to carry out four primary services for the organisation as well as for the employees working with them. The functions are; communication, motivation, decision making and leadership development. Most managers go for team formations for achievement of these objectives.

World –wide interest and researches have attempted to find out - "who is a good leader" and "what is leadership". Till now, there is no single universally definition of a leader and leadership. Peter Drucker had simply said, "a leader is one who has followers."

Since we are more concerned with business and workteams, we may quote a few definitions or sayings by Indian business leaders:-

(1) Leaders lead by love, trust and example.

(Dhirubhai Ambani, Reliance Industries)

(2) Leaders think big, never compromise on fundamental values, look ahead, self – confident and have the best around themselves. They are committed to quality and play to win.

(Azim Premji, Wipro)

(3) Leaders are those persons who have trustworthiness, fearlessness, live their life to make differences to the society.

(Narayana Murthy, Infosys)

But, then, leadership also needs to be precisely defined. Four basic leadership styles are frequently referred to and an effective manager as a good leader have to follow them. These are; (i) directing, (ii) coaching, (iii) supporting and (iv) delegating. It has been observed that those who make it to higher managerial rung frequently fail. They stay in leadership roles for shorter and shorter periods. They fail to mobilise team members behind the concept of a mission of where your organisation should head to.

One familiar description of leadership is " a process whereby an individual influences a group of individuals to achieve a common goal."

Another statement says, "it is the process of guiding and directing the behaviour of people in the work or in any other environment."

The guiding principle in true leadership is the "Use, by a leader, of personal abilities and talents in order to have profound and extraordinary effects on followers".

A few Commandments of Good Leadership

A checklist of a few commandments of Good Leadership Qualities is given here. The "Success Mantras" are not by themselves conclusive and the list goes on expanding with the passage of time.

- The first quality requirement is that *a good leader should be able to win the trust of all colleages.* The values and virtues of good leadership should be known and visible all around.
- Good leadership should be able to take *quick and unpleasant decisions based on ethics and truthfulness.* There may be some initial setbacks but team members will eventually come to recognise the correct steps. However, effective and fact based communication must be at place to remove misunderstanding.
- *Good leadership is a learning process.* Good leaders never hesitate to learn even from subordinates. They admit mistakes readily and they proudly claim, "We are perpetual learners." The team members as followers will appreciate and mould themselves to the benefit of the organisation as a whole.
- *Good leadership is always on the look out for exceptional team members.* Without being discriminating they should be able to recognise, train and nurture talent.
- *Good leadership demands effective communication skills.* Clarity and focus are part of such abilities. Leading the teams and dealing the host of complicated issues at hand will put immense sellectual challenges for the leadership in organisations. They have to screen out unnecessary details and focus on what really matters.
- *Great leaders possess an uncanny ability to judge people* . They understand who will work best in what kind of slots. It is a task cut for good leadership. But this will require higher IQ as well as EQ and intuition coupled with experience.
- *Ability to understand and ability to get on well with people at all levels* . No flattery, but a mix of humility, tolerance and abundant common sense.

- *Good leadership calls for ability to motivate.* The whole team to do what the leadership wants them to do. It is the process of arousing and sustaining goal – directed behaviour. And this accounts for team members' intensity, direction and persistence of efforts on their own.

Finally, an oft repeated quote given by 6th century Chinese poet and philosopher Lao – Tzu can be referred to once again (See Chapter IV).

Example: Leadership at the CEO Level

Harvard Business Review came out (January – February 2013) with an exhaustive research study on "100 Best – Performing CEO's in the World". The study evoked acclaim, as well as criticism around the globe. HBR frankly stated (three researchers were Morton T. Hansen, Herminia Ibarra, and Urs Peyer) that the rankings were primarily based on long – term performance rather than achieving short term goals. The 2013 version of the CEO scorecard provided an objective answer.

One interesting issue was: who were up in the new listing and who were down. We will take up five names in the list of 50 global CEOs. The five Indian CEOs who figured are:

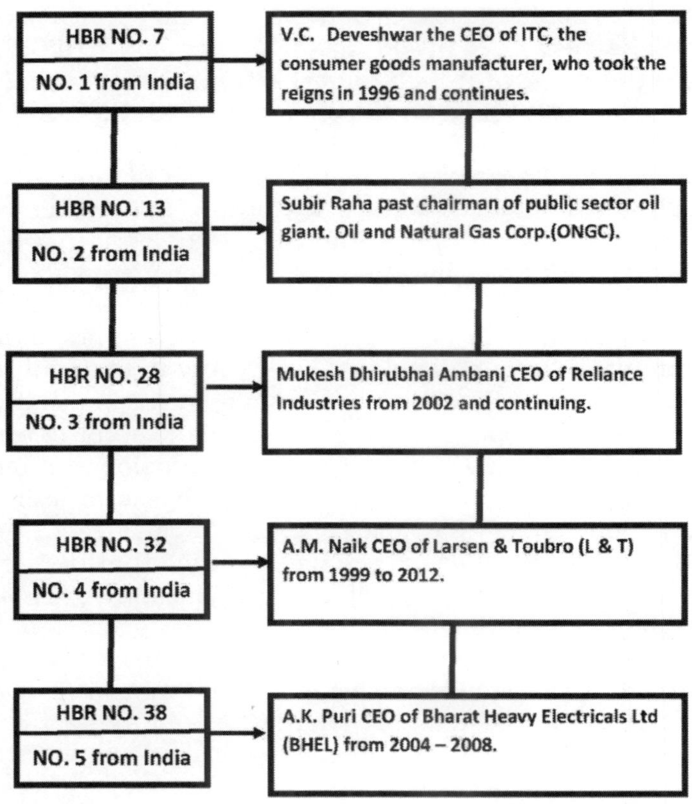

Apart from their significant contributions to respective companies in terms of total shareholders return and higher market capitalisation changes, they scored the highest in respect of corporate social performance. Of course, it comes as no surprise that the best performing CEO over the past 17 years was Steve Jobs of Apple who was No.1 on HBR list in 2010 as well, from 1997 to 2011, Apple excelled on all fronts of CEO's as well as its company's performance.

The most noticeable area of the Indian companies was to deploy their people to get best results.

The CEOs and the senior managers succeeded in making star teams out of countless star players. Appreciably, the star teams of these organisations, which included their CEOs, did extraordinary work. Additionally, these companies followed basic best practices for talent management through organised teamwork. Thus they were able to make their all – star teams exceptionally effective.

The Other Side of the Picture: Case Study on Indian Call Centre Employees.

Many an exploratory study has been carried out in the Indian Call Centre Industry to find out the work environment, employee- employer relations, their particular attitudes and the emerging professional issues. One author, B. Ramesh titled his book as "Cyber-*cooling in BPOs"*. A. James and B. Vira in their study through the book *"Unionizing the New spaces of the New Economy"* researched on the efforts of the trade union leaders to bring them under the union fold. On the other hand, D. Mc Millin tried to find out the "*Outsourcing Identities: Call Centres and Cultural Transformation in India"*. By these references we are trying to pinpoint the challenges, ironies and complications in the overall BPO industry scenario in India.

The Indian Call Centres have long been associated with high stress work environment and they were being called "*new – age sweatshops"*. The employers created 9 -10 hour shifts with two 15 minutes breaks and one 30 minute break with 5 day work weeks. Any kind of failure to fulfil organsiational or task – related requirements resulted in punitive actions by the management. The punishments started with verbal warnings, then warnings in writing, stoppage of increment, suspension and termination at the end. Were all these actions led the employees to seek redressal through union actions, go – slow, strikes etc.? Not the least.

Indian BPO employers have argued all the time that the formation of unions would only discourage foregn direct investment in the Indian economy. In the worst, all the BPO industry would be forced to shift their operations from India to other countries. They further argued that since the employers provided similar or even more improved work environment than the Western Countries, no scope for grievance for Indian BPO workers. Moreover, the employers reasoned that the modernized and updated human resource management system in the industry take the best care of the interest of the employees.

It is also true that the BPO employees, by and large, expressed their dislike of the traditional unionism and their normal tactics. The employees felt that they conduct themselves with dignity and current union practices were not in keeping with their professional standards. They felt slogan shouting, dharnas (picketing) and striking work were not their tools of expressing resentment against the employer. They felt agitated over some academics calling them as "Cyber Coolies" as they felt so much pride in their professional identity.

The state governments as well as the central authorities didn't want to lose the existing BPO industries and they maintained studied silence. The central trade unions, although they had some initial interest, lost their zeal to unionize them, since practically no BPO employee came forward to embrace them.

Discussion Questions

(1) How far do you agree that trade unions are irrelevant for BPO sector employees as the employees themselves are not enthusiastic about unionization? Do you think that BPO employees are able to look after their own interest as successful workteams in their organisations?

(2) To what extent it is acceptable that BPO employers provide exceptionally good work environment and their HR wings are constantly vigilant about the level of satisfaction at work levels.

(3) Many an authority on the subject strongly feel that techno – bureaucratic controls stressing professionalism in Indian BPO sector do not go uncontested. Do you agree? Why or why not?

(4) Is it possible that BPO experiences and style of functioning can be extended in other industries with the increase in literacy and education among employees? Do you feel self – reliant workteams can look after themselves and their interests independent of union control? Give your views.

CONCEPT DEVELOPMENT QUESTIONS

(1) What are the essential characteristics of effective teamwork? Do you feel that there could be a number of failure factors in achieving the objectives of group factors? Provide details alongwith one corporate example.

(2) How do you relate human relations to successful teamwork functioning? How do you propose to handle human relations problems in organsiational as well as in other team activities? Discuss and provide your suggestions in this context.

(3) It has been felt that functional groups can significantly contribute to improved performance at all levels in any team – based

organisation. Do you agree or not? Give justifications to your answers.

(4) What do you understand by the term "Leadership Matrix"? What are the guiding commandments of good leadership qualities? Provide your answers with a few examples.

SUMMARY

Achieving group teamwork calls for attention to training and development, skill development and also nurturing communication abilities. A number of failure factors create serious impediments in the process. Briefly these are frustrations, employee issues, absence of good leadership, levels of hierarchy in the organisation and inability to communicate effectively.

Effective team work should ensure intergroup and intragroup relations and group meetings must be productive and stimulating for all group members. All must express their views and opinions honestly and openly. Discourage negative outlook and promote a positive environment, all around. At the same time involved groups should be well aware of the aims and objectives of group exercises. Suggestions and recommendations by groups will be meant for speedy execution and ensure rewards for goods suggestions. Since most group exercises in organisations are held during working hours all participants have to be conscious about good time management.

Good teamwork and human relations go hand in hand together. It is the development of joint purpose and motivation in a group. And this concept is applicable in industry, business or in any work environment. Any disagreement, dissatisfaction or conflict situation should be replaced by cooperation and control measures instantly. All members have to appreciate the value of discipline in good teamwork.

Another area to be attended to is the need for transition from directive style to interactive style of communication. All barriers to communication have to be removed and promote free and frank opinion among all team members.

Leadership in teams and in the organisation is of priority importance. Members look up to their leaders who will guide them, lead them and inspire them for better performance. The questions being asked are: "Who is a good leader and what is leadership". The examples of business and industry leaders and what they feel can be referred to as guiding principles. A few of the commandments of good leadership are worth emulating. In essence these are the success mantras but such qualities are not conclusive and go on expanding with the passage of time.

KEY TERMS

Adept	:	Skillful.
Arrogance	:	Aggressiveness, presumptuous, unduly or overbearingly forward and confident.
Capitalise	:	Use to one's advantage.

Cohesion	:	Intelligible and articulate, disagreement to agreement.
Discontent	:	Dissatisfaction, grievance.
Distort	:	Misrepresent, inaccurate.
Elusive	:	Difficult to pin down.
Exasperated	:	Irritate intensely.
Exploratory	:	Enquire into to find details.
Hierarchical	:	System of status or authority.
Humanistic	:	Philosophy based on liberal human values.
IQ and EQ	:	Intelligence Quotient and Emotional quotient.
Ingredients	:	Component part in a mixture.
Mantra	:	Originally vedic hymn term used as set of rules to follow.
Matrix	:	Mold in which a thing is cast or shaped.
MIT	:	Massachusetts Institute of Technology, USA.
Morale	:	Determination of a person or group.
Perpetual	:	Lasting forever, continuous.
Profound	:	Having great knowledge or insight.
Punitive	:	Intented to inflict punishment.
Relentlessly	:	Oppressively constant.
Retaliations	:	Attacking in return.
Spur	:	Stimulus or incentive.
Stimulating	:	Thing that rouses activity.
Zeal	:	Earnestness or fervour.

REFERENCES

Adair, John, "The Skills of Leadership: The Effective Communicator" Jaico, Mumbai (2002).

Hindustan Times Weekly Feature, April 15, 1999.

Harvard Business Review April 2013 and Feb 2013

Indian Journal of Industrial Relations Vol. 48 NO 3 January, 2013.

James A. & Vira, B, "Unionizing the New Spaces of the New Economy? Alternative Labour in India's B.P.O. Industry", Geoforum (2010)

Ludlow, Ron & Fergus Panton "Effective Communication" Prentice – Hall of India New Delhi – 110001 (2000).

Mc Millin, D. "Outsourcing Identities", "Call Centres and Cultural Transformation in India" Economic and Political Weekly (2006).

Naresh, B. " Cyber Coolies in BPOs", Economic & Political Weekly (2004).

Sengupta, Sailesh, "Business and Managerial Communication" PHI Learning Pvt. Ltd. New Delhi – 110001 (2011).

Sengupta, Sailesh, "Management of Public Relations and Communication," Vikas Publishing House Pvt. Ltd. Noida – 201301 (Second Reprint 2009).

Time Business, Times of India, New Delhi 1st February 2010).

Part—II

I

Crisis and Management of Risks Many Sides of the Same Coin

Nature and form of crisis

Crisis may come in all kinds, shapes and forms. Some involve loss of life or property, or both. For that matter, no company or organisation ________ profit or non-profit, commercial or non-commercial, Government or a local body_____is immune to crisis. It may be a product related crisis, which may include a manufacturing mistake, a packaging error, tampering of products, a Government inquiry, a lawsuit, a boycott or a consumer action or protests by activist groups.

Many more crises result from events such as bankruptcy or a high rate at which people enter and leave employment or even a scandal. Crises must include an industrial accident, any form of labour dispute like strike and lockout or closure, a corporate acquisition or reorganization, stock market crashes, explosions and fires and similar circumstances.

A crisis may also occur owing to acts of nature like flood, earthquakes, drought, epidemic etc. internally major corporate crises are characterised by low productivity and operational inefficiency that tend to threaten the basic goals of an organisation.

What is a crisis?

Interestingly, Webster's Dictionary defines crisis as a turning point for better or worse. The message is clear that the particular situation could turn out to be both good and bad. For example, an industry which falls 'sick' will create a situation of overall crisis for the management, employees, shareholders, suppliers, distributors, financial circles and many more publics with whom an industry has to interact.

The other side of this gloomy picture is that some persons will consider it as an opportunity to turn the organisation into a viable unit. Indeed, calamity and opportunity are two extreme sides because people involved in the business are ready to clutch at a straw, they would be, in their own interest, ready to do something for the organisation.

The moral of the situation thus leads to any opportunity and nurtures the unit back to health provided all aspects of the crisis are handled with understanding, efficiency and business acumen.

Responding to a Crisis

"How does a crisis occur and how should an organisation respond to a crisis" is no doubt a topic of recurring debate. It may be difficult to anticipate or predict a crisis and initiate remedial measures. But it is necessary to recognise the early warning signs of a crisis, study the nature of the crisis and be able to measure the magnitude of damage in practical terms that the crisis may cause.

Most companies, in reality, do not contemplate any crisis management that might be required of them, should even a small disaster occur. A number of incidents in recent times, such as Bhopal Gas Tragedy, The Chernobyl nuclear explosion, the IC 814 hijacking case, the World Trade Tower collapse or the London underground bombings and host of industrial and non-industrial happenings are in vivid memory. All these have shaken organisations, Governments and other bodies from their complacency and forced feelings of immunity.

A crisis brings risks into focus, the organisations instantly fall under media scrutiny, and it reflects internal impact on employee morale turns the community and opinion leaders into direct antagonists and drags the organisation into prolonged legal battles. In addition to financial losses, the company or the organisation suffers almost irreversible setbacks in reputation.

Risk Management

To address crisis management in the coming decades, it is necessary to begin, in right earnest, to pinpoint your organisation's vulnerabilities. Where are the greatest risks? Try to discover potential trouble by an appropriate crisis audit. What specifically could happen? How likely is it? How severe would the impact be? And look for worst case scenarios.

No organisation as well as no business is free of risk. Risk, in the broadest sense means exposure to adversity. In business, when we say risk, we generally mean the eventual possibilities of incurring commercial

When I say business as usual, I mean no crisis heppening for some time....!

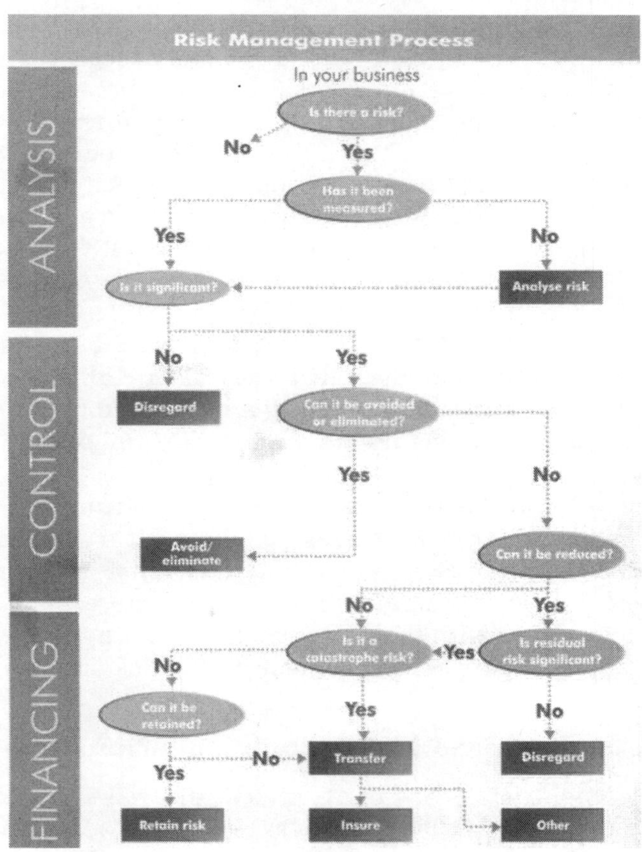

losses and reputational setbacks. Therefore, if we cannot avoid risk, we must learn to minimise it and take measures to reduce its impact.

Obviously, risk is ever present in every aspect of our lives and in the lives of every organisation ________ production risk, marketing risk, distribution risk, financial risk, personnel risk and so on. For many companies, clearly, risk management is part of the strategic competitive picture, as important to profitability as R&D or capital investment plans. Risk has to be managed continuously. Or else it is going to affect the business and diminish competitiveness. For all such reasons, risk and crisis are increasingly part of every aspect of a business or a non-business operation.

Information-Communication-Truthfulness.

Few communication problems loom as ominously as do those related to how risk levels will be successfully announced and discussed in public. One risk communication model indicates that if people receive credible and clear information regarding assessed risk levels they will accept the conclusions and recommendations of reliable assessors.

Crisis and communication are really the two broader sides of the same coin. The communication plan, preferably formulated by PR and Management professionals, should be put into operation as an ongoing process but must be set in full motion at the onset of the crisis. Bhopal gas tragedy is an extreme example of deliberate and confused "do nothing" attitude on the communication front, whereas ONGC Bombay High old gas flare up case showed how free flow of communication led to understanding, appreciation and success.

Another example of disastrous failure on all fronts is the recent hospital fire in prestigious AMRI Hospital in Kolkata on 9th January, 2011. 91 lives were lost and nothing much could be done, except that some local youths lunged forward voluntarily and saved lots of patients in distress.

Here comes the role of media in the crisis situations. The larger the crisis the greater the media interest. And isn't it true that media creates public opinion? The increasingly dangerous, unstable society of the 21st century means that organisations must strive more than ever to develop relationships of trust with their publics. Indeed, the split-second reporting of tragic events presents new challenges for the risk and crisis management teams.

Issues to be discussed and Recommendations to be given

1. "Whether visible or latent, crises and risks are to be managed, because otherwise organisations cannot remain viable or competitive." Do you agree? Give reasons with examples.
2. Do you think that appropriate crisis planning and crisis management should result in improved productivity through fewer

bottlenecks or interruptions in work? Explain various facets of Planning and Management of crisis and risk factors in organisations.

3. Enumerate the benefits of Effective Risk Management in terms of increased profitability. Explain how the process can help to identify exposure to risks and why risk management is considered a necessity for survival.
4. Many past crises are examples of deliberate and confused “do nothing” attitude on the communication front __ Discuss and give your own recommendations about communication strategies (before, during and after)

Introduction

Webster’s dictionary defines Crisis as a **turning point for better or worse**. The situation could turn out to be both good and bad. For example, an industry, which falls ‘sick’ will create a situation for overall crisis for the management, employees, shareholders, suppliers distributor and many more public with whom the industry has to interact. The other side of the gloomy picture is that some persons will consider it as an opportunity to turn the organisation into a value unit. **Calamity and opportunity are indeed the two sides of the same coin.**

Most companies, in reality, do not contemplate any crisis management that might be required of them, should even a small disaster occur. The operation of a business or industry might get disturbed by a crisis triggered off by accidents, environmental pollution, and product defect or failure, hostile take-over, strike, lock-out or closure, stock market crashes, explosions and fires and similar circumstances. Internally, major corporate crises are characterised by low productivity and operational inefficiency that tend to threaten the basic goals of an organisation.

It can also be a situation where, in the eyes of the media or general public, the company did not react to one of the above situations in the appropriate manner. For example, Bhopal Gas tragedy, Exxon oil spill, Tylenol disaster. The crisis brings risks into focus: these risks can be political, social, economic or financial in nature.

There are also certain crises over which companies may not have any control, such as:

- Unknown hazards from products or wastes
- Natural disasters (floods, droughts or earthquakes)
- Ownership battles.
- Technology problems.
- Civil unrests (riots, civil wars general strikes and political violence)

Truly, a crisis can originate outside a company or within a company. It cannot always be fully predictable, but the management can defuse the crisis at the right moment with proper handling. Poorly handled, crisis also can threaten future sales of product or service. A single event can threaten to obliterate all the equity of past market development. By planning ahead, one can be prepared for the unthinkable. The following steps are recommended:

- Asses you crisis vulnerabilities
- Develop a crisis prevention plan
- Establish an early warning system
- Prepare a crises communication plan.
- Learn basic media relations skills
- Work closely with public relations and communication persons in anticipating and responding to crises.

CRISIS PLANNING

Crisis planning involves a few essential steps, not in anticipation of crisis but to be prepared mentally for such situation and be able to minimise damages to the organsiation and the community.

The basic **steps** are:

1. Prevent a disaster by all possible means. (Remember: Accidents do not happen they are caused)
2. The company should be alert and vigilant at all times with its eyes, ears open to read the warning signals before the disaster strikes.
3. Prevention mechanism should be frequently tested and made foolproof. The company has to clearly identify the specific problem areas and sensitive issues within or even outside the organisation.
4. The company should prepare, circulate and train relevant people in the organisation according to model crisis procedures. No one should feel isolated and confused about their role and duty when the need arises.
5. Planning and communicating well in advance and at appropriate points of time can contribute to the prevention of crisis and even when it occurs minimise the damage to life and property. The Bhopal Gas Disaster is a classic example. If the Union Carbide had a crisis management group and had the group members communicated the remedy that the released chemical (MIC) could be neutralized by water, possibly many victims could have been saved just by placing water soaked rags over their mouths.
6. Crisis and communication are really the two sides of the same coin. The communication plan should be put into operation immediately at the onset of crisis. Communication is an ongoing activity, and it must be ensured that communication process is in full and effective existence at all times without any hindrance of any kind.

Again, Bhopal gas tragedy is an extreme example of "do nothing" attitude on the communication front, whereas ONGC Bombay High Gas flare up case showed how free flow of communication led to understanding, appreciation and success.

7. Last but not the least, it is important to treat employees with respect both as valued resources and as people, especially for the reason the employee can contribute very substantially to managing a crisis.

COMPLIANCE

When a crisis occurs, the company needs a system that will advise the initiatives that can be addressed during a crisis. This will allow acting in a responsible manner to fulfill the purpose and intent of existing legislation.

It can also provide a framework for anticipating future legislation. An effective system for compliance can be developed only if one knows what laws and regulations pertain to their operation. In order to accomplish this task, a survey of all operations should be undertaken.

The survey should include:

- General Administrative Information.
- Management Awareness and Control Programmes.
- Identification of Hazards/Potential Crises.
- Business Characterization.

Once the survey programme has been developed and implemented, it must be evaluated and kept up-to-date.

PREPAREDNESS

Preparedness means all measures taken to prevent, prepare for, respond, mitigate and recover from a crisis. Preparedness consists of four critical aspects:

- Preparation and prevention.
- Detection and Classification.
- Response and Mitigation.
- Reentry and Recovery.

Mistakes in Crisis Management

The main cause of corporate crises, say experts, is management. In all research, one can see that the majority of crises have their origins within companies and organisation and managements are the causes of the majority of crises.

These are the seven biggest mistakes in crisis management and crisis communication:

(1) No issues/risk audit

A company should identify issues that can affect it through an issues audit before it begins to plan for a crisis. Issues should be prioritized and stances worked out. "A sensitive monitoring system is absolutely essential for an effective crisis management programme," say many an expert crisis handlers.

(2) Ostrich mentality

This phenomenon occurs when a company hopes that no one learns about its crisis. This is where companies cater to whoever is advising them to say nothing or to do nothing. The company senior officials feel that they don't have to do anything instantly but will face the situation when it comes. Such an attitude leaves no time for preparation by the management and the results are mostly suicidal. They assume that they will have to react when and if necessary with little or no preparation time.

(3) Are you ready at all times?

The company managerial team as also their communication professionals need to pass through rigorous vulnerability tests together with risk audit from time to time. Similarly, scenario planning is an essential aspect of crisis preparedness and they must undergo training schedules in association with expert advice from consultancy services.

(4) Poor ability to communicate openly

The biggest mistake communications practitioners make in crisis communications is allowing them to be overruled by the lawyers "The role of the lawyers is to "enable" companies to do right thing, not to block companies from doing so." Many companies still view the media as adversaries. They need to recognise the media as a crucial conduit to carry their message.

Apologise promptly and remember that the most credible company spokesperson is the most senior person .Key executives must be trained to deal effectively with journalists in a crisis.

(5) Not listening to stakeholders

Organisations have to receive and encourage continuous feedback from their clients and customers, employees and their unions, investors, industry leaders and other stakeholders including communities and their leaders as a matter of urgent importance. Interactions and open dialogue with various stakeholders will enable the companies to identify potential crisis situations.

(6) Establish formal crisis communication plans

Before the onset of any crisis companies need to establish well – thought out crisis communication plans. At the same time there will be the need for a training and policy manual. Crisis management teams are similarly to be put on stream with total management involvement. Update company telephone and key media lists are another instrument of crisis handling measure and should be available at any given moment.

(7) Failure to test procedures

Crisis communications procedures and plans must be tested realistically and reviewed regularly. Companies should identify weaknesses so they can strengthen organsiational capabilities to respond to crises. Frequent simulations ensure readiness to handle a crisis.

What is Risk management?

The definition of risk management should quite simply be. "The art or act of handling the possibility of loss or opportunity".

In another way we can define it as "the overall coordination of an orgnaisation's response to a crisis, in an effective, timely manner, with the goal of avoiding or minimizing damage to the orgnaisation's profitability, reputation, or ability to operate during a crisis situation".

POTENTIAL BENEFITS OF EFFECTIVE RISK MANAGEMENT

- Supports strategic and business planning.
- Enhances communication between departments.
- Supports effective use of resources.
- Promotes continual improvement.
- Helps focus internal audit programme.
- Fewer shocks and unwelcome surprises.
- Reassures stakeholders.
- Quick grasp of new opportunities.
- Increased reassurance for the public.
- Increase ability for the public and government to make appropriate choices in the face of adversity.
- Increases the level of safety and confidences.

Effective risk management is a critical component of any winning management strategies. The application of pre-post loss mitigation technique combined with varying level of properly designed insurances and risk management programme allows an organisation to actually take an additional risk management programme while growing more securely. It allows an institution to take on activities that have a higher level of risk and therefore could deliver a greater benefit because the risk have been identified and understood and are being well managed, thus the residual risk is thereby lower.

NECESSITY OF RISK MANAGEMENT

- Improved product quality.
- Increased ability to deliver on time.
- Improved asset efficiency due to fewer breakdowns.
- Reduced costs by limiting legal actions.
- Improved reliability leadership to an unchanged reputation.
- Less possibility of incurring commercial loss.

HOW RISK MANAGEMENT HAS CHANGED

Old Risk Management Approach	New Risk Management Approach
• Heavy reliance on audits • Reactive detection and correction approach. • High cost. • Low involvement of company personnel.	• Involve all employees. • Focus on enterprise risks-those affect the company's objectives and competitiveness. • Build risk management into all management activities. • Become proactive: Stress prevention instead of correction. • Leverage risk management and control. • Set acceptable exposure targets and keep risk control costs low.

A CHECK LIST FOR RISK MANAGEMENT

Risk management/programmes work best when senior management assesses risk tolerance and division managers monitor specific risks.

- Set up a board-level risk management committee to monitor company-wide risk and assess company exposure.
- Determine the company's risk tolerance for major factors.
- Develop a cross-departmental management team program to monitor risks.
- Assign risk management responsibilities to appropriate departments and operations.
- Assess risks at the lowest possible divisional or operational level. Develop strategies to mediate where appropriate.
- Make risk assessment integral to the achievement of any objective, and reward employees for dealing appropriately with risk.

(***Reference: Global Finance***)

RESPONDING TO A CRISIS

- The special communication plan should be put to use immediately at the onset of the crisis.
- The information process goes into operation-informing employees, relevant authorities, concerned publics and obtaining help and assistance to fight the crisis.
- Media action plan would be a critical factor as the media and the organisation become interdependent during and after the crisis. It is dangerous and sometimes suicidal to pull the wool over the eyes of the media.
- Never leave any public out of the information process who may be concerned with the organisation and its welfare or who may be hit as a result of the crisis.

- Company's chief spokesperson must be identified who must be available to the media from time to time. In fact, there is need for several spokespersons as the company has to deal with the media, government, employees, local population, shareholders etc.
- The role of Corporate Communications is not restricted to routine functions related to a crisis situation. It would be instantly necessary to get hold of essential technical details, arrange photographs, collect statistical information and study historical data as input for crisis-handling procedure. Sometimes, media including the television would prefer to interview, in addition to the top management, shop-floor employees, citizens and opinion leaders and it does not ultimately pay to oppose. It is better to co-operate and sensitively handle opposite points of view.
- Co-ordination, both internally and also at the external level, is a key factor in the management of a crisis. The ability of the affected unit to mobilise resources and without waiting for corporate approval is another important factor in the successful implementation of the contingency plan. The corporate office has to provide adequate technical and financial support without wasting time. The delegation of authority in advance and co-ordination of the essential components of the management function could be highly advantageous.

Role of PR Communication

The overall image of an organisation is intertwined with an effective communication plan especially at the time of crisis. So, it's important that PR and Communication must be considered essential part of management rather than trouble shooting apparatus. In dealing with crisis, PR and communication shall begin with sending, monitoring and analysing possible public response to the orgnaisation's policies, motives and actions. The first and foremost thing is to make a MAP (Message Action Plan).

- MAP is an easily read document, containing PR and communication plan which allows quick understanding of that must be done, how and by whom.
- It is a strategic planning representing overall plan.
- MAP reduces plan into basic component.

The 3 golden rules to crash down the crisis are:-

1. Management co-operation to initiate any corporate communication plan. It is necessary to tell corporate management that the purpose of the communication plan is to respond adequately in the moment of crisis, so that people are ensured that the communication machine is always in existence and not any offshoot of emergent situation.

2. Respond properly to media. Anticipate what media wants to know. Avoid "no comments" situation or any debate on subject. Infact, be available

to media, select credible person and train him or her to tell your side of story quickly and honestly. Give enough evidence to support your side.

3. Internal communication is a must:- Inform employees on matters of concern and confer with them and their representatives about the crisis. A good internal communication plan will be source of encouragement for them to be involved, generate a sense of belonging and further motivate them to increase productivity level of an organisation.

ROLE OF COMMUNICATION

The ability to manage the communication factor is an essential element of crisis management. The communication strategy should pinpoint important stakeholders, their information needs and how the need could be satisfactorily fulfilled. A few steps, therefore, like crisis survival, doomsday communication and managing the communication function are worth consideration.

Step one: The first golden rule for initiating any corporate communication plan is to stress to corporate management that the purpose of communication is to respond adequately in the moment of crisis. It has to be ensured that the outside world has the feeling that the communication machine is always in existence and it is not an offshoot of an emergent situation.

Step two: The company and its communication must ensure that the **company is in a position to anticipate what media may want to know**. More often 'Press Hostility' arises mainly because of the inadequate preparation, half hearted information and lack of public awareness of basic issues concerning the corporation. Companies must understand and appreciate that the media serve the public for survival and success and the company could not do just without the media for the broader relationship with the public.

Step three: Providing information to the employee systematically on matters of concern to them as employees and confer with them and their representatives about the ongoing crisis. A well-structured employee's communication programme will be a source of encouragement for them to be involved in a company's crisis situation.

Some other steps that can really help a company out of crisis situation are:-

- Effective media relations by the organisation.
- Not evading journalist's question with "No Comments"
- A good image lends credibility in minds of target audience.
- Press kit should be prepared containing all the essential background information about the organisation.
- Preparing stand by statements on issues and incidents where journalist may require comments.

Conclusion

A good management, which wants to be one up, needs to grapple with the problem and find solutions. If one alternative is not working the other may be tried. It may take time, or the problem may not be solved at all. But at least the management can have the satisfaction of making the maximum effort. They cannot be idle spectators who watch from the sidelines. The experience gained during the struggle can be of immense gain in the future. To sum up, it is very true to say that no organisation can survive without crisis management plans, action programmes, and appropriate responses before during and after the crisis. In a trying situation the organisation is able to realise its strengths and weaknesses.

The Meerut Fire case, the Pepsi and Coke pesticide controversy and the Cadbury Worms Case have taught these organisations how to manage crisis and to maintain their image, at the same time.

Thus, crisis can either lead cohesion of an organisation or its break-up.

Hence, crisis and management of risk are instrumental in the success or failure of an organisation. If problem is solved, the rating of the management as a whole goes up several times in the corporate world. After all, it is good to think of how history would describe you: as a fighter or a spectator.

CASE STUDY

David Vs Goliath in the USA
Ralph Nader takes on "General Motors"

THE CRISIS

Ralph Nader discovered that the new Covair Compact Car lacks safety measures. When he questioned the company he was brushed aside.

THE PUBLIC

Media ignored him when he tried to criticise the car in the press. This did not deter him. His documented book "Unsafe at any speed" hit the book stalls and became an instant best-seller.

THE COMPANY

General Motors hired private detectives to shadow Ralph Nadar in an attempt to besmirch his private life and thus to destroy his credibility and bonafides. The company failed miserably in the face of strong public support in favour of Ralph Nadar.

THE RESPONSE

The chairman of General Motors, James M. Roche, was summoned before a Senate Committee investigating the safety of automobiles. It was his candid apology that helped GM to salvage shreds of its shattered image and the entire Covair range of cars was withdrawn from the market.

THE CONCLUSION

(1) "The man in the street" could now pronounce his verdict on a mighty corporation and bring it to heel.

(2) "Consumerism" had struck its first successful blow at the citadels of private sector power in the USA.

(3) Today, Government, organisations and individuals are vulnerable to pressures from public, hitherto largely ignored.

(4) Faced with the crisis of survival, the communication part of the task of informing the public that the right thing will be done seems as important as ever.

II

Challenges of A Different Kind Managing And Retaining New IT Professionals

The Problem

Companies in the Information Technology Sector, in India and elsewhere, are facing the problem of finding the right talent and then to keep them. There is also a constant dearth of IT professionals. A recent survey points out that almost 3 jobs out of every 10 jobs go unattended because of shortage of employees.

Whenever an employee leaves the organisation, the professional takes along with him the means of production, which is his knowledge. N.R. Narayana Murthy, Chairman of Infosys Technologies, puts it with telling effect, "My assets walk out of the gate every night"!

To retain the IT employees the companies come out with innovative HR techniques but still Human Resource Development practices have a long way to go. No doubt, over the years, HR functions have matured from the staff to a line, and have been implemented with various degrees of success in many of the sectors of the Indian economy.

Experts define knowledge workers as "Key employees who create value added areas" (and often transport those assets in their heads when they change employers). In order to manage and retain these "Key employees" the HR mangers have to look into their needs and aspirations, their likes and dislikes, which will keep them away from quitting.

Now, what do Indian companies need to do to adapt themselves to the fast-moving changes? Tom Peters, the great guru of management, during a recent visit, said he observed dramatic changes in India. He added, "You can make a strong argument that this will probably the century in India". Tom referred to IT revolution in India as a young people's revolution. His warning is, "You have to allow relatively younger people much more freedom."

In the Indian IT sector, nevertheless, it is time to counter the general assumption that Indian knowledge workers are too independent-minded to be managed beneficially. On the other hand, it can be argued that the very diversity of the Indian workforce could be a great advantage to IT firms, not a handicap. Narayana Murthy and Azim Premji have stated with great conviction that Indian workpeople needed good HR management and good motivation. In return, they can bring more commitment, creativity and high-quality performance to their work than their counterparts in other countries.

At a time of great organsiational change, and a stated commitment to people on the other, it may be often difficult to assess important trends and issues in human resource management. The current need is to provide an entirely new model for organisations to structure themselves to deliver successful patterns through inventive HRM practices. It eliminates the prevailing hierarchical organisation of command and control; and replaces it with a horizontal organisation that manages the basic core processes. It has to create and deliver to full satisfaction of the organisation and its knowledge workers together as a single entity. Is it really possible and does it stand up to measurable success?

Issues to be discussed and recommendations to be given

1. Discuss the concept of strategic HRM and the human reality factors in relation to Indian Software Industry. How far the present HR practices are integrated with the management processes in the Indian IT Sector and how successfully?
2. Discuss the principles of managing the Indian IT Industry and how far the new HR standards have been suitably applied in this sector?
3. Can you provide appropriate industry examples as to how they are able to attract and retain their professionals without much of conflict and clash of interests? Give details.
4. Discuss the expectations of the New Age Workers and give your recommendations and conclusions.

Strategic HRM: The Human Reality

We need to have an informed, accessible and dispassionate look at how leading corporates handle their people management in ICS (Information and Communication Systems). We need to know how some of the national and international blue chip companies, well known for

Managing and retailing IT professionals is a major challenge today for IT industry globally.

their HR commitment ____________ Wipro, Infosys, TCS, Hewlett Packard, BP, BT, Microsoft, etc. look towards various partnering arrangements within. In turn, we have to examine:

- The environmental factors that shape the orgnaisation's approach to HR vis-à-vis knowledge workers.
- The links between what is intended and what is realised.
- The way HR interventions impact on the individual.
- The influence HR strategies have on everyday management behaviour.

The Environmental Factors

The effective management of knowledge assets is a key requirement for securing competitive advantage in the information economy. Yet the nature of knowledge assets, however, remains poorly understood. One needs to explore and understand how knowledge and information assets differ from physical assets and how to deal with them at a strategic level within an organisation.

Highly proficient IT professionals are hard to come by and harder still to retain for the simple reason that they own their means of production which is their knowledge. For example, a worker in a manufacturing industry does not own the means of production. It is also true manufacturing is a highly automated job with much lower skills required from the worker. The case of the IT industry is just the opposite; here the knowledge worker holds the key because he is no way less than a machine. If he is not available, the system cannot run on its own. He owns the means of production and thus commands value and respect within and outside.

Integration with the HR Practices

Do traditional HR practices support the needs of the new breed of IT professionals? For leaders in the HR area, especially for themselves, the key issues are:

- Skills needed to manage change successfully, particularly during organsiational transformations.
- Discover how to motivate, lead and manage people and teams and also make sure their personal styles are the most effective for their careers.
- Regulate change to maximize effectiveness and minimize resistance.
- Understand factors that have an impact on team climate, individual motivation and organsiational performance.
- Above all, HR managers have to develop an agenda for improving the effectiveness of individual style.

Integration with the Management Processes

The Information and Communication Systems (ICS) recognize that the strategies and business opportunities in an organisation are strongly influenced by its technology base.

In essence, information and communication systems are important business resources that must be integrated with the management processes of organisations. And the knowledge workers are the most important ingredients in this entire value system. Moreover, the concentration is designed to meet the ever growing national and international need for highly skilled and imaginative IT professionals. If these issues are not properly attended to, they will not be able to use ICS technologies in the world of electronic business for competitive advantage.

Obviously, the aim is to create organsiational advantage in global markets. The area of interest must include the economics of information capital, human interaction at every stage of progress and strategies to support meaningful developments inwards and outwards.

It is time organisations realised that information and communication technology is changing knowledge workers and their work, causing massive organsiational change. Systems are now more likely to fail for organsiational reasons than for technical reasons. Leading companies like IBM, Microsoft, Infosys and Wipro have studied the human side of effective implementation of new systems.

They constantly ensure, their HR teams more so, to attend to the human side in every aspect of information technology.

Many such organisations are now evolving toward an integrated self-managing, team oriented culture. This structure emphasizes group-problem solving, interpersonal communication and leadership among peers. High technology induces and allows them to do things differently and to do different things. There has to be an entirely new focus on theories of motivation, evaluation and feedback, compensation and incentives, cultural and group influences.

The Indian Software Industry

In an unexpected and sudden reference to India, the legendary Bill Gates stated, “the software industry will create millions of new jobs in the years ahead. India, more than any developing nation, is seizing this opportunity and will become a huge exporter of software expertise”. “In fact”, he predicted: India is likely to be a software superpower”.

The industry has gained significance in the Indian Economy with sustainable growth rates, increased contribution to FDI (Foreign Direct Investment), employment and experts. Despite the uncertainties prevailing about the overall economic scenario in 2011, hiring activities in IT/ITES Segment in India may increase by 7 – 8 percent in 2012 (outsourcing firm Elixir Consulting). This sector alone is expected to generate as many as 3, 00,000 new jobs in 2012. The experts are predicting even greater upsurge in the coming few years and thereafter as well. Adding to the cheers of the job market, the employees in all segments could expect double digit salary hikes during 2012 and in subsequent years, IT/ITES included (Executive Search firm Global Hunt).

One more survey says that the IT enabled services (ITES) industry in India will touch a whopping **5 – 25** billion US dollars employing over **1.5** million people in the next few years (People One Consulting). The Group recently conducted a study to benchmark HR practices in this industry. The accent of the survey has been on (i) Designing the right pay package and (ii) Honing skills to perfection. The findings conclude with the conviction that India is well positioned to derive benefits from the ITES market and become a key hub for these services. This phenomenal growth and expectations are due to the availability of highly competent and cost effective IT professionals, the knowledge workers.

Another distinctive characteristic of the software sector is that they have only the expertise of their staff as assets with which to trade. The task of the leader in this sector is therefore to recruit, train, empower and retain the best and the brightest professionals. It is vital for companies to recognise certain market realities. In the software sector it is an employee's, market due to the worldwide shortage of software professionals. 2.5 jobs out of every ten are currently unfilled and will remain vacant till 2012.

Hence for practitioners and HR managers, an important variable to probe is what kind of Human Resource practices are required which provide both nurturance and control of the IT professionals in the companies which attract them.

A sound Human Resources Management (HRM), based on norms of social welfare, contributes substantially to better employee relations, higher productivity and consequently better profitability to the organisation. From the days of "command and control" we are in the era of mutual trust, based on social equity, equality and justice. Better tools and training are abstract aspects of productivity management. Social welfare brings in the human aspect.

The chart below typifies the principles of managing IT professionals.

1. **Return the devotion of your knowledge workers**

   An Indian company has enshrined the principles of sound HRM in the object clause of its memorandum and articles of association, extracted as follows:

   Objects incidental to the main object:

   - To meet the orgnaisation's social, civic and economic obligations and responsibilities.
   - By attracting, training and retaining employees and affording them jobs, wages, standards of living, amenities, working conditions, job satisfaction, stability of employment and opportunities for advancement and participation in company's activities in return of their loyalty, initiative, skill care, effort, attendance and spirit of team work.

This illustrates the commitment of the organisation to its employees and the impact of mutual devotion.

2. **Meet their Basic needs**

   Consider for a moment, that, if your employees are spending all their time with you and your organisation, where else should they go to get their needs fulfilled? Further, your meeting their needs keeps them captive from gathering reactive ideas from outside.

3. **Meet their self-actualization needs**

   Human needs are diverse: basic and self-actualization. Human awareness to their rights is raising every day. India won its independence to call off servility and "salamming" culture. Every man looks for mutual respect from everybody else, not less in his work place. Man-Management methods should aim at satisfying such needs in the current context. These have been taken for granted.

4. **Training**

   A number of organisations feel that training is a waste of time or is a holiday to their employees. It is not that every point discussed at training programmes is to be implemented, but just one point or two taken is adequate reward for the training. Remember you have no time to train your people yourself. At the same time you are weary of their mistakes. That is not fair. Train them to improve work knowledge. A knowledgeable worker is an asset to an organisation.

   Besides, look at the exchange of ideas in inter-company meets, and above all the pride of participation in a training programme for the employee.

5. **Advancement**

   All work and no pay make Jack a dull boy in his work place. Who does not look for advancement in life? Advancement is not mere normal and special increments, but also advancement in status. Take the military for instance; a cadet could rise to be a General with a number of rungs in the ladder of promotion. An organisation should provide the steps; and men will climb the steps to reach the top.

6. **Security-Now and After**

   An employee having spent all his life for his organisation has the right to security. First by his continued employement, and next after his retirement. Assured employment can come only from the organsiational stability and profitability. The theory of corporate profits is to be understood in the proper context, as representing efficient working and progressive advancement without which the organisation will collapse, sooner than later, whatever the sector it is in: manufacturing, service or information technology.

Essential and supportive needs take care of employees during their employment, but one looks for his old age security too. Terminal benefits like gratuity, provident fund, pension, etc. are the prime sources and if he decides to leave early, a voluntary retirement scheme should work. Provide subcontract jobs to efficient retired employees-it will be an added advantage to them; besides, employer's investment on such efficient men would not go waste.

CASE EXAMPLE

Inside Microsoft: Keeping a Tab on Employees

During my early days at Microsoft, I found that Bill Gates wasn't the only top executive who was frustrated with the inefficiency of the company's business practices. In one meeting, Steve Ballmer, the head of sales, questioned his managers on the number of employees assigned to different tasks in the division. After receiving varying answers, he blurted out, "Look, maybe we should suspend the meeting for three hours. All of us can go back to your building and count heads to find out how many people you actually have." He was kidding-but just barely.

In many companies, human resources is one of the most difficult areas to track, and Microsoft was no exception. With the slack way we counted employees and with the company trying to keep up with 30% annual revenue growth, divisions and units were hiring like crazy. When asked about head counts, manager's answers usually were, to put it charitably, poetic.

After implementing a companywide human resources management information system, we can now track the number of full-time employees, as well as temporary or contract workers, by geographical division, business unit, or function. We can compare those numbers with the levels in previous fiscal years, with the authorized level for the current year, and among divisions or functions. This information, like the company's financial information, is available to executives anywhere via their PC and a phone connection. Furthermore, the system includes a new-employee authorization tool, which allows a manger to quickly get a recent hire up and running in all key systems, including e-mail, payroll, company benefits, and employee services.

But the new systems didn't just correct a deficiency; they also strengthened two of Microsoft's core competencies: recruitment and performance assessment. One key to the company's success has been its ability to attract and retain good people. Given the importance of this activity, top management should be able to monitor it. The system provides historical and current data on hiring targets, offer and acceptance rates, and attrition, sliced any number of ways.

Another of Microsoft's strengths is its employee evaluation and reward system. Under a performance appraisal and compensation approach that

Bill developed in Microsoft's early days, managers give employees numerical performance ratings, which closely follow a bell-shaped curve. Employees with high ratings receive aggressive salary increase. Those with low ratings get below-average raises and, just as important, are helped with strategies for improving their performance. If they aren't able to bring up their rating over time, they are encouraged to find another job that might be a better fit, be it inside or outside the company. The system ensures that star employees are disproportionately rewarded, and it forces managers to constructively deal with poor performers.

But to keep such a process robust, managers must execute it religiously. Our performance management information system helps impose the necessary discipline. When the vice presidents enter their employee's ratings every August, the system compiles reports on how those ratings match the bell-shaped curve. If the ratings stray too far from the curve, the performance evaluations won't be approved until individual ratings have been adjusted. The system also reports whether proposed salary increases-individual and average –fall within guidelines tied to the curve.

The performance management system has a major factor in the adoption of performance appraisal practices. And the umbrella human resources management system, like the financial management one, has almost eliminated the variety of information systems-including at least 18 HR-related databases –that had proliferated throughout Microsoft.

(***By Robert J. Herbold former Chief Operating Officer, Microsoft in Harvard Business Review***).

Well Knit Organisation

Hiring good people is tough; but as every senior executive knows, keeping them can be even tougher. Many talented professionals leave their organisations because senior managers don't understand the psychology of work satisfaction; they assume that people who excel at work are necessarily happy in their jobs.

Deeply embedded life interests do not determine what people are good at –they seek after activities that make them happy. At work, that happiness often translates into commitment. It keeps people engaged, it keeps them from quitting.

We must remember that calculators and computers do not have feelings human beings do have, therefore, they have to be dealt with empathy and compassion with great care. We talk about MIS, etc., but how much we know about the health, morale and attitude of our human resource? With a view to sustain high performing organisation we must listen to juniors, sometimes some of them may come out with some winning ideas.

Ability – meaning the skills, experience, and knowledge a person brings to the job, can make an employee feel competent.

Values – refer to rewards people seek-money, intellectual challenge, prestige or a comfortable life style.

Life interests-people with same ability and life interests may pursue different careers based on their values. Like ability, values matter. In fact, people rarely take jobs that don't match their values. But after a short period of success, they become disenchanted, lose interest, and either quit or just work less productively.

This stands the reason why life interests are considered to be the most important of the three variables of career satisfaction.

You can be good at job and you can like the rewards you receive from it. But only life interests will keep most people happy and fulfilled over the long term. And that's the key to retention.

Information Technology Industry Rallies Round New HR Standards

Almost all kinds of organisations are affected by information technology. Innovation, creativity, flexibility, and the ability to react quickly have become crucial because of the pace of change and potential threats from competitors. Competitive advantage, always a prime requirement in the private sector, is rapidly becoming more important in information services. If the last decade witnessed Indian IT companies queuing up to get Software Engineering Institute (SEI) assessment to meet the software development quality standards, the new millennium has seen a greater emphasis on HR strategies like the People Capability Maturity Model (PCMM).

Mastek, which has a software development centre in Bangalore, has entered the elite league of PCMM level companies.

Today there are not many Indian companies, engaged in PCMM assessment process. And, their efforts have just started yielding results.

"PCMM has just happened in India and it has a long innings to play. There have been a great reception to it here", says, Patric David, head of people consulting practices at QAI, a software standard certification entity.

The PCMM is a maturity framework developed in 1995 by the SEI, to help software organisations focus on improving capability of their workforce. The PCMM guides organisations in improving their ability to attract, motivate, develop and retain talent needed to steadily improve their workforce capability.

People, apart from being one of the biggest assets of the knowledge industry, also pose to be a huge challenge to this new economy to grapple with. Attracting quality manpower, retaining them and improving their skills is a crucial component of any company.

The early birds to adopt PCMM have been the Indian Infotech Companies. Besides Mastek, other companies in for PCMM include Aptech, Datamatics, Wipro, Seimens Information Systems Ltd.

The criticality of PCMM can be gauged from the fact that Aptech gave first preference to PCMM over any other available technique.

However, experts caution that PCMM is not a recipe for retaining people, rather its objective is to address people oriented issues which ultimately serve the purpose of retaining manpower.

Maximizing Human Resource Capital – An IT Industry Perspective

Human Resource Management in the IT industry has to deal with several "market dictated" employee satisfaction parameters. Most global and domestic IT companies have focused on creating a conducive working environment for its employees. In the Indian context the programmes, processes and the practices have been mostly reactive and in just few exceptional cases, proactive.

The Right Working Environment

It is not only the compensation package but the overall corporate culture, management style and working environment that play a major role in retaining the IT professionals in an organisation. The companies should focus on creating global employee networks that transferred knowledge (applications and technologies) and best practices on a continuous basis. The companies should leverage the power of internet to do this in a more effective way.

Remodeling the Organsiational Hierarchy & Importance of Change Anticipation

The Infotech age has blurred boundaries and also has done away with traditional organsiational structures, systems and skill sets. IT companies have now developed a pool of executives who are used as business developers or fire fighters in short and medium term assignments across the continents.

Continuous and overlapping change has become a way of life in the corporate environment. This scenario has created a certain amount of stress within the high-profile IT organisations attempting to take control of the technology environment.

The solution for this can be in anticipating for change in the technology. But it demands a strategic perspective from the training and human resource professionals in the organisations. The companies have to take steps to train the workforce ahead of anticipated technological developments.

Designing Innovative Reward Packages

The Infotech revolution did start a wave of huge and even 'obscene' compensation packages for talented IT professionals. Although this has tapered off to some extent, the monetary packages of Indian Infotech professionals are the highest in the services sector. The Infotech companies have realized that higher compensation packages are essential for enthusing the employees and retaining them. In the IT industry HR professionals plays a dual role:

1. Retaining the employees through well structured compensation packages.
2. Designing innovative compensation structures so as to arrive at an optimal mix of basic salary, performance incentive and stock options.

Soft rewards or indirect rewards in form of educational assistance, corporate training, and employee bonding initiatives also form a sizeable part of the employee reward structure.

Monitoring – The New Mantra

The marked shift towards e-business has changed to very dynamics of employment because of far-reaching changes in skills and knowledge. Numerous firms are therefore now investing in their core human capital. IT firms the world over have started incubating and funding business ideas from their employees. The company selects the idea that corresponds to its core business model. Incubating strategy not only helps firms to retain their best talent pool within the organisation but also helps them to move up value chain in the business they are in.

Attracting and Retaining

Since the demand for IT professionals is greater than the supply, the success of a company is dependent on its ability to attract and retain the workers. The key areas of consideration, while making hiring decisions, must include degree of learn-ability, fit with organsiational culture and values, and, decidedly, educational excellence. Since technology in IT industry keeps changing very fast, companies like Infosys, Wipro, Hewlett Packard, Satyam Computers and a few others emphasize on learning capabilities, aptitudes of the new entrants more than just knowledge on current technologies.

What IT companies really need from new recruits is to attract individuals with honesty and integrity, commitment to customer, and a belief in professional excellence. They need to turn their attention to a wide variety of areas such as:

- Technical competencies and customer focus.
- Functional fitment.
- Cultural fitment.
- Achievement orientation.
- Ability to work as a team member.

Companies are increasingly getting aware of the simple truth: the success and survival of the organisations depend entirely on knowledge workers. It is also true that many progressive IT companies have adopted smart and innovative HR practices and are able to overcome the challenges.

Retaining the knowledge workers is a much bigger challenge than hiring them. Elton Mayo in "Human Relations Theory" talks about the informal social setting of the organisation which boosts up the workers to work willingly and proudly. In a formal setting, workers feel being treated as just machines. In an informal work environment they feel being treated as humans. Their self-dignity is respected and this leads to cooperation with employees.

Designing the Right Package

Orgnaisations began wooing the knowledge workers by giving them handsome bonuses and employee stock options (ESOP). Now ESOP is regarded as a vital employee retention tool in the IT industry. Some of the Indian companies have started offering equity shares to their employees. For example, Infosys offered stock options to 7,853 employees thus creating 1773 rupee millionaires and 213 dollar millionaires. Hughes Software Systems employs 1300 people and created 215 rupee millionaires. In Hewlett Packard (HP) all employees are eligible for stock options; around 95 per cent of them own stock in the company.

In spite of everything being in place, sometimes companies still don't get the results they want. Despite reward systems: group-sharing practices and many more incentives, companies complain that many knowledge people do not willingly come forward to share knowledge with each other. But isn't it true that human beings are never identical and there is some fundamental uniqueness in every human being? KM manager, therefore, need to be very sensitive and aware of these differences and consciously avoid blindly following a set or a uniform path.

Peter Drucker in his treatise "They Are not Employees Anymore" (Harvard Business Review) stated convincingly:

"In a traditional workforce, the worker serves the system; in a knowledge workforce, the system must serve the worker"

He added, "Leaders in knowledge – based business must spend time with promising professionals: Get to know them and be known by them, mentor them and listen to them, challenge them and encourage them."

EXAMPLES:

1. ***Wipro Case: High on Hire***

   "At a time when the Indian software sector is seeing a rebound and more hiring, thanks to increasing outsourcing or IT spending, the Bangalore-based Wipro Technologies saw as many as 517 techies leaving the blue chip company. Wipro had recruited more than 1270 young people a few years ago.

   The company came out with the explanation that 317 were asked to leave for failing to meet performance benchmarks, and the remaining 200 left on their own for better prospects or in pursuit of professional advancement.

The new recruits included many freshers who were hired at campus level during the period, but their joining letters were deferred due to the slump in the IT industry, the company stated (The Telegraph).

2. ***Wipro:Challenges on Offer***

On a somewhat different plane is Wirpo's Corporate website that promises "challenge for the mind, reward for the soul". Forming an integral aspect of the sales pitch of this Infotech major are its technology offerings, designed to attract the young, enthusiastic, technical whizkid. "Freak out with Wipro" invites a visual. The offerings.................. freedom, rewards, excitement, ambition and knowledge.

A crisp and clear profile description asks for focus on customer satisfaction, self-confidence, cross-cultural comfort, perfection and discipline. The returns................ Challenging assignments, world class work environment, professional management, opportunities to train and learn, and exceptional rewards. Using carefully chosen words, the website communicates the essence of what the organisation stands for and what an employee can except to be recognized as .... "We believe that being a Wipro-ite is a badge of honour."

Technical career paths are highlighted in detail. Candidates can visualize their growth from a team member (or developer) to a module leader (involving customer interaction and team management), a project manager, and a SBU head. Using an elaborate resume search tool, candidates can choose from over a combination of 30 functional specializations', 6 experience levels and 12 countries. (***Human Capital***)

New Age: New Workers

Many other corporate websites make painstaking efforts to include value-added features to leave a lasting impression on potential candidates. Texas Instruments' internet recruiting page is a one-stop shopping mall not just for a career at TI, but for any career. Those interested in becoming a "Tier" can undergo a lengthy Fit Check that is designed to ensure better matches between potential employees and IT.

Intel, on the other hand, posts its hottest job listings online, and they remain on the website for a maximum of 30 days. New listings are added every week, and resumes submitted electronically are reviewed daily. The idea, quite simply, is to make the Intel name as visible as possible to those surfing the web-a demographic group that ties in perfectly to the company's goals and interests.

Companies, therefore, must not underestimate what is required to and maintain a corporate website that creates an impression and gets results for HR.

Measuring Effectiveness

The major difference between financially successful companies and others is that successful companies measure their rewards strategy, policies and procedures on periodic basis. One more characteristic that goes with the successful companies is on the reward mix used by them. They have realised that people are a source of value and competitive advantage.

They use a wider range of recognition awards and continuously promote a culture of performance through productive incentives. Though not so prevalent earlier, more and more in the successful category of companies are regularly measuring the effectiveness of their reward as well as retention plans.

The Strategic Rewards Survey "Playing to Win" by Watson Wyatt reflects the process with the following highlights:

- Indian high-performing employees rank opportunities for development and compensation as the top two criteria when accepting employment.
- Lack of developmental opportunities and job flexibility are the two top-ranking factors contributing to retention problems, according to employers.
- Financially successful companies in India are able to link rewards to business strategy.

Conclusion

Performance of knowledge-based companies depends on running the institutions so as to attract, hold and motivate knowledge workers. This is possible by satisfying their values, giving them social recognition and turning the subordinates into fellow executives and, finally from employees to partners.

By rewarding employees for performance sends a powerful message, that employee contributions are vital, and performance is being recognised and acknowledged.

No doubt, financially successful firms report significantly fewer incidences of attraction and retention difficulty.

III

Managing Productivity
Right Decisions at The Right Time
How Proactive Steps Lead to Survival and Success

A process good manufacturer was operating in a highly competitive environment. There were altogether 14 companies in this particular industry and their production was almost 20 percent higher than the market demand. The industry had adequate production capacity. There was keen competition between these companies and each company was trying to increase production in an effort to reduce the cost of production and pass it on to the consumer in some from or the other to gain a marketing advantage.

The Proposition

The company operated six days a week with Sunday being a holiday for all production workers. Therefore, there was no production in the plant for 52 Sundays in a year.

As the company was working on all the three shifts, the only way to company could increase production, without adding any more plant and machinery was to increase the production week from six to seven days. The seven-day work week would yield an additional 18-20% production, without additional capital investment.

The cost of installation of additional plant and machinery was considered uneconomic under the present marketing conditions and poor return on investment.

Feasibility Study

A feasibility study was worked out, and the study team was of the opinion that introduction of Sunday working could boost the production and bring down the cost of production as the fixed overheads could be then distributed to additional volumes, thus bringing down the unit cost. A preventive plant and machinery maintenance programme was recommended to avoid any plant breakdown, as Sundays would no longer be available as routine plant maintenance days.

The Personnel Department worked out the manpower plan to put the plan into operation. The man power planning indicated that the extra work force required would be a small percentage of the total labour force and thus it would contribute to further saving of labour costs in proportion to the additional production to be achieved by this extra day production.

The Problem

However, the introduction of seven day work week required the staggering of day-offs for all workers. In other words the work force who so far enjoyed Sundays as weekly day off would now have to stagger the day off on week days so that some workers get Monday as off day, some have their day off on Tuesday and others on other days of the week in turn. In this system the existing labour force could be employed for certain key production areas on Sundays as well. The manpower planning for each day was worked out very carefully in consultation with the process department and other supply departments of the plant.

The personnel department was ready to discuss the proposal with the labour union as their cooperation was vital in putting this new system to work. The new proposal would require each worker to change their Sunday life style which they were accustomed to for a good many years. Sundays are normally a day of visiting friends, going to movies or attending to miscellaneous household work. For some it was helping children with their studies. For others it was just a day of relaxation when everyone was at home, an opportunity of a family gets together.

The dilemma was what would happen if the union did not accept or if the union executives were unable to make the workers accept this proposal.

Communications Opportunity

The company had just recently recruited a few middle management trainees for different operations.

The management saw in this proposal an opportunity to test their communication skills. The first attempt was to find out to what extent the employees were aware of the marketing situation faced by the company, and whether they could visualize that this situation, if not remedied in time could affect extra earnings, which they received each year by way of bonus.

Research

The middle management trainees interviewed a cross section of the employees which consisted of workers, supervisors ad junior management level personnel. The interviews were unstructured and often took the form of informal discussions at various times of working hours. The trainees were able to conduct these interviews informally without arousing curiosity as to the real reasons behind these interviews.

Feedback

The feedback received from the employees revealed that most of the employees were unaware of the seriousness of the competitive situation and in any case they had never given a thought that this could in any way affect them personally. Difficulty in the marketing situation was something remote to them. If it should bother anybody it should be sales people and it was up to sales and marketing people to sort out their problems.

Based on the feedback the management trainees formulated a new communication programme to create awareness on the following aspects:

1. Marketing situation is highly competitive.
2. Reduction in the cost of production would be a marketing advantage.
3. Cost of production could come down if the volume of production could be increased without a corresponding increase in the cost of production.
4. All employees should co-operate with the management to bring down the cost of production.

At this stage, it was decided that the communication programme should not make any mention of the proposed plan to include Sundays as full working days. It was argued that once the employee understanding of the problem is achieved, it would create a proper environment when further plans could be discussed.

On the basis of this requirement, the management, assisted by the Communication Staff, decided to make use of slide and sound presentation techniques.

The audio-visual presentation was formally presented to the floor workers in groups of 25 to 30 persons. Question and answer sessions immediately following the presentation revealed that the employees understood the situation, and they were ready to cooperate to improve the marketability of their products.

Some workers were very critical that the situation had been allowed to reach this critical stage. They felt that the management should have taken proper steps to correct the situation at the appropriate time.

When the reports from all presentations came in, the personnel management came to the conclusion that the employee's awareness to the problem facing the company was fairly high, and they were in a mood of cooperation to protect their own interest, the bonus at the rate received in the preceding years, and to expect further increase in their pay packets.

About two months later, when the management presented their seven-day-work-week programme to the union, it was accepted without any prolonged discussion.

Issues to be Examined and Recommendations to be given

1. Examine in detail the pros and cons of the ideas of employees involvement in the "management of change"?
2. Evaluate the value of face to face and upward communication in the context of the complexities of management –employee relationship.
3. "Productivity is not only about people working hard but working willingly, enthusiastically, knowledgeably, proudly and efficiently" – Can good employee communication contribute to job satisfaction and help to increase productivity?

Brief Outline of the Case Scenario

Introduction

The case study deals with the effective use of communication to overcome a crisis situation in the company and how effective communication helped in involving employees in solving the productivity problem. In the changing and highly competitive market scenario, internal communication and employee involvement has gained an added importance and is now referred to as "internal marketing". Unfortunately, in most companies the standard of internal marketing is low. While executives recognise they also need to convince employees of the power of the brand. Information is doled out to employees in the form of memos, newsletters and so on and so forth, but it's not designed to persuade employees what makes the company special or unique. The intent usually is to tell employees what the company is doing, not to sell them on the ideas.

But by applying many of the principles of consumer communications to internal relations, leaders can guide employees to a better understanding of and even passion for the brand vision-which in turn, enables employees to 'live' the vision.

Co's Plan of Action

- Increase productivity so as to reduce the cost of production and thus gain a good share in the market.
- Rise in production time from six to seven days a week so as to achieve production rise from 18-20%.
- A plant and machinery programme to be launched to avoid plant break down as a result of increased use.
- Involve management trainees to find out employee awareness about the market situation and their response to the situation.

- Appreciation of the situation by conducting informal interviews.
- Get proper feedback from employees in this regard.
- Take corrective actions so as to avoid such problems in the future.

Dilemma faced by the company

The main problem faced by the company is how to five a practical shape to the above proposals. As per the proposal the middle and lower level manpower would be required to put extra efforts on six days a week and perform better and better. Personnel department would be required to convince the employees and their trade unions to put this system to work.

Employees' viewpoints

- Unaware of the seriousness of the competitive situation they are facing.
- Unable to feel that they are personally affected too.
- Problems faced by the company were remote to them.
- They are ready to adjust once the situation was made clear to them.
- They will expect increase in their earnings (pay/bonus/incentives) on account of productivity gains.
- They are of the opinion that the present decisions should have been made way back-much before the current problems had set in.

Communication Requirements

Some of the ways in which managers can communicate will during any organsiational changes are:

- Communicate consistently, frequently, and through multiple channels, including speaking, writing, video, training, focus groups, bulletin boards, and more.
- Communicate all that is known about the changes, as quickly as the information is available. (Make clear that your bias is toward instant communication so some of the details may change at a later date. Tell people that your other choice is to hold all communication until you are positive about the decisions).
- Provide significant amounts of time for people to ask questions, request clarification, and provide input. (How many of you have been part of a scenario in which a leader presented changes, on overhead transparencies, to a large group and then fled? This is bad news for change integration!).
- Clearly communicate the vision, the mission, and the objectives of the change effort. Help people to understand how these changes will affect them personally. (If you don't help with this process, people will make up their own stories, usually more negative than the actual truth.).

- Recognize that true communication is a "conversation". It is two-way and real discussion must result. It cannot be just a presentation.
- The change leaders or sponsors need to spend time conversing one-on-one or in small groups with the people who are expected to make the charges.
- Communicate the reasons for the change in such a way that people clearly understand the context, the purpose, and the need. Several people called this, "building a memorable, conceptual framework," and "creating a theoretical framework to underpin the change".
- Provide answers to questions only if you know the answer. Leaders destroy their credibility when they provide incorrect information or appear to stumble, when providing an answer. It is much better to say you don't know, and that you will try to find out.
- Leaders need to listen, just listen. Avoid defensiveness, excuse making, and answers that are too quickly given. Act with thoughtfulness. The power of real listening could not be over emphasized.
- Hold interactive workshops and forums in which all employees can explore the changes together, while learning more. Use training as a form of interactive communication and as an opportunity for people to safely explore new behaviours and ideas. All levels of the organisation participate in the same sessions.
- Communication should be proactive. If the remour mill is already in action, the organisation has waited too long to communicate.
- Provide opportunities for people to network with each other, both formally and informally, to share ideas.
- Publicize rewards and recognition for positive approaches and accomplishments, and celebrate each small win publicly.
- Last but not the least; make sure to involve the employees in the "Management of change".

Q -1. PROS and CONS of the idea of employee involvement in the "management of change".

Why do employees resist change?

Resistance to change is a very natural reaction. Managers need predictability, routine, familiar patterns to survive. They try to preserve the status quo at all costs. Change threatens items in head, heart and guts.

1. Psychological resistance to change: Loss of security, loss of familiarity and unpredictable environment.
2. Changes diminish status: Innovations threatens the individual status within organisations–Example–Fired; or merger with a company and closure of a department or promotion of a subordinate.

3. Change threatens economic position: Change depresses in economic positions of those involved with it. Example: Change in wages or salaries.
4. Difficult to change culture, rules and procedure of an organisation as it requires time and energy.
5. Inadequate communication between the employee and employer: In this kind of situation the need for change should be recognised.

Facilitating change

As organisations need people and people also need organisations, people can use organisations and organisations can use people to reach their objectives by communicating properly with each other. When the objectives of the organisation are made clear to the employees, the workers are motivated to work in that direction. It should be made clear that the organisation cannot survive if its objectives are not reached; and if the organisation does not survive, there would be no chance of employment opportunities in it. The employees and the management should develop the link of communication for better mutual understanding and encourage each other to achieve their self-interests.

The progressive employers are convinced that there ought to be some ways of effective communication between the management and the workers to develop better employee satisfaction and a sense of security. If the insecurity and frustration of employees is successfully dispelled by the management, the employees feel motivated for better working.

The management must be able to communicate with the employees regarding the financial state of the organisation and should motivate them for better worker in order to make the organisation financially strong enough to support its employees.

Participation, cooperation and teamwork of the management and employees can yield best results because of their common commitment to goals that encourage better performance. Participative managers communicate with their employees. They ask for the opinions, views, suggestions and recommendations of the employees in the decision-making process so that they work together as a team.

In participatory management, the manager retains the ultimate responsibility of his unit, but he shares the operating responsibility with the employees who actually perform the work. This gives a sense of involvement and satisfaction to the employees who work with high morale to achieve the objectives of the organisation as the manager seeks participation of the employees in policy matters and decision-making.

The employees in any organisation are actually engaged in operative functions. The procedure and operation of any work is better known in those who are always in touch with it. The employees, especially the lower staff, come across many procedural or operative difficulties. They may also conceive a new idea which may bring smoothness and effectiveness in their work and thereby the productivity may increase, if such ideas are properly attended and applied by the organisation.

It is essential to set objectives before the workers. They must understand the purpose behind their work as well as the objectives they are to achieve, so that they may work hard to reach them. It is natural that they get job satisfaction when they complete their work successfully. The workers must be well informed about the plans and polices of the organisation and how they are to be brought into actual practice. If the management does not clarify their plans, polices, procedures and the objectives to the employees, it will be difficult for them to motivate the workers and to expect quantitative work from them. The employees must be informed about the background, history, efficiency contributions, benefits and targets of the organisation.

Belonging and Motivation

When workers are invited by the management to participate in the decision-making process, they experience a sense of belonging to the organisation and it motivates them to work better. It is found that the business organisations, which encourage their employees to offer their suggestions for the improvement of the working procedure and overall development of the organisation, were successful because they could thereby motivate the employees. These employees cooperate with the plans of the management and earn their confidence by inviting them to participate in the decision-making process. The employees are motivated when the management appreciates and accepts the suggestions given by them.

The management and supervisory staff have to persuade the workers for better and hard work.

Nobody likes to mend his views and actions, if he is forced to do so by compulsion or repression. It is natural that force, compulsion and repression bring resentment and anger of the receiver. Therefore, it is better not to impose views on the others. It means the receiver must be prepared to accept the message. If your ideas run contrary to the views and beliefs of the receivers, it is better to start with the points which are agreeable to the receiver. When the receiver is prepared to open his mind and accept some of your ideas, you can gradually convince him the other points.

It is always better to avoid the topics which are strongly disliked by the receiver and which are likely to bring his resentment. Such topics are risky in the sense that a mere mention of them might suddenly snap the communication link between the communicator and the receiver. Therefore, selecting an argument which might strongly appeal to them in such a way that they readily accept them. Having prepared both the receiver and the message, the next step is to present the message in a proper way. The persuasion is likely to be effective and successful if the ideas are put forth step-by-step in a forceful but courteous manner. The arguments must be organised carefully so that the easy and pleasant ideas come before the relatively difficult and unpleasant ones.

Advantages of Employee Involvement in Change Management

- Participation may result in better decisions. Workers often have information that higher management lacks. Furthermore, participation permits a variety of different views to be aired.
- People are more likely to implement decisions they have made themselves.
- They know better what is expected of them, and helping make a decision commits one to it.
- The process of participation may satisfy such non-pecuniary needs as creativity, achievement, and the desire for respect.
- Participation improves communication and cooperation; workers communicate with each other instead of requiring all communications to flow through management, thus saving management time.
- Participative workers supervise themselves, thus reducing the need for managers and so cutting overhead labour costs. Participation teaches workers new skills and helps train and identifies leaders.
- Participation enhances people's sense of power and dignity, thus reducing the need to show power through fighting management and restricting production.
- Participation increases loyalty and identification with the organisation. If participation and rewards take place in group setting, the group may pressure individuals to confirm to decisions.
- When union and management leaders jointly participate to solve problems on a non-adversarial basis, the improved relationship may spill over to improve union management relations.
- Participation frequently results in the setting of goals. Goal setting is often an effective motivational technique, particularly when workers set their own goals.
- Participation leads to employee becoming aware of the functions of an organisation and the strengths and weaknesses of the organisation in a better way.

Disadvantages of Employee Involvement in Change Management

- Workers may be less informed than managers, and the promises upon which they make their decisions may be different. The rewards motivating workers to share their ideas may be larger than the value of the ideas themselves.
- Once becoming committed to a decision, employees may be reluctant to change it.

- Not everyone has strong desires for creativity and achievement, or they satisfy these sufficiently off the job.
- Participation is time consuming, and if groups make decisions, reaction to changing environments may be particularly slow.
- Retraining of employees and managers can be expensive.
- Once a precedent of participation is established, withdrawal of the right to participate becomes difficult.
- Cohesive, participative groups may unite against management to restrict production and prevent change.
- Sharing information with unions raises their bargaining power, so companies may lose. Cooperating with management may lower unions' legitimacy with members, so they may lose as well.
- Goals workers set for themselves may be low.
- In case where the workforce is not well educated the idea of employee involvement generally would give opposing ideas to the management.
- Due to lack of holistic view employees may tend to maximize the gains of their individual departments. Thus not thinking of the organisation as a whole.
- Ideas from all the employees may not only be difficult to collect but would also lead to chaos and conflicting ideas.

Some more disadvantages.

After The Shock

As one era ends, another begins. According to HARRY WOODWORTH and STEVE BUCHHOLIZ in their book. "After Shock: Helps people through corporate change (1987)" – change is viewed as the end of a golden "era". The employees may accept change intellectually but accepting it emotionally is a much more difficult process. Once the change process has been implemented, adjusting to it becomes the problem. Here the management plays a major or a very important role.

Four main reactions

1. Disagreement or withdrawal-employees normally leave the job if they find it difficult to adapt to the changes.
2. Dis-identification-unable to adapt, the employees do not identify with the new environment. It results in unwillingness to adapt new methods and make new associations.
3. Dis-orientation- employees loose their significance of where he/ she fits into the new structure.
4. Dis-enchantment- This involves people in the realization that what is gone is gone and now they cannot do anything about it. At this moment they gather up their energies for negative involvements against the organisation like back-stabbing, sabotage, grapevine etc.

Listening and communication is important to avoid the aftermaths of these changes. For this the organisation should owe the classification of the perceived losses and relevance of employees. Management at this juncture should share the purpose of change with the employees. A mutual agreement can also be undertaken which ascertains the commitment to change.

Q-2. Evaluate the value of face to face and upward communication in the context of the complexities of management–employee relationship.

"Communication is a two way process". This is a universal rule which applies on the whole universe. Management – employee communication is no different. The prime objective of setting up a communication system in industries is to exchange facts and information in a manner which is acceptable to all concerned and which will lead to willing and cooperative action. Saying that "Communication is the life blood of an organisation" would be an understatement.

With the advancement of technology the changes have become a regular feature in an industrial undertaking and if the communication system is carefully planned and applied it will reduce worker's resistance and acceptance of new ideas and changes will be a much easier process.

Effective Communication is also important is executing a personnel programme and then controlling the activities with the help of feedback information. Communication grows best in the climate of trust and confidence. It satisfies the need of self expression of the people who work and also those who get the work done from others. Effective communication leads to higher productivity and job satisfaction. With effective communication

"We come alive"

"We gain at work – in home and in society".

At work the job becomes more meaningful, interesting, rewarding and easy going. At home the family life becomes fuller, richer and happier. Socially also it takes new dimensions as one develops a new look a view challenges.

The communication climate of an organisation includes the nature and content of upward, downward, lateral and external communication. Establishing open and clear communication with each other, with employees and with stakeholders outside the organisation sets the stage for a fruitful exchange of ideas and information throughout the entire organisation.

Some ways in which a manager can encourage upward communication

- **Manager should listen more:**
  Manager who listen to employees have a much more efficient workforce. There are many benefits to listening to employees. Employees are able to voice concerns and deal with them before

they become lingering problems. They also feel valued which raises productivity and lowers turnover. In addition, the manager will have a firm grasp on how everybody feels. Lastly, once employees feel they have been heard, they become much more attentive and responsive to concerns the manager has.

- **Regular meetings:**
  Employees are people and, like it or not, people tend to keep their feelings about their job bottled up inside. They can be upset about something and the manager won't even have a clue that anything is wrong. As a result, the problem festers as resentment and anger build up inside while productivity and motivation decline. The cure for this cancer is for managers to regularly schedule meetings to listen to employees about anything related to their jobs.
- **Open door policy:**
  Most managers will probably say, "Well, I have an open-door management policy. Employees are free to set up a time to talk to me anytime they want." Although this is true, employees don't think that you really want to hear what they have to say. Employees fear if they voice their opinions that the manager might become upset label them as complainers or do nothing about it. Managers should listen without judgement and stay neutral. Employees should be heard without fear of being reprimanded. In addition, managers should never choose sides or ridicule another employee.
- **Management by walking around:**
  An even more effective "open door" is for the managers to walk through their own doors and get out among their people. By walking out through the door, the manager cannot only discover key information from employees but also use the opportunity to project a supportive atmosphere.
- **Questionnaire can be handed out:**
  Questions should be asked to clarify exactly how employees feel and to obtain more detail when needed from employees who are not comfortable being direct and who don't feel comfortable speaking in front of a big gathering like a departmental meeting.
- **Suggestion boxes:**
  Managers should also listen to employees to get ideas on how to improve the business. Employees know more about their jobs than anyone else, but they are usually the last ones to be asked how things could be done better. Besides being the experts at their jobs, employees can bring a fresh perspective to analyzing the problems of the business because they have a different set of life experience. That is valuable. In fact, asking employees how to improve the business is tantamount to getting high quality management consulting advice. Most workers would cherish the opportunity to give input on decisions that affect their jobs.

The message being communicated from Managers to employees is that "You are important and we value what you have to say. "That is one of the highest compliments that a manager can give an employee.

Some ways of encouraging face-to-face communications

- **Face-to face meeting:**
  It is estimated that managers in companies spend almost half their time in meetings. They may be one-to-one or group meetings. The bigger the company, the more meetings there are likely to be. Meetings we useful because they allow instant feedback and discussion to take place.
- **Presentations:**
  A manager often accompanied by members of his or her staff, uses a presentation to explain a project or a plan to colleagues. Visual aids, such as transparencies projected on to a screen, are often used to illustrate points in the talk. Presentations are also given externally to clients or potential clients. For example, an advertising agency might make a presentation of its campaign to a client. Presentations allow a large amount of complex information to be communicated to a number of people at the same time. They also provide opportunities for feedback and discussion.
- **Parties in a social group:**
  Picnics, sports, events, hobby groups are some events through which recreational time is provided to the employees together. Celebrating creates camaraderie and also lets people know that you want them to have fun and enjoy themselves. Parties are useful because they create an informal environment, which makes the flow of communication easy for the employees.
- **Discussion groups:**
  In discussion groups (also known as forums, newsgroups, or conferences) employees can converse and build relationship with their colleagues. Such forums are being used to help create knowledge-building communities, and simply to provide a means for soliciting information and "chatting".

And a quote here:

"Communication is really all anyone ever gets paid for. Ultimately..... and if you cannot effectively communicate ...... you will pay.... Not get paid..."

Q-3. "Productivity is not about people working willingly, enthusiastically, knowledgeably, proudly and efficiently" Can good employee communication contribute to job satisfaction and help to increase productivity?

Productivity refers to efficient utilization of resources. While the productivity in an organisation can be improved by better application of materials, improved process of machinery, faster production lines and application of more energy from the worker, this is not all. The attitude of the top management has to be right in order to give the right direction. The attitude of the lower level of people has to be tuned to that of the higher level of management so that the right message is picked up. A right direction leaves a prolonged impact on productivity.

Good employee communication can contribute to job satisfaction and help to increase productivity. Effective communication provides better understanding of what is to be done, how it is to be done.

In the face of recent economic uncertainty, organisations are looking for ways to reduce expenses. For many, this can mean curtailing communication activities. During tough times, company leadership often sees communication as easy prey-overhead that can be painlessly cut; a quick fix for reducing a top-heavy budget without negatively affecting bottom-line profits. What's worse, at such times, company leaders often assume a stony silence with their employees, thinking "no news is good news," while in sharp contrast, the media continue to weave tales of shaky economic conditions through the pages of the morning paper.

Although such actions are all too common, savvy communicators know better. Pulling back on communication activities in learn or unsettled times can result in a wide range of long-lasting negative effects, none of which is in the best interest of organsiational prosperity.

For example:

Confusion:

A vacuum develops where once there was information flow, leading to a perplexed and troubled workforce. Now, when it's more important then ever for employees to know how the organisation is doing, what's expected of them and how to act accordingly, they are hearing less and less. This can lead to ...

Distrust and suspicion:

In the absence of information, inevitably, employees will begin to wonder, "What's going on?" "Why aren't they saying anything?" Why is everything so quiet?" "Is the company going to fold" In the midst of all of this questioning – voiced or silent – you are bound to see...

Productivity Decline:

A basic way to express productivity is productivity equals output divided by input i.e., productivity is the ratio of output to input, or simply output over input. When their eyes are taken off the task and they are more concerned with their own welfare than with the task at hand, employees are not motivated to be the contributors they once were.

Loss of line of sight:

Employees no longer see the connection between what they do each day and how it affects the success of the company. And when line of sight diminishes, so does commitment to doing a good job and helping the organisation succeed.

Add it all up and you have an unhealthy work environment where you are at a high risk of not only loss of productivity, but also loss of your best people as they seek out seemingly more stable positions with more "supportive" employers.

Because of these negative effects, there's a strong argument to be made that communicating well and often is a prime factor in not only increasing productivity but also job satisfaction.

While productivity issues may need more study to determine if there are serious problems, many managers have found that communicating key information and changing their point of view have helped improve productivity.

Communicate Universal Outcomes

Few people would agree to spend every working day travelling to an unknown destination with no road maps. Yet that is, in effect, what many companies ask of their employees. While most organisations have developed vision and mission statements, few have stated them in ways that are helpful to their employees. Their vision and mission are just words on a corporate brochure.

Try to describe clearly the outcomes the organisation wants to see. Tell people what the organisation envisions for the future – what it looks like, who's involved, what are the products and services. If you can describe the outcomes you envision, you will more easily be able to figure out how to reach them, and you'll know when you've done it.

Provide Context

Without other information, employees make assumptions, which then become the underlying structure for decisions and actions. The danger comes when the assumptions are not correct or cause confusion. Valuable time is wasted and resources are used up. Before embarking on any new venture, explain the context. Why are we taking this step? What purpose does it serve? How does it fit with where we want the company to be five years from now? Be sure everyone understands the context of an action before you take it.

Make clear what success looks like

Just like vision and context set the stage for effective action, when employees know what they will need to do to be successful, they can be more effective and productive and hence will be more satisfied with their jobs. Ask, "What does success in this role book like? What indicators will tell us the person is successful?" Then communicate the success factors in terms of behavior – this is what you need to do, as well as measurable outcomes – this is what you need to produce or achieve.

Agree on individual expectations

When determining what success looks like, get the employee's input. What does it look like to him or her? What will the employee need to do in order to achieve success? Then get the person's agreement to the goals, and commitment to the desired outcomes.

Learn that conflict and Dissension are Gifts

It's natural to try to avoid conflict and to want to maintain agreement and harmony. However, if problems are being covered up or issues swept under the carpet, it's only a matter of time until things begin to fall apart. When people disagree, argue, or even get angry, it is a wonderful opportunity to make changes and find new ways of doing things. Put the energy created by conflict to good use – generate new ideas, find creative solutions, be innovative.

Recognize Regularly

Everyone contributes every day. Yet how often are those contributions recongnised? There is a direct correlation between recognition and praise, and employee satisfaction and retention and productivity. Recognition doesn't have to be expensive or cumbersome. Studies have shown that the rewards that mean the most are those that are personal, immediate, and sincere. In other words, when you say "thank you", "you did a good job", or "I appreciate all your hard work". Employees feel valued. They also feel motivated and are likely to be more productive.

If organisations and its employees can follow these simple steps, it's likely that the organisation will be more productive. In addition, because some of these steps force the management to think things through and communicate more clearly, chances are there will be less confusion and more focus on what's important.

BENEFITS

Communication performs four functions:

1. Motivation
2. Emotional expression
3. Information control
4. interdependence

In any group organisation we need to maintain some firm control, stimulate or motivate the members to perform, provide for emotional expression and interdependence along with making decision choices on the basis of information.

Only a proper understanding of these basic functions of communication can make an organisation work effectively.

According to HERBERT G. HICKS

"Motivation is a complex process. It involves external rewards such as wages and salaries, recognition and promotions. It also includes internal rewards such as satisfaction with a job which is nicely done and challenges of a job to be done". A manager must provide the "Right Mix" satisfactions if the individual is to be motivated in the desired direction.

For Example:

NTPC organizes yoga classes for all round development of its workers. The employees attend computer classes so that they learn the basics of the language and keep a pace with the changing environment. With every increase in production charts they give a token of encouragement to every worker. The estimates come in limelight with a mere glance on their production charts. The production increased from 4863 units in the year 1998-99 to around 5050 units in 1999-2000 and went on increasing by around 200 units every year in the subsequent years.

The workers must be well informed about the plans and policies of the organisation and how they are to be brought into actual practices. It should be presented in such a way that the employees must feel a sense of pride for being the employees of a good business organisation. Workers should be initiated by the management to participate in the decision making process. By this they experience a sense of belonging to the organisation and it motivates them to work a better deal.

Management should also experience and accept the suggestions given by them. They may also conceive a new idea which may bring smoothness and effectiveness in their work thereby the productivity may increase. Even when superiors accept the suggestions of the subordinate, the moral of the employees is raised. There must be mutual understanding between the employer and the employee and also between the senior and junior staff. They must come together in an informal atmosphere and discuss their views as well as opinions.

If the workers get job satisfaction, social recognition and sense of belongingness to the organsiation, he is certainly motivated for better work which ascertains the development and welfare of the organisation as well as the people working with it.

Conclusion

Good employee communication does contribute to job satisfaction and also helps increase productivity:

(a) It creates a "we" feeling of pride,

(b) It enhances the performance and hence paves the way to job satisfaction,

(c) If information is correctly and properly distributed, it imparts knowledge to employees, so that they can be aware of the situation and work accordingly,
(d) It motivates employees,
(e) The feedback is immediate. Therefore, the communication can be planned and the employees can be easily made to work.

Therefo**re, even lesser input would result in a better output due to communication, enhancing productivity.**

It's a famous saying:

Watch your thoughts; they become your words,
Watch your words; they become your actions,
Watch your actions; they become your habits,
Watch your habits, they become your character.

Your attitude is always showing, so develop a positive attitude and see the people working with you build it up continuously.

IV

Marketing and Advertising Need to Join Hands Together

The Company

ABC Electrical is a manufacturer of electrical motors. Originally ABC was engaged almost exclusively in the production and sale of small motors manufactured to customer specifications. These motors were used by makers of appliances, hand tools and toys. This market was stable but very competitive. ABC then decided to enter the market of precision machinery.

The precision machinery market was specialized and catered to variety of customers such as control systems for defence products, manufacturers of high speed printers and industrial equipment. Products used in these applications required extremely high quality and accuracy. Government contracts need special specification and designs to meet stringent requirements. ABC's attention to details, quality and customer satisfaction gave the corporation an excellent reputation with various clients in precision machinery industry. This market represented 20% of the corporation's revenues and approximately 30 per cent contribution to profits. Due to high reliability requirements, prices were not major criteria in selection of sources.

Sales and Distribution

ABC has approximately 1,000 active customers on its roll. In the last fiscal year, the fifty largest customers accounted for 40 percent of net sales. ABC's customers included industrial clients, government agencies and precision machinery manufacturers.

Sales to original equipment manufacturers were made through five regional sales managers who were supported by 15 sales engineers and 15 marketing executives. High precision motors sales were primarily made by advanced engineering department which was responsible for preparation of proposals and quotations. The department is assisted in its operation by 5 marketing executives.

Advertising and Marketing Campaign

For the last two years, ABC spent Rs. 50, 00,000 to 75, 00, 000 on advertising. Twenty percent of the advertising expenses were made on corporate image advertising as well as direct marketing messages in various trade journals and business newspapers. Rest of the advertising was carried on television, radio and magazines and was aimed at the consumers at large. The strategy was to make consumers aware of the ABC products used in their day-to-day appliances and tools.

ABC had four major competitors and they were getting active in the small electrical motor market.

Three months ago, ABC management went through major reorganization. A new president was appointed to direct the operations of the company. He reviewed the business expenses and questioned the advertising expenses directed at consumers. He said the ABC manufactured industrial products which lost its identity in the products made by other corporations. Since the ultimate customer never associated ABC motors specifically with any brand names, the consumer advertising was a total waste. He was thinking of giving orders to eliminate all of the consumer-oriented advertising.

Progress Test

1. Is it possible to create demand for ABC's products with advertising directed at the ultimate consumer?
2. How should ABC structure its advertising for its products?
3. What media would you recommend to reach new customers?
4. How far sales promotion measures could be helpful in achieving the objectives in addition to advertising efforts?
5. How much should ABC spend on corporate image advertising?

QUESTIONS – ANSWERS

No.1

Is it possible to create demand for ABC's products with advertising directed at the ultimate consumer?

Answer:

Yes, certainly the demand for ABC products can be created by successful advertising campaign. Indeed, advertising is an important means of mass communication which can really work miracles in selling and marketing.

However, electrical motors being an industrial product, ABC's clientele consists of industrial clients, government agencies and precision machinery manufacturers. Since motors manufactured by ABC are not directly bought by the ultimate consumer but by makers of appliances, hand tools and toys, advertising directed at ultimate consumer might not be of much help. The ultimate consumer would not know which machinery is used in the appliances bought. Hence, it is advisable to direct the advertising at the manufactures of appliances and other equipments so that they use ABC's electrical motors and precision machinery in their products, which are supplied to the ultimate consumer.

No.2

How should ABC structure its advertising for its products?

Answer:

After choosing the message, the advertiser's next task is to choose the media to carry it. Both advertising and marketing should join hands together to organise the campaign process. In fact, they should listen to each other and choose the best to achieve common objectives. The steps here are deciding on the desired reach, frequency and impact; choosing among major media types, deciding on the media timing and finally is the decision of the geographical media location. Media selection involves finding the most cost-effective media to deliver the desired number of exposures to the target audiences. The effect of exposures on audience depends upon the exposures' reach, frequency and the impact. Media planners make their choice among the media categories by considering the following variables:

- *Media habits of the target audience.*
- *Products*
- *Messages*
- *Cost*

ABC Electrical deals in industrial goods. Despite a good advertising structure for its products, they need to restructure it. They should go for Industrial Advertising. Industrial advertising doesn't sell only on emotions like most consumers advertising does. It has to provide sound reasoning for buying the product in question. Thus, to make the ads convincing, ABC should make use of case histories and testimonials. While drafting the copy, demonstrative aspects should be emphasized. They should show the product utility for the user. If necessary, the proof of the product capabilities can be placed directly in the reader's hands. For e.g. actual copy to demonstrate the capability of a copier.

For different product groups, they should follow a single advertising format, so as not to give an impression that they originate from different small companies. They must allow readers/ viewers participation in ads by encouraging Quizzes etc. For such advertising long copy is recommended because ads with really long copy actually tend to get read more thoroughly than the ads with shorter copies.

Apart from trade journals they should go for other media of advertising like catalogues, brochures, direct mails, exhibitions etc.

NO.3

What media would you recommend to reach new customers?

Answer:

Medium is a channel of communication, such as newspapers, magazines, radio and television. A medium is a vehicle for carrying the sales messages of an advertiser to target prospects.

Effective advertising refers to informing the public about the right product at the right time through the right medium. Conveying a right message through a wrong medium at the wrong time would be a waste of resources. Therefore, the right media selection is the crux of the success of the entire advertising campaign. But advertising and marketing need to brainstorm together and then decide about the correct steps towards fulfilling organsiational needs and aspirations.

Media selection decision refers to the selection of a specific medium of advertising, such as the newspaper, a magazine, the radio, or television, the mail service or outdoor advertising.

Today multi-media campaign is the most effective form of advertising. All the possible media like newspapers journals, magazines, television, radio etc. should be used to advertise a product. Since ABC deals in industrial product, the most recommended media consists of newspapers, journals and magazines. This is because of the fact that their clients are not the ultimate consumers. No doubt, other media like television and radio etc. should also be used but more percentage of budgets should be allocated to advertising in newspapers, journals and business magazines. Electrical motors and precision machinery being industrial products which are not bought directly by the ultimate consumer, the manufactures of appliances etc need to be made aware of the existence of the product and should be encouraged to use ABC motors in their products like high speed printers.

No.4

How far the sales promotion measures could be helpful in achieving the objective in addition to the advertising efforts.

Answer:

It should be most appropriate to understand advertising and sales promotion. As we know, advertising is a paid form of non-personal presentation of ideas, goods, or services by an identified sponsor. Sales promotion is necessarily a key ingredient in the marketing campaign. Whereas advertising offers a reason to buy, sales promotion offers an incentive to buy. Sales promotion includes various tools for consumer promotion (samples, coupons, cash refund offers, price-offs, premiums, prizes and so on). Sales promotion tools are used by many organisations including manufacturers, retailers, trade associations and the non-profit organisations.

Sales promotion tools vary in their specific objectives. A free sample stimulates consumer trial whereas a free management advisory service aims at cementing a long-term relationship with the retailer. Sales promotion basically yields a faster and much more measurable response in sales than advertising does. The biggest advantage of the sales promotion tools is that loyal brand buyers tend not to change their buying pattern as a result of the competitive promotion.

The importance of sales promotion cannot be under-estimated. Therefore, both advertising and sales promotion would be helpful in achieving the objectives of ABC.

No.5

How much should ABC spend on corporate image advertising?

Answer:

Advertising expenditure decisions are often arbitrary and at time merely a guess. That is why we find gross inadequacy of funds at one extreme and wanton extravagance at the other. Advertising is an extremely vital force in the success of marketing endeavours.

Corporate advertising aims at building a positive image for the firm in the eyes of internal and external public. Corporate image comprises the knowledge, feelings, ideas and beliefs associated with a co's activities. It may introduce products indirectly or may introduce the sales people indirectly. It cultivates or tries to promote a spirit of friendliness towards it among the public. A favourable corporate image can also be of advantage in dealing with distributors, employees, competitors, suppliers, the government and, also, financial circles.

For the last two years, ABC spent Rs, 50, 00,000 to 75, 00,000 on advertising. From this, 20% of the advertising expenses i.e. around Rs. 10, 00,000 to 15, 00,000 were made on corporate image advertising in various trade journals and business newspapers and rest on television, radio & magazines and was aimed at the consumers at large.

As per our point of view, as the company deals in industrial products, the money spent by ABC on corporate image advertising is not quite sufficient and they should go for around 35 to 45% increase in corporate advertising because cultivating a good reputation among potential customers will have good payoff, i.e. it will help their salesmen to get a 'foot in the door'.

So we suggest that the company should curtail their expenses on the consumer oriented advertising and concentrate more on corporate advertising.

V

Rethinking Celebrity Endorsements Leveraging the Brand and Effect on Product Sale

The use of celebrities in mainstream advertising is a common marketing communication strategy. For many years, marketers around the world held an unwavering belief that celebrity endorsements are a great way to sell a product. In such an approach, the advertiser gets a lot of help from personalities that possess certain phenomenal characteristics to tell the product's story. All the popularity, glamour and charisma attached to a movie star, a sports hero, a TV personality, or even a politician are sold and purchased as the product's own.

The use of celebrities began more than half a century ago, when Bob HOPE first pinned the Texaco star to his chest and Ronald Reagon hawked Chesterfield Cigarettes. Since then, numerous companies have paid large sums of money to align themselves and their products with big-name celebrities in hopes that their popularity and fame might entice consumers to buy. However, many marketers are re-evaluating the value of celebrity endorsements.

Critics argue that the use of celebrities has become too risky and they rarely do much to help business. A number of celebrities have been involved in major controversies that some feel have detracted from their value as endorsers. In 1991, basketball star Earvin (Magic) Johnson was a highly paid spokesman for several companies when he announced he was retiring from basketball because he had contracted a serious disease. Some argue that basketball superstar Michael Jordan's endorsement value declined when he was linked to sizable gambling debts. The Florida Citrus Commission paid actor Burt Reynolds more than $ 500,000 to be its spokesperson but decided to drop him when his nasty divorce from actress Loni Anderson became the talk of the tabloids.

And speaking of products that don't exist, remember that refrain of a company called Home Trade? "Life Means More". Presumably, it meant more to Sachin, Hrithik and Shahrukh, who so valiantly plugged its indefinable and totally mysterious "product". More than just defrauding the Nagpur Cooperative Bank, more than just cheating millions of small investors, more than just helping to sell something they nether believed in, nor had any proof it even existed.

Advertisements are money. Celebrities who endorse things that go bust can quietly get away with impunity, count their millions, and never be the worse for having perpetuated the fraud.

And then there is singer Michael Jackson, who has received endorsement fees of $ 20 million from Pepsi over the past decade.

Critics also argue that celebrity endorsers do little to help sales. L.A. Gear paid millions to Michael Jackson a few years ago to design and promote a line of offbeat sneakers, which were a total flop. Some ad experts argue that consumers have become too skeptical about celebrity endorsements and many are losing their trust in the celebrities themselves.

Not everyone agrees with the negative assessment of celebrity endorsements. However, Pepsi officials note that while that company was sponsoring three Michael Jackson tours and features him in its advertising, it picked up two market share points on archrival Coca Cola, each point worth an estimated $ 500 million in annual sales. Executives at Sprint claim that "Murphy Brown" star Candice Bergen has helped the company develop an image that separates it from AT & T and MCI and its market share has climbed nearly two points since it began using her as a spokesperson.

Some advertising people think the marketers who want to use celebrities have Hollywood tinsel in their eyes and a desire to rub elbows with the stars. But if marketing executives can't prove that the use of a celebrity makes sense, their company may join the ranks of those which have an across the board policy against hiring celebrities. The President of one such company says, "If you want the best shoe for yourself, you don't really give a boot if Michael Jordan wears it. We'd rather put the money into our factories than into the hands of celebrities".

According to surveys by Centre for Media Studies, film stars and sports persons are relied upon more for brand promotions in India. Some of the Indian examples of celebrities used to endorse brands would include the magic of Lux as a beauty bar. The positioning of Lux as "beauty soap for film stars" holds true because of its association with films celebrities almost

Celebrity
Endorsements : Leveraging The Brand

anywhere in the world. Other examples would be the whole host of Cricketers (Kapil Dev, Sachin Tendulkar, Sourav Ganguli, Rahul Dravid, Yuvraj Singh, etc) film stars (Amitabh Bachhan, Sharukh Khan, Hrithik Roshan, Amir Khan, Akshay Kumar, Katrina Kaif, Karishma and Kareena Kapoor etc) and a range of well known models.

In India, the testimonials by either a known or even an unknown individual has been a successful technique for decades. A celebrity personality, indeed, continues to grab more attention for print ad or a TV commercial in India, as it is happening elsewhere in the world. Obviously, many marketers believe strongly, in the value of celebrity spokespeople as the money paid to them has soared to record levels. Marketers look for celebrities who will attract viewers' or readers' attention and enhance the image of the company or the brand.

The use of celebrity in advertising however is no guarantee of awareness. For mathematical reasons, not every celebrity ad or commercial performs above average. One Gallup & Robinson survey says that more than one in five commercials and one in six print ads fall 20% or more below the category norm in terms of recall. This should be applicable in India too. The obvious question is, why?

PROGRESS TEST

1. Discuss the ethics of celebrities endorsing products to promote brands. Do you think celebrities hurt their reputations by endorsement? Why or why not?
2. Discuss the pros and cons of using celebrities as advertising spokespersons. Provide examples of two celebrities you believe are very appropriate (or inappropriate) for the brands they are endorsing and explain why.
3. Most marketers choose sources with high credibility both in India as well as in the West. Do you agree that celebrities actually transfer their personality traits to the brand's personality? Try to develop some theory on celebrity usage.

Celebrity Endorsements – What, Why, How?

Marketers try to match the product of the company's image, the characteristics of the target, market, and the personality of the celebrity. The image celebrities project to consumers can be just as important as their ability to attract attention. A new perspective on celebrity endorsement has been developed recently by **some experts**. ***They argue that credibility and attractiveness don't sufficiently explain how and why celebrity endorsement works and offers a model based on meaning transfer.***

According to this model, a celebrity's effectiveness as an endorser depends on the culturally acquired meanings he or she brings to the endorsement process. Each celebrity contains many meanings, including status, class, gender, and age as well as personality and lifestyle.

The meaning transfer model has some important complications for companies using celebrity endorsers. Marketers must first decide on the image or symbolic meanings important to their target audience for this particular product, service, or company. They must then determine which celebrity best represents the meaning or image to be projected. An advertising campaign must be designed that captures that meaning in the product and moves it to the consumer. Marketing and advertising personnel in most cases, rely on intuition in choosing celebrity endorsers for their companies or products.

Marketers may also pretest ads to determine whether they transfer the proper meaning to the product. When celebrity endorsers are used, the marketer should track the campaign's effectiveness. Does the celebrity continue to be effective in communicating the proper meaning to the target audience? Celebrities who are no longer in the limelight lose their ability to transfer any significant meanings to the product.

Celebrities

Celebrities are individuals or characters who are known to a large portion of the general population, primarily because of the publicity associated with their lives. Most celebrity endorsers come from the entertainment world or the sports world or Talk show hosts, business personalities and a host of male and female models. The term celebrity itself need not exclude individuals who may be controversial as long they are used carefully to convey a certain image.

Advertisers offen develop and use fictitious characters to serve as spokespersons for their brand. Fictitious characters could be actors, actresses, animal's personification or fantasy creations. We can classify fictitious characters as celebrities because their use involves an essential element of celebrity endorsement. That is they have certain distinct personalities that communicate unique meaning to target segment.

LAY ENDORSERS

Lay endorsers are unknown individuals or characters that appear in ads. They are selected to closely resemble the target segment, enabling the target segment to identify with the endorsers and the message. However, for some products such as washing powders or toothpaste and services such as insurance and health care, these lay endorsers may be chosen because they personify the aspirations of the target segment. Lay endorses may be real or fictitious and are (initially) at least – unknown. Brands such as Surf Excel, Arial and Dove have relied on lay endorsers.

Marketing and Advertising

In the fast moving world of marketing and advertising, celebrity endorsement has become a very essential part. Any company that wants to create a new advertisement for his or her product do not want to do it without a celebrity. For celebrity do have a greater impact if they speak about a product. For we all believe that they are the experts. And everybody believes in what experts say for we do try to imitate a celebrity. For example, if Sharukh Khan does an advertisement for Mayur Suitings rather than any other model doing it, the product does have a greater impact as everybody feels that the big bollywood star has a faith and belief in the product. So the product cannot be bad at all.

The Forms of celebrity endorsement:

A product can be endorsed by a celebrity in different forms based on purpose, the advertisement media and the expected appeal. Following types of endorsement forms have been identified to be heavily in use at present.

(1) As spokesperson for eg: Amitabh Bachhan in KBC.
(2) In print & electronics for eg: Sharukh Khan in Omega & Pepsi.
(3) In outdoor media like hoarding eg: Aishwarya Rai in Lux.
(4) The use of brands in movies: Eg Hero Cycles.

Reasons for endorsement:

(1) When the concerned brand has close substitutes available.
(2) When there is a need to create a clear differentiation.
(3) When the brand has to make an entry into market and the life cycle of brand is feared short. In such cases, the rationale is to make quick money and exit.

Why celebrity endorsement:

(1) A celebrity helps leveraging a brand, in other words makes a brand stand out.
(2) It facilitates instant awareness and communicates instant attention.
(3) Adds new dimension to brand image.
(4) Convincing clients.
(5) Celebrity values define and refurbish the brand image.

Why celebrities want themselves to be endorsers:

(1) Firstly, of the huge compensation involved in the marketing process.
(2) To get an enhanced level of acknowledgement, Kaun Banega Crorepati helped to stabilize the fast declining careers of their hosts by providing strong audience recognition.
(3) Endorsement breeds endorsement: Not only does the subject end up getting better offers but the avenues in related & unrelated fields also open up; for Eg: Most of the cricketers have already been made to walk the ramp, a lot of models have already made way into the movies.

Problems with using celebrity:

- Celebrity has ups and downs in careers that affect the performance for the brand.
- Sometime public may not like celebrity if it lacks credibility.
- Possibility that target audience may not respond positively to the use of particular celebrity.
- Increases cost of product.
- Major controversies distract their value as endorsers.

Task One:

Ethics of Celebrities Endorsing Brands. Do they Hurt their Reputations...............?

Now we move on to ethics. Ethics is a choice between good and bad, right and wrong. It is governed by a set of principles of morality at given time and a given place. Ethics is related to group behaviour, setting the norms for an individual to follow in consistence with the group norms. Advertising too has its ethical values.

As advertising is a social process, it must honour the traditional norms of social behaviour, and should not affront the moral senses of a society. In order to enforce an ethical code we in India have Advertising Standards Council of India (ASCI). It is a non-profit organisation set up by 43 founder members who are involved with advertising in one way or the other. It puts forward a regularity code. ASCI proposes to adjudicate on whether an advertisement is offensive and its decision will be binding on its members. It processes to deal with government if there are any disputes.

The celebrities knowing little about the products they hawk and we, as consumers, tend to rely on their knowledge as “experts” even though their expertise is usually far removed from the products they endorse.

For example:

Amitabh Bachhan doing advertisement for the ICICI Bank, where he speaks about the different facilities of the bank like the ATM facilities of the bank, their mutual bonds, the ICICI Prudentials. So we consumers do feel that when such a big personality can have trust on this bank then why we cannot have similar trust on this bank. And this has really led to the sales boost up by more than 50% of their financial products. But here ICICI Bank also backed up the celebrity by proving themselves in front of the consumers by providing all the services that the celebrity had promised to them. So we can say that they hold or seek some public responsibility or public trust and this justifies greater scrutiny.

A celebrity cannot escape moral responsibility by saying that he just appeared in the ad and did not endorse the product. Strange logic indeed! After all, these celebrities are paid millions of rupees for their appearance and endorsement. Because of their popularity they exercise considerable influence or readers and viewers. To say that they are concerned only with endorsing and not responsible for anything else is the height of hypocrisy. The celebrities who appear in all sorts of ads for money are luring gullible public buying into trash. It is well known fact that film stars appearing in ads for cosmetics and toiletries never even touch them, let alone use them! The celebrities should never betray the confidence of the public just like that.

For Example:

We can take the Home Trade ad. "In the sad case of Home Trade, one must conclude to some extent that the advertisement gave legitimacy to the enterprise, as did, indeed those featured in the advertisement in spite of the fact that none of them actually endorsed the brand. As home Trade was a complete fraud and lot of people invested in this product, so it was the ethics of the celebrities that had been hurt as these celebrities hardly had any knowledge about the product. But, wasn't it their business to know all about it? They cannot turn the business of business as well as its ethics as their own personal business ethics.

However, the ethical issues are very complex and it therefore requires a conscious effort to deal with each situation.

Social Responsibility:

The celebrities should not endorse products like cigarette, cigars and chewing tobacco. Specially when medical evidence about the harms that these products cause is an open secret.

On the other side the celebrities must do endorsement for health awareness programs.

For example the awareness programmes about AIDS, Hepatitis, Cancer, Drug Addiction etc.

The best example of this type of endorsement is by the well known actress Shabana Azmi who did the campaign for AIDS awareness programme.

Puffery:

Puffing means exaggerated claims by the advertisers about the product. According to ASCI consumers expect exaggerations and inflated claims in advertising to a reasonable extent. Now the celebrity should use his/her analytical skill to decide on this issue before endorsing the particular brand. As the consumers rely on endorsement to make buying decisions, the endorsers must be qualified by experience or training to make judgements and they must actually use the product.

If endorsers are comparing competing brands they must have tried those brands as well. Though, determining whether the endorsement is authentic may not be easy. Is Hrithik Roshan a regular coke drinker? Is he qualified to judge the quality of the product? These are all million dollar questions.

Whether the celebrities hurt their reputations by endorsement depends on the particular situation. If the celebrity is on the epitome of popularity and he endorses any brand people take it positively which further adds glitter to his popularity.

On the other hand, if the celebrity is not so popular people take it negatively, that he is running short of funds and this is doing some ad campaigns to make the proverbial quick bucks.

Task Two:

Pros and Cons of using celebrities as spokespersons. Examples of celebrities as appropriate or inappropriate.

The Pros – The Positive

Celebrity endorsement has always been a matter of hot pursuit for the marketers, which works very well to draw attention of the customer. Using celebrities provide weight and recognition to the ad. Simply, well – known the celebrity, well-known will be the ad.

Various Pros of the celebrity endorsements are:

1. The advertisement catches an immediate attention of the fans (potential consumers) of the celebrity used in the ad.
2. Some people take the celebrities as their role models. As a result when celebrities endorse any particular brand people blindly follow their footsteps.
3. Generally the audience relates the product and themselves to the celebrities. They think that whatever the celebrity is saying is right or if Sharukh Khan is endorsing Santro it has to be number one because Shahrukh is number one and he believes in the best!
4. The influence of ambition psyche lead people to ape the celebrities in their day to day activities. Many even dream to become like a celebrity some day. Some know they wouldn't become as good as the celebrity but sharing common belonging makes them feel better. In the process the brand is the gainer.
5. Celebrities could build, refresh, and add new dimensions to brand by transferring their values and images, thus enhancing the value and the image of the brand itself.
6. Research had indicated that target prospects are more likely to choose goods and services endorsed by celebrities than those without such endorsements. Celebrities thus facilitate instant awareness and immediate attention.
7. Celebrity expertise is perceived relevant by a very large segment of the present as well as the potential customers. Expertise is the knowledge that the communicator seems to possess to support the claims made in the advertisement. It is universally understood

that a well known celebrity is better suited to claim expertise to influence the consumers' mind. At the same time our own Sachin Tendulkar would be a much better option for Reeebok advertisements in India.

8. Common people in general perceive celebrities as their trustworthy models. They look forward to them for objective and honest information about products as well as services. Similarly, between non – endorsed and celebrity – endorsed items they depend more on trustworthy celebrities for their choice.

The Cons – The Downside

There can be some negative consequences to using celebrities as endorsers. Despite the potential benefits they can provide, celebrity advertising increases the marketer's financial risk. Let us now go through the discrepancies in the present system of endorsement.

1. Large companies may not have a problem spending millions to acquire the fame and glamour of a movie star or a sports icon, but the small one may have to struggle to afford it.
2. Sometimes celebrities overshadow the brand. Examples galore when many campaigns have to be aborted due to effective communication.
3. Not only that celebrity advertising leads to heavy advertising budget, the implicit costs remain uncovered. Mostly, the tangible and visible costs are considered.
4. Owning to unavailability to dates, long term contracts have to be signed whereas the life of the celebrity might not always be long term.
5. When a negative image of the celebrity is portrayed, a tainted picture is also painted for the company or brand, making it difficult to gain consumer trust' to support the organisation or buy product.

   Ever wonder about the risk a company takes when hiring a celebrity endorser? Just ask Hertz, which found themselves the unwilling sponsor of an accused murderer on O.J. Simpson.
6. Advertising of non-social products: When youngsters watch celebrities endorsing such items, they get induced towards these products as these celebrities are their role models. Examples: Red & White Cigarettes (Akshay Kumar), Bagpiper Whiskey (Sunny Deol).
7. Celebrities alone do not guarantee success as consumers now a days understand advertising, know what advertising is and how it works. People know celebrities are being paid a lot of money for endorsements and this knowledge leads them to cynicism about celebrity endorsement.

Example 1:

Coca Cola Ad campaigns with Hrithik Roshan

The Appropriate One

The Hrithik Roshan ad promotion for Coca Cola in the desert in Rajasthan is an appropriate and sensible one.

The celebrity use for the product somehow is related to the product with appropriate projection and ambience for the product to be used.

The celebrity as shown in the ad is an actor who dances well. But the villagers don't recognise him and after watching him dance on his song suggest him to go for films.

This ad promotes not only the product as it is needed in that hot and dry weather but also promotes the celebrity further.

Example 1:

Pepsi's ad campaign with Amitabh Bachhan.

An Inappropriate one

The Pepsi ad showing film star Amitabh Bachhan begging for a Pepsi bottle was totally irrelevant and meaningless with no correlation between the products and the celebrity. He is the superstar, a hero and people look up to him with high regard.

The Pepsi people seemed to have shifted from their crux as earlier they used to talk young celebrities such as Juhi Chawla, Shahrukh, Karishma, Rani Mukherjee, Ajay Jadeja, Sachin Tendulkar and so on ..... for their ad campaigns.

Now suddenly they changed their strategy and took Amitabh Bachhan, an old man craving for a cold soft drink bottle with no valid reason in somebody else's house. Decidedly, he is not the suitable person who can promote that product even if he had been a great star and a famous celebrity.

Task Three:

Do celebrities actually transfer their personality traits to the brand's personality? Some theory on celebrity usage.

Yes, celebrities actually transfer their personality traits to the brand's personality. The brand managers try to select the celebrity whose personality or image matches with the brand personality. Whenever the choice is not appropriate the endorsement is a fiasco.

First, what are personality traits? Personality traits are enduring characteristics that describe an individual's behaviour: shy, aggressive, timid etc.

What is personality?

It is a set of relatively stable characteristics or dimensions of people that account for consistency in their behavior in various situations. We can judge various personality traits like outgoing, intelligent, happy, practical, released, independent in a personality. In celebrity endorsements many, celebrities display or transfer some of their traits to the personality of the brand.

The positive example:

Certainly, in recent memory, there are instances of happy confluence of commercial interest and subliminal desire. Lux soap, for one it's gone all awry now, and trying to be everything that other beauty soaps are, but at one point, the association was pretty clear. Fair- Skinned actress = Lux beauty soap: Hema Malini's smooth cheeks were once intrinsically, irrevocably linked to that innocuous pink bar of glycerin and fatty acids. The question about whether celebrity advertisements work is not so much a question about celebrities, but about the advertisements themselves.

A cynical public is constantly assaulted by the endless flow of the sales pitch: and yet, in those multitudes of messages crowding our thought waves, there is information that manages to get across, there are lifestyle imprints that manage to stick, and products that manage to get sold. The point, therefore, about celebrities in advertisements, is the point of advertising itself, everyone does it, so it isn't up for analysis and examination as much as simply something that is permanently there.

What is fascinating about ad-culture is the narrative structure it adopts, the way in which advertisements have come to be whole spectacles in themselves. Shahrukh Khan's visibility hinges not so much on the number of films he has recently acted in, as on the number of advertisements he has starred in, and their frequency of deployment. People talk of the new Pepsi ad as if it is the new mega hit from Karan Johar, and watch it with the same curiosity.

Take the folks who diligently churn out visual images of Shahrukh plugging Pepsi and Hyundai cars. We can believe that someone out there will go out and buy Pepsi because it is suddenly very cool, now that Shahrukh is drinking it. But a car? Is it conceivable that Mr. Sharma in Delhi sits down one evening to watch his favorite television soap, happens to catch Shahrukh blow up a building and zip away in his Santro, and then adds 'Buy car' to his shopping list for the next day? Naturally, not.

But the folks who sell the car know that. They're working on a much larger principle. A thought – control process that includes worlds such as 'concept', 'lifestyle', 'equity' and 'recall'.

In that sense, a car advertisement itself is working on this principle with or without Shahrukh Khan. With the actor, it is shrewdly magnifying its effect. In mapping out the equation Shahrukh = Santro, it makes the consumer think of the Santro, every time she sees one of the million images of Shahrukh that pervade her everyday existence. Thus celebrity inclusion does induce the ultimate multiplier effect.

Say, for example, when the most beautiful lady that is Ms Aishwarya Rai asks you to Donate Eyes for a social cause she Infact is transferring her own personality to the advertisement as she herself has got lovely eyes. Or when Shabana Azmi campaigns for AIDS she is transferring her personality to the social cause. When the beautiful actresses of Bollywood show that their beauty and the reason of their soft-soft is the LUX beauty bar, they are Infact relating their beauty with that of LUX.

Conclusion:

Oftentimes celebrities are caught in a scandal that has to do with this or her own actions. Information about the negative event, including the response of the firm and the response of the endorser, become part of the brand and organsiational associations. Negative information becomes more important. There are two types of endorser response:

(1) Denial and accept responsibility and take corrective action.

(2) When the endorser denies or dismisses the negative information on the organisation related event, consumer evaluations of the endorser will be lower than with other response strategies.

(3) When the endorser accepts responsibility and takes corrective action for a negative organisation related event, consumer evaluations of the endorsers will be higher than with other response strategies.

For celebrities that are blameworthy for scandals, the credo is "lie low" and wait until the scandal disappears from the news before quietly firing the celebrity (typically, the company doesn't renew the endorser's contract). For companies sponsoring a highly blameworthy celebrity stronger action is often warranted. In these cases the company often makes a public statement that distances the company from the endorser.

In the aftermath of a scandal for which the endorser is highly culpable, the celebrity is not necessarily "blacklisted" forever, although it may take time before advertisers accept the celebrity back into the fold.

In short, the link between product endorser and company is a tenuous one which must be managed with diligence by a company that chooses to associate itself with a fundamentally imperfect human being.

The person who is involved in communicating the marketing message in either a direct or an indirect manner is known as the source. Celebrity endorsements are expensive for firms and therefore there must be careful consideration taken in the selection process. There are many differing views on what characteristics make a celebrity endorser a good source.

Admittedly, the effectiveness of a celebrity endorser depends in part upon the meaning he or she brings to the endorsement process. Demographic characteristics are relatively easy to establish but it is more subjective categories such as expertise, likeability and trustworthiness which are used more regularly to determine the effectiveness of a source. On the other hand, it may be advisable to put the cultural foundation of endorsement theory into perspective when analyzing the social implication of internalizing the traits of unattractiveness, untrustworthiness and unbelievable factors of the endorser.

To conclude, one can say that one must not rely too heavily on the fame of the celebrity. One must look for the genre of consumer that he/she represents, as eventually celebrities are what they are because of huge set of consumers think that they are that way. These celebrities represent the apparitional values that consumer wants to articulate. So the celebrities are here to turn the brands into celebrities. Are you ready for it?

VI

Depicting Women in Advertising Influencing People: Myths and Mechanisms

Any review of Indian or global ads suggests that the overall trends seems to be favour of portraying women in domestic roles or as decorative sex objects. Even today, the concept of male reward or male approval continues to be alive and strong but sickening. Indecent representation is global occurrence, it's not an Indian monopoly as such.

The most guilty culprits are the toiletries, men's wear and cosmetic ads which sell the idea that the be-all and end-all of women's existence is the attentive male. Is it not disgusting that the so called accomplished women portrayed by the ads would have to rely on their boy friend's or husband's say-so to validate their most routine purchase?

This comes up even in the context of new thinking that the customer is no more the king. The old rule is changing fast and marketing and advertising specialists are claiming that the customer is now the "Queen". The question whether the man or woman is important has been the focus of debate often and long. The available evidence so far gives women leading position as buyers. The truth is established owing to two reasons: (i) the position of women as controllers of income and wealth and (ii) their influences as purchasers for the family. It is entirely truthful that the age of the Mrs. Consumer has arrived. This puts Mr. Consumer in the back stage of decision making in the household buying behaviour.

There is no doubt that over 70% of the decision is made by the housewife. But essentially only those women are considered to be the ideal wives who care about their husband's shirts, trousers, and cholesterol. For example the ad showing the wife roasting fluffy chapattis from some readymade brand Atta. The wife is only too happy to please him via fluffed out, soft, chapattis. Many women and particularly the activists feel that these are all damaging, insulting, humiliating to the image of the women.

Ads tend to underscore and reinforce the already negative feelings many women have about themselves, thanks to the male-centric society we live and work in. Sexist models have changed our women. Women models unwillingly lend themselves to becoming both the seller and the sold. Pretty and attractive, passive and docile women models are selling a culture which, in its glossy perfection, is almost an unattainable fantasy. And all these lead to greater frustration for an already-disadvantaged segment.

According to Piyush Pandey, since advertising agencies in India are predominantly run by men, portrayal of women in indecent or superhuman roles has been inherent in the content of Indian advertising. Studies have shown that whatever the product being advertised __ cosmetics, fabrics, tyres, luggage or stationery, women are mostly projected in glamorous and enticing roles. Portrayals in which women are realistically depicted as useful contributors to the world of politics, business, economics and development are sadly lacking.

Although there have been some positive changes in the portrayal of female characters over the years, the traditional view of femininity and objectification of women still persist in advertising. From a global perspective, it is felt that derogatory representation of women in the advertising media is a social and cultural problem. In a survey, a number of women were asked if ads like Fair & Lovely affect the self - esteem of women in general. More than 80% of them voiced their protest against the ad. They felt such ads make women likely to believe that man attribute the highest value to attractiveness, and the women who are not extremely attractive and fair looking cannot do well in life. This advertisement was considered so offensive that it had to be pulled off air following protests by the women's organisations.

We may not deny the fact that advertising has to get attention. It has to cut through the clutter of other ads and get noticed. To this end, advertising uses a variety of attention advices, one of the best known of which is sex. But how far all such ads are functionally effective? For example, advertisers who import sex into an ad and use it purely as an attention-getter when it has got no intrinsic relationship with the product may yet attention. But, contrary to popular consumer belief, this device stands little or no chance of being effective if it is not directly relevant to an advertisement's primary selling point.

WHAT WILL FANTASIA DO TO YOU?
Get the taste of strawberries. The smell of strawberries. Get strawberry pieces inside! That's rich, creamy Strawberry Farm from Fantasia. Grab a tub at a Creambell outlet nearest to you. You'll surely become a fan.
FANTASIA
PREMIUM ICE CREAM
STRAWBERRY FARM

The truth has to be told emphatically that an ad that compels attention but fails to register the brand and its message is next to useless for any advertiser. Another point to be noted is that derogatory representation of women in the advertising media is a social and cultural problem. To conclude, according to a United Nations research report on advertising and the portrayal of women, advertisers have been held responsible for projecting women in a derogatory light, and as an inferior class of human beings.

Progress Tasks

1. Please try to find out whether the women of today can relate to the female characters depicted in the ads. Do you feel that despite improvement of status of women in real life, women in advertisements are still largely portrayed as objects without a voice?
2. How far is it true that only those ads which are aimed at females and contain exclusively women characters allow females to assume an authoritative role? Otherwise, again, is it true that the male characters are always in position of authority? Provide examples with exceptions, if any.
3. Do you think that including female models in ads of products increases their brand value as well as sales? How far is it necessary to use female models in ads of products not related to women at all like men's razors, aftershaves, male-wears etc.?
4. It is generally felt advertisers frequently commit deliberate mistakes by issuing offensive ads while depicting women and thus create and perpetuate stereotypes. Do you feel that the media have an obligation to serve as ethics watchdog of the advertising it airs or prints?

Introduction

The study involves imperative analysis on how popular myths and mechanisms are employed by the advertisers to influence masses in order to promote their product. The expose of females in advertisements is not only divergent to their reality but also indifferent to their needs and true position in the society.

For example, as the study pointed out, Advertisers seem to be oblivious of the fact that customer is no more the "king" because now the customer is a "queen". We all know that the purchase decisions in most of the family units are taken by the female members of the household. They are the ones who manage the inflow and the outflow of financial resources in the family. It has to be kept in mind by the endorsement designers that advertisements have to be created in order to persuade and please the women instead of the men because ultimately the formers are the ones who take the purchase decision. But sadly only those females are seen as virtuous homemaker who care about their husband's shirts, trousers, cholesterols and take great pleasure in running after kids, play excellent hosts, washing clothes in the endorsed washing machine and detergent or storing "food or provisions in the "favourite" refrigerator.

Clearly, such themes corroborate and reinforce the unreal notions of women in the male centric social order that we are a part of. Attractive, giggling, submissive female are clearly canvassing a culture which is hyped as euphoric but is again not based on fact. In fact, this culture is seen as great peril to socially developing status of women by many feminists and thinkers. For example, says Piyush Pandey (a prominent name in ad industry) puts right words to it.

"Since advertising agencies in India are predominantly run by men, portrayal of women in either indecent or superhuman roles has been inherent in the content of Indian Advertising Portrayal of women in which they are realistically depicted as useful contributors to the world of politics, business economics and development is sadly lacking."

Facts of the Case:

- Media as well as advertising suggests that the trends seem to be the favour of portraying women in domestic roles or as decorative sex objects.
- The evidence so far gives women leading position as buyers.
- The position of women as controllers of Income and Wealth.
- Their influences as purchasers for the family.
- Over 70% of buying decision is made by the housewife.
- Advertising agencies in India are predominantly run by men.
- In advertising women are mostly projected in glamorous and enticing roles.
- Women fell ads like Fair & Lovely affect self-esteem of women, such ads make women likely to believe that men attribute the highest value of attractiveness and women who are not extremely attractive and fair looking cannot do well in life.
- To this end, advertising uses a variety of attention getting devices, one of the best known of which sex.
- Most of the time women are involved in advertising where she is not supposed to be present. For example: Men's wear, perfumes, toiletries, cosmetics and so many others.

Question:

1. **Please try to find out whether the women of today can relate to the female characters depicted in the Ads. Do you feel that despite improvement of status of women in real life, women in advertisements are still largely portrayed as an object without voice?**

Yes, it is true that despite the improvement of status of women in real life, women characters shown in the media are fictitious and offensive at times. Women are shown in derogatory light and in stereotypical role which are difficult to relate with. Women are shown as decorative sex objects, having no voice or opinion of their own. This is indeed degrading the image of women and projecting them as inferior human beings.

The aspect of advertising that is most in need of analysis and change is the portrayal of women. Women are shown almost exclusively as housewives or sex objects. The housewife, pathologically obsessed by cleanliness, debates virtues of cleaning products with herself and worries about "ring around the collar". She feels guilt for not being more beautiful, for not being a better wife and mother.

The sex object is a mannequin, a shell. Conventional beauty is her only attribute. All "beautiful" women in advertisements, regardless of product or audience, conform to this norm. Women are constantly exhorted to emulate this idea, to feel ashamed and guilty if they fail: and to tell their desirability and lovability are contingent upon physical perfection.

If we take the example of Indian culture, despite the improvement of status of women, they are not able to express them right. In India, as we all know, dowry is a big problem. A woman who left her house, mother, father as well as her surname, even then she does not get the right that she deserves. If a woman is not able to collect money she is tortured by her husband and family members. In many cases man killed their spouses. Why? This is a big question. We are taking an advantage of women because they are supposed to be inferior. We always want to see women as a domestic housewife. She can't walk openly in the society.

It is felt in the society as a whole that female should be more attractive and fair. If a girl is not looking more attractive, she is not able to take right place in the society. As we can see in daily life at the time of birth of girl people are not enjoying. However, at the time of birth of a boy, people organise a grand party.

In '50 – '60s women were depicted merely helpless, who could not do anything on their own, aside from cooking and cleaning of course.

In '70s – '80s, ads world witnessed women being used as sex symbols and thereafter, till now, they are still used as sex objects except that ads have become more skin revealing thus giving women an unrealistic view of typical women.

- It was perceived that the models should look a cut above the average women;
- Some thought that the women should always look beautiful and men could be ordinary.
- Even women are advertising for the clothing by wearing next to nothing, it is hard to understand how it sells clothes.

Past are the days when women were treated as beauty of household, now that they not only walk on the ramp with men hands in hand but are posing stiff challenge in every walk of life, may it be politics or society or anywhere else.

Indian Women Criticize 'Fair and Lovely' By We Correspondent

Skin lightening is coming under increasing criticism in India.

NEW DELHI, India (WOMEN'S NEWS) – Two attractive young women are sitting in a bedroom having an intimate conversation. The lighter-skinned woman has a boyfriend and consequently, is happy. The darker-skinned woman, lacking a boyfriend, is not. Her friend's advice? Use a bar of soap to wash away the dark skin that's keeping men from flocking. Hindustan Lever Limited, one of India's largest manufacturing and marketing conglomerates, discontinued two of its television advertisements for Fair and Lovely Cold Cream, after a yearlong campaign led the all India Democratic Women's Associations'. Increasing public criticism may be initiating a change in cultural attitudes towards skin whitening in India, a country where the fairness industry accounts for 60 percent of skincare sales, bringing in $ 140 million a year. The company is the subsidiary of Unilever PLC, based in London.

Fair and lovely, one of the Hindustan Lever's "power brands" is marketed in over 38 countries. Its frequently-aired ads typically show a depressed woman with few prospects gaining a brighter future by attaining a boyfriend or job after becoming markedly fairer (emphasized by several silhouettes of her face lined up dark to light). On its website the company calls its product, "the miracle worker", which is "proven to deliver one to three shades of change".

The ad targeted by the women's association shows a woman, whose father had lamented not having a son to support the family, landing a well-paying job as an airline attendant after using the product.

Hindustan lever failed to respond to All India Democratic Women's Association's complaints first sent in March and April 2002. The women's association then appealed to the Human Rights Commission, which passed its complaints on to the Ministry of Information and Broadcasting. The government issued notices of the complaints to the company. Activists credit this intervention, rather than "sudden awakening to the feelings that women have when they see those ads", with triggering the company's about – face. "We are not for heavy – duty censorship" they said, but "when the companies don't respond we have no alternative".

Hindustan Lever, shortly after pulling its ads off the air, launched its "Fair and Lovely Foundation," vowing to "encourage empowerment of women across India" by providing resources in education and business. Sangeeta Pendurkar, the company's skincare marketing manager, announced that the company believed millions of women who, though immensely talented and capable, need a guiding hand to help them take the leap forward."

Question:

2. **How far is it true that only those ads which are aimed at females and contain exclusively women characters allows females to**

assume an authoritative role? Otherwise, again, is it true that the male characters are always in position of authority? Provide examples with exceptions, if any.

In the modern commercial world advertisements play a great role in attracting, commercializing and thereby selling any existing or new products/services. In this competitive world, advertisements have attained a major role in products or services acceptable by the users and ultimately making it a habit of end – users in daily life.

It is very much true that only those advertisements, which are aimed at females and contain exclusively women characters, allow females to assume an authoritative role. We observe females are seen in all products whether it is women oriented and targeted or not. All cosmetics, household goods, jewellery, microwave ovens, soaps, fabrics etc, related commercials and advertisements are women targeted advertising. Females are depicted and contained exclusively women characters in these ads. A very few ads reflect women self-esteem and authoritative role of women.

Studies have revealed that whatever products are being advertised women are projected in glamorous and enticing roles. In today's world Mrs. CONSUMER is in the backstage of decision-making in household buying behavior. The position of women as controller of the family is in forefront now.

Clearly, times have changed in twenty years, since the bulk of research on impacts of gendered depictions on advertising effectiveness was done. More women work outside home, earn and control significant amount of money and make large important purchases (e.g. mobile, car, oven, vacuum cleaners).

In the recent past, women have started acknowledging their independence with the help of education. Now, they have started earning for themselves. Their role form housewife has changed to breadwinner of their family as well. With increased power of money that she earns, women have also gained somewhat the status to influence the buying decision of family.

She seeks to search for her identity, has become more extrovert and outgoing relating to her needs & demands. This change in role of women in society is also being depicted in advertisement. Hence, women are also becoming a potent target customer. This also reflects the need of authoritative portrayal of women in advertising world.

Women are often showcased in very stereotypical roles such as in submissive roles of family roles, and in lower physical and social positions than man. Studies reveal that actual position of many women in society may have improved considerably, yet images of women in advertisements have not changed appreciably. In modern times a sign of status for a man is to have a physically attractive woman by this side. The more attractive the woman is the more prestige she will bring to her male partner/spouse. So, the advertisements definitely undermine the importance of Femina, in its derogatory representation.

Advertisements for products where women play a decisive role in selection of the family are the examples, which depict authoritative role of the women. For example, a decision as to select edible oil, which is safer & healthier for heart of family like Sundrop, Suffola edible oil. A very strong social role is exhibited in the ad where a celebrity like Aishwarya Rai spreads the messages of "Donate you eyes".

Here female authority and elegance is pertinently exploited to pass out a social message as well as exhibit dominance where their family's welfare is an issue of concern. Women certainly take advantage of situations where role of mother, housewife or an educator is needed. They substantially perform their role in doing no compromises where family and a being's welfare is involved. Thus crying out more significantly for social issues of peace and prosperity for whole world.

To some extent it is true that those ads which are aimed at females and contain exclusively women characters allow females to assume an authoritative role. For, example NAKSHATRA & ASMI ads which are exclusively meant for women and also women are the targeted audiences mainly. The ad which says "WEAR YOUR NAKSHATRA AND CHOOSE YOUR MYSTICAL POWER FOR THE DAY.

But if we take the example of "PINK SCOOTI" ad where Priety Zinty says "PINK SE PANGA NAHI LENEKA" also shows women in authoritative role.

But in the ads of HOME APPLIANCES though women are showed as the main buyers but ultimately it is the man who makes the decision as to what to buy and what not to buy.

Now if we take the example of TATA SALT which shows the man in the authoritative role. The ad goes like this: the child wants to eat pizza, mother decided to make it at home and so she buys all ingredients along with TATA SALT. After she makes it the whole family sits for dinner but no one dares to taste it before the male character. In this add it is shown that if the male had refused the pizza the whole world of the female who is his wife would come to an end. But there can be no denying the fact that in the present male-dominated society male members of family does final decision- making authority in the most of the products for the use of family. In such decision-making process, opinion or consent is sometimes taken from the female members but the final authority of selection & decision making remains with the males only.

Hence it can be concluded that portrayal of women in stereotypical domestic or decorative objects is both cultural and social problem. Such situation is prevalent not only in India but also globally. Yet things are strongly changing for of women slowly. To make a commendable change in current position where ads underline the role women as pretty and attractive, docile and passive. A wholesome change in mentality and perception of society is essential. For accomplishing this women need to be educated and trained. They must be well aware their role in society and family to bring about a change in patriarchial mindset.

Question:

3. **Do you think including female models in ads of products increase their brand value as well as sales? How far is it necessary to use female models in ads of products not related to women at all like men's razor, aftershaves, males wear etc?**

Advertising basically has four vital uses-informative, innovative, persuasive and competitive. Every other day market is flooded with various new products as also the ads to promote them.

Advertisement plays the role of the mediator by the way of coining slogans and visuals to make the products catch the public attention and the most used and exploited idea in this regard now are females.

Feminity is the new selling idea for the ad makers. They term Feminity as a situation or culture in which the dominant values in the society are caring for others and quality of life and who best to portray this? Answer of course is the woman. And that's probably the reason why we get to see more and more ads which are predominantly women-oriented. Hence, it will be no exaggeration if we say that the women are the queens of ads.

But the question of debate is whether including female models increases product brand value as well as sales.

As of sales we can say 'yes' but as of brand value we need to ponder over. For example, keeping aside those products which are female oriented such as lipstick, shampoos, beauty salons, cooking oil, face creams etc. Let us take a peep into products which do not require projection of women at all such as man's razor, aftershaves males wear etc. in such ads do we require women, the products being male oriented? Your answer maybe 'no' but then why women are present in such ads? A point to think over. Various arguments have been given in this regard.

- Women view more television and are more sensitized to programme difference or to advertise a new product.
- Secondly, a woman has more decision making responsibility.
- Thirdly, women in a persuasive role have a far reaching impact than men.

They may not be professionally perfect but who cares about perfection when they see a glamorous and a desirable charming lady on screen. The whole stress is to a make the advisement eye-catching i.e. if the advertisement succeeds in making an appeal to the prospective buyer, moving him to enquire, to develop keen interest and ultimately decide in favour of buying the product the female part has served its purpose. For example, men's ethnic wear. In this ad we see a man in centre wearing an ethnic wear and two ladies by his side holding his arm. Is this not the use of women as a SALES PROMOTION COMMODITY?

- Fourthly, the ads in which women are used get retained in the minds of the user or the consumer for a longer period.

So we can conclude that although women are mainly used as an object of sex and sensuality it has become more or less the need of the hour to use female models in ads in which they are not related.

But one possible remedy for unnecessary exploitation of women can be compliance with a code of conduct, failing which regulation by government through laws is the only answer.

Moreover it is more of a social and cultural problem. It is basically society's outlook towards women which needs to be changed. Women are not an object of attention-getter or ne used only to import sex but are much more than that, society should be ready to explore other horizons of women. She's much more than what the advertisements show.

Question:

4. It is generally felt that advertisers frequently commit deliberate mistakes by issuing offensive ads while depicting women and this create and perpetuate Stereotypes. Do you feel that the media have an obligation to serve as ethics watchdog of the advertising it airs or prints?

In this age of liberalization and opening up of our economy to global market forces, women and young girls have become an important target for the media. In print and electronic media we find two broad trends- either woman are commoditized for the sale of various products or they are presented in typical stereotyped roles like Saas-Bahu quarreling or proudly involved in domestic work, etc. both these trends are highly objectionable as they demean and devalue their status and work and help to build a particular mind set which provides legitimacy to the social devaluation of women. This is particularly true of advertisements where images of women are carefully constructed by big advertising companies to reinforce and obtain public sanction for certain value codes which will serve their interests and create more profit.

The problem is that multinational companies and big capital involved in advertising are either guided by market norms or they try to exploit patriarchal and traditional popular sentiments for their own vested interests. It suits their needs to offer mindless stimulation, to reinforce women's subjugation and at the same time to promote a consumerist culture to create more demands for their products.

Although women are making a mark in every field but we rarely come across an ad where a woman's talents, contributions to the society or struggle for existence are shown, even when a working woman is shown, she is depicted as if her sole concern is to seek the attention of a male. That sends out a very wrong message to the viewers of our society which is till male dominated. For example, a 'Revlon nail polish' or a 'Ponds' lotion can bring about 'revolution' in a woman's world! No need to struggle and shout against various discriminatory social practices and structures.

Also justification, rather glorification, of eve-teasing in an increasing number of ads, all in the name of fun and entertainment, is an area that requires serious probing. This is one aspect that has been a cause of increasing violence against young girls, especially in educational institutions.

There is an equally dangerous trend of showing women as repositories of retrograde patriarchal values like son-preference. The old "fair and Lovely" ad – "kaash mera beta hota!" and other such ads present the demand for dowry in subtle, overt or covert ways: grandmother expressing pleasant surprise and satisfaction at the granddaughter becoming so fair in colour, a woman expressing sharp jealousy and envy against another in favour or disfavor of a particular product and so on..... The portrayal becomes all the more objectionable when the woman is shown as "modern" and 'presentable' in her looks, her attire, and behaviour. She is looked at, presented and defined from the male view point only.

An LIC policy ad talks of the necessity of insurance for a daughter's marriage and a son's education – 'Bete ki padhi aur beti ki shadi ke liye'. This kind of stereotyping reinforces the notion that the only future for a young woman is marriage while that of son is individual development through higher education. That is at a time when young girls are faring much better in the entire examinations-just look at the recent results. The ads also trend to legitimize customs like dowry and need for insurance at such a time. Young women in India today are struggling to gain recognition of their creative faculties and desire for more educational opportunities, and for an independent career.

To top anything else- woman are lesser human beings who can be mocked at, trivialized, cut to size through jokes, through gestures, through maxims, through all kinds of devaluing practices – all in the name of 'culture' . A 'Titan' watch discount offer which is intended for offer a new watch in place of the old one and the husband taking a dig- 'How I wish that 'old' wives could be replaced by 'new' ones'. A person buying 'Babool' toothpaste – "buy one get one free" offer – The husband is shown in a comfortable monarch like position-being served by a wife each on either side and commenting- 'Doesn't this offer apply to wives as well"? The makers should be punished on the charge of propagating bigamy.

These days's media loves to concentrate on men .... "Their concerns, their activities, their achievements, their woes", she says that it generally disregards women and their interests and is hence "sexist". And with the media depending heavily on advertisements for revenue, it happily plays host to sexist ads.

Sharda J Schaffter, writer of gender in India Advertising, has made some observations that "Does a woman need to be always tall and slim, young and light-skinned with silken skin and mob of gloriously shining hair? Is all this calculated to catch a man, and once she has caught him, to spend the rest of her life preparing mouthwatering dishes and washing his shirts until they outshine the sun —- as ads persuade us to believe?"

She points out the dangerous repercussions of sexist advertisements in a "caste-conscious, tradition-bound, superstitious, feudal an intensely patriarchal Indian society. She maintains that while there is nothing demeaning in a woman being represented as a homemaker "the profusion of such ads gives birth to an ideology" which implies that women should be primarily homemakers, and nothing more.

Some of the pertinent questions she raises include:

- Do advertisers turn women into commodities that please men, or do they portray them as human beings conscious of their own worth?
- Are women shown preponderantly serving others or as pursuing profitable careers?
- Are they shown as objects of men's fancy, relying on their largesse, or as persons of value, capable of managing their own lives?
- Are they show silly, stupid and mindless, or are they portrayed intelligent, strong and assertive, capable of successfully undertaking responsibilities and contributing to productivity in society?
- Are women shown fanatical about cleanliness around the house?

She has also question about the need to irrelevantly divide the women's body into segments-lips arms, leg etc, and represent her as an inveterate, irrational shopper. While Quoting the experience of Nelia Sancho, a former beauty queen of the Pacific from the Philippines, Sharada points out how the woman was expected to only smile and look pretty at an event. "When after the preliminary greeting nobody tried to have any sort of intelligent conversation with her, she realised that she was only a pretty object beautifying a room."

National Chairman, RMG DAVIDS, finds the stereotypical role of women that exists today is more of a preserver who brings harmony into a home. In India, Advertising stereotypes are becoming two-dimensional. A mother brings a glass of milk for her son doesn't imply she is serving her son. Rather, it brings out the finer nuances of the mother-son relationship, which is important for the ads and the product.

Hence, advertisers should be more responsible while making ads and should ensure that there is absolute gender equality. Also the media has a very significant role to play in shaping social attitudes. Hence it cannot cater to the interest of a miniscule section only. It certainly does have a social obligation and responsibility in the development and reinforcement of opinions which lead to a better and more equitable society.

CONCLUSION

Consistently throughout Asia, women have been portrayed in the media as victims, subservient, nurturing, sacrificing and objectified sexualized beings. This not only inaccurately represents the diversity of women's lives, roles and experiences within this complex region, women's contributions to the political and economic development of society are often neglected.

The role of women in our society has changed dramatically in last 3-4 decades. It will be erroneous on our part to accept the traditional role of women in this modern world, women are now playing diversified role in the socio-economic context of our society. They have emerged as a powerful influence group. The change in the educational, social and cultural set up has given new dimensions to our social structure and mind set.

The perpetuation of stereotypes in images and representation solidifies women's traditional roles and unequal gender relations in multiple ways. Most visibly, women are seen as mourners at tragedies or as victims of violence. **The Global Media Monitoring Project** found that out of the small number of women who were interviewees in news stories (14%). 29% of them were as victims of accidents, crimes or other events. This does not only represent women as helpless subjects without a voice. It also fails to emphasize men's role as perpetrators in instances of violence against women. Further, the dissemination of these messages affects women's self-confidence, mobility and subsequently access and particulars in public spaces (for fear of assault).

Today, advertisers seem to have finally cottoned on to the fact that nowadays Urban Indian Women are decision makers. They are an important and burgeoning consumer segment that can also be tapped for such product as automobile, computer, financial plans, and home loan.

Indian women's transition from homemaker to home loan taker and the representation of that transition in the media cannot be ignored.

As Charulata Ravikumar, executive vice president of Bata Enterprise, pointed out

"Today more and more advertisers are looking at consumer segmentation that is not gender specific but mindset specific."

At the same time, much of the advertising portraying women perpetuates their secondary role in Indian society and also invents fresh circumstances that characterize women as inferior to men. The Advertising Council of India encourages people to bring to its notice through elaborate procedures about the ads that contravene regulations so that action can be taken to redress the situation. But an ad cannot be separated from its import and effect. Once the veil is lifted and contents are unmasked, neither the most regretful retraction nor the most penitent apology can undo the damage caused.

The task ahead is to frame a moral outlook that challenges the patriarchal social order. Sharada J Sehaffter, in her book, lists several guidelines for non-sexist language and advertising codes to ensure fair portrayal of women.

VII

Ethical Perspective: Benetton Ads.

Using Advertising to Appeal to Social Consciousness

In recent years, many creative people complain, advertising has become bland and boring because advertisers are too concerned about offending and restrict themselves to ads that are politically correct. However, not all advertisers are worried about their ads offending; some are even deliberately creating controversial ads. Critics call this new genre shock advertising and claim that its intent is to elicit attention for a brand name by jolting consumers. However, Benetton, the Italian- based clothing manufacturer whose ads are well known worldwide for their shock value, says it has a different reason for using this type of advertising. Benetton's creative director, Oliviero Toscani, says the controversial images are designed to raise public awareness of social issues and position the company as a cutting-edge, socially conscious marketer.

Benetton has been regarded as a renegade of the advertising world since 1989, when it ran a print ad featuring a black woman nursing a white baby. Other shock ads have featured such images as a black man's handcuffed to a white man's, a priest kissing a nun, an AIDS patient and his family moments before his death, a boatload of refugees, an automobile ablaze after a car bomb, and naked adults with naked children.

One of the latest images is a symbolic picture from the war in Bosnia. The idea for the ad came when a young woman who fled Sarajevo after her family was killed in the war wrote Toscani and asked. "Why don't you do something about what's going on in my country." Toscani had Benetton representative visit a morgue in the war-torn country and contact families of slain soldiers, seeking permissions to photograph their possessions left behind as a reminder of the war's horrors. Toscani selected a slain soldier whose father attached a note to his uniform that read: "I, Gojko Gagro father of the deceased Marinko Gagro, born in 1963 at Blizanchi in the province of Citluk, would like my son's name and all the remains of him be used in the name of peace and against war. "The ad, which was photographed by Toscani, shows a single arresting image of a bloody camouflage uniform. The copy in its author's native Servo – Croatian, is Mr Gagro's letter, Toscani has stated, "The language in the ad belongs to a dictionary the Western world doesn't want to open".

Benetton's shock ads often ignite criticism and stir up industry debate over their purpose. Peter Fressola, a Benetton North America spokesman said. "Yes, we mean to shock some people with our ads. But people who are shocked by this have been living in a cocoon. They need to be shocked into seeing what's really going on in the world. We believe that when many people see an image this powerful, it can raise their collective consciousness. And that can result in action." Critics argue that the real goal of the Benetton ads is to generate publicity. Some accuse Benetton of exploiting human suffering to sell its products. The Benetton ads are controversial even in more liberal European countries. Advertising self regulatory bodies in Britain, France and Spain have condemned the ads and urged magazines in these countries to reject many of them. The Vatican newspaper, L' Osseratore Ramon, ran an editorial denouncing the Bosnian image ad as "advertising terrorism." However, Amnesty International applauded the ad for drawing attention to the war and Sarajevo's daily newspaper asked Benetton for posters of the ad to plaster across the city.

Toscani sees the negative reactions to the Benetton ads as nothing less than a debate between advertising and art. He argues that in the art world, debatably offensive images are accepted, while in other realms such as advertising they are not. A Benetton spokesperson said Toscani wants to explore the limits of art and advertising - where one begins and other ends and how tolerance shifts from one realm to the next. However, an attorney for France's self - regulating advertising body replied. "Advertising versus art or whatever, Benetton always has an explanation. That's not the point. The point is they've broken the rules." It is likely that Benetton will continue breaking the rules and shocking people. Of course, it may also get them to think about some of the world's problems in the process.

Progress Test:

(1) Do you consider that the Benetton Add carries "a big idea" as its main concept? Why or why not?

(2) Many people believe that some advertisers are going too far in their efforts to break through the advertising clutter and have an impact on consumers. Give your views in relation to Benetton ad.

(3) Examine this ad vis-à-vis the following:

Clothes of the killed Croatian soldier Marinko Gagro, 1993. The genesis is passed on in different versions, th
anonymous postal package at Toscani with the petition for publishing a photo - up to the claim, this motive is arra
completely in a studio. Benettons version is following: Toscani had in view of the war in Bosnia. The general pub
gave him an idea to that motive and he engaged the Benetton-office for Bosnian affairs to procure the uniform of
together with the approval-explanation of the relatives to be allowed to use the clothing as a Benetton photo-mot
photo, as ad and poster world-wide, evoked most vehement criticisms: the *Osservatore Romano* wrote about "pi
and the *Society for Threatened People* interpreted the campaign as a violation against the UN-Convention to the
genocide.

The general opinion postulates that topics like Aids, racism and war must not be amalgamated with product pla
strictly content separation of the editorial part from advertising is demanded. Then actually a fixed, reality-distar
remain to advertisement. Benetton does not show pictures in a happy world of consumption - and subjects like A
the Mafia, death penality, birds in tar and graveyards of soldiers do not say anything about its sweaters... The
press-photos in the spring- and autumn-campaigns of 1992 got the reality in its negative manifestations into th
advertisement indeed.
The extended public attention on Benetton-posters effected as well a deficit in significance of usual advertisem
for prohibition and censorship was explicable for simple reasons of self-preservation therefore...

*"The arguments of the Benetton-company could be credible in one case only - by concentrating economic str
with the same methods against worldwide disgraces which are denounced - beside and beyond of company-adv
the way they are represented,"* has been the commentary of M. Kissler (Center of German Advertising-Council).

Source (text and illustrations): Gefühlsecht - Graphikdesign der Neunziger Jahre, page 114, Verlag Edition Bra
1996. ISBN 3

CRITICS WITH INHERENT DRAMA

THE CREATIVE FORCE BEHIND THE BENETTON IMAGES IS PHOTOGRAPHER OLIVIERO TOSCANI, WHO BEGAN WORKING FOR THE COMPANY IN 1982. ACCORDING TO TOSCANI HIS EMPLOYER IS ACTUALLY A ROLE MODEL FOR OTHER ENTERPRISES. 'THEY TELL ME THAT I HAVE TO DO A PIECE OF COMMUNICATION. I THINK THAT THE COMPANY OF THE FUTURE, THE ONE THAT IS TO SURVIVE IN THE FUTURE, IS THE COMPANY THAT WILL HAVE A SOCIAL-POLITICAL RESPONSIBILITY,' HE TOLD SCOTLAND ON SUNDAY. IN DESCRIBPNG HIS RELATION WITH THE CLOTHES GIANT, TOSCANI LIKES TO COMPARE HIS SITUATION TO THAT OF AN ARTIST SUCH AS MICHELANGELO WHO WORKED FOR THE ROMAN CATHOLIC CHURCH. IN FACT HE THINKS THAT 'COMPANIES ARE THE NEW CHURCHES'.

BEYOND ITS UNIQUE ADVERTISING CAMPAIGNS, BENETTON IS ALSO ENGAGED IN DIRECT HUMANITARIAN ACTION. TOGETHER WITH THE FRENCH ANTI-RACIST ASSOCIATION, SOS-RACISME, IT HAS RAISED DONATIONS FOR SOME OF THE POOREST AFRICAN COUNTRIES. THROUGH THE 'ITALIAN ASSOCIAZIONE PER LA PACE' IT HELPS SUPPORT WAR VICTIMS IN BOSNIA WHILE IN SOUTH AFRICA THE COMPANY HAS ORGANIZED A SERIES OF CULTURAL WORKSHOPS AND SEMINARS. IN 1996 BENETTON IMPLEMENTED 'THE COLOURS OF PEACE', A PROJECT TO SUPPLY 130,000 SCHOOL CHILDREN IN EUROPE WITH BOOKS AND POSTERS TO ENCOURAGE THEM TO BE TOLERANT AND TO RESPECT OTHER CULTURES.

UNITED COLORS
OF BENETTON

UNITED COLOR
OF BENETTON

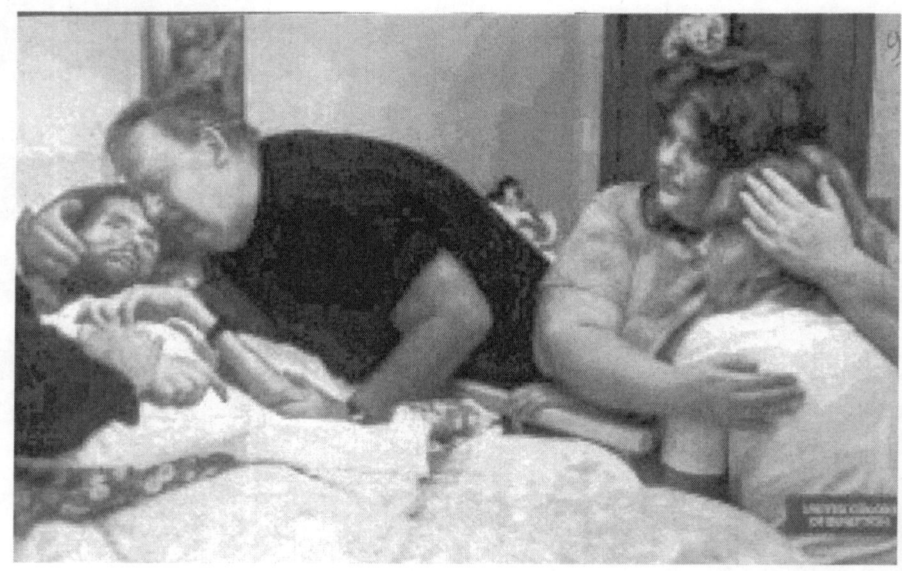

(a) Copy thinking and copy style
(b) Advertising objectives
(c) Inherent Drama

(4) Can you spell out any other effective creative strategy to appeal to social consciousness?

Historical Background

The Benetton family (comprised of three brothers and a sister) established the Benetton chain in a small Italian town called Treviso. To support his family, Luciano Benetton (born 1935), dropped out of school to sell apparel. His sister Guilana (Born 1937) worked as a knitter on a local factory. Recognizing the potential for new business Luciano and Guilana decided to start their own apparel company. They started off small by selling sweaters and as the business grew, the remaining two brothers joined in the activities of the company. Each of them took responsibility for one aspect of the business. Luciano concentrated on marketing, Guiliana directed the design department; Gilberto (born 1941) handled administration and finance and Carlo (born 1943) managed production.

As the business picked up, the company entered into an agreement to open a store for the exclusive marketing of apparel. The first store was opened in 1969 and was an immediate success, the same year; it went overseas by opening a similar store in Paris. Unlike most small producers, who opted for the widest possible distribution, they decided to create a network of exclusive distribution and used sub contractors. The chain soon expanded across the world and established strong brand equity. The company is listed in Milan, London, Frankfurt, New York, Toronto and Tokyo stock exchanges. The company operated in about 120 countries through more than 1000 retail stores.

Now let us have some information regarding production and distribution system of Benetton.

PRODUCTION: Consistently high quality is one of the fundamental characteristics of the Benetton production process from the raw material to finished garment.

Production Process includes:

1. **DYEING:** Since the beginning, dyeing has always been a crucial phase in the Benetton production process.
2. **COMPUTERISED KNITTING MACHINES:** Benetton is the world's largest consumer of pure virgin wool and operates with a structure of computerized machines that are programmed to operate all knitting phases.
3. **SEAMLESS SWEATER:** One of the Benetton's innovations is the computerized knitting procedure capable of producing a complete seamless sweater in half an hour. Thanks to the software program conceived by Benetton specialists.

DISTRIBUTION: From the very beginning, Benetton decided to maintain direct control of logistics phase and has invested in automating processes in order to achieve total integration within production cycle.

Distribution Process includes:

1. **AUTOMATED SORTING SYSTEM:** System through which flat and hanging garments are automatically sorted over 110 million items a year, packed and sent directly to automated distribution system.
2. **AUTOMATED SHIPPING:** Automated distribution system covers an area of 20,000 square meters, with a total of 40,000 boxes and is able to handle 20,000 incoming and 20,000 outgoing boxes.

The group's ability to engage with society is evident in Fabrica, which is Benetton's Communication Research Centre. Fabrica's challenge is both an innovative and an international one. It is a way of marrying culture and industry, using communication which no longer rely on the usual forms of advertising, but transmit "Industry culture" and company's intelligence through other means: design, music, cinema, photography, publishing and Internet.

Analysis of Benetton

Range of Advertisements

Until the 1980s, Benetton advertisements were of the traditional form and largely focused on its product and logo (stylized knot of yarn with word Benetton printed under it, contained within a dark green rectangle).

In 1982, Luciano Benetton hired Oliviero Toscani, a prominent fashion and advertisements photographer. He was given the responsibility to head the advertising department of the company.

Toscani's first theme featured teenagers and kids from culturally diverse nations. Colorfully dressed in Benetton attire the kids engaged in a variety of playful acts. It was from these advertisements that the world famous inspirational trademark "*United Colors of Benetton*" emerged.

In 1988, the company started mixing culture and legends. New advertisements featured Adam and Eve, Joan of Arc and Marilyn Monroe, Leonardo De Vinci and Julius Caesar, with the slogan "United *Superstars of Benetton.*" Similarly campaigns were also done with the animals – a wolf and a lamb with the tagline "*United Friends of Benetton.*"

This type of advertisements created confusion in the minds of the viewers, which gave rise to questions such as:

- **What does this image mean?**
- **Why does this image appear with a Benetton logo?**

In the late 1980s, it showed a black woman breast feeding a white baby. This ad received severe criticism because many people thought that Benetton was reminding the black community of the US and UK of the times of slavery when black women were forced to breast – feed the babies of white.

Another ad which created furore among the black groups in the US, when it showed an angelic looking white child embracing a black one whose hair shaped into devil's horns.

Throughout the early 90s Benetton advertisements featured a cemetery, many different brightly colored condoms, a baby with an umbilical cord, a priest and a nun kissing, etc.

The advertisement featuring the priest kissing the nun seriously offended the Pope of Vatican and the religious sentiments of many.

In 1992, Toscani combined advertisements with politics to further promote the Benetton image. He selected the photojournalistic images concerning the AIDS Crisis, Environmental Disasters, Political Violence, War, Exile etc.

The HIV ad showed close up of various parts of the human body (pubis, arms, stomach, and bottom) tattooed with the English abbreviation "HIV Positive". The tattooed mark was similar to the numbers tattooed by the Nazis on Concentration Camp prisoners.

Benetton advertisements also promoted homosexuality, they showed two smiling men cheek to cheek and two women – one black and the other white holding an Asian baby wrapped in the same blanket etc.

Other controversial advertisements included a black stallion mounting a white mare. These advertisements were severely rebuked by the government, media, and the general public.

In Jan 2000, Benetton released its death row advertising campaign, which featured prisoners who had been sentenced to death. The booklet included photos of 26 inmates and interviews in which they discussed about life and their punishment.

"Big Idea" as main Concept

Q.1 Do Benetton advertisements carry "a big idea" as their main concept?

When we discuss marketing strategies in the present day and age, we immediately think of advertising, why is that? Firstly, it is considered as one of the important elements of marketing. Advertising is one of the few elements that tend to roll most of the different aspects of marketing into one. It is a division of the general promotion process, along with personal selling, sales promotion and public relations. In order for a company to succeed, it is almost necessary for them to advertise their product.

Advertising is very common and there are many techniques used to entice consumers: unfortunately, some advertisers go to extremes to persuade consumers, which can create social problems. One such extremist is Oliviero Toscani, better known as the photographer and creative director of Benetton advertising. However, Oliviero Toscani is not an extremist in the sense of irrationality, but he is rather quite an organized, intelligent and original creator, whose marketing strategies for Benetton have been known as controversial and somewhat politically incorrect.

Benetton's advertising campaigns and social communication strategies are a clear echo of the present-day culture and society. The "United Colors or Benetton" campaign transformed the traditional notions of advertising. Benetton advertisements definitely carry "a big idea" as their main concept. Their goal is not only simply sell their products, the brand name or to create a desire of purchase, but also to promote social concerns, critiques and ideologies. Benetton claims that, "our strategy of advertising is to 'communicate' to consumers, rather than to sell to them." All over the world, Benetton stands for multi – culturalism, world peace, racial harmony, a progressive approach towards serious social issues and colorful sportswear.

It is interesting to see, how controversy has accompanied every advertising campaign that Oliviero Toscani has created for United Colors of Benetton. In this case, promotion of the product is not the only motivation for the advertising; almost equally important is that the advertising campaigns are hoping to promote the company. This was mainly achieved by creatively explaining the company's philosophy to the clients.

In place of the product, Benetton presented powerful and problematic visual images of social issues of global importance such as: environmental disasters, peace, Aids, terrorism, murder, struggle against racism and capital punishment, in their advertising campaigns. This strategy was born of the company's wish to produce images of global issues for its global consumers. The company's strategy was that issues, not clothes, played the lead role. Through time, they opted to utilize issues that appealed and concerned both young and old.

So, Benetton does have a latent "big idea" underlying its main concept. Benetton supposedly believes that it is important to take a standpoint in the real world instead of using their advertising budget to carry on the myth that, "they can make consumer happy through the mere purchase of their product."

We can understand their "big idea" through the given example of Benetton advertisement that shows, what was supposed to be a bloodied clothing of a Bosnian war victim. There can be no other better way to show what war does to precious human lives. Similarly, other advertisements featuring bloody victims of war, a black woman nursing a white baby, a black man handcuffed to a white man's arm, an Aids patient and his family moments before his death are just the finest images capturing human feelings at their emotional best.

There are two views regarding this advertisement:

(1) The people who are associated with Benetton, believe that they mean to shock people with such advertising and that when many people see an image this powerful, it can raise their collective conscience which can then result in action.

(2) On the other hand, critics accuse Benetton of exploiting human sufferings to sell its products. Advertising self- regulatory bodies in Britain, France and Spain have condemned and rejected this advertisement. They have denounced this advertisement as "advertising terrorism"

Sarajevo's daily newspaper, however, applauded Benetton for drawing attention to the war and asked Benetton for posters of the advertisement to plaster across the city.

We can say that Benetton's advertisement does have a "big idea" that it dramatizes the world's worst issues, while simultaneously grabbing people's attention and thus, exposing and selling their brand.

Advertising Clutter

Q.2 Many people believe that some advertisers are going too far in their efforts to break through the advertising clutter and have an impact on consumers. Give your views in relation to Benetton Ads.

In today's world where advertising is at its boom, we as consumers are constantly exposed to the advertisements of various kinds with the sole objective of grabbing our attention. These ever-increasing number of advertisements ensure the survival of only those advertisements which are different from others.

Thus, in order to gain attention, advertising agencies are always in a lookout for new, interesting and different ways which will make them stand out from the rest of the crowd.

May be, to have its own individual identity among others, Benetton became the first company to eliminate the picture of its products from its advertisements in 1989. This is a very bold step on the part of Benetton, because no other company has been able to follow its footsteps even till now.

Instead of their products, Benetton uses powerful images of Aids victims, racism, war, diseases, religious intolerance etc.

This attempt of theirs' has been successful enough because such advertisements have become synonymous with Benetton's corporate image. This has registered them in the minds of the people who identify advertisements relating to social messages with Benetton.

Despite claims of Benetton that profit was never a motive and raising social conscience is their single goal, Benetton advertisements have been widely criticized for their in – your – face advertisements for years and years. But, this surely has helped them break through the advertising clutter.

The company's President – Luciano Benetton insists that if he cannot offer solutions to the existing problems at least he can make the people more aware and may be this will lead to action when such advertisements will raise collective consciousness.

Thus, though Benetton is known for provocative advertisements aimed at sparking awareness of controversial social issues, they are also giving chances to people when no one else is willing to listen to.

All these efforts of Benetton surely shock the people all over the world who find it difficult to view the realities of the world. This also has an ever – lasting effects on the minds of their customers who associate this brand with social service. This will definitely take this company a long - way as the impact of these advertisements is simply unforgettable.

So, in the end we can say that Benetton advertisements have not gone too far in breaking away from the advertising clutter and have always broken the rules and will continue to do so and shock the people. But, in the process, it may also get them, to think about some of the world's problems. They are trying to put a human face back on those whom society dehumanizes and this has enabled them to march miles ahead of their competitors, and have also helped them ensure a place in the hearts of the people who associate them with social service.

Q.3 Examining the symbolic picture of a slain Bosnia solider.

All Benetton advertisements have a typical style of depicting a socially relevant image through their advertisements, which convey a social message. Throughout the world Benetton has been known for its shocking advertising. Benetton has worked on various themes such as Racism, Aids awareness campaign, Death penalty and War. These are designed in such a way so as to jolt the consumer and make him or her to think about the issue.

For instance, in its advertisement against racism, three hearts are shown with white, black and yellow written across them. The message that it conveys us that underneath our skins we all are the same.

Benetton came with its Aids awareness campaign at the time when people were not aware of the causes of transmission of the disease. In another advertisement photos of blood like those used in Aids testing places are shown. Names of the famous world leaders are shown on the vitals in an attempt to show that no one is immune to virus.

At this time when Aids was known to be transmitted only between gay men and HIV drug users, Benetton wanted to create awareness about the desease. Benetton has always attempted to shock people and open their eyes to the realities of the world. In one of its advertisements against war, it shows a single wresting image of a dead soldier's uniform, who died in Bosnia war. This image conveys the horrors of war and is thus, a symbolic image.

Thus the advertising objective was to create an impact and promote unity and brotherhood in the world. Also, by doing such advertisement, Benetton wanted to position itself in the market across the globe as a socially conscious brand. Benetton with its logo "United Colors of Benetton" wants to sell its product to everyone irrespective of what race they belong to. But since the clothes are very expensive, it only caters to high- income group. This shows that though they raise global social issues their market is highly segmented.

Copy Thinking

1. Copy thinking is the process of thinking about the final ad process. It is the innovative art in the making of an advertisement.
2. In words of Luciano Benetton, "Good advertising does not just circulate information. It penetrates the public mind with desires and beliefs."
3. Benetton uses one of the most innovative and courageous copy thinking in its advertising.
4. Over the years if has avoided the usage of beautiful models and has put up images from the real life. Images which demand attention such as the World war 3 placing beautiful models will never inspire anyone for a long while but presenting the ads in Benetton's style may at least make a few people think seriously about issues.

Copy Style

Copy style is the final outcome of any advertising procedure. It is the advertisement itself which appears in a newspaper or in any other mass media.

As William Bernbach puts it in a forthright manner, "all of us who professionally use the mass media are the shapers of society. We can brutalize it or we can lift it into a higher level."

This is what exactly Benetton is doing. Their sole objective is to raise the level of consciousness of our society. Benetton ads carry a social message and that goes into the heart of their advertising efforts.

Q.4 Any other effective creative strategy to appeal to social consciousness.

In the social marketing approach to communications, activities to achieve objectives are based on formative research to uncover the facts related to the intervention, implementation, and testing of messages and behaviors with the target groups themselves, and evaluation to determine the success of the intervention. Research is conducted to understand the cultural, attitudinal, economic, and logistical resistances that prevent people from carrying out the desirable behaviors. Such data provide critical information to formulate better – targeted and more effective messages, which eventually lead to better reception by the public - the ultimate beneficiaries.

Well – designed communications are creative. They do not merely convey information in a conventional, factual manner, but deliver a message based upon the knowledge, attitudes, and perceptions of the target group. Based on formative research, an attractive "image" of fortified foods or supplements is portrayed and supported via mass and interpersonal communication. Messages contain effective appeals or motivational statements. What is of greatest concern to mothers? Is it their own health, the health of their babies, the difficulty of adopting a certain behavior, or religious or cultural beliefs about certain behaviors?

Messages must address and respect these concerns, and at the same time appeal for behavior change. Many creative approaches and methodologies of social marketing are similar to the manner in which commercial advertisers approach product promotion. Advocacy, a component of social marketing, involves raising the consciousness of decision – makers at any number of level from officials of UN agencies to national political leaders and technocrats, from provincial leaders to village panchayts.

Inherent Drama

"Everyone dies but not everyone fully lives". Writer, thinker and philosopher George Bernard Shaw with these words made us realize that perhaps we are not living our lives to the maximum. We tend to neglect the realities of the society and the world drastically. By its advertisements. Benetton tries to bring the reality of the society to the people and at the same time become close to the people and being talked about in the society.

Benetton works on controversial images only, because the company says it wants to raise the social consciousness of the people who are living in their cocoon and by this they can bring in result in action. Benetton always claim that their images have the power which can raise the collective consciousness or words for the united world. Their ads are so shocking that Oliviero Toscani, the controversial photographer behind Benetton's advertising campaigns, has been hired by the World Health Organisation in its effort to combat smoking.

Mr. Toscani will create hard – hitting advertisements for the organisation, which is campaigning for a worldwide ban on tobacco promotion. Mr. Toscani developed a reputation for his ability to shock. His campaigns for the fashion retailer used controversial images such as depictions of Christ's crucifixion and photographs real prisoners on death row in the US. It's just the drama of creating publicity and image so that everybody thinks that Benetton has always taken care of the world problem rather than selling its product.

In fashion industry their primary target market consists of young people. Younger consumers are less likely to perceive shock ads as offensive or in bad taste and may even help create favourble attitudes toward these companies because of their edgy, rebellious tone. When viewing advertising as art it becomes difficult to say where one ends and the other begins. If one views the Benetton ads as a form of art this suggests that there should be a wide tolerance for the types of images used. Some people question this position however, since advertising is instrusive in nature and the public cannot control what images they will be exposed to in the media. Advertising must often respond to a different set of standards since consumers often have no way to controlling their exposure to the images used in advertising and these images may often be offensive to many.

Benetton has always had an image as somewhat of a renegade in the advertising world because of the shock approaches the company often uses. However, the company is known for being very socially concerned and trying to make consumers realize the realities of the world in which they live. One might question whether the type of publicity Benetton is getting from its shock ads is really beneficial to the company. On the other hand, most of its customers are young people who may identify with the issues and causes the company is raising in these ads.

Conclusion

Benetton advertising campaigns addressed social and political issues. Oliviero Toscani said "I am not here to sell pullovers, but to promote an image."

Benetton is one of the strongest brands in the world and adding to it is the popularity of the company's advertising strategy. The biggest accolade that the company received was for its practice to separate its products from advertisement.

Benetton is well known across the world for its usual advertising techniques and themes, most of them bordering on controversy and debate. Benetton utilized "shock values" and the reality of photographs to grab viewer's attention and to make their brand name memorable.

Benetton advertising campaigns address social and political issues like racial integration, Aids awareness, war, poverty, child labour, health etc.

The campaign tried more to "communicate" to the world about these issues rather than to "sell" apparel and accessories.

The company strives to promote itself as a socially responsible business by supporting social organizations and discussing moral issues in its print campaign throughout the world. The company opted for a communication strategy in which issues and not clothes play the lead part.

Benetton team said "Unlike our traditional ads our image usually have no copy and no product, only our logo. They do not tell anyone to buy their products nor do they imply it. Some of the positive as well negative perceptions about Benetton way of ad making are:

Positive:

(1) Benetton advertisement does have a big idea. To put in David Ogilvy's words, "a big idea is one which makes you gasp as you see it the first time and is unique". In addition to this they are using social messages to promote their product.

(2) Benetton advertisements show a minor image of society and do not go for promoting their products.

(3) They are focusing the social issues still prevalent in the modern society.
(4) They are able to present their United Colors of Benetton theme.

Negative:

(1) Benetton does focus the social issues but not focusing on the real nerve of the business that's selling and so, facing certain problems in today's market of great competition.
(2) They are able to shock people through their advertisements, create awareness but are not able to persuade people to purchase product. True, by their very strong nature of copy writing and copy thinking they have been able to present a unique idea and versatility. All their copy themes have got some inherent drama which is able to bind the viewers at once.

Benetton seem to take the virtuous stand for the betterment of humanity and thus create a sense of power in the viewer who agrees with the safe politically correct message even if the message is made with shocking images, by empowering the viewer, the consumer, the company associates itself with engineered feeling of empowerment and righteousness. Through the use of such images, Benetton as a company has become icon for this kind of protest in advertising which tries to claim the ability to encourage collective consciousnesses towards a more desirable world order.

According to Benetton workers it is the press, religion and politics that are most to blame for creating a climate of intolerance. The press by showing negative images of conflicts, politicians for not resolving disputes and religion for frequently being the source of dispute. 'If journalists would be artists, and if politicians would be artists, the world would be different', Toscani told Scotland on a Sunday. And in his introduction to **'Enemies' Luciano Benetton wrote: Conflicts aside, people want to live, buy and sell,** fall in love. That which is divided by politics and religion, is united by the daily, normal qualities of life and relationships. There's a world where bombs scatter death among ordinary people; **sometimes when they're running one of the most ordinary errands,** like shopping,: this is exactly where we've tried to record the deep longing for peace of two people divided by an endemic conflict.'

VIII

The Big Idea Came in A Blue Moon

Pradeep Kar stunned the readership of the Sunday Times of India on April 20, 2000. That included virtually the majority of Indians who read English language newspapers.

A blank first page, with only a few small lines informing you that the most important news is on the last page.

Turning to it instantly (easy to do), we were informed about his web site with the new spelling of India, ensuring that the name was remembered.

The ad grabbed your attention, ensured recall, and the inner pages 2 and 3 had illustrative photographs of the contents of the site.

Many people consider that this is the greatest ad they have seen for decades, that this was innovative genius at its peak. Others decried the ad as well as the newspaper for its unprecedented decision.

With Microland and his new dotcom, Pradeep has VC investors, who are at a roll call of the most successful and eclectic names in the world, beating a path to his door, wanting a piece of his action. And he is hardly forty years old! What other great ventures he and his wife Kalpana were going to conceive and incubate only he and his wife can dream of ....

Advertising Task

1. "Creative advertising, non-creative advertising .... Why isn't anyone talking about good advertising? That's what counts." Examine this statement in relation to Microland advertisement in the Time of India.

The Sunday Times of India April 16, 2000

Page: 1

THE SUNDAY TIMES

Breaking 162 years of perfect tradition, catch the headlines on the last page today.

Page No.2

It happens

Chat

Cinemaa

e-campus

Women

Sports

Page No.23

only in Indya

travel

smart search

e-mail

Singles club

and e-cards, news, astrology, discussion boards, newsletters, music, help. Drop in at

www.indya.com

indya.com™

Page : 24

indya

India changes its name today

India changes forever, Indya.com™ launches today. Signifying not only an errant spelling change, but unleashing a bold new face of a nation.

In news rooms, chat sessions, across e-mail, the world meets a new identity.

Speaking sports and movies. Discussing astrology and travel. Women and a singles club-co-existing.

All this and more at Indya.com. A whole world with a strong indyan accent.

indya.com™

It happens only in Indya

2. Do you think best advertising should have a touch of audacity about it (makes you turn around and say, “arre what is this! It most jolt you out of your slumber). Give your views with justification and with one example.
3. Does this particular ad insult the readership, landing up being irritating? Give your views on Times of India decision to break 162 years of their own tradition.

Gateway to the Topic

Ideas are driving the economy and are changing the world. Finding an idea is something like passing through a tunnel; in search of light at the end. But the big idea just flashes in the brain unexpected all of a sudden.

Big idea means an “Artistic Impression”. An Idea may come from an average person but big idea comes from an exceptional person who is full of fanciful ideas and that’s what makes him different.

The words like idea and business are interrelated because every business starts with an idea. No matter what that idea is, a well thought out business plan is what turns it into reality.

Today, in the competitive environment, big idea is of great relevance. It’s the big idea which helps the product to sell today and build brands for the future.

Though the big ideas are elusive but still they are pursued by the ad agencies, since the advertisements have to build brands alongwith “creative brilliance” and thereby start selling.

Just a few years ago, there was an example of sheer brilliant idea that created a storm in the market, in ‘Times of India’, the Sunday Edition of April 20, 2000. It was given by Mr. Pradeep Kar. The first page was blank with a few lines indicating that the most important news is on the last page which was regarding his web site with the new spelling of India – ‘Indya’. What was it? It was his big idea which he presented in front of people through a creative advertisement. It was a great success in the year 2000 and the bell still continues to ring. This was something that normal people had never before seen. The impact was so strong that it created a stir in the world of advertising.

According to market sources, Microland paid somewhere in excess of Rs. 3 crore to buy out the entire Times of India front page and three inside pages and turned the pages into an advertisement for their portal. Indya.com got what they wanted – ATTENTION! The ad was something no one could ignore. Some called it an excellent way of branding, some a foolish way to blow out money.

Breaking 162 years of tradition ....was it really worth it? Was it a big idea? Was it so creative? Or was it creative at the cost of readership? Many people considered that this was the greatest ad seen for decades. On the other hand many believed that this kind of ad was the most unethical thing which the company and the newspaper had done.

But whether the ad was ethical or not, creative or not, a good ad or so, appropriate or not so appropriate or whether others should follow suit or not .... we are going to find out in the next few pages.

Task One

Creative advertising, non creative advertising .... why isn't anyone taking about good advertising? That's what counts. Examine the statement in relation to Microland's advertisement in the Times of India.

Firstly, let us try to understand

- Creative advertising
- Non-creative advertising
- Good advertising

Creativity is the range of abilities. It is a complex process whose outcome depends on the forces within the individual and outside. In an Ad, creativity is essentially planning, thinking and making big ideas. The big idea flashes in the brain all of a sudden. Creative process which generates "the Big Idea" helps the product to sell today and build the brand for the future. Eg like Amul "Utterly Butterly delicious", Raymond's "The Complete Man". In these Big Ideas there's proposition of creativity and effectiveness. So in every advertisement creativity has to be an inherent component of the ad.

Non-creative advertising is something where the presenter wants to publicize with the help of a celebrity or an exotic location without giving much importance to the basic concept or the requirement of the audience. The ad generally lacks the essential ingredient to be different. These ads are used generally with the content of matrimonial, classifieds etc where only a limited crowd is interested. The fact cannot be denied that the business could be easily enhanced with use of creative advertising but absence of willingness for difference doesn't allow the scope for improvement.

With relation to the Microland's ad in Times of India.

As we discussed about the good advertising, this ad is surely a good example. This ad has a pinch of creative-mindedness in itself but still the main attraction is its catch which is the excellent presentation. The presentation of the ad scores over its creativeness. The creator "Pradeep Kar" went beyond the limits of imagination. Leaving the first page blank itself caught the attention of readers, some in irritation, some in curiosity, in some way or the other it made an impact on their mind.

Good copy can't be written with tongue in cheek, written just for a living. You have got to believe in it. – David Ogilvy

The Times of India hit two targets from a bullet –

- They made a lot of money from the stunt.

- And also the expected damage to brand was safeguarded as they had very correctly calculated their brand equity, which was good enough for the task.

Thus the faith was restored.

If it does not sell it is not creative – David Ogilvy

The campaign must be considered to be a success as the objective was achieved and selling of the site was very profitable.

Task Two

Should best advertising have a touch of audacity about it?

What exactly is Audacity? Is it some kind of a thrill? Is it an excitement? Or is it when one feels energized. Or is it a combination of all these and many more feelings as well as sensitiveness. But one thing goes for sure. Audacity stands for some bold, daring act, even bordering on impertinence.

"If wooing the people is what advertising is all about, then knowing what will interest and excite them is a must to win them over". And for that if we have to add audacity, there is no harm to it. Because that's how the generation of today want it to be bold, daring and captivating. Something which jolt them out of their slumbers.

Make an effective, discreet use of sex appeal. There are various kinds of misconceptions among the people about the use of the female form and sex in advertisement. While some people feel that the female form can sell anything, others dismiss it as something cheap and vulgar, and still others feel that it proves more a distraction than as aid. A scantily clad girl showing her smooth, velvety skin may be very good for advertising a hair removing cream or a cleansing milk but you cannot use the face of a beautiful girl or her curvacious body to sell shock absorbers, unless your imagination is so fantastic that you can justify her presence in the advertisement.

Therefore, best advertisement should have a touch of audacity about it. Good advertisement depends on big ideas. Big ideas can drive companies and brands to extraordinary levels of achievement. An idea that doesn't make a difference is not an idea at all. The bigger the difference, the bigger the idea.

Unless and until the advertisement contains the big idea, neither it will attract attention nor induce action.

Moreover, in this era of cut throat, audacious competition advertisements are the necessity. If the advertisement is not daring then the company may lose sales to its competitors. So, in order to penetrate and survive in the market an advertisement has to.

It became a point of discussion at every corner, every desk, and every home. Breaking the 162 years of tradition of front page headline was itself a big idea. Then by giving the punch line – "India changes its name today-INDYA" stunned everybody. Prefect creation with excellent presentation appealed the nation and made itself an ad to remember. In short "creative brilliance by creative genius" or "the big idea."

Good advertising is the trend of the hour which makes one still at it. Each one has a personal opinion about good advertising. On a whole, good advertising is but a blend of different spices.

As thrill for Y-generation, romance for couples, cartoon animation for kids.

Good advertising must:

- Appeal to the psychology of the target group – the same advertisement cannot appeal equally to the men and women, the old, the young, and the kids, the rich and poor.
- Conform to the latest fashion- it is useless highlighting things nobody cares for.
- Have a visual or / and auditory effect – Advertisement in print media should carry attractive visuals: advertisements in electronic media should have jingles or catchy dialogues.
- Be as brief as possible.
- Have both repetition and variation – repetition for continuity and as a valuable recall aid: variation to save the advertisement from monotony.
- Explain how the product is unique and why it should be preferred to others.
- Stay for longer duration.
- Provide another step in the constant process of Evolution

We often use the word creative and non-creative in the world of advertising. But the term creative and non-creative are always considered different from good advertising. In reality, creative and non creative are the important chapters of good advertising. Now even if we create a good ad, still sometime we find something missing. It's the "catch". The instinct that holds you and something which makes an ad perfect. A creation without "catch" is a waste**. Amitabh Bachhan's BPL campaign, home trade's "life means more" campaign.** Even the presence of celebrities couldn't save the fate of the ad which lacks the "catch".

In a country like India where 100 million people holds 100 million opinions, the only motive of the ad is to capture the % mass of the audience. **Hutch which gives standard ads to attract the standard crowd of metro cities. Whereas Airtel, Bsnl etc. being all India company their ads try both rural and urban market by giving more user friendly ads.**

I do not regard ad as entertainment or an art form, but as a medium of information – David Ogilvy

The intention of the ad in the case is not less than being informative. The vital information needed to pass on was the launch of a new web site

www.indya.com is audacious. In this regard we can take the examples of Coke, Pepsi, Limca, Thumps up and so many FMCG products. For dealing with all these aspects of Microland and Times of India joint adventurism, celebrated words of William Bernbach could be relevant:

"Why should anyone look at your ad? The reader doesn't buy his magazine or tune in his radio and TV to see and hear what you have to say ....Then what is the use of saying all the right things in the world if nobody is going to read them? And, believe me, nobody will read them if it is not said with freshness, originality and imagination"

So true, ads should have a sense of audacity about them otherwise we tend to ignore them. Just imagine when in morning breakfast table we try to catch up with headlines, we capture only 3 or 4 ads out of 50 odd ads published. The reason being those 3 or 4 ads were creative in their content and execution.

So we must realise:

"An advertisement is an intrusion: the reader basically doesn't like ads and tries to avoid them if possible. So as an advertiser we become obligated to reward the reader for his patience and his time in allowing us to interrupt the editorial content".

Thus there are two points to be noted:

- It's not debatable that ads should have a sense of audacity about them..... else they will be lost in scanning process.
- But worth noting is another point that audacity should be in good taste else it will not be cherished by readers but criticized.

Task Three

Does this particular ad insult the readership, landing up being irritating?

Now as far as the reaction of the readers is concerned it is different for different readers. This is so because it depends upon how one perceives a given situation.

Some readers decried the advertisement as well as the newspaper for its unprecedented decision. According to them: newspaper is information medium and using its first page for an ad is a bizarre decision. They found the ad irritating and felt that the ad only represented the lust of Times of India to make easy money.

Contrary to this view, some readers felt that the advertisement was the innovative genius at its peak. According to them: there is no rule that the first page of a newspaper cannot be blank or cannot be used for an advertisement. They found the advertisement very refreshing, creative and different from the monotonous routine. They welcome that change wholeheartedly.

The decision of the Times of India was indeed a bold decision. When they broke their own tradition they proved that even though they had set one trend they still dared to set another trend. Thus they managed together into their fold more and more readers and made the ad a highly memorable one. This is what the big idea does. It is indeed great advertising.

Conclusion

Advertising represents a very substantial sector of our country's economy. Its images and messages fill our lives, its brilliance on a good day stimulates out minds and its success dents our pockets. As far as the good advertisement is concerned, it has a memorable, catchy, dynamic style and a very clear message that promises a great benefit to the consumer. In the profession good advertisement captures the big idea and lasts for a long time. A good advertisement will attract attention, stimulate interest, carry convictions and most importantly induce action.

The best part of big idea is that it is remembered for a long duration. Analysis says that the average life span of any advertisement now a days is too short with just a few exceptions but of course we have some advertisements which have deeply looked into our lives and it is next to impossible to forget them. Remember Lalitaji of surf: remember that caption "Did u cherry blossom your shoes today", Amul – The taste of India, Nokia's – connecting people, Eveready's – Give me Red, Pepsi's – Yeh Dil Mange More etc. all these advertisements which can be aptly called "Big ideas".

The big idea helps the product to sell today and build the brand for future by contributing a lot to the brand equity.

Now there are some grey areas of concern. Like sometimes it can happen that the exact message about the product is not conveyed to the viewers in proper sense and in adequate time.

The Big idea should be flexible enough so that the whole campaign can be built around it. So the innermost concept rather than the intellectual concept of big idea should go hand in hand with the product. There should be creative solution to the consumer's problem and it should sum up the brand proposition creatively and efficiently.

In this regard Microland's advertisement satisfies all the criteria and indeed was a wonderful launching ad. Though printing the ad on the first page was considered by many as unethical act still it was a good advertisement and was creative and audacious also. To say in a nutshell, in assiduously quiet way-the Microland's ad was the loudest.

Even though the change of India's name or spelling is decried universally, the ad gave India a new identity. It was no more the age of old India, it was INDYA.

India for the Y – generation. Generation that loves to chat, travel, music, enjoy cinema and generation of e-mail and e-campus. This ad brings to surface new questions and people responded to them, by waking up and shunning the darkness of the night and welcoming the New Dawn.

IX

Fall Of Advertising............Rise of PR
Fact ....Fiction.........or Machination

INTRODUCTION

PR and Advertising are two important fields of communication in the Corporate World. PR and Advertising share differences and similarities between each other. They complement each other and at the same time are at loggerheads too.

Reality in modern world cannot be observed by an individual with just his or her own eyes and ears. One has to depend on the ears and eyes of third party sources that stand between them and reality. Media outlets are the vital links that add meaning to most lives. This link has to be credible enough to be believed. We have no control over how the media presents our information. If they decide to use that information at all. They are not obligated to cover an event or publish a press release just because it is sent to them. Hence it is the job of the personnel in the PR that they create a favourable image in media.

Given the current scenario, where a consumer is exposed to numerous advertisements per day though different media, it is very difficult to create an impression of your brand in the consumer's mind merely by advertising it.

The intention of most advertisements is to inform, persuade or remind about a product-usually with the intention of making a sale.

Whereas the intention of public relations efforts is often to create good – will, to keep the company and/or product in front of the public, or to humanize a company so the public relate to its people or reputation rather than viewing the company as a non-personal entity. And once the people relate to the product or the brand and have confidence in it, this automatically helps in increasing it sales, and thus, the profits of a firm. However, today PR itself is being used as a primary tool to inform the people about a brand as well as to maintain it, and advertising provides further help in doing this

POINT COUNTER POINT

ADVERTISING

1. Advertising is any paid form of non – personal presentation of ideas, goods and services by an identified sponsor.

   —American Marketing Association
2. Advertising is the greatest art form of Twentieth century.

   —Marshall McLuhan
3. Advertising is a mass paid communication, the ultimate purpose of which is to impart information, develop attitude and induce action beneficial to the advertiser — generally the sale of a product or service ——— **Russell Colley**
4. Doing business without advertising is like winking at a girl in the dark, you know what you are doing, but nobody else does.

   —Stewart H Britt
5. Advertising induces people to buy things they do not need and perhaps cannot afford.

   —Kenneth Galbraith
6. Advertising .... A funny business, it is half a business, quarter a profession and quarter an art.
7. You cannot bore people into buying a product

   — David Ogilvy
8. Advertising is one of the most value destroying activity of modern business civilization.

PUBLIC RELATIONS

1. Public Relations is a philosophy and function of management expressed in policies and practices which serve the public to secure its understanding and goodwill.

   — Public Relations Society of America
2. Public Relations is the attempt by information, persuasion and adjustment to engineer public support for an activity, cause, movement or institution.

   — Edward L. Bernays
3. The Fundamental purpose of public relations practice is to establish a two - way of mutual understanding based on truth, knowledge and full information.

   — Sam Black.

4. Public Relations is a service, a craft that must be adapted to the needs of whatever business your company is in.
   — Arthur Roalman in "Profitable Public Relations).
5. PR can provide professional services in promoting products, services, images or ideas by arranging opportunities for exposure in the media.
6. Public Relations can be an organisation's most valuable resource for building brand value, maintaining vitality and establishing credibility.
7. Skillful PR strategists are keenly aware of the value of customer service, loyalty and return - on – investment (ROI), and have the means to deliver.
8. Where customer satisfaction is the catalyst to the healthy CRM environment, and survival of the best is prevalent in a cut throat competitive scenario, Public Relations is the call of the day.

MODERN PR

The functions of modern PR are as follows:

1. Counseling and advising on key management decisions.
2. Providing Strategic inputs to management on the whys and how's of running their business.
3. Provide counsel and strategic advice on all aspects of communication.
4. Management of brand and corporate image.
5. Implementation of events and promotions to further the image of corporates and brands.
6. To act as the interface and decision – maker on all communication being made by a brand or corporate to any and every one of its external and internal target groups .These include:
   - Media relations and management of media messaging.
   - Customer relations and management of employee messaging.
   - Financial stakeholder relations and management stakeholder messaging and many more.

ADVERTISING V/S PR

Advertising and PR are two different functions. However, many businesses do not know the difference. Since spending one's advertising budget and PR budget effectively is crucial one cannot accomplish this important goal unless he/she understands the difference.

When thinking of advertising, billboards, glossy spreads, quarter - page newspapers advertisement and other forms of highly visible promotional material comes to mind.

Press releases, news conference, professional networking and exhibitions or trade shows are examples of PR work. PR will never go for showy displays as advertising mostly does but it is equally important in today's business scenario.

AI Ries and Laura Ries in their "The fall of advertising and the Rise of PR" gives an account of one of Aesop's fables.

"The wind and the sun had a dispute over who was the stronger of the two.

Seeing the traveler down the road, they decided to settle the issue by trying to make the traveler take off his coat. The wind went first, but the harder the wind blew, the more closely the traveler wrapped his coat around him.

Then the sun came out and began to shine. Soon the traveler felt the sun warmth and took of his coat. The sun had won.

Advertising is perceived as an imposition, an unwelcome intruder who needs to be resisted. Advertising is the wind.

PR is the sun. You can't force the media to run your message. It's entirely in their hands. Prospects think the media are trying to be helpful by alerting them to a wonderful new product and service."

PR is a management function. It is concerned with the overall functioning of the organization. It wins at image building of the organization/product/services and is directed towards both internal & external public. PR is a two - way communication.

Advertising is a marketing function, primarily concerned with the promotional functions. Advertising, a one way communication process, is optional for an organisation.

CONCLUSION

In today's fast paced life, cluttered and fast changing media environment, getting your message across with impact to the target audiences, requires a well thought out strategy that must include an innovative and attention getting idea; which is possible only through effective PR.

India is a pasture land for PR with almost 70% of its population living outside the urban areas, with the clutter of advertisements in every media and with the lack of credibility in PR is the be all and end all of communication.

PR and Advertising work together in a series. A brand has lot of PR potential when it's new and different. With effective PR campaign, a new category and a new brand can generate enormous amount of publicity which in process helps in the building of the brand. Word of mouth plays major role in the Indian scenario. After the brand has been established advertising should be used to reinforce those ideas that had already been established earlier by PR. Advertising can serve as a reminder.

Advertising should try to become credible by using ideas that already exist in the consumers mind as a result of the PR campaign. But the future belongs to PR. Speed, accuracy and efficiency will be the key attributes of PR in the coming years. Technology will serve as a major role in the next stage of evolution of PR in India.

Marketing activities take the brand to the people while the PR activity brings people to the brand.

PROGRESS TASKS

1. It is commonly said that advertising today is the "Soul of Modern Business". Is advertising the only affective way of enhancing the sales of products or services up the charts? How far is it safe to rely only on advertising given the clutter and their low credibility in the competitive market environment.
2. Discuss following two statements in relations to PR & Advertising. How far they are truthful and relevant?
   (a) "PR sows the seed, Advertising reaps the harvest."
   (b) "PR can start a fire, Advertising cannot, Advertising can fan the fire after it has been started".
3. Please make an assessment of the comparative role of PR and Advertising towards brand building and provide relevant examples in the Indian context.
4. How far public relations in India is able to take on the role of creating, introducing and popularizing a brand, a company or in launching a public service campaign? Do you think that time has come not to bank only on Advertising but also in investing heavily on PR activities as well?

QUESTION:-

It is commonly said that advertising today is the "Soul of modern business". Is advertising the only effective way of enhancing the sales of products or services up the charts? How far is it safe to rely only on advertising given the clutter and their low credibility in the competitive market environment?

INTRODUCTION:-

In today's corporate world, both Advertising and Public Relations are important fields of communication. Both play a vital role in the market. They go hand in hand & share differences and similarities with significant and noticeable variations.

In reality, one has to depend on the ears and eyes of the third party source i.e., media that stands between reality and individuals.

If we give a glance on the present scenario, the intention of advertisements is to inform, persuade or recall about a product or a service for making a sale through media.

On the other hand, PR is to win goodwill of the organisation, product, and services and is directed towards both internal and external public.

Therefore, marketing activities take the brand to the people while the PR activity brings people to the brand.

A LITTLE MORE DEATILED STATEMENT ABOUT ADVERTISING AND PUBLIC RELATIONS MAY FOLLOW:-

ADVERTISING:

Advertising is a form of communication that typically attempts to persuade potential customers to purchase or to consume more of a particular brand of product or service. Many advertisements are designed to generate increased consumption of those products and services through the creation and reinforcement of "Brand Image" and "Brand Loyalty". For these purposes, advertisements sometimes line up their persuasive message with factual information. Every major medium is used to deliver these messages, including television, radio, cinema, magazines, newspapers, video games, the internet and billboards. Advertising is often placed by an advertising agency on behalf of a company or other organisation.

PUBLIC RELATIONS:-

Public Relations (PR) is the practice of managing the flow of information between an organisation & its publics. Public Relations – often referred to as PR – provides a wide and meaningful exposure to audiences using topics of public interest and news that do not require direct payment. Because public relations place in credible third – party outlets, it offers a third – party legitimacy that advertising does not have.

Now, corporates all round the world have come to acknowledge the truth that the most effective marketing strategy encompasses a much more comprehensive plan of direct actions. These include a communications mix of marketing tools that should cover both Advertising & Public Relations in a big way.

The two work hand in hand to produce desired results. Public Relations can be regarded as a bigger activity than Advertising because it relates to all the communications of the total organisations, whereas Advertising, although it may cost more than Public Relations, is mainly related to the marketing/sales function. It is wise business practice for public relations to work with Advertising, rather than relying solely on Advertising to break into a new market or to introduce a new and unknown product or service.

FUNCTIONS OF PUBLIC REALTIONS

PROFESSIONAL PUBLIC RELATIONS OPERATES IN EVERY SPHERE OF LIFE:-

1. Government – National, Regional, Local & International.
2. Business & Industry – Small, Medium, Transnational (across, beyond)

3. Community and Social Affairs.
4. Educational Instns, Universities, Colleges etc.
5. Hospitals and Health Care.
6. Charities and good causes.
7. International Affairs – Political, Social, Economic, any other.

WE CAN SAY PUBLIC RELATIONS PRACTICE IS:-

(More so in the new context)

1. Counseling based on an understanding of human behviour.
2. Analysing future trends and predicting their consequences.
3. Research into public opinion, attitudes and expectations and advising on necessary action.
4. Establishing and maintaining two ways communication based on truth and full information.
5. Preventing conflict and misunderstanding.
6. Promoting mutual respect and social respectability.
7. Harmonizing the private and the public interest.
8. Promoting goodwill with staff, suppliers and customers.
9. Improving industrial relations.
10. Attracting good personnel and reducing labour turnover.
11. Promotion of products or services.
12. Maximizing profitability.
13. Projecting a corporate image and identity.
14. Encouraging an interest in international affairs.
15. Promoting an understanding of democracy.
16. A new dimension has been added by the rapidly advancing technology and electronics explosion.

PR person must keep with the pace, equip adequately with the knowledge of the latest development. More important – be able to communicate effectively in the different areas of the new knowledge and trends.

In addition to general public relations policy, it is essential to have specific policies for specific publics. Policies are required for employee relations, stockholder relations, buyer, supplier, dealer relations, educational relations, consumer relations and press relations. A Primary responsibility is to ensure that PR policies are understood, accepted and intelligently applied in developing good relations with people inside as well as outside the organization. The execution of public relations policy is the responsibility of everyone connected with an organisation.

TRUE DIMENSIONS:

Whatever the nature and purpose of the organisation, the dimensions of PR activities are wide and all – pervasive.

PR performs at least fourfold role to enable the organisation appreciate its multi- dimensional existence:-

1. To establish and maintain a correct image of the organisation, its personnel, products or services.
2. To monitor outside opinion and convey this intelligence to management.
3. To advise management on communication problems and techniques.
4. To inform publics about policies, activities, personalities, products or services.

   It must be admitted that the success of the above role implies a proper appreciation of the value of PR by management, and of the need for PR – minded management.

POLICIES OF PR

To achieve good public relations an individual or an organisation should place the interests of the people first in every decision and action. Good actions are not enough. They should be effectively communicated to the public to gain their understanding and acceptance. There should also be enough feed back to know that the public have a balanced and fair view of the organisation.

PR DISTINGUISHED FROM ADVERTISING

(British) Institute of Practitioners in Advertising defines Advertising this way – "Advertising presents the most persuasive possible selling message to the right prospects for the product or service at the lowest possible cost".

How does public relations differ from advertising? Let us consider some of the major differences between these two forms of communication. These distinctions are based on the fact that PR is not a form of advertising and it is, in fact, a much bigger activity than advertising. Not until this is fully understood we will have a clear idea or image of PR.

Public Relations is neither "Free advertising" nor "unpaid for advertising". There is nothing "free" about PR: it is time consuming and time costs money. This money may be represented by either staff salaries or consultancy fees. If a story appears in the news column or bulletin, its value cannot be judged by advertisement rates for space or time because editorial space and radio or television program time cannot just be calculated in terms of money.

Advertising may or may not be used by an organization, but organization is involved in public relations. Public Relations embraces everyone and everything, whereas advertising is limited to special selling and buying tasks such as promoting goods, buying supplies or recruiting staff. Public Relations has to do with the total communications of an organisation: It is, therefore, more extensive and comprehensive than advertising. On occasion, PR may use advertising _ that is why PR is neither a form of advertising nor a part of advertising.

OTHER DISTINGUISHING FACTORS:

MESSAGE CONTROL:

A distinct difference between PR and advertising is their extent of message control, when, where and how an advertisement will come is quite controllable: Ad space purchased in the right format means one has total control over what messages are communicated.

On the other hand, while the process of creating messages through public relations is controllable, what occurs after the message has left its source or origin is often uncontrollable. The most common uncontrollable factor is how the media views your information as newsworthy.

SHELF LIFE:

Until recently, TV advertisements have had a shorter life than press releases archived on the internet. For now this is probably still true.

Corporate organsiation are also posting their commercials on the corporate web sites to extend the shelf life of their ads. Stored press releases and news articles still rank high in terms of longevity.

IMPLIED ENDORSEMENT:

No matter how interesting an ad might be, it is recognized as a self – serving communication. The only implication here is that someone paid you to have your message passed to the consumer.

PR ensures the credibility of indirect third party endorsements. You get free coverage of a story about your company through the print or the electronic media. This means you are not paying to get advertising placed, but the publication is freely giving space to a story about your company.

COST:

Advertising costs huge amounts of money. Whether you advertise on a billboard or in prime time television ads will consume the budget faster. For companies, PR is a better method for direct and personal communication with a target audience.

QUESTION

Discuss the following two statements in relation to PR and Advertising. How far they are truthful and relevant?

- “PR sows the seeds, advertising reaps the harvest”
- “PR can start the fire, advertising cannot, advertising can fan the fire after it has been started”.

ANSWER

The statements definitely hold true. As the cliché goes, for any building to be built, what is most important is the foundation on which it is being built.

But somehow the final appreciation or criticism which comes forth is that for the building and not for the foundation per se. The significance of the foundation get hidden somewhere beneath the grandeur of the mansion.

In very similar terms, in the realm of mass media, PR is the foundation while advertisement is the building. The base for any endeavor is first conceptualized by the PR division and then based on that, the ad department builds on it, the plot and the storyline for the same.

EXAMPLES-

Take for example, Pepsi's advertisements. The concept of "Youngistan", i.e., to capture the youth, major consumer of the drink, must have been thought about by the PR department. Then, the ad department must have devised the plot. Popular youth icons of today, Ranbir Kapoor & Deepika Padukone were roped in as the main protagonists. Then, sponsoring shows like "Yeh hai Youngistan meri jann" on MTV also formed a part of addressing the youth.

Advertising is a marketing function which is used to catch the attention of the customer with the help of use of pictures. Inherently, advertising is done with the purpose that is not to a build a brand value but to 'defend" it. It has been built primarily by PR. That is the reason advertisement has lost its influence to put a new brand in the mind. Reasons why advertisements have lost their influence.

- People look at ads in whatever manner they want or the way they read a novel or watching a T.V. serial.
- Because of "too much ads", "too much clutter" begins in the market.
- As a result its effectiveness as a tool of persuasion, awareness creation and information is vanishing.
- It had credibility but is losing rapidly. Why is the motivation of sale of a product lacking today?

Now, what is PR and how is it prevailing?

"PR can start a fire, advertising cannot, advertising can fan the fire after it has been started"

This is a true statement, PR can start a fire, and it means if you don't have a simple idea to drive your company or brand then a PR person can help you.

PR person knows what the demand of the public is and what their requirement is and thereafter the company launches its product. After launching a product a constant reminder is given to the public through advertising.

Why is it said PR starts a fire:

1. PR plays a vital role in brand building.
2. Credibility is obtained through factual information.
3. Makes a significant impact on shaping public opinion and provides instant credibility due to the power of the press.

4. Advertising can be a tool of PR; however PR is not the tool of Advertising.

PR is a management function. It is concerned with the overall functioning of the organisation. It wins at image building of the organisation/product/services and is directed towards both internal and external public by constant two way communication.

A new brand must be generating favorable coverage in the media or it will not have a chance in the market place.

What others say about product is more powerful than what you are saying about it yourself. That's the way PR in general is more powerful than advertising. And that is why over the past two decades PR has surpassed advertising as most powerful force in branding.

When you have a good brand with right qualities, public will believe you and certainly they will hear what you are saying about your brand. Credentials are particularly important in this process.

THE LAW OF HYPE

When things are going well, a company doesn't need the hype. When you need the hype it usually means that you are in trouble.

Press releases, news conference, professional networking, exhibition or trade shows are examples of PR work, PR is not as flashy as advertising but it is as important and much more.

Once again we may refer to Al Ries & Laura Ries example of Wind and the Sun.

Advertising is perceived as an imposition, an unwelcome intruder which needs to be resisted. Advertising is the wind.

PR is the sun. You cannot force the media to run your message. It's entirely in their hands. Prospects think that media are trying to be helpful by alerting them to a wonderful new product and service.

So this is the general rule that PR comes first and Advertising is the second.

QUESTION

Please make an assessment of the comparative role of PR and Advertising towards Brand building and provide relevant examples in the Indian context.

Answer:

Advertisement is a paid form, the ultimate purpose of which is to impart information, develop attitude and induce an action beneficial to the advertiser, generally, the sale of a product or service.

ROLE OF ADVERTISING THROUGH CONVENTIONAL APPROACH–

1. The company develops a new product or service.
2. The company researches the new product or service to make sure it offers consumers a significant benefit.

3. The company hires an advertising agency to launch the new product or service with a "big bang" advertising campaign.
4. Over time the advertising builds the new product or service into a powerful brand. Particularly here, Advertising needs the help and support of PR to reach and fulfill its intended objectives.

According to Russell H Colley "PR is a philosophy and function of management expressed in policies and practices which serve the public to secure its understanding and goodwill."

When thinking of advertisements, billboards, glossy spreads, quarter page advertisements and other forms of promotional material comes to mind.

Press releases, news conferences, professional networking, exhibitions or trade shoes are examples of PR work.

In the fast paced life, cluttered and fast changing media, getting your message across with the right impact on the target audience requires a well thought out strategy that must include innovative and attention getting idea which is possible only through effective PR.

A brand has a lot of PR potential when it is new and different. With effective PR campaigns, a new brand can generate enormous amount of publicity which in process helps in brand building. After the process has been established by PR, advertisements should be further used to reinforce the ideas that have been already established by PR i.e. advertisements can serve as a reminder.

The recently launched APPLE iphone is very good example of this. The iphone gained a lot of publicity before it was launched with help of PR campaign that is almost became a craze with the Indian youngsters.

Image makeover is another important aspect of brand building. It is done to improve the already established image of a brand/product or when it has gone through a bad phase. When coca cola was going through the pesticide crisis, its brand ambassador appeared in front of its plant on screen trying to assure it to be a safe drink. People were invited to come and watch it being manufactured.

PR is more trustworthy, reliable and credible. Since it involves a 3rd party endorsement and use of word of mouth, it gains the consumers' trust better. Advertisement is self-appreciation and people believe it to be a pitch, self praise to get the product sold.

Again it is more entertainment oriented and PR is related with providing the right information, knowledge and truth. It helps in retaining the brand name in the customer's memory for long. What PR does is to personalize or humanize a product so that the consumer relates to it better. The advertisement impression is often short lived.

Advertisement often assists in reminding the product to the consumer and not the brand whereas, PR tries to upgrade both. For instance, 'Colgate' toothpaste is a well known product in India but consumers are less aware of the 'UNILEVER' brand attached to it. The same is the case with 'Mazza' mango juice which is attached to Coca Cola brand. This has prompted the companies to bank not only on Advertisement but also PR.

Sometimes the beautiful product that we see in advertisement is a result of PR brain. It is the PR intellectuality which has made it possible for the largest car manufacturing company in India, Maruti Suzuki to cater to the needs of different segments of the target.

EXAMPLES IN INDIAN CONTEXT:

1. **Café Coffee Day (CCD):** One coffee hut which is famous throughout the country without giving any "big bang" on the T.V. by showing commercials.
2. **State Bank of India:** It first made the creditability in public's mind published itself through 3rd party and now when it has established the 2nd step it took by maintaining the brand through advertising.
3. **Coca - cola:** Same in the case of Coca – cola, it established its reputation & then advertises it to maintain its relative position.

Other examples are Bajaj, Hero Honda, Taj Group of Hotels, PVR Cinemas, Godrej, Naukri.com, Nestle India, Philips India, Tata Group of Industries, etc.

QUESTION:

How far public relations in India is able to take on the role of creating, introducing and popularizing a brand, a company or in launching public service campaign? Do you think that time has come not to bank only on advertising but also in investing heavily on the PR activities as well?

Answer:

PR is a good way to build relationship with employees, customers, investors, voter, or the general public. All organisations who have a stake in how they are viewed by the concerned public, employ various levels of public relations.

In India words of mouth play a big role. So, therefore, PR in India is able to take on the role of creating/introducing a brand or launching a public service campaign.

Also India is advertising a lot but also investing heavily on PR activities as well; as it is launching campaigns for illiterates who are not able to understand the advertisements.

Public relations in India although called a 'sunrise' profession have gained its own ground. From the time when a PR professional was just a facilitator of meeting to being the role person who holds the responsibility of maintaining a good image of the company, PR has definitely come a long way.

Coming to the question it is evident that today's major brands are born with PR not advertising.

Let's have a look at the recent past. Look at what PR did to the Iphone. PR makes it a craze everywhere. How many advertisements did we see before the launch of the Iphone in India?

Brands like Mercedes Benz hardly do any advertisements. They are purely confident on their PR strategies.

Leaving along the brands, let's look into some of the major PR campaigns in the recent past.

The TOI Lead India Campaign is a superb example of a highly successful PR campaign.

It has also bagged several awards including the "Cannes lion" award for the best PR campaign. Also the very recent "teach India" campaign from the Times of India has been a successful one.

Moving to the second part of the question, definitely time has come not to bank only on advertisement, but also to rely substantially on PR for effective audience participation.

One simple point would be that advertising is far too expensive in comparison to PR. Another major reason would be the overdose of advertisements. The actual message sometimes remains undelivered. As a bigger message has to be covered in a smaller amount of time, it is better in invest in PR. It is more profitable for an investor to invest in PR rather than advertising.

Advertising has been more than extensively used in the past and more and more at present but PR has been underdone. PR consists of many activities, which are called tools of

PR: publications, events, news, community involvement, image and identity setting, lobbying and social investments.

When a customer sees an advertisement, he/she knows it is an advertisement only. PR has a better chance of getting a message through.

Furthermore the message can be fresh and more believable. PR is better equipped to create 'Buzz" about a new product or service.

GROWING PERSONALISED MARKETING

Indian companies are spending far more today in terms of money and effort, lifestyle and other values through creation of large database and thus are inclined more towards personalizing their offers and communication.

Companies such as GM (India), Glaxo India, Maruti Udyog, Citibank, Appollo Tyres and even Air India are leveraging the databases to convert their existing customers into lifelong "Clients". The approach followed by these companies suggest that:

1. Causes for customer desertion.
2. How to convert one time sale into prolonged relationship through customer interaction.
3. Latest methods of personalized communications and marketing.

4. Newer approaches for sharply focused and clearly – targeted programmes.
5. Optimum use of available resources.

Campaigns like AIDS, Peace, Family Planning, Education, and Polio were successful in India for the reason that they were supported by good advertisements and effective PR. In India PR organisations are now organising workshops, skits, play in schools and colleges with the help of their institutional management for creating awareness of these campaigns among youngsters and for illiterate people. They organise camps or plays in the villages or the doctors make them aware of the diseases.

Therefore, advertisements get their inputs from PR. So we cannot completely agree with the statement that advertising is the soul of modern business or that it is the only way of enhancing the sale of products or services up the charts. PR is gradually taking over the place of advertisement and is on its way to become the soul of modern business.

Then, again, take for instance, the IIFA Awards a few years ago. Instead of the customary red carpet, the stars were greeted by a "'green "carpet. Now, here comes the role of the PR department. Green carpet signified "Campaign against Global Warming". Thus, the theme for the ceremony was decided by the PR. The seed was sown by them. It was allowed by the ad department. By implementing it by way of the green carpet. Together with this, some celebrities furthered the cause by adorning a green gown. Thus, the green carpet and the green gown were advertisements for the cause of global warming which was put forth by the PR department.

Hence, the PR and ad departments are complementary to each other.

CONCLUSION

In today's fast paced life, and changing media environment getting messages through direct communication is more important.

The role of public relations is to pique the interest of a target market, not necessarily to persuade them to buy. In order for public relations programme to work, the message must be of interest not only to the public but also the media. The object is to develop a message that the media will deem of great interest to their audiences. Therefore, the key to effective public relations messaging is newsworthiness.

PR and advertising must go hand in hand. Both are dependent on each other. But PR comes first anytime than advertisement.

Advertising should become more credible by using ideas that already exists in the consumers mind as a result of the PR campaigns.

So the future belongs to PR. Speed and accuracy is the strong features of PR.

Marketing activities take the brand to the people while PR activity brings people to the brand.

X

In – House PR Department and Outside Consultancy

Strengths & Weaknesses in the Light of Organizational Needs

Background

ABC Corporation is a multi - unit organisation for mass production of colour TV sets and Audio – visual equipments. It has its corporate office at New Delhi. You have since been recruited by the company as an Executive in its Public Relations Department having a total staff strength of 10 persons from Chief of PR to middle and lower level of employees.

The Problem

Although the company was enjoying considerable reputation in the Industry and consequent buyer support, it has been observed that the image was suffering a down - slide for unknown reasons. The company wanted a fact – finding survey to identify the causes of erosion of buyer confidence and, thereafter, recommendations for effective steps including campaign outlines to prevent any fall in its market share.

The senior management of the company has full confidence in the ability of its In- house PR Department but, considering the seriousness of the problem, feels that a competent outside PR Agency could possibly do this job better.

The Task

The management has asked you to assess the present situation and make a detailed study of the problem and make appropriate recommendations in respect of the following:

(a) Carry out an overall survey of the challenge confronting the company and identify the reasons for the present situation.

(b) Pinpoint relative strengths and weaknesses of both In – house PR and outside PR consultancy.

(c) Recommend appropriate steps either to engage an outside PR consultancy or pass on the responsibility to In – house PR Department. You may also suggest a combination of both but must justify your recommendations adequately.

You are free to assume sales figures, expenses, PR budget, etc, as long as they are logical and realistic.

ANALYSIS OF THE PRESENT SITUATION

The ABC corporation was the largest manufacturer of the colour TV sets and Audio – visual equipments in the country in the 80's. The company enjoyed considerable reputation and substantial market share due to its products quality. Another reason for the success of the company was the absence of any real competition in the market and the absence of new technology in the domestic sector.

During the 90's, when the Indian economy was liberalized, a large number of multinational companies (MNCs) entered the country to tap the ever – expanding market. During the initial years of liberalization the ABC didn't suffer any major setback but from 1995 onwards the sales figures started falling drastically, it has already fallen from a high of Rs. 800 Cr. To Rs. 500 Cr. In the previous year without any sign of recovery.

The technology which was being used by the company was primitive as compared to the latest technology brought in by the new entrants in the industry. The introduction of new, more sophisticated goods in the market gave the consumers a variety of brands to choose from.

The ABC Co. did not take up an appropriate action to retain its consumer base. The new competitors in order to establish themselves in the market were slashing down their prices, coming up with exchange schemes, longer warranty period and assuring the consumers of an efficient after sales service. The ABC, due to a long period of reigning at the top of the market, had a laid back attitude. The advent of MNCs along with their aggressive advertising campaigns saw a huge chunk of consumers going in for new products. Their efficient after sales service and innovative marketing along with technological factors caused a considerable damage to the identity and the image of the ABC Corporation.

The company had an in - house Public Relations Department, but owing to the seriousness of the situation the company thought of engaging a outside PR Agency which could possibly handle the problem better.

Possible Reasons for the Downslide in the Image of ABC Corporation:

(a) **Inadequate PR Efforts –** It is quite possible that the PR efforts of the company was not well planned. They did not keep themselves abreast with the changes in the market scenario. They may not be working in co – ordination with other departments of the company.

(b) **Rise of Competition in the Market –** There has been a sudden spurt of competition in the market for which the company was not prepared. If they had a planned strategy, it is quite possible that downslide of their company's image could have been avoided.

(c) **Press Relations not given due Importance –** Well balanced media and press Relations are a major PR function. They have to be maintained in order to create the right image in the eyes of target public audiences. Failure in this respect might have led to the creation of a hostile press and media.

(d) **Lack of proper fact finding –** there was inadequate fact finding. It is extremely essential for a corporate PR department to get these facts straight which means enough knowledge and information.

(e) **Insufficient efforts to maintain Customer Relations –** After sales customer relations is an important aspect of marketing strategy of any company. The after sales services provided by the corporation were not satisfactory.

(f) **Lack of good feedback –** Feedback which is a part of the research methodology has to be constantly carried out by the PR department. If this aspect is not paid enough attention it could inevitably lead to downfall of the corporation. If they receive a regular feedback they can anticipate and work out their plans accordingly.

INADEQUATE PR BUDGET

Insufficient flow of the funds and resources from the company for PR activities may lead to PR being ineffective and inefficient.

(a) **Stagnant Technology -** To keep abreast with the competitors, it is necessary to have updated technology. Must keep pace with the moving times.

(b) **Rift between Management & Employees -** There has to be absolute harmony between the management and its employees. There has to be healthy communication both upward as well as downward. It is quite possible that the PR dept. failed to bridge the gap between these two. This could have led to a decline in the working standards.

(c) **Community Relations:** It is of immense importance to maintain good community relations. If the corporation fails to do that successfully it can have negative impression in the minds of people.

STEPS TOWARDS PRODUCTIVE SERVICE

In addition to effective and efficient PR, ABC must initiate efforts as under to rejuvenate Co's overall working.

1. To be above competition, the company has to offer quality products, better or equal to the other competitors.
2. Because of increase in selling price, the company has to increase both scale and scope of their production to reduce the selling prices.
3. The design and appearance should be improved so as to attract maximum buyers.
4. New schemes like exchange offer, easy finance, longer guarantee period should be introduced.
5. After sales service and on the spot services should be increased and effectively carried out.
6. More information about the products should be conveyed to the consumers by increasing advertisements, both in print as well as in the electronic media.
7. Trade fairs and buyer – seller meets should be organised from time to time.
8. Offer more dealership to retailers in different parts of the country.

RELATIVE STRENGTHS & WEAKNESSES OF IN – HOUSE PR AND OUTSIDE CONSULTANCY

IN – HOUSE PR

PROS	CONS
1. Organisations having people oriented structures will require in – house PR more to promote and maintain good relationship with emphasis on people aspects at all levels of working.	1. As a result of loyalty to the organisation, many PR persons lose unbiased behaviour, an essential requirement in the profession.
2. In – house PR provides full – time service with continuity of functions. They have direct access to decision-makers within the organisation.	2. In – house PR people normally do not have, nor are they interested in knowing, the good aspects of PR activity in other organisations.
3. Management can easily ensure value for time and money spent on PR activity in diverse fields.	3. Chief Executives of many orgnaisations are easily lured by the slick talk and appearance of Consultants while ignoring the in – house PR capabilities.
4. Relations with the media will be more direct which will ensure immediate feedback and prompt action.	4. Employment conditions prohibit doing away with inefficient PR persons and in effect they become redundant.

5. PR personnel become identified with the aims and objectives of the organisation. They protect the interest of the organisation better in important PR activities like crisis relations and consumer communication.	5. In – house PR persons normally fail to elicit information of value from various sources involved and are at a disadvantage pertaining to national or global communication matters.

PR CONSULTANCY

PROS	CONS
1. Consultancy firms are like advertising agencies who can be dispensed with if found inadequate or inefficient.	1. Lack of continuous functioning is a hindrance to effective build - up of reputation and attachment for the consultant.
2. They normally possess wider range of experience and exposure by working with many organisations.	2. Lack of sufficient knowledge about the organisation for which the consultant is working.
3. Consultants can provide unbiased, impartial service facilitating correct assessment of situation by the management e.g. in emergencies like strikes, natural calamities, consumer resistance etc.	3. While dealing with the press and the government, a consultant will be needed to make frequent reference to the management for seeking approval.
4. They will have locational advantage enabling companies situated at distant places for maintaining line of contact with the government, media and other agencies.	4. Partial service and divided loyalties of consultants create barriers of communication for an organisation.
5. Consultants are better equipped to collect a host of information from the multiple sources which will be of value to the management. They are also able to reach across the world for global communication matters.	5. Most consultants employ inexperienced personnel with lower salaries resulting in half – hearted performance by them.

IN – HOUSE PR

Strengths

Total access and total understanding of the product, the company's philosophy, and the company's goals are the main attractions to having PR professionals on the payroll.

The in - house pro has the advantage of doing "PRBWA" – PR by Walking Around, based on the MBWA (Management by Walking Around) theory. Essentially, PRBWA gives the PR professional the chance "to uncover new ideas and trends in their company" by having conversations with the key players.

Casual conversations with product managers and talking to executives in the cafeteria help to gauge the pulse of the company's plans far better. That's a perspective that is nearly impossible for outside counsel to gain, no matter how close the relationship is between the company and the account team.

PR professionals on staff can also focus their efforts on their company exclusively. Their time is not spread between the numerous accounts they oversee.

Weaknesses

Corporate PR professionals are working within the same framework every day, which can be boring for a creative individual. If the people in the corporate PR department do not actively seek out input they can become stale.

Another pitfall to avoid in corporate PR is letting company loyalty and job security impede your media relations instincts. Corporate PR professionals must remember to view their company from the outside.

The PR people become insulated and can lose touch with how their company is truly perceived. In the event of an emergency, some corporate PR people fall down when it comes time to handle crisis communications. They immediately assume a defensive posture, break nearly every rule of crisis communications, alienate their media contacts, and ultimately do more damage than good for their own company.

OUTSIDE PR CONSULTANCY

Public relations firms help secure favourable public exposure for their clients, advise them in the case of a sudden public crisis, and design strategies to help them attain a certain public image. Toward these ends, public relations firms analyze public or internal sentiment about clients; establish relationships with the media; write speeches and coach clients for interviews; issue press releases; and organize client - sponsored publicity events, such as contests, concerts, exhibits, symposia, and sporting and charity events.

Strengths

In a tight market, it allows a company to have a well – oiled PR machine with an experienced staff, media connections, and the ability to get your message out quickly. The client gets the benefit of the combined experience, knowledge, and skills of professionals. Rarely can a company find a person or a small team that has the level of expertise one can find in a truly professional agency.

Another plus to hiring an agency is it brings an outside point of view to the table. Companies benefit from the objective viewpoint that an outside agency brings. Pushback is hard to do, and possibly suicidal, when you're an employee of the company. In the long run, that impartial viewpoint will strengthen a client's PR programme and make the company look savvier.

An agency has the advantage of being able to offer a "fresh approach." They don't deal with the same message day after day so they are open to new ideas and can offer immediate marketing solutions. Agencies also have so many resources available that they can often launch a campaign more quickly and effectively than an internal department. That's very important when each day counts.

By outsourcing PR duties, companies can focus on what they do best, and concentrate their resources on reaching their business goals, leaving PR to the professionals.

Outsourcing offers a lot of flexibility, especially in times like this, strategic marketing is a company's best weapon. If times are tough, you don't want to disappear from sight, you want to be even more visible. Increasing awareness is the key.

Another bonus to agency PR is that they're easier to fire. If an agency does not produce, the contract can be cancelled, therefore not exposing the client to any long-terms HR risks.

Using consultants is advantageous, because these experts are experienced, well – trained, and abreast of the latest technologies, government regulations, and management and production techniques. In addition, consultants are cost effective, because they can be hired temporarily and can objectively perform their duties, free of the influence of company politics.

Weaknesses

PR firms often tell clients that they need a lot of excessive unnecessary things to get press. Most reporters don't like external PR personnel who are not in touch with what is going on inside the company.

It would now be advisable to prepare a comparative chart of pros and cons of each mode of service.

Finding Appropriate Steps

Do you hire permanent expertise in – house or use an outside consultant or agency? This decision depends very much on the type of your business and the stage it is in. Generally, however, you can use the same process you use in hiring other professionals, such as accountants. Are your needs routine, ongoing and clearly defined? Then perhaps you're ready for in – house staff.

More likely, however, you don't yet know your public relations needs, and you need an outside professional with diverse experience to guide you in determining the scope of your opportunities .You can always retain a consultant to help you decide what kind of help you need and assist you in finding it.

The key when selecting an agency is to pick a specialized agency versus a "generalist ship." A company should look to hire an agency whose experience maps back to the client's industry, so that the agency can deliver turnkey expertise fast.

All these situations are common to growing businesses. All represent tremendous risks and opportunities. And anyone of these situations is all the evidence you need that it's time for your company to review its public relations game plan.

A first step in that decision process ought to be a careful financial analysis; the salary, benefits and overhead costs of an employee versus the fees and expenses of the consultant. If the requirement actually justifies a full time staffer, the employee is likely to be less costly than a comparable consultant.

Probably more significant, however, is the level of knowledge about the organisation an employee will develop compared to a consultant. Day - in and day – out, this detailed knowledge of the organsiation and its products or services produces significant benefits; work is produced more efficiently, it is more likely to be suited to the organisation's culture, and it is more likely to be produced within budget and time constraints. As a spokesperson, an employee is more likely to be perceived by stakeholders as representing the policies and embodying the values of the organisation.

However, a single individual or small team will not meet all requirements, and it probably is not cost – effective to try solving all communications needs in- house. But a skilled and knowledgeable in – house communicator also is the best intermediary with outside consultants.

IN – HOUSE OR CONSULTANCY OR BOTH: RECOMMENDATIONS

Public relations is not sales, hype or spin, and it is more than sending out press releases or holding press conferences. It is the process of strategically planning, organizing and distributing information in ways that meet your company's goals. When practised best, PR works hand – in – hand with other marketing techniques such as advertising, direct mail and special events. But it is much more than a mere tactic. It is an essential process for any growing business, especially if it's a business that seeks to differentiate itself in a highly competitive industry.

Public relations help to overcome executive isolation, something that can affect every organisation sooner or letter. An inescapable assignment of every public relations practitioner is opening the eyes and ears of management to what's really happening "out there."

Here's the dilemma: You have a great product and you need some press. Needless to say, you don't have a huge PR budget, but you're still expected to produce results. Where is your money best spent - on an agency or by hiring a small team in – house?

While the jury is still out on this question, there are some pros and cons to weigh.

By all accounts, a mutually beneficial interaction between the in – house PR and the external PR consultant would be for the ultimate good of a company whether in the private or in the public sector.

Why should PR managers be ready to pay handsomely to consultants for which they themselves are paid? Indeed, this is a question which many find hard to answer. They don't think counseling or PR strategies can be entrusted to outsiders. Many more experts in the field feel otherwise and claim that potential business for consultancies appears limitless. In a world of accelerating client needs, there is no denying that PR consultancies can make genuine and far – reaching contribution towards professionalizing public relations practice. And, truly, consultants in other disciplines are freely commissioned by managements for advice and fresh ideas. And this is done without any reflection on insiders. The same guidelines should apply as well to PR if the profession is to be treated on par with other management disciplines.

PR – In – house department will help to

- Protect the interest of the organisation better in important PR activities like crisis communication, Investors relation and consumer communication. This is already prevailing in the organisation.
- Maintain relations with media will be more direct, ensuring immediate feedback and prompt action, which is very much required to overcome the problem.
- Be sure about the sufficient knowledge about the Organisation.
- Engage in the full time service with continuity of functions, with direct access to decision makers within the organisation, which is very much **needed in the situational crisis.**

WHEREAS PR consultancy will help to

- Possess wider range of experience and exposure by working with many organisations. Collecting host of information from multiple sources which will be of value to the management.
- Provide unbiased, impartial service, facilitating correct assessment of situation by the management e.g. Consumer resistance, which cannot be assessed by the management itself.

Regardless of the choice, PR, like any facet of a business, has to bring results. Whether a company hires its own PR team or hires an agency there has to be a return on investment. This must go beyond simply reciting how many column inches or minute of news coverage a company receives. The PR efforts must contribute directly to a company's goals and ultimately its bottom line. Does a company want to increase sales? If so, by how much? Does a company want to enter a new market? Introduce a new product? Unveil a new service? Whatever it might be, the PR team or agency must bring results.

Views and perceptions are endless and, possibly, meaningless. Each discipline has its own advantages and disadvantages. Each can survive separately at well as in a combined manner. The pros and cons of each in the light of organsiational needs are well worth a look.

XI

Event Marketing and Event Management New Medium of Promotion

Background

Gone are the days when a cocktail of resources were brewed to put up a show-fare, conferences etc. leaving its success to fate. Last decade has seen growth of event management in the service industry as a profession requiring skill and expertise at par with and at times more than any other profession today. In India, although the concept of event management is catching up fast, it can still not said to be a fully matured industry and happens to be in its infant stages. This promising industry is a viable option for budding professionals of PR and Mass Communication entrants into the field. They have before themselves an unexplored land of plentiful job and self-employment opportunities. Hence this topic comes as one of the most appropriate subject of study for a student of public relations and communication activities.

OBJECTIVE:

The aim of the study should be to minutely know the tenets of event management to analyze it for its strong points & shortcomings and finally evolve it into a comprehensive guide for entering this field. As a student of PR management one will come to know about new promising lucrative career option for a mass communication professional.

Content of the Study

1. Types of events
2. Growth of event management
3. Event management methodology
4. Importance of event management in Indian service and entertainment industry.
5. Career growth for fresh aspirants.
6. Marketing Aims.
7. Problems and Conclusions.

Methodology:

Both primary and secondary data.

The concept of Event Marketing and Event Management is discussed here in some detail without any specific questions on the subject.

Introduction

Philip Kotler, The Marketing Guru defines events as occurrences designed to communicate particular messages to target audiences. One leading Indian Event Agency defines events as something noteworthy which happens according to a set plan involving networking of a multimedia package, thereby achieving the client's objectives and justifying their need for associating with events.

Event and sponsorship may sound almost similar, one supporting another as form of promotion. Strictly, sponsorship consists of the giving of monetary or other support to a beneficiary in order to make its activities financially viable, sometimes for altruistic reasons but usually to gain some advertising, public relations or marketing advantage (Frank Jefkins)

In essence, sponsorship and Publicity are highly interlinked. Such publicity are done by others for the organisation i.e. newspaper report, programme sponsorships etc.

Examples:-

(a) Femina is being published by associating itself with Miss India contest.

(b) LG is being publicized by associating itself with Indian Cricket Team. Thus in such cases, publicity through sponsorship makes the organisation and product popular amongst the people. They may not give details about the product but make people more and more familiar with the name of the company. As a result, the company establishes itself as "Company as a Brand," leading to reminder and recall factors towards their brand products.

Another independent example is that of Walmart – the world's foremost chain of retail stores in the US. The founder-wizard of Walmart, Sam Walton, prefers not to advertise in TV or print media but is only involved with the Event Management to promote itself.

Progress Test (Refer to content of the Study)

1. Discuss the growth of event management and types of events. Do you have any suggestions for expanding the scope and coverage of event marketing in India?
2. Discuss the importance of event management in Indian Service and Entertainment industry and methodology of its operations.
3. Do you think that there is considerable scope of career growth for freshers in the event industry in India? How far public relations and sales promotions are involved in event marketing and management and how far these activities are able to extend their hands of support to event organisers?
4. Identify the problems and challenges faced by this growing industry in India and give your conclusions on the subject.

Growth of Event Management

Events are acts of news development. The essential ingredients are time, place, people, activities, drama, songs and music and showmanship. In fact one special event may have many more subsidiary events. These could be banquets, luncheons, contests, speeches, and many others as part of the buildup. An event involves a mass of details skillfully blueprinted, presented, dramatized and reported.

The corporate look out for cost effective way to satisfy the customer or consumer expectations and distinguish themselves from the competition has made events management one of the fastest growing area. Business houses today are too willing to spend sizable chunks of money to promote their own brands. They don't care even if the amount goes as high as Rs. 50 lakh or more on a single event. And greater the event in terms of popularity and participation greater such enthusiasm and money spent on such occasions.

Owning liberalization and free market operations the multinationals and even the domestic companies will pool their efforts and money to produce an overall show and an overall publicity campaign that attracts strong public interest. One may wonder how every element-sound, light, music, anchoring and many more – are timed perfectly in clockwork way in a film award function or a fashion pageant. Truly, this is the magic of event management for any observer or bystander.

These are the unique means of marketing, advertising, sales promotion and brand building and involve planning, organising and executing live events to create awareness about a particular product organisation or cause. The event could be just about any significant or not so significant occasion – a fashion show, a musical night, a corporate seminar or conference, cricket, football, tennis or any other sports event, Commonwealth or Olympic Games, a product launch or even a wedding or birthday bash.

Today it is much of an organised sector. This sector broke away from main stream course and started for a niche itself in the industry. But it is very difficult to pinpoint exactly when this has happened. It was around 1996 that it rapidly gained importance as a professionally managed niche of marketing.

The below diagram shows that in the beginning the IMC used to handle all the activities such as Public Relations, Advertising Events, and Sales Promotion etc. But now each activity has specialized in its own area and today we have separate agency for advertising, public relations and for event management as well. But all such activities come under the total Integrated Marketing Communication functions of any organised corporate entity.

IMC

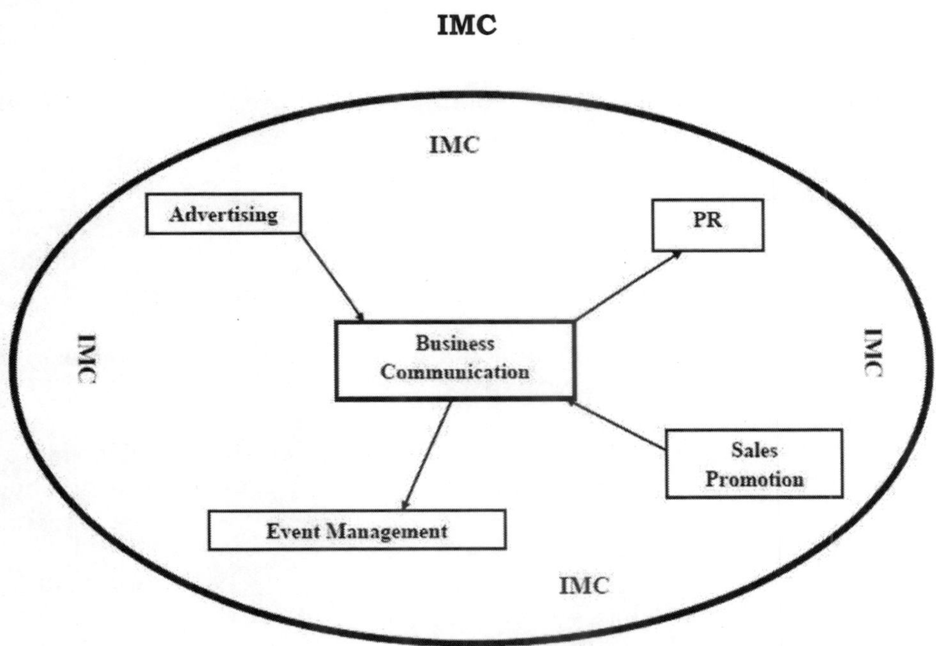

IMC – Integrated Marketing Communication

Types of Events and Sponsorships

These may be considered under the following items in two major groups:

1. Corporate Events

(1) Launching and promotions of Brand or Product.

(2) Launching of public issues in the form or shares, debentures or mutual funds by corporate houses to raise money from the public, domestic as well as global for investment purposes, Includes road

shows, media conference, organising annual general meeting and so on.

(3) Dealer/Customer meets – interactive and sales promotion activities.

(4) Exhibitions, Seminars, Conferences.

(5) Annual events/fashion shows/special celebrations.

(6) Movie premiere and promotion.

(7) Parades, pageants processions, athletic competition, showmanship and musical extravaganza.

2. Commercial Events

(1) Cultural event, special shows.

(2) Concerts and similar programmes, DJ nights.

(3) Awards programme.

(4) High – end parties.

(5) Wedding management.

(6) Celebrity management.

Similarly the spheres of sponsorship include event management as well as direct sponsorship. The occasions are of a varied nature and cover many of the following areas:

(1) Sports events:

Which could be sponsored by corporate houses to reach mass consumer market almost effortlessly. In fact, more sponsorship money today is devoted to sports than to anything else.

(2) Exhibitions:

Public, trade, tourism, fashion are often sponsored by business, or a magazine or by a newspaper.

(3) Education:

Another new area of interest is the interest in varied forms of education, particularly in business and professional studies anywhere in the world.

(4) Charities and Public Service:

Sponsoring a film, a charity show and any particular effort to do some public good as a part of cooperate citizenship ideas.

(5) Professional Acclaim and Award:

This may be direct participation to attract media attention or by organising contests by the sponsoring companies.

(6) Community Relations:

By participating in local events such as carnivals, flower shows, village fairs, club activities, public toilet construction, range of inaugural functions and direct community welfare activities in cities, towns and villages.

The events have to be effectively conceptualized by the creative team ______ the actual presentation and visual impact. A special theme is created for the event. This is then reflected in every piece of communication, décor and music. Besides loads of creativity, what one requires are excellent communication, networking, organsiational, logistical, marketing and presentation skills. Many of these qualities can be acquired on the job.

Public Relations and Sponsorship

The Indian experience, factually speaking, is that many corporations, driven by a sense of public responsibility, have undertaken projects and built institutions which have yielded rich public relations benefits. To give one of the foremost examples, Jamshedji Tata, the Founder of the Tata Group fervently believed that, "what comes from the people must go back to the people". He went even further and announced that all the wealth of the Tata's was essentially a public trust.

In recent years, The Unilever Associate in India, Hindustan Unilever, had quietly and with no fanfare done much outstanding public service. ITC, the diversified corporate today, has been a major sponsor of sports and cultural events even if largely for public relations gains. A large number of Indian public sector giants, SAIL, BHEL, NTPC, ONGC, IOL, and other oil companies have taken up greater number of key issues for intensive corporate activity through sponsorships, events and public service communications.

Sales Promotion:

Similarly, Sales Promotion closes the bridge between advertising and sales, assisting media advertising and personal selling to clinch the sale. Various inducements come in handy which are:

(a) Contests.
(b) Games.
(c) Sweepstakes/Lotteries.
(d) Coupons (Newspapers, magazines, direct mail, coupons).
(e) Displays.
(f) Sponsorship of entertainment events.
(g) Samples for distribution.
(h) Demonstration as products and services

We have to accept the fact that all promotions bear the communicative aspects of marketing. Promotion is an effort to make the public aware of a product, service, idea or an image by a business organisation. Sales promotion personnel use displays, shows, exhibitions, demonstration and most prominently by organising events to encourage consumer response and dealer effectiveness.

Importance of Event Management

With the changing consumer lifestyle, sudden media explosion and an advent of the entertainment economy, competition for brand promotion has increased tremendously. In this scenario, events have emerged as effective tool for brand promotion.

In today's cluttered marketing environment simply airing your commercial on television or radio will not assure success. Today's market place is too segmented. Because of that segmentation, it has become necessary to find ways of reaching the public that go beyond the 'traditional.' It was becoming increasingly expensive to reach people and increasingly tough to break through the "jungle of jingles". Event Management provides an opportunity to leverage the brand in mass media through public relations.

The event management has started to play a great role in the integrated marketing communication. Before, the 80 – 20 (80% of advertising and 20% of event management) ratio was existent in the industries, now it is 50 – 50. As a cause of the changing trend of the Indian service and entertainment industry event management has picked up enormously.

Event management has helped to reach out to the customer more intimately and interactive, which is much cheaper than the conventional form of communication. It helps in the easy recall of the brand or product through the event, rather than by advertising which is giving the competitive advantage and which was not realised before by advertising through the conventional forms.

This is for sure going to give a growth prospect for the event management industries which is going to happen to be 20 – 80 ratios of advertising and event management in the near future.

Other Relevant Information

Departments

Typically, a good-sized firm would have a staff of 30 – 40 persons grouped in three main departments.

- The service department
- The creative department
- The production department

Career growth for a fresher

The career growth in this field is tremendous and one can achieve success through own merit. One can earn a lot in this career, but it involves back-breaking work. There is no stipulated amount and earning largely depends on the success of each show or event. One can earn name and fame within a short span of time like three years. The starting salary of a fresher generally ranging from Rs. 10,000 – Rs 20,000.

Though having such positive aspects of this career, this industry has some **negative aspects** also, these are:

- The salary problem
- No time limit for working hours
- Sometimes a deterrent for a woman

- Perfection has to be there.

A single error can ruin the whole show.

In recent times, numerous event management firms have come up and they are able to find good business and creative opportunities to succeed in the race for perfection. Apart from fresh entrepreneurial endeavors, most leading advertising and public relations agencies have separate event management cells. Additionally some of the high profile corporate houses also have their own in-house event outfits.

Many of the independent event management firms would employ 40 – 50 people grouped in several main departments. If it's a major event, they go for even outsourcing and subcontract part of the work like catering, music, security, and advertising to other firms. Many freelance coordinators as well as painters, artists, musicians earn a decent living just by working for event managers. All these activities provide ideal opportunities for freshers to learn the ropes. In these ways, the shows therefore go on.

In India such change concept in production and marketing are for too many as in the advanced countries. Wipro, Reliance, Videocon, Tata, UB group from Breweries to Airlines, are other notable examples.

(1) Launching a new product. As a strategy of launching a new product, events and sponsorships are excellent vehicles. There is also a kind of public test for performance. The experiment can be applied to many new products like cricket bats, racquets, tyres, cars, bikes and sportswear.

 The aim of fulfilling marketing objectives through events and sponsorship can be equally good for positioning a product, supporting dealers, encouraging product or service use and even in international marketing tasks.

 The aims and objectives of marketing in relation to events and sponsorship are quite distinctive. The following responsibilities are particularly noteworthy.

(2) Pinpointing a change in marketing policy. Many well known companies are firmly established in a particular product field and a change or diversification into other product or service field may create problems of a quick acceptance. In such situations, which are essentially marketing policy decisions, established companies largely opt for participation in events or sponsorship of major events.

The history of ITC is a good example. Its transition from Imperial Tobacco Co to India Tobacco Co and finally to just ITC Ltd is known. In the process they diversified from Tobacco to Hotel and Hospitality and to a range of lifestyle products. They never compromised in terms of quality and excellence and were able to mark its distinctive presence in the corporate world.

Media relations and media coverage have a good role in event marketing efforts. For example, every trade and industrial show, any event or sponsorship occasion will attract large groups of media personnel. They are eager to know about new ideas and new trends about products or services. This is an easy as well as opportune moment to make media and the public aware of the marketing, sales promotion and the company's image or identity factors.

Marketing Aims

Although all the promotional strategies may be blended together to achieve organsiational objectives, Marketing has certain obligations and aims of its own. Strictly speaking, PR, Sales Promotions, Advertising have their similarities and differences and this applies to marketing in a big way.

We have to take note of the communicative aspects of marketing most particularly. Promotions are an effort to make the public aware of products or services as well as to make them increasingly popular.

The marketing objectives of Events, by cooperative and coordinated orchestrations will try to stimulate ultimate sales through persuasive communication. The involved professionals can make such events bright and interesting by infusing a high level of imagination and creativity into event marketing as well as into advertising for promotion.

The public relations functions extend not only by news coverage through identified media, but through collaborations of all kinds. These include travel advertising to attract people from other places, inserts, stickers and many other devices to project the event to more people. All steps and attempts are to be directed to providing substantial exploitation benefits to the events, TV networks, print media and sponsor.

Marketing Objectives of Events

It is said that "Business is Marketing" and thus the winner in the race will be the one who satisfies the customer needs in a variety of ways. Thus Sales Promotion, Public Relations, Advertising and Marketing are now addressing themselves to winning the goodwill of target audiences on long term tenure. All these pay dividends in an unending way.

PR can play an increasing role in the total marketing effort by helping in press relations, organising exhibitions and fairs, producing persuasive literature.

Event Management Methodology

The methodology usually consists of conceptualization, planning, budgeting and execution of below-the-line activities such as exhibitions, stage shows, music concerts, celebrity appearances, fashion or charity shows, conferences, weddings, product or brand launches, and sports shows.

Companies approach event managers with a vague idea and a budget in mind and the rest is entirely upon the event manager to develop and improvise to turn ideas into success.

As soon as the idea takes a proper shape and the budget provisions are made, the event manager will coordinate with sponsors and performers and will finalise the agreement with them. The arrangements will include travel plans, security, accommodation for the performers if there is show.

Mostly, the three departments of the Event Company will arrange these activities.

1. The Technical Department: The technical professionals will be given the responsibility of production and organisation of the event. These functions are – lighting, acoustics, video, venue management and logistics. They have also to procure relevant permits. Management of the venue includes commissioning security personnel, managing the banquet area, refreshments and hospitality.
2. The Marketing Department: The functions of marketing refer to coordination with sales and marketing teams, public relations, advertising, publicity and all aspects of mass communication elements. All of them together will sell the concept to the client and market the event to the media, sponsors and the public. As we all know, the Miss India and Mr. India contests as well as film and TV shows attract big company sponsors to these programmes. They derive considerable benefits in terms of brand promotion and brand recall through such events.
3. The Creative Team: Conceptualizing the event and creative presentation go a long way to capture the mind of the audience or the viewers. They put their best in the areas of presentation, communication, décor and music. Background in advertising graphics, commercial art and multimedia skills will be helpful for gaining necessary skills and needful application. The Event Managers and the executive team members today are qualified professionals and there cannot be any compromise in terms of performing abilities.

In this module of event planning-identification of the type of event to be planned (a product launch or a conference or some other event), and then drafting a rough budget, target audience, promotional campaign, publicity and other arrangements are involved.

These include:

- Identification of event
- Budgeting
- Catering of the need
- Venue
- Security
- Hiring and rentals
- Publicity and promotion

Identify the Event

The first job is to identify the type of event to be planned, whether it is going to be a product launch or a conference or a wedding or some other event.

Then there is need to sit and draft a rough script of the budget, target audience, promotional campaigns, publicity, and other miscellaneous arrangements.

During this one must be able to answer the five basic questions:

1. **Who** is the target audience?
   First you have to find out who are the people who will be coming for the event. This is very important because the whole event rests on the kind of people who are going to be invited.
2. **What** type of event?
   Next turn give the attention to the type of event going to be set up.
3. **When** do you wish to stage the event?
   Here we decide on the date. Date can be fixed as to whether to stage it next month or after a few months or one year or even more than that.
3. **Where?**
   When you are planning the event then the important factor would be the venue. If it is a wedding/party it has got to be a hall, conference rooms for a product launch. Depending on the nature of the event one has to decide on the venue.
4. **How?**
   It should decide about the framework of the objectives to be met. How long should the event last? – Think about the duration and how does the event fit into your overall marketing programme?

Be clear whether it is going as a stand-alone or a one-off event that is separate and distinct from the other activities. Alternatively it could be part of a wider campaign-just one aspect of other ongoing advertising and marketing work.

Catering

Now the importance of catering really depends on the kind of event. If it were a wedding or a party then a major chunk of the entire plan would go for catering itself. While selecting a caterer check out his/her credibility from various sources. After having it, sort out details regarding payment, mode of payment dates and other useful information.

Get well these details in writing and get it signed from the concerned person so as avoid any problems in future.

Venue

The choice of the venue naturally depends on the kind of event. If it is a fashion show or a product launch, then chances are high that it would be held in a star hotel. Before deciding on the venue you should first decide on your target audience.

Security

Security is another big issue that is dealt with by event managers. In India, shows usually have to end before midnight at the latest, even earlier in some places.

It should be ensured that it is safe and secure in all ways. Especially if it is an event which is bound to attract a lot of attention like a musical concert of a film based ceremony or such other events. For this you need to ensure that the event is fireproof and free from any obnoxious incidents.

Hirings and Rentals

By hiring and rentals one refers to the other professionals who will be working along with you like a photographer, decorator, videographer and a host of other people who will be helping out with the event.

When you are hiring them remember to do the following things:

(a) Get a contract letter made
(b) Decide about the advance to be paid to the person
(c) Try negotiating as far as possible
(d) List down your terms and conditions before signing the contract
(e) Take into account their terms and conditions
(f) When you fix the money, you should also fix up the timings
(g) Check out for their credentials before signing them on.

Explain them as to how you visualize the event. These are experts who will understand what you are wanting from them and accordingly co-ordinate with you.

You need not be an expert in everything but should know how to co-ordinate with all these people and bring out the best in each one of them.

Publicity and Promotion

If you know how to plan and organize your event, should also know how to market it. If there is something very peculiar or special about your event then has to be main thing to be highlighted. A product launch for example requires a sales promotion campaign either before or after the launch. In that case the product is advertised through banners and media and even door-to-door canvassing. Effort is taken to ensure that people sit up and take notice of the event. Sometimes it could be an event like an award ceremony, which is to be shown on television. You then have different companies making a beeline for sponsoring their respective products in due course of the programme. This is the publicity and promotions work.

Managing Events

There are at least seven steps in planning for a well organized event-whether corporate, social, dedication or just a meeting or a conference.

1. Setting the goals. Determine the specific objectives, the audiences that the event is meant to influence and the ways in which the effects can be further extended.
2. Begin your planning very early. Time is the crucial factor in planning, organizing and finally in its effective execution.
3. Delegate responsibility for each activity separately and assign the tasks of coordination at a different level. Provide a "backup system" if something goes wrong at subsequent stages, check and double check and nothing must go wrong.
4. Apply "MBWA" theory (Management by Walking Around) and get the employees to be enthusiastic and knowledgeable about the whole exercise. Form committees to distribute workload but overseeing is the key factor.
5. Create good understanding with the hosting company or the sponsors and use company professionals as and when possible. They know what they want and won't mind to extend cooperation. Many times they may even allow their trained and experienced staff to work with you. They include copywriters, visualiser, exhibit specialists, creative talents and design personnel.
6. Consult and make the company agreeable to bear the expenses, to provide giveaways, souvenirs, prizes, awards, product samples and so many more to ensure higher attendance and to make the event memorable. Be imaginative and provide different kind of attractions for different target audiences.
7. All appropriate logistics have to be planned out and put through with utmost care. These include parking area, transportation, signs and printed maps to guide visitors.
   Publicize and advertise to keep the expected audience informed and to create awareness and interest among more and more people.
8. Mail thank-you letters after the event is over. Never forget those who helped and worked hard to make the event successful. They include people both inward as well as outward.

Problems and Conclusions

Events and sponsorships are big business today. Games absorb hundreds of millions of advertiser's pounds, dollar and rupees. But how effective are they? Would the money be better spent on above the –line advertising? That also has come under serious doubts. The debacle of the Indian Cricket team on several occasions are the most glaring instancs.

With huge financial outlay, sponsors of the events need to quantify the success or failure of their sponsorships. One way of doing this is by researching and measuring the actual results in terms of desired benefits. From research angles, events have several dimensions. These include the specific objectives, the audiences that the event is meant to influence and the ways in which the effects can be extended. The results of the exercise may be observed, too, in a variety of ways, in terms of awareness, sense of participation and of enhanced relationships with the key audiences.

What is needed, if event managers are to account for all the labour and expenses, is a disciplined, systematic approach to the planning and evaluation of events.

An event usually can have unforeseen challenges. To do a post event evaluation one needs to make at least two lists. These are

(1) Areas of Improvement (include what went wrong, if any)

(2) What went right

We always begin with "Areas of Improvement". Maintain a judicial attitude and be brutally honest. Admittedly, every event, every single event, without exception can be improved. Find out if you had a problem that could not have been foreseen and how do you avoid it in the future. Secondly, finish cataloguing what was good about your event. This helps you prepare your list of thank you notes to send out.

Producing and organizing events are entirely a team effort. Cultivate the atmosphere by showing appreciation and always acknowledging their contribution. Indeed, there's always a new challenge, and there's always something new to learn.

XII

Saying no to Polybags .... Campaign Against Plastic

The Present and the Future

One of the so –called greatest man-made inventions which has eased everyone's lifestyle is Plastic. It was invented because of its superior qualities over traditional materials. Since its inception, it has taken every aspect of our day – to – day life. It's present in varied forms, be it household appliances, stationery, pipes, plugs, packaging – it's practically omnipresent.

In the past few decades, plastics bags, which were initially known to be harmless, of all colours and sizes have become indispensable part of our lives. Their wide usage for various purposes that is whether for storing groceries, milk, food or clothes has increased their numbers from some thousand to infinite today. The bell rang when polybags started taking form of nuisance for the society as it led to reduction in the soil fertility, death of cattle and other animals both on land and in water, choking of drains and air pollution came to the fore. Now the inventors realized what grave mistake had they done.

The fact remains that the polybags have proven to be irreplaceable in case of consumer durables and for other household purposes. The unhindered use of polybags has become a hot topic for debate and discussion. So much so that the environmentalists have raised their voices in concern against this menace. In fact, to help reduce the problems caused by this environmental unfriendly product, a lot of campaigns have been initiated. But it seems that there is more to be done in terms of creating awareness and implementation and of course research on the topic if the menace has to be got rid of once and for all. It's for the future generation that we want at least clean drinking water and clean air to breathe. The cry is to save the environment and all this has to be done fast, better late than never, but let's make sure it's not too late.

Plastic: The Material

Plastic are a group of synthetic resinous or other substance that can be molded into any form. Plastic are polymers; a polymer is something made from many units. It's like a chain, each link of the chain is a — "mer" or basic unit that is usually made of carbon, hydrogen, oxygen and / or silicon. To make the chain, many links or "—mers" are hooked or polymerized together. Many common classes of polymers are composed of hydrocarbons. These are specifically made up of small units bonded into long chains. Carbon makes up the backbone of the molecule and hydrogen atoms are bonded along the backbone. Example of polymers that contain only carbon and hydrogen are polypropylene, polybutylene, polystyrene, polymethypentene etc.

Even though the basic makeup of many polymers is carbon and hydrogen, other elements like oxygen, chlorine, fluorine, nitrogen, silicon, phosphorous and sulphur are also found in the molecular make-up of polymers. Polyvinyl chloride (PVC) contains nitrogen, Teflon contains fluorine, polyester and polycarbonates contain oxygen.

There are some polymers that contain silicon of phosphorus backbone instead of carbon and are called inorganic polymers. Amorphous polymers have no long – range order or form in which the polymer chain arranges them, these kinds of polymers are generally transparent. This is an application for many things such as food wrap, headlights and contact lenses.

Polymers are divided into two distinct groups – thermoplastics and thermo sets. Majority of polymers are thermoplastics meaning that once the polymer is formed it can be heated and reformed over and over again. This property allows for easy processing and facilitates recycling. Whereas on the other hand thermo sets once formed cannot be re – melted, in fact re – heating causes the material to scorch.

The basic problem associated with the material known as plastic is that it cannot be decomposed, meaning it can deteriorate but could never finish off completely.

The Origin of Polybags:

The word plastic has originated from the Greek word ***Plastikos*** *which* means easily shaped. Plastic is a petroleum based product. Polybags are

IF YOU CAN'T PUT IT BACK

DON'T TAKE IT AWAY

made from both recycled and virgin plastic. They are generally made from LDPE (Low density poly ethylene) or HDPE (High density polyethylene)

Increased Plasticization and more Polybags:

As we have stated before, plastic in made of both virgin and used plastic, therefore the actual amount of plastic produced depends on the availability of fresh and waste plastic and of course the demand for these bags. Considering the amount of plastic waste which will be made available through increased consumption of plastic there will be no shortage of specific waste of polybags. Thus the only way out the vicious circle is by decreasing the demand for this material.

Problems Associated with Polybags:

There are various environment and health related problems associated with this material. The lists of hazards are as follows:

1. **Polybags choke drains:** Being flimsy and light polybags are blown by the wind and ultimately they land in the drain, thereby blocking them. As a result of health hazards and consequently infections and diseases.
2. **Lead to animal's deaths:** Dustbins, sidewalks serve as handy eating joint for cows, which swallow polybags along with organic waste. As a result the creature dies slow and sure death.

Polybags kill animals by obstructing either small or large intestine. If the blocking is complete the animal is unable to digest the food and as a result it throws up everything it eats, Toxins are released into the body by the plastic themselves as well as by food that may still be in the alimentary canal, overloading the digestive system and thereby by poisoning the animal. In case of partial blocking, the toxification remains, but the animal continues to survive until there is complete blockage. Occasionally, polybags remain in the stomach of the animal and this result in a feeling of fullness. The animal then does not eat and gradually starves to death.

Creations other than cow especially marine creations like turtles swallow plastic floating in the seas and choke too. Zoos across the country including national zoological park of Delhi have banned plastic bags and have been quite successful in limiting their numbers.

In Delhi, one veterinary surgeon operated upon a cow and removed 4000 polybags from its stomach. At Sanganeer in Jaipur about 5 – 7 stray cows handed over to the Gaushala or cow shetter die every day of swallowing polybags.

3. **Polybags reduce carrying capacity of the soil:** Polybags are non-biodegradable, this implies that they neither dissolve nor disintegrate into the soil; instead they lie there and at best are weathered into smaller parts. Being non – porous, they don't allow the free – flow of water, resulting in water-logging and deprivation. Also the material is such that it doesn't allow the free flow of air

and thus chokes the plant. This draws the conclusion tha the local ecology gets damaged greatly.

4. **Food hazards:** Among the various health hazards that crop up, toxic dyes -, which are used to colour, polybags – is the most important of the Polybags are mostly made in informal recycling sector with or almost no controls exercised. The dyes used cause extensive damage to workers health that usually scoops them up with his bare hands, thereby ingesting and inhaling them.
   The main cause of concern is that chemicals used in the dye which leach (leak) out into the food products stored in them and in this way they make way into our system. The two most commonly used dyes in plastic are based on the heavy metals, lead and cadmium. Lead is a neurotoxin, which causes severe learning disorders in children and neurological disorders in adults. Cadmium is a nephrotoxin that affects the kidneys and bones, both of these are used in the production of red and yellow polybags. Even the transparent ones are made so using titanium dioxide as a bleaching agent.
5. **Limited recyclability:** Plastic recycling is linear, not cyclic, which implies it can only be recycled a certain number of times. This is usually not more than four to five times at best, depending on the type of plastic, the technology employed and the use it is put to. Thereby the more plastic we use, the more waste there will be. In turn it will be down cycled into new products like polybags, even when these products are finally disposed off through landfills, incineration and other methods, they continue to pollute and remain in our environment in other forms.
6. **Leads to air pollution by burning:** When Polybags are burned they release carbon monoxide and carbon dioxide as well as carbon particles, which increase the local particulate matter. All these affect human health and the environment.
7. **Mosquito breeding**: Stray polybags are deep enough to act as receptors of water, sufficient enough for mosquito breeding. During cleaning and anti – mosquito operations in recent years, they have also being targeted, along with tanks and water coolers.

Tasks:

1. Examine the issues affecting sanitation, health and environment by hazardous use of polybags in India. Do you feel that the present set of rules and notifications should be able to tackle the problem of increasing plastic consumption?
2. How far the anti – plastics campaign is successful in sending out the right signals to users and producers of plastic bags? Is a total ban feasible or alternatives to polybags could be more acceptable?

3. Provide recommendations towards increasing awareness about the menace of polybags and suggest corrective steps.

TASK ONE:

Issues affecting health and environment by hazardous use of polybags in India. Do the rules and legislations address the problems of increasing plastic consumption?

Polybags Recycling in India:

The Bureau of India Standards (BIS), New Delhi has formulated Indian Standard Specification entitled "The guidelines of Recycling of Plastics". This Indian Standard was necessitated with a view to disciplining recycling practices in the country, as also to promote codification and marketing plastic products.

According to the plastic industry, there are not enough resources for all the people on this earth to consume at the present rate, so morality as well as prudence dictates that we must make better use of materials in the first place and reuse them when the product life expires a discussion that is increasingly being reinforced worldwide by legislation.

Therefore, designers now have new responsibility, as it's no longer enough to consider just styling, cost efficiency, safety and utility. We must now add material conservation, recycling and disposal; the first thing to consider is the recycling method, as given below.

Types of disposal methods/ recycling methods:

(1) **Conventional disposal:** The product is dumped in a landfill site where it may remain indefinitely. This solution is environmentally unfriendly and is being phased out by public opinion and recurring landfill costs.

(2) **Mechanical recycling:** Products are sorted, cleaned and reprocessed into pellets ready for the production of new products. The process is very suitable for thermoplastics.

(3) **Feedstock recycling:** Products are broken down into basic chemical constituents that can be used to synthesise new chemical products, whether plastic or otherwise.

(4) **Energy recovery:** Products are burned under controlled conditions to recover stored energy; Plastic has a higher calorific value than coal. The process is suitable for low – value mixed soiled wastes.

(5) **Treatment and dumping:** Products are pre – treated to reduce volume and to remove pollutants before disposal in landfill.

Landfill solutions are no longer accepted. Product reuse applies only to special cases, energy recovery is in some ways a last resort and feedstock recycling usually implies a high – volume supply of a single type of polymer. That leaves mechanical recycling as the likely route for most thermoplastic products, and this has a number of consequences for designers.

Most important is the need to identify plastic at the end of product life. Different plastics may be completely incompatible and if they are mixed by a failure to distinguish between them, the values of the waste are reduced to zero. Even experts find it difficult to tell one plastic from another so we need a standard way to mark plastic products with the identification marks.

Problems of polybags recycling:

When we talk about recycling in India it's very important not to forget the fact that polybags recycling in India takes place in the informal sector. Here recycling takes place in hazardous conditions, further, the manufacturing and recycling of plastic bag is itself not without problems.

The following are some basic issues related to polybags recycling:

(1) Reprocessing can be hazardous: Although PE is less toxic then PVC and considered inert, studies reveal that under light, heat and pressure, it can decompose and release hazardous chemicals, thus it's dangerous for the health.

(2) Dirty bags are uneconomical: Very dirty plastic bags including those which are used to dispose garbage in are seldom recycled as they don't serve any purpose and are uneconomical. Thus they are rarely collected, mostly they remain in the soil.

(3) The workers suffer: The incomplete combustion of PE causes the release of carbon monoxide and harmful smoke; this affects both, the workers health and the environment. In shanty recycling units where no temperature monitoring is carried out, this becomes an even greater problem as there is little or no ventilation due to which the workers are forced to inhale contaminated air.

(4) Polybags are marginal for rag pickers: Around 200 – 350 polybags make up a kilo and the selling price is usually between Re. 1 – 1.50. In fact, many discarded polybags don't reach garbage bins and are found either stuck on trees or in sewage pipes or lie embedded in the soil. In case the bags are dirty, they have to be washed which is a highly labour intensive job. This makes it an additionally unattractive proposition for rag pickers.

Substitutes for Polybags:

Since polybags have become a necessity of life due to its multiple use and excessive demand. It seems difficult to find an appropriate substitute for the material. But then something has to be done to tackle the polybags menace, therefore a range of possible substitutes is given as follows:

Paper:

There are several kinds of paper bags that are available and which can be put in different uses. Recycled or handmade paper is very expensive and therefore even while being suitable can't be used as a proper substitute of polybags. Handmade paper bags are more suitable as shopping bags rather than as inexpensive temporary packaging material. Nevertheless other kinds of paper bags can compete as alternative to polybags. The strongest contenders are paper bags from used paper. These paper bags are generally manufactured in cottage industry, which is often done by women on a piecemeal basis. This industry has shrunk considerably since polybags took over the market. Thus it has become overly expensive to produce reused paper bags.

The demand for reused paper bags can be created encouraging and increasing the industries demand for them, also by generating awareness against polybags can help for the same. The government can help to increase the demand for these bags by making them available at central distribution and procurement agencies such as ration shops. Others steps that the government can take to encourage reused paper bags could be either by imposing fiscal measures to restrict polybags such as taxes or by reducing duties on imported paper, this will also bend down prices of domestically produced paper and enable this industry to substitute polybags more efficiently and viably.

Cotton:

There are two types of cotton bags one is made of new cotton and the other one from old cotton. The latter is based upon household practices that put old cotton cloth to a number of uses, including bags. Many economists consider manufacturing bags form new cotton cloth as an inappropriate use of an expensive material. It is estimated that cotton shopping bags cost twice as much as jute bag of the same size. However, old cloth is more appropriate material for shopping bag.

Jute:

This one material that is touted as the single most important alternative to polybags, although it's an appropriate substitute. Many changes are required before it can actually become a viable alternative, such as increasing the production of jute per man day in order to compete with plastic. Also by providing material from Yarn Bank Schemes which provide jute at mill gate rates would help small groups to source the material without having to incur the cost of expensive transportation.

Legislations – in favour or against?

There has been a spate of legal acts restricting the use of polybags since 1994, when the first such legislation was passed in Himachal Pradesh. In 1999 the Union Ministry of Environment and Forests formulated the Recycled Plastic Manufacture and Usage rules. It was based on the recommendations of the Plastic Waste Task Force, which included government officials and, members of the Plastic industry, constituted in 1996. Despite objection from several environmental groups and citizens the proposed notification was made into the final rules as mentioned above.

These rules however have some flaws. This legislation lacks both the radical steps of some of the state legislations as well as the strength required for such restriction. This can largely be attributed to the fact that it was primarily the result of discussion of the plastic waste management committee, which comprises members of plastic industry and government officials.

Such a notification will be unable to tackle the problem created by polybags across the country, because it does not address nor solve the core problem of increasing plastic consumption.

The main issues regarding the notification are as follows:

(1) Increase in the use of virgin plastic: The notification has ordered that plastic bags made from both virgin and recycled material be at least 20 microns thick. This is a substantial increase from the current 6 -7 microns.

The reasons given for this is that currently polybags are not being recycled as rag pickers find them too thin and light to be profitable enough to pick, clean and sell. In fact, it can take up to 350 bags to make a kilo which finally sells for only between Re. 1 to Rs. 1.50. It's expected that thicker plastic bags will lead to increased profitability for rag pickers.

But it's quite obvious that thicker bags from virgin material meant that more plastic polymer is being used for an existing consumer product. This also translates into an expanded market and hence, profit for the plastic producers. At the ground level therefore the Notification has actually expanded the market for plastic.

(2) Polybags as dumping ground for recycled plastic: The plastic production in India is growing astoundingly, with the demand trebling every 10 years. The domestic demand is expected to increase from 1.88 million tonnes in 1995- 96 to over 5 million tonnes in 2004-2005 and around 10 million tonnes in 2012-2013. Of this 52% will go into packaging. The huge amounts of waste that is, and will be generated, will pose a major problem of waste management.

The rules encourage the use of plastic by accommodating a part of it through recycled material polybags.

(3) No move away from the plastic: Another conspicuous feature of the rules is that they seek to replace polybags, acknowledged as creating a variety of problems, by other polybags. Notification makes no mention of other material – cloths, newspaper bags, jute, - which could be encouraged by local authorities thereby reducing waste.

No additional notification offering incentives to those creating alternatives is being considered or planned.

Also, polybags are seen as an essential part of the contemporary lifestyle and no structural changes in the packaging have been attempted. It's interesting to note here that 52% of all plastic go into packaging.

(4) **Weak provision for recycling:** The recycling of plastic bags is to be undertaken in strict accordance with the guideline for recycling of plastic, issued in 1998 by the Bureau of Indian Standards. However, no systematic charting out of a course of action about how this can be done has been specified. Given that several factories are actually shanty recycling units, that follow no norms and use stolen electricity etc, it's difficult to see how these guidelines can be implemented. This fear is amplified as the laws inherently encourage polybags production and plastic consumption rather than minimizing it. This helps build a perception of the sector as profitable and therefore worth investing in.

No penalization has been clearly spelt out in this notification, as it has been in the case of other similar legislations even in smaller Union Territories such as Lakswadeep.

(5) **Concern for rag pickers as an excuse to expand the markets:** The plastic industry has paid specific and disproportionate interest in one of the facts relating to polybags that they contribute to the rag pickers livelihood. Also dirty plastic bags, such as those used for garbage disposal are hardly touched by rag pickers. This fact of polybags was used as the rationale for thickening polybags, so that henceforth they would become lucrative and be picked up. These linkages to livelihood and recycling have served very well to actually justify and legitimize the new thick plastic bags. The thickening is actually a means of increasing the market for plastic in the first place. Clearly, rag pickers have been used as a means of increasing the market for profit by the plastic industry to justify their own ends.

No aspect of the legislation however actually contributes to their empowerment to lessen their vulnerability or occupational hazards. What it does is allow the industry to tint its commercial interest with false social concern. A recent survey of the polybags manufacturing factories in Delhi has revealed how little impact the legislation has made on the ground level scenario. Colored bags continue to be manufactured and even factory owners agree that there is no way mere legislations can be implemented in such factories without market changes.

No doubt the Governments at the Centre as well as in the states have taken certain steps especially the civic bodies in many metros and smaller cities. They have initiated measures discouraging the use of polybags and anti – plastic garbage dumps at various places. The Central and State Pollution Control Boards unanimously believe that the key to finding solutions to the polybags menace will be by generating awareness.

A senior authority in the Bio – medical Waste Cell of Delhi Pollution Control Board threw lights on some of the gravest problems regarding polybags and its solution. According to him, plastic as a material cannot entirely be blamed, as its application in various utilities is indisputable. Also, polybags constitute only 10 % of the total plastic production in the country, so a ban on polybags will not severely affect the profit of the plastic industry. Admittedly, plastic is a very essential part of our lives and its not advisable to stop using it altogether.

However, one fails to understand why so much fuss is created over the issue of banning polybags. One can argue with lot of reasoning that 10 – 15 years earlier people used cloth, jute, paper bags for most of their work and liquids were stored in metal or glass bottles. In reality, our society is very flexible and it will be able to adapt itself to the new scenario if legislation is passed to restrict the use of polybags.

The main reasons for the polybags menace is not just particularly related to plastic material itself. In fact, it's the civic sense of people that lacks miserably. Used plastic bags can be seen strewn across the street which make it all the more difficult to be managed and given for recycling purposes. In cities and towns and even in villages people keep on littering polybags anywhere instead of disposing them properly. Legislations may not be a problem but it's the civic sense which has to prevail in order to take care of the menace once and for all.

Is the Plastic Industry Responsible for its products?

Primary polymer producers, that is the plastic industry have refused to take responsibility for the life cycle of their product. In fact, they have even refused to acknowledge the havoc caused by polybags during their life cycles. In the specific context of polybags the industries argument has been that the problem is not with the material, but with the users and the municipalities.

Therefore, in the case of management of polybags in India, the plastic industry has been shifting responsibility. The solution is focused around better waste segregation and collection.

Containing polybags might stop them from flying around at the first stage of collection. However, it does not improve recycling status and toxicity among a host of other problems that polybags pose. Dustbins placed at certain spots do not change this situation and neither have they addressed the issue of many plastic being non – recyclable. The question arises, where do these polybags go? At best they reach large municipal garbage dumps or uni – engineered landfills. From here they can and do fly beyond the landfill perimeter to other places. Polybags throw into larger municipal dustbins for garbage disposal are untouched by such schemes.

Imagine a consumer who has just thrown away polybags and a suitable biodegradable alternative. Both of these will affect sanitation, health and the environment in totally different ways. Undoubtedly polybags will cause more havoc. This specific impact of material calls for a greater producer responsibility for the entire life cycle. In India the responsibility is being abdicated and shifted to other sectors. Token gestures in guise of responsibility have been made, but without changing the larger picture.

In order to bring about a genuine change what is required is that the government agencies take firm steps and, in fact, be backed by political will in their endeavour.

TASK TWO:

The aftermaths of the anti – plastics campaign. How far a total ban is practically feasible.

The Anti – plastic Campaign

It was in early 1998 that the National Foundation for India organised the "Say no to polybags" campaign.

The Campaign worked on a few basic presumptions, which are given below:

(a) Information is available, but this needs to be collected and analysed to form a larger picture. Some local studies need to be carried out.
(b) The information must be fed to the general public, through various channels.
(c) Information of various kinds is itself a powerful weapon and must form a basis for this campaign.
(d) Public attention is critical to making a change. This action must also encompass dissemination, in the public sphere of the information received and it's understanding by various publics.
(e) Public action can only lead to pressure on various sectors, but not necessarily in the complete action required to create a change. For this, various other measures have to be undertaken simultaneously.

In addition, workshops and puppet shows are important methods, which can be used in order to educate the children and the public about the harmful effects of polybags, like:

(a) The burning of the material could cause serious air pollution problems as it leads to dissemination of harmful gasses while burning.
(b) Children are made aware about the fact that polybags are non-biodegradable which makes them harmful for the land in the long run.

(c) Also they are advised to use alternative to polybags in order to curtail the production of the material.

The basis of the 'Say no to polybags' campaign was that a shift in usage patterns can be brought about not by bans, fiscal, measures or restrictions alone but by the consumer's own comprehension of the problem and their role in creating and tackling it.

The campaigners were convinced that an issue like polybags pollution which affected the lives of thousands of people daily, needed to be taken to the consumers through broad – based discussion. Hence, there was a need to mobilize public opinion. Mobilizing public opinion in a focused fashion is seen as more productive vis-à-vis lobbying with government agencies or organisations like traders' associations or even helping flood the market with alternatives.

The best partners would be consumers themselves, as they would have the power to decide to minimize their usage and adopt alternatives. However, 'consumer' is an umbrella expression, encompassing a wide range of people from homemaker to government, employees, professionals, shopkeepers, students, workers etc.

In order to be effective, it was necessary to focus on one specific, homogenous sub-set within this comprehensive group of consumers. NFI chose to engage directly with schoolchildren as schoolchildren are not only open to new ideas and are concerned about environment and lifestyle but are also direct users of the material. In fact, if they say no to polybags themselves their sheer numbers would help reduce the consumption of polybags significantly. They would grow into a generation sensitive to the impact on the environment due to their changed lifestyles, leading to long term attitude changes. Lastly, they could influence other consumers through a strong ripple effect.

Partners in Progress:

In order to make the cause of awareness on the issue of polybags a number of partnerships can be created, especially with agencies that are concerned about the issue. For example: National Foundation for India did pioneering and highly laudable work in this direction. These are as follows:

(a) FM Radio Station: FM radio station is such which counts among its listeners not only schoolchildren, but also adults, young and old. Hence, the message is transmitted to a wider audience. The biggest advantage of using Radio is that is reaches out to the biggest segments who would otherwise remain untouched.

(b) Television: Doordarshan, the state – owned, channel, can play an important role in spreading awareness regarding the polybags menace; it's highly effective as its viewership includes remote parts of the country, which are also affected by the issue. DD also funds certain projects with social value or in the public interest. Commercial TV channels should also join hands in these directions.

(c) **Print Media:** The Print media play a critical role in spreading awareness regarding the problem of plastic bags. In fact some newspapers launched a campaign on the issue and used it to put pressure on responsible agencies, following up on the statements by the officials and inviting readers to participate more proactively. This also implied that the newspapers would have a long – term interest in the issue and would be willing to accommodate updates etc. A snowball effect was observed in the print media. Reporting by a few newspapers led to much more, independent work by other newspapers, magazines etc and lent synergy to each other.

(d) **Posters:** Posters have a strong ability to carry the campaign to the most inaccessible areas and venues. Many schoolchildren made posters by hand or had them printed and used them very effectively.

(e) **Plays:** Street plays are performed at every nook and corner by schoolchildren. This kind of activity could be adapted to situation, venues and audiences.

(f) **Leaflets** and Fliers: After verbal discussion and other exposure, one – page fliers were the first written information that students and parents received. A flier war important since it put all the basic arguments down in one place and could be used by the students in various activities as well as to circulate. The perceived authenticity of the written word also seemed to be important.

(g) **Direct Contact and Talks:** Speaking directly to students and members of the public in a discussion format is mutually beneficial. Also by meeting and discussing the issue with the specialists it can help to clear doubts and confusions in the minds of students and teachers as well as others.

(h) **Panel Discussions:** On radio and television, these serve to reinforce the message and also help project the issue to a wider audience.

(i) **Stickers and Banners:** Colorful stickers can prove to be very popular inside and outside the school. They seem to excite schoolchildren; they could relate to them and were handy tools for them to state their message both on personal belongings and other places.

(j) **Using Popular Themes:** In order to make the message short and basic popular themes are founded very useful. It also becomes much more interesting for the audience when joke, puns, popular songs and tunes are thrown in to convey the message.

TASK THREE:

Suggestions and Recommendations towards increasing awareness about the menace of polybags and corrective steps.

Pro –active steps

In schools and colleges, the teaching staff, with the help of students, parents and school managements have to plan a series of activities as part of the campaign. These should be designed to help children become familiar with the issue of polybags as well as with the larger issues of packaging and waste.

A difference in approach will be needed vis-à-vis street children keeping in mind their specific needs. Although many of them are also rag pickers, they do not perceive polybags as materials with high returns. For street children, it is difficult to ask them to stop using polybags especially in absence of shelter from rain or for storage. Hence, the emphasis has to be on post – usage management.

Findings of a Survey

The results of a survey by one organisation among the school children in Delhi is a real eye opener.

"Out of Hundred schoolchildren questioned in the survey a whopping 86% of them were aware of the 'Say no to polybags campaign. But only 27% of them had ever participated in any anti – plastic campaign.

A "Social purpose" was understood to be the prime reason to the campaign. While most of the ill effects were known to students the only area which needed to be given more attention was its characteristics of 'limited recyclability'.

Paper bags followed by Cloth and Jute bags were said to be the best alternatives to polybags but the students agreed that these needed promotion to increase their use.

While many students said they used alternatives to polybags the latter could not be totally eliminated, as not enough alternatives were available in the market. Availability and carrying capacity were found to be the most important criteria while using a particular kind of bag. Being environmental friendly was important, but the significance is diminished if such bag is not easily available.

Half of the students felt that creating awareness among people would help to check the use of polybags. 30% also felt that some sort of legislation restricting the production of polybags was necessary.

The best part about the survey was to find out that most of the students who did not get a chance to participate in an Anti – plastic would love to do so if given an opportunity."

After going through all the pros and cons of plastic bags as a harmful material, its effects, its uses, and legal angle, one could easily derive the right conclusions. In order to curb the menace that the material has caused to the society and the people, some recommendations are given as under:

1. Increasing awareness among people. Under this a few specialized categories have been identified.

(a) Increasing awareness through television specially through channels like Discovery and Cartoon Network which children watch. For others messages should be aired on local city cable channels.
(b) Increase awareness through newspapers/ magazines.
(c) Increase awareness through poster/banners/ wall writings.
(d) Increase awareness through rallies.
(e) Increase awareness through mass contact programmes.
(f) Increase awareness through debates/sessions in schools.
(g) Increase awareness among the housewives and people residing in slums as they use polybags extensively.

2. Polybags should be used only when really necessary.
3. Polybags should be phased out only after making alternatives available adequately.
4. Polybags should not be littered at various places and should be given for recycling.
5. Colored polybags should not be used.
6. Polybags should not be burnt.
7. The price of polybags should be increased.

Ban or No Ban

A Ban does not solve the problem though it does send out strong signal to users and producers of plastic bags. Regardless of a ban, the following steps must be undertaken:

1. Creating incentives, fiscal and otherwise, for the usage of alternatives to polyabags.
2. Creating similar incentives for better and reduced packaging.
3. Invest in research and development of better packaging.

XIII

'CRY – Child Relief And You'
Public Relations In NGOs

Non – Govt Organisations (NGOs)

An Introduction

Year of Establishment

NGO's are non – profit, social service organisations formed by certain individuals or group of individuals who voluntarily join hands together to work for the betterment of the weaker sections of the society. At the beginning of the 20th century only a few NGOs were in existence. Since 1920, there has been a significant increase in their number, agencies existed prior to 1900. The study of the National Institute of Public Cooperation's and Child Development (NIPCCD) which investigated the status of voluntary efforts in the country indicates an upward trend in the growth of NGOs during the period 1953 – 80.

Source of Inspiration behind the Origin of NGOs

Organisations do not emerge out of vacuum, be it in the government or non – governmental sector. They are most of the time associated with a purpose or an inspiration which is rooted in a personal mind. Ideological or religious fervor or some other belief system of the founder's personal interest.

During the modern times, some people may be motivated to help the poor and the needy of the under privileged children, adults, elderly people, sometimes to satisfy their ego or to get public recognition or may be even to derive tax concessions.

Legal status of NGO's

A non – governmental organisation which functions in a community has to deal with various persons. It is difficult for the community to deal with each member of the Board individually. Therefore it's necessary that an agency should have a recognizable public standing and legal status.

Most of the welfare agencies are registered under the Indian Societies Registration Act (XXI OF 1860).

Aims and Objectives

Every organisation has its own of arms and objectives towards which they work. Similarly, NGOs too have their own aims and objectives depending upon their area of activity. Some of them can be discussed as follows:-

(1) Emphasis on need to educate, enlighten and develop the character of individuals (including children) and development of the community life.

(2) Aims at improving the economic and social conditions of the poor.

(3) Non – formal education and training.

(4) To provide aid to destitute women by imparting skills so that the beneficiaries can support themselves in the long run.

(5) Making efforts to make bonded child labour and children of commercial sex workers free.

(6) Undertake constructive activities, aimed at relieving the poor.

(7) Creating awareness on exploitation of poverty, need of education etc.

(8) Upliftment of a particular section of the society or case or community.

(9) Serving people in distress – the destitute, mentally or physically challenged people.

(10) Social justice to the weaker sections of the society.

(11) Providing formal and non – formal education, adult education, pre-schooling, health education and kindergarten.

Issues for Discussion and for Recommandations

1. Examine the functioning of NGOs and particularly about 'CRY' and its mission as well as vision. How public relations is involved in 'CRY' operations and in all spheres of its activities? Discuss all relevant factors.
2. How far the 'cause marketing' concept is applicable to 'CRY' and how it has helped the NGO to fulfil its objectives?

Child Relief by Organisations.

3. Discuss the method of external and internal communication in NGO organisations and in 'CRY' and also about advertising campaign process in 'CRY'.
4. Provide a short note about media relations in 'CRY'. Also provide 'conclusion' about this case briefly.

PUBLIC RELATIONS IN NGOs

Non Government Organisations or NEGO's are created by certain individuals or groups through voluntary efforts to bring a change in the system or to serve the weaker sections of the society

These organisations are of three types:

(1) Organisation working to bring about a change in the system by fighting against exploitation and oppression.
(2) Organisation working towards reforms.
(3) Organisation providing service and charity.

Therefore, many of these organisations have to deal with such aspects as human rights, injustice to women, bonded labour, child labour. Welfare or orphans etc. in doing this, these organisations may become the target of attack if their policies are not explained to the public properly. For this, it is important to have PR activity, which is the promotion of communication both within and outside the organisation, to project its image and earn the goodwill of the public. Besides, PR is needed for their very sustenance as most of these organisations depend on public support for finance and funding.

Doing good work is not enough. It has to be made known to the public. That is what PR can do PR effort is to earn goodwill, present a responsible image and motivate the public in favour of the NGO.

PR in NGO's is necessary for the following:

(1) NGOs or voluntary organisations depend on public support for funds and manpower.
(2) They need to keep people informed of their activities.
(3) Awareness campaign must therefore be carried out for public support.
(4) Only sustained communication can help generate funds.
(5) Media relations must be cultivated for publicity and to create public awareness.
(6) Relations with government has to be established.
(7) Interaction with other related organisations is necessary.
(8) Propaganda by vested interests has to be effectively countered.

7x7 x You = Infinity. The story of CRY

CRY is a Bombay based Indian organisation started in 1979 by seven young Indian people who met around a dinner table and contributed seven rupees each. They had strong conviction to do something for the underprivileged children in India. That is now CRY was born.

Those seven people were joined by seven others, soon 14 became 1, 400. Today, the freedom movement has grown to over 1, 00, 000 people and cover various organisation in 17 states across India. To date, CRY has collected and disbursed over Rs. 50 crores to more than 300 child development initiatives, helping change the lives of more than 9, 00, 000 children all over India.

The CRY mission

"To enable people to take responsibility for the situation of the deprived Indian child and so motivate them to confront the situation through collective action thereby giving the child and themselves an opportunity to realise their full potential".

CRY focuses on the rights of under privileged children – street children, bonded labour, the girl child, children of commercial sex workers, prostituted children, tribal children, physically and mentally challenged children and children in juvenile insitiutions.

For poor families, the small contribution of a child's income at home that allows the parents to work can make the difference between hunger and a bare sufficiency. These children are offered jobs because they can be paid less and they usually don't show any physical resistance when they are abused. Parents of such children are usually uneducated or unemployed or underemployed. Therefore, CRY believes that the only way to make a permanent difference in the lives of these children is through education. This needs to involve both society and the state in implementing the plans and procedures of the organisation.

CRY – The link between the Child in need and you (Individual Organisations).

There are hundreds of voluntary organisations working with children all over India. As most of these are non profit organisations, they face a common problem – lack of resources. On the other hand, there are people who are able to help and are willing to help, but don't know how to.

In this situation, CRY acts as a link between these organisations and the people who want to help them CRY do not run its own projects. Instead, it provides support to organisations that do.

Public Relations in CRY

"Publics"

Publics are in indispensible part of any organisation. It includes people dealing with the organisation inside as well as outside the organisation.

- **Employees:** CRY has 218 full – time employees across five locations in India i.e. Delhi, Mumbai, Banglore, Chennai and Kolkata. They are paid a regular salary.

- **Media:** CRY has been receiving constant support from the media through editorial coverage of the issues and providing free advertising space or mailing lists, sometimes free of cost or at discounts. These gestures provide CRY a powerful tool to bring the situation of India's children to the attention of decision makers and opinion leaders.
- **Volunteers:** NGOs depend heavily on volunteer help as an ongoing part of their operations. Volunteers often perform work that requires less skill or specialized training than that of paid employees.

Why do people volunteer? Some people do because of the gratification they drive from helping others or to repay obligations towards the organisation or for some it's a way of meeting interesting people.

A common way of recruiting volunteers is to help current ones to help recruit additional ones among their friends and acquaintances.

At present there are hundreds of volunteers all over India. Apart from India, CRY has 'CRY' Inc", a network of over 600 committed volunteers based in United States, who work to gather suppor for the cause of Indian Children.

Community and cultural events are the main activities of CRY Inc. it managed to collect Rs. 2.5 crore in the year 1999 – 2000. This network has now also extended to Middle East, U.K. South East Asia and Australia.

In total, the contribution made by Indians overseas in 2004 – 2005 was Rs. 4.4 crore of the total Rs. 18.4 crore.

Activties/ functioning of CRY

In 1989, the United Nations defined its Charter of Child Rights. These rights include the:-

1. Right to survival covering the following rights
    - The right to life.
    - The right to health.
    - The right to nutrition.
    - The right to name and nationality.
2. Right to protection from exploitation, abuse and neglect.
3. Right to development through education, early child care, leisure and recreation.
4. Right to participation in access to information, respect for children's views and freedom of expressions.

In India, there are thousands of children who do not have access to some or any of the above mentioned rights.

CRY uses the money, time, concern, goodwill and skills of thousands of individuals and organisations towards child development initiatives run by committed organisations and individuals that strive for Child Rights. They can be broadly classified into –

- Individuals
- Organisations
- Government
- Society at large

CRY reaches out to them through:

1. **Direct Action:** This includes direct work with children and their communities through financial and non – financial help to child development initiatives all over India by Individuals and organisations. The main emphasis is laid on education, healthcare, vocational training, awareness programmes for children as well as income generation programmes.
2. **Networking and Policy Influencing:** Involves getting together with other individuals and organisations doing the same kind of work to enhance collective impact at the field and policy level.
3. **Capacity Building:** Helping to build up the necessary skills, structures, attitudes, knowledge in order to enhance child development efforts.

CRY and its Wings

The main wings of CRY are:

(1) Resource Generation Unit: The main function of the resource generation unit is to generate funds from two main sources i.e. from the sales of its products – greeting cards, stationary, calendars etc, and donations from concerned individuals and organisations

Maximum funds are received from individuals, accounting normally for over 60% of the total funds. Motives of such people may be need for sell esteem, habit, concern for humanity on tax advantages.

Support a Child

CRY focuses mainly on education and health care. Therefore, under this scheme, one can support a child's education and health care for a year.

Instead of making donations, an individual can support a child, several children or even an entire community. The following are the schemes under sponsorship programme.

Education – Rs. 600 for 1 child. Rs. 1800 for 3 children. Rs. 3000 for 5 children

Education and Health Care – Rs. 1000 for 1 child. Rs. 3000 for 5 children.

Support a physically or mentally Challenged Child

These children need specially trained teachers, psychotherapists, special teaching aids, special vocational training to make them independent.

Most importantly, their community needs to be taught to accept them. CRY supported initiatives help to do these things for these special children.

Contribution – Rs. 2500 for 1 child. Rs. 5000 to 2 children Rs. 10, 000 for 4 children.

Sponsor a Balwadi:

Balwadis are pre schools for children under 6 years.

They help to ensure that children do not get into child labour or pretty crime.

Children in Balwadis are mainly taught through plays and are also provided with supplementary nutrition.

Contribution Rs. 30, 000 for a year.

Sponsor a Non – formal Education

These centres provide education and vocational training to children between 6 and 14 years who are not able to attend regular schools. NFE Centres prepare children for enrolment in regular primary schools.

Education is imparted through innovative teaching methods and special curricula.

Contribution Rs. 26,000 for a year.

Sponsor a Teacher

Teachers play a vital role in the development of the children who attend the NFE and Balwadis. Besides this, they also act as link between the projects and the communities in which they are located by sensitizing and educating parents about children's right and ensuring that their children are enrolled into schools.

Contribution Rs. 12, 000 for a year.

Sponsor a Health Worker

Their main function is to activate non functioning or underutilized government primary health care centres. A health worker spreads awareness about basic health care and health – related issues through audio – visuals discussions and lectures on topics such as:-

- Ante – and post natal care.
- Nutrition, hygiene & cleanliness.
- Precautions against common diseases like tuberculosis, diarrhea, HIV, AIDS.
- Educating midwives on curbing foeticide and infanticide.

They also help organise immunization and other medical camps. To help them with their work, they are provided with regular training and support in terms of medical supplies and equipment.

Contribution – Rs. 14, 000 for a year.

Donations to & Collecting Donations for the Cry Material Bank

CRY collects materials which can be used directly by underprivileged children or by the organisations that help them. The CRY Materilas Bank, in Delhi and Mumbai, then disburses the materials at a minimum cost to development initiatives working with underprivileged children and communicates.

Corporate Partnerships

Organisation can choose to build a partnership between CRY and itself. Today, there are more than 400 corporate partners associated with CRY all over India.

Partnership can be formed through one or the other following ways:-

Cause Marketing

This is the best method to market a product or products related to a cause and thus help CRY or any other NGO in that matter. A couple of ways are:-

(1) Donating Proceeds from the Sale of a Product or Service: Special promotions are carried on by organisation and individuals, from which a percentage of the profits is donated to CRY. For example, British Airways, launched its new look for the 21st century will ads in leading newspapers. They invited people from all over Asia to pledge money for children CRY received Rs. 7,00, 000.

Nokia, the electronics manufacturer, set aside a part of its revenues from the sale of every Nokia 5110 cellular phone sold over a four month period. This raised Rs. 637, 500 for CRY. S. Chand gave Re. 1 from the sale of every copy of select titles they published in a number of years.

(2) Providing a Platform for CRY: Payroll giving scheme – the free a child movement. Thise scheme helps those individuals who would like to contribute for under privileged children. It is an easy and paper free work. Therefore, it encourages employees to donate money by sanctioning an automatic deduction from their monthly salaries. However, the success of this scheme depends upon the consent and participation of both management and employees.

Material Donations

Instead of or along with money the organisation can also donate material to the CRY material bank (In Delhi and Mumbai). This bank disburses materials at a nominal cost to development initiative working with under privileged children and communities. The material can range from note books to stationery, office equipments, old toys and clothes. CRY also accepts office furniture. IT equipment or any kind of infrastructure for its own use and thus save money.

For e.g. Nokia, besides contributing towards cause marketing efforts also donated cellular phones to CRY. Delhi.

Mahindra & Mahindra has donated an Armada Jeep to CRY Mumbai to replace the old jeep.

Other organisations that have contributed to the materials banks are – HPCL, ICICI, the American Consulate, and Mumbai.

(2) Development Support Unit: This is the second most important unit of CRY which work with the underprivileged children via various projects.

The main function of this unit is to act as a link between an individual or an organisation and the selected projects on which they want to work. Besides channeling the funds to the project, development support unit is also responsible for monitoring its working through qualified social development professionals.

DS unit focuses mainly on health & education in selected areas, other areas being vocational training etc.

For e.g. American Express Bank, Delhi, has adopted a CRY supported project which works at Tigu, a slum in Delhi, focusing on education for children and adults. Motorola Bangalore supports "SNEAHA", a project working for the uplift of tribal and communities in Bellary, one of Karnataka's most backward districts.

Recently, NIH organised a special event on computer literacy for around 40 children of REAP (Rural Education Assistance Programme). A CRY – supported programme.

(3) Youth Wing: This unit comprises of students from various fields who interacts with other students at school and college levels to spread plays, puppets, concerts, workshops etc.

In 2001, 2 medical students from Lokmanya Tilak Municipal Medical College, Mumbai started working for CRY. They collected material like toys, curtains etc for their pediatric ward. Now, they organise weekly programs through films, puppets and talks for the children.

Frank Anthony Public School, Bangalore, made and sold cards and donated the money to a CRY supported project. CRY youth wing organised a summary camp for school children and underprivileged children.

Doon school organised a classical music concert in Mumbai and donated Rs. 2 lakh from the proceeds of the ticket sales.

(4) Support Wing: Support wing is divided into various departments such as HR department, Finance department, Administration department, Communication department etc.

These departments are there to help the other wings in their day to day activities.

INTERNAL & EXTERNAL COMMUNICATION

It is very important to establish and maintain a regular communication between a NGO or any organisation for that matter, and its publics. The diversity of membership in many organisations makes the communication difficult. The key public s are sometimes scattered and are poorly defined. Often communication budgets are not adequate for a well planned sophisticated communication programmes, specially in NGO like CRY.

One of the most effective communication by CRY among its publics is through various periodic as well as non – periodic publications.

PUBLICATIONS: This word is derived from the word 'public' and refers to 'any notes, compositions, etc. generally in a printed form which reaches out to a large number of people through sale, distribution or exhibitions'.

All the publications are sent from Mumbai to all the branches with inputs from different regions. The following are the various publications by CRY:-

1. **House Journal:** "A House Journal is a periodical publication which tires to establish a regular communication between an organisation and its employees and other public."

   A house Journal contains information on achievements of the organisation in various fields, articles on its plans and policies, news on cultural and social functions, etc. Here the quality of CRY's House Journal is worth mentioning.

2. **News Letter:** Theoretically, there is no difference between a House Journal and a Newsletter. The only difference is that a newsletter contains only the news items of an organisation and is a cheaper version of House Journal.

   CRY publishers its newsletter by the name "CRY in Action". It contains all the details of the events, news, programmes that took place in the preceding period.

3. **Annual Report:** AR primarily presents the achievements, policies, programmes, the new milestones and the new targets of the company. An annual report is the most important publication of an organisation expecially for NGOs like CRY which has to maintain transparency of the 'source' as well as 'application' of funds.

CRY Publishes its annual report at the end of each financial year which generally contains:-

- Chief Executive's address to the publics
- Director's report on activities of the year
- Performance review
- Organsiational structure & changes
- Trustees overview
- Financial statements
- Projects list undertaken in different stats.

The financial statements consist of a summarized 'Income & Expenditure Account' of a year and a summarized 'Balance Sheet' which gives information on the 'source' & 'application' of funds.

4. **Brochure:** "A brochure is a non – periodic promotional back grounder publication produced prestigiously in the format of a small booklet or a magazine and which is published on important occasions."

   CRY's brochure generally contains introduction on CRY, how it works for the underprivileged children and how an individual as well as various organisations can donate towards or support CRY's activities and various projects.

5. **Folder:** "A folder is a single sheet non-periodic promotional publication produced prestigiously and which is folded into convenient sized pages for mailing or distribution purposes".

   The folder published by CRY informs people what CRY is and what it actually does for the underprivileged children. Since the information is printed on a single sheet folded into desired pages, the topics are covered in brief. They are sometimes sent to various people through mail and sometimes distributed manually.

6. **Catalogue:** "A catalogue is a complete list of things like products etc., usually in an alphabetical or other systematic order".

   Every year CRY brings out its catalogue of a wide range of cards designed by famous and talented artists, designers and photographers. It also contains a list of a variety of attractive products such as handcrafts, toys, stationery and gift articles created by NGOs working with underprivileged children, adults and women.

   First of CRY's fund came from selling of a few greeting cars by the founder and his few friends who dedicated their lunch hours to sell them at offices in Mumbai. They were able to raise Rs. 30, 000 and CRY was able to support its first project for deprived children. Today, CRY cards are one of the main sources of income. The CRY's paper products business has now grown to a Rs. 4 crore operation involving design, paper purchasing, printing, warehousing, marketing and sales.

   Tie up with Archies: CRY has now tied up with Archies Gifts and Greetings Limited, one of the leading name in the stationery business in India. CRY has consolidated its manufacturing and retail distribution contracts with Archies. CRY greetings and other products are now available in almost 10, 000 retail outlets across India compared to the few hundred outlets in the past.

7. **Sponsorship forms and Donation Coupons:** Sponsorship forms are basically documents with some blanks to fill up.

   While filling up these forms, a person has to give information on his profile for e.g. name, address etc., and has to tick on some options given in the form. Donation coupons are detachable tickets or forms entitling the holder to make a desired amount of donation to the organisation for the children.

These forms and coupons are usually distributed along with the brochures, folders, etc. or are sent to various individuals and organisations through mail:

8. **Books:** There are number of books released on CRY, one being. 'The Indian Child Book 2001'. This book is designed to disseminate information about the situation of vulnerable children in India against the rights they have been ensured by the UN convention of the rights of the child and the constitution of India.

ADVERTISING IN CRY

Advertising refers to "any paid form of non – personal presentation of ideas, goods and services by an identified sponsor".

The medium of advertising may be print, electronic or any other and the communication is usually one- sided i.e. from the advertiser to the public.

Ads usually aim at creating awareness, about a product or services or an issue and to build an image of the organisation in the public mind.

Similarly, the advertisements released by CRY focus mainly on issues related to the plight of underprivileged children such as child labour, etc, and initiates people to donate generously and help the cause.

CRY's ads are generally sponsored by various business organisations. This is done to build a positive image of the organisation.

CRY ads are generally sponsored by various business organisations. This is done to build a positive image of the organisation.

CRY has its PR agency which handles all advertising activities and releases them too. Each region has its own PR agency.

One of the small sized ads had the picture of a small child with a load of bricks on his head. The copy conveyed that if only Rs. 300 were donated, the child would not be using his head, as he did (in the ad), bringing out very clearly that it was expected of the people to donate such a nominal amount in a year to achieve the objectives.

CRY, however, has not been able to generate enough funds since past few years to advertise on a regular basis either in the print or on the electronic media, because advertising on a large scale requires a huge amount of money.

Media Relations

Media relations is one of the most important PR functions of any organisation whether in electronic media such as Television, Radio or print media such as Newspapers, Magazines etc.

CRY holds its State Education Conventions annually which is organised by the National Alliance for the Fundamental Rights in various states like UP, Karnataka, West Bengal, Maharashtra and other states throughout India. CRY has been receiving constant support from the media since a long time, from editorial coverage of the issues to coverage of important events, seminars, conventions to free provision of advertising space and mailing lists. These small gestures provide CRY a powerful tool to bring the situation of India's children to the attention of decision – makers and opinion leaders.

Conclusion

The role of NGOs tend to be significant in bringing out the development and the upliftment of the weaker sections of the society. Therefore, it would be wrong to express NGOs as mere non – governmental voluntary organisations.

True, voluntary organisations are not only non – governemental and non – profit but they have their roots in the local communities and neighborhoods, securing participation of people in meeting their aims and objectives.

They are transparent in operation, free of bureaucratic control and accountable to local communities. But today, it has become important to be bureaucratic to survive, grow and be successful in any endeavour.

CRY has a very well defined organisational structure of its own. Since NGOs have been established by the founders with different motivations, once the founder disappears from the scene, the next generation of leaders may not share the same level of commitment. In such situations, an institutional structure fills the gap, thereby ensuring stability.

The main purpose of any study, therefore, has to be: firstly, to describe the profile of NGOs taking CRY as a case study in regard to its basic characteristics, missions and area of activities. This study deals with how CRY came into existence and how it tries to extend its helping hands towards the underprivileged children of the society.

Secondly, the most important, to describe how NGOs (CRY) conduct their PR functions. No doubt, CRY does commendable jobs and works for not only the underprivileged children but also the society as a whole. But the good work done has to be communicated through various channels of internal and external communication.

Another important and powerful source of communicating with the people is publications, both periodical as well as non – periodical, such as House Journals, Newsletters, Brochures, Folders. CRY also maintains its transparency and accountability through Annual Reports. It also organizes various events, seminars, conventions etc. on a regular basis and also advertisers on T.V. and newspapers.

The best thing is that CRY does not work in isolation on various issues but works with various NGOs, especially providing financial help to them, on different projects in different parts of the country. The main objective of CRY is not only working for the underprivileged children but also to educate, inform and spread awareness among the parents, community and the society as a whole on issues such as education, health, hygiene etc. however, inspite of its effort. CRY should put more stress on the communication work as many people in India are unaware of what exactly does CRY work for and more importantly, how it operates to achieve its aims and objectives.

XIV

"Visuals Speak Louder Than Words"......... Augmenting Undertanding and Enjoyment

What is Audio?

Simply, it's something which we hear in the electronic gadgets. What we hear in a Television ad is also an audio. The web definition of Audio is – "it is the sound part of a programmed or the sound recorded in a videotape. It can be sound, music or a narration." A recent example of such ad can be of TATA TISCON. In this ad a "pundit" is recommending a woman about this product during the house warming ceremony. Though it's very clear the product they were talking about but the problem is that we cannot see the product and the ad is quite boring. It may not gather public attention.

What is Video?

In simple words, the picture of a programme or a picture recorded in a videotape is what we mean by video. It is something which brings our eyes into action.

Here we have divided video into two distinct categories:-

1. **Simple Visual**
2. **Audio visual**

Explanation:

1. **Simple Visual:-** These are the print ads that we see in newspapers and magazines. There is a better scope of making these ads more

Visuals signify the importance of TV programmes.

creative and meaningful than radio ads. There is a presence of visuals in it with the absence of Audio. Examples can be that all the ads that we see daily in all the newspapers and magazines for almost all the products of all the brands existing in this world.

2. **Audio Visuals:-** With the invention of Television the scope of Audio Visual ads has increased. This is the medium that has brought competition in the market for product, brought competition among various ad agencies across the globe for its survival. Audio Visual ads are a combination of both Audio and Video. Ads have become more realistic, creative and understandable with the help of Audio Visuals. It doesn't keep any product out of it. In today's world it has become a race to prepare ads to attract viewers and the combination of Audio and Video provide the perfect platform to sustain.

Audio vs. Video

Video means something in front of our eyes. It includes both simple visuals (in the printed form) and audio – visuals. Before, it was only the audio, with virtually no video at all. But now it is video all the way. People all over the world prefer to "see" rather than just to hear.

Design in front of the eyes

We remember more of what we see because aptly, "Seeing is Believing". If anyone goes to the rural areas where the education is not very prominent and tries to make the rural people understand some concept with the help of some technical stuff, then most surely the show will be a damn failure.

This is why in the rural areas, people take resort of puppet shows, road shows, drama etc. in order to make their campaign a success. Same goes for the infants, who do not understand much.

Appropriate visual example not only enhances understanding but also renders enjoyment. Also, the chance of retaining an information is increased manifold.

Target Audience

It is easy to make someone understand about the focus of a product through a visual than just by an audio.

If only a message is aired in the radio, telling a few words the product then it would have been very difficult, if not, virtually impossible for people to understand about the target group. They would have gone to the market and many would have got flummoxed after knowing about the fancy price of a product which could have been targeted at the upper middle class and the upper class segments of the society.

Why Visuals?

Visuals are usually more important than copies; they're more effective in attracting readers attention and can instantly present the product or service in a dramatic and motivating way.

Show rather than tell, and don't forget that call to action. Television has made the term "Call today!" a very popular call to action in all advertising. That's what sky rocketed MTV to success. They added visuals to songs.

A good way to figure out the importance of visual this simple example can also be given. A person can always understand what he has been told about the product in words but he can never realize what the product looks like, but in a visual ad you can even know all the things about the product, what the advertisers want to show you as well as you can also see the outlook of the product.

Given below are few points which make Visuals a clear – cut winner:-

1. The audience's attention is focused more completely. Visual aids provide one mechanism to direct & focus attention.
2. Visual aids make you more persuasive. A recent study found that presenters using computer – generated visuals (multimedia) had more credibility, demonstrated greater professionalism, and proved to be more persuasive than individuals using overhead slides or text.
3. The receiver retains the message better. Research has clearly shown the people retain more of what they see hear compared to what they simply hear. For example, research has found that message retention after three days is only 10 % following oral presentation, but is 65% following an oral and visual presentation.
4. People have come to expect visuals. Today's world is very visual compared to just a few decades ago. The average person is visually oriented and accustomed to visual presentations. Thus, a strictly oral presentation is tiresome to the majority of the people.
5. Visual aids help establish organisation for presentations. One of the most effective uses of visual aids is establishing overall organisation for the presentation. Audiences look for order in everything they experience. Organsiation aids comprehension and retention. If the structure of a presentation is shown at the beginning of a presentation, a cognitive framework is established for what is to come. If the visuals outlining the presentation are used throughout the programme, it will also aid in organising the new material as it is presented.
6. Visual aids add variety and emphasis to your presentation. Effective teachers use a variety of different teaching methods and technologies as they teach. Visual aids help provide variety.

7. Visuals help you to be concise. You are forced to distill your ideas down to their essence when using visuals. Visuals force you to order and sequences the ideas you will present.

Another example would be a very simple explanation about the human psychology.

Why that is when they are trying to teach little children about health, food, hygiene issues in schools they take help of dramas.

That is because human psychology is somehow more fascinated towards moving objects and colors.

And child inside us never dies. So the love of visuals also stays with it.

PROGRESS TASKS

1. How far is it true that visuals generate a better effect on the audience as far as retention or remembrance and even enjoyments are considered? Please provide examples to find out the comparative retaining capability of Audio and Video messages.
2. Does the maxim hold true that "a picture is worth a thousand words"? Give examples of better targeting with visuals to prove the response factors. Please try to provide examples of application areas in various professional campaigns (Marketing – PR – Advertising).
3. Please provide explanation of concepts relating to audio and visual presentations. Is it true that though audio can explain matters almost properly, an audio – visual or even a visual is much more impact – making?

QUESTION:-

How far is it true that visuals generate a better effect on the audience as far as retention and enjoyment are considered?

Provide examples to find out the comparative retaining capability of audio and video ads.

Answer:-

Let us begin with understanding what audio & visuals are.

Audio can be defined as, "the sound part of a programme or the sound recorded in a videotape. It can be sound, music or a narration." Video is the picture portion of a programme or a picture recorded in videotape.

Video can be divided into two categories:-

1. **Simple visual:-** For example the print ads we see in the newspapers and magazines.
2. **Audiovisuals:-** Audiovisual is a combination of both audio and video. In today's world it has become a race to prepare ads to attract viewers and the combination of audio & video provide the perfect platform to sustain.

Why do we need visuals?

1. **Complexity of the human mind:-**
   We are human beings because we have the power to think, analyze, interpret and judge things the way we wish to. It is not easy to grab the attention of creative minds unless there is a mechanism to do so. Visuals are the right mechanism to hold on to the attention of the people. We have a natural attraction for moving objects. Also it's the easiest way to grab the attention of children, even while educating them about something.
2. **Presence of various sensory channels & their correlative function:-**
   We as humans have the ability to see, smell, touch, feel and taste. In order to enjoy the benefits of the world we live in it is important for all the sensory channels to function in perfect coordination.
3. **Facilitation of better interpretation:-**
   Let's take an example over here. As consumers we wish to buy a new computer. How much ever we might hear about it, we are satisfied only when we see the product in front of our eyes. Moreover, if someone tells us that the color of the product is grey, it is difficult for us to visualize the exact colour in our mind till we actually see it.
4. **Creating a better impact for a longer period of time:-**
   When we simply hear something we may not remember it for a very long time. We may remember a speech, but we will not remember the exact description of a place. For example, we will not remember the details of our friend's college, which we have not visited. But we would certainly remember every minute detail of the college we studied in.
5. **Natural attraction towards colours:-**
   We all love colours. It is not possible for us to lead a colourless life. That is why even though black and white television was popular initially; the need was felt to introduce colour transmission.
6. **Inner belief in what we see:-**
   It is said, "Seeing is believing". We always tend to believe something completely only when we see it. Even though other's opinions do influence us to a great extent, we form the final picture in our mind only after a firsthand visual experience.
7. **Visuals foster creativity and imagination:-**
   Since visuals help in holding on to the attention span of the audience, it ends up adding variety to any presentation. Once we are attentive, we tend to concentrate better, indulge in deep analysis and therefore end up making the current visuals even more creative the next time. It gives lot of scope for creating something new.

8. **Visuals help us to be concise:-**
   It is said. "A visual speaks a thousand words". Explaining something in words takes much longer to get conveyed desirably to the audience. But a visual end up explaining the concept briefly and in a much short span of time.
   Mankind, since the time of their development did not have facility of visuals. There was not technological development and our ancestors survived on sounds and symbols. Even then they managed to communicate with each other to move in groups and satiate their hunger. Yet because of all the above reasons an obvious need was felt for a system of visuals.

Video means something in front of our eyes. It includes both simple visuals and audio visuals. Before it was only the audio, with virtually no video at all. But now it is video all the way. People all over the world prefer to 'see, rather than just to hear.

Even the advertisers have caught the nerve of the masses. The ultimate aim of advertisers is to create a need amongst the masses to leave an impact of the potential and the current customers. There was a time when audio or more preferably the radio was the only channel for effective communication.

But television has changed the entire scenario. Visual ads today are more effective in communicating and delivering the messages. They do not only work on the rational appeal but touch the emotional appeal as well considering the emotions of envy, fear, anxiety, happiness etc.

WHAT WE SEE...........IS WHAT WE BELIEVE...........

This fits well for the visual advertisements. Consumers are able to see, evaluate and analyze the product by viewing it. The advertisers work on the formula of getting attention of the consumers first and then develop their interest.

This has led to a shift of nature of ads from:

RATIONAL APPEAL TO EMOTIONAL APPEAL

Wherein consumers feel very much related and connected with the visuals. This is so because visuals are more effective in attracting the attention and can instantly present the product in a dramatic & motivating way.

Another reason to support the view is the

HUMAN PSYCHOLOGY

It is human psychology because of which somehow we are more fascinated towards moving object and Feel attraction for colors.

Sensory appeal impacts us more and has more retention ability. This is the reason that even when kids are taught, visual aids are always used.

Even their books are full of colour pictures. You will never find 'A' for 'APPLE' written without the picture of apple actually.

It is for the simple reason that we are able to memorize things easily if we can relate to them and feel a certain level of enjoyment as well. Let's take another example: If anyone goes to the rural areas where the education is not very prominent and tries to convey a message through lectures using technical terminology, then surely the show will be a failure.

But if the same thing is explained through a puppet show, road show, dramas etc the campaign will be a success.

Let's relate this fact to our own life: we all listen to radio 24 by 7 these days. But how many audio ads are we able to retain and memorize when compared to visual ads.

Or let's take into account the very famous POLIO CAMPAIGN by Mr. Amitabh Bachhan. What do you think had been more effective .... Just to listen to his voice which could have been mimicry also or the actually see the great actor on the screen with his pleasing and convincing face.

It is for sure easier to remember and is more entertaining to observe the actions and gestures of celebrities, models and actors than to just hear their voices.

Why Video Messages Have More Retention than Audio Ads?

(1) Video is a comprehensive technique.
(2) Evocation of experience in Video Ads.
(3) Demonstration of products.
(4) Emotional content.
(5) Product is close to reality in Video Ads.
(6) Familiar, Friendly faces.
(7) Possibility of distortion in Audio Ads.

Why Visuals Make A Greater Impact?

(1) Recall Value.
(2) Visual Aids provide variety and effective presentation.
(3) Visual presentation is very organised sequential affair.
(4) Visuals combine knowledge with entertainment.
(5) Design in front of the eyes.

Advantages of Audio and Visual Presentations

(1) The audience's attention is focused completely.
(2) Audio – visual presentation is more convincing, more credible and generates greater professionalism.
(3) The receiver retains the message better.
(4) People have come to expect visuals.
(5) Visual aids help establish organisation for presentation.

(6) Visuals add variety and emphasis to the presentations.
(7) Visual helps you to be concise.

All the above points prove that Audio- visual presentations are much more impact making than the oral ones.

QUESTION:

Does the maxim hold true that "A picture is worth a thousand words"? Give examples of better targeting with visuals to prove the response factors. Please try to provide examples of application areas in PR and Advertising campaigns.

Answer:

We all are aware of the controversy regarding the leading Cola giants, Pepsi and Coke. Both the companies faced a major loss when the rumour spread the consumption of their products was a health hazard. Sales dropped. Schools banned the sale of Coke and Pepsi. Regular consumers began refraining from consuming the product. There was nothing that the companies could do. They could not package their product afresh and bring it back in the market since just with a few days the company had lost its credibility. So what did the company do? Simple. The CEO of Pepsico personally came on NDTV and declared his product safe. Coke roped in Aamir Khan to come on television and give proof the Coke is not harmful. Coca Cola also roped in Smriti Irani, the favorite 'Bahu' for millions and the perfect homemaker, to come on screen and declare Coke as a safe family product. Instead of creating public relations through the radio, they chose the easiest medium to reach the masses, Television. Within a few days people were back to quenching their thirst with their favorite soft drinks. A similar PR campaign was conducted by the government to convince people that consumption of eggs and chicken is safe. Where on one hand consumers had almost turned vegetarian, watching their favorite stars consuming eggs and chicken tempted them to resume their consumption. Had they simply heard suspicious consumers may have even considered the voice to be imitated!!!

Similarly in ad campaigns, advertisers would not have taken pains to go out of their way to buy space in newspapers or on television to advertise their products. Simply advertising via radio would have been much simple. Yet the advertisers know the mind of their consumers. They know that Kareena Kapoor's voice on the radio would not make a deep impact as much as her beautiful appearance would make on television. Or let's take the example the exact color of a new lipstick that has been launched in the market? It can be done only and only through visuals, whether the advertiser uses the print media, or the broadcast media. How would another advertiser launching a new computer impress his consumers with the intricate details of his brand? Most effectively by the broadcast media. In this age with one product is being sold by innumerable brands, how consumers would differentiate the logo of one brand from the other unless they form a visual picture of the logo on their mind. Can brand create an image just by audio advertising? Certainly not. The recent efforts being made by advertisers to bring forth their product to the consumers via the usage of internet and television, it speaks of how important visuals are for creating and maintaining brand image.

Concepts Relating To Visual Presentations

We often hear of the pen and sword analogy. But nothing cuts through the clutter of the prospect's mind like a picture.

"The saying that a picture is worth a thousand words is usually applied to the effectiveness of a picture in understanding what was communicated; it may also apply to the effectiveness of the picture in remembering what was communicated." One reason for this effect is that visual images are processed in two parts of the brain rather than just one. A pile of evidence supports that people learn more deeply from words with pictures than from words alone and overall, several studies combined have shown a median percentage gain of 89% effectiveness. Some of the theory behind the gain you get when words and pictures are combined is that we use our brains more fully, processing the content more deeply, because we actively connect the words to the pictures. In other words, our brains work to make sense of the combined pictures and text, and that processing leads to more meaningful and memorable learning. That's the theory, anyway.

In previous generations, graphics were generally illustrations, accompanying the text and providing elucidation. For today's generation, the relationship is almost completely reversed: the role of text is to elucidate something that was first experienced as an image. And even seemingly simple ideas can take a lot more time to convey if you don't use pictures.

Visual aid makes one more persuasive. A recent study found that presenters using computer generated visuals (multimedia) had more credibility, demonstrated greater professionalism, and proved to be more persuasive than individuals using overhead slides or text.

One of the most effective uses of visuals aids is establish overall organisation for the presentation. Audiences look for order in everything they experience. Organisation aids comprehension and retention. If the structure of a presentation is shown at the beginning of the presentation, a cognitive framework is established for what is to come. If the visuals outlining the presentation are used throughout the programme, it will also aid in organising the new material as it is presented.

While some speakers can hold their audience's attention without one prop or graphic, they are the exceptions. Today's listeners almost demand that certain types of presentations use visuals. If your audience members can't visually relate to what you're saying, they'll tend to shut out and stop listening.

The Benefits of Using Pictures

Using pictures as part of a reviewing process can produce these benefits:

1. The process of creating helps individuals to sort out their own thoughts and feelings – after which they are able to express themselves more clearly (with or without the picture they created)
2. The process of creating pictures co – operatively (in pairs or groups) encourages people to talk to each other in some depth and detail about their experience of the activity being reviewed.
3. Whatever is created through pictures serves as a visual aid or confidence booster in helping people to communicate their experience of the activity to others?
4. Pictures expand the 'language' of reviewing, open up new channels of communication and generally help to develop communication skills.
5. The picture may speak for itself, sometimes communicating more about an activity than a verbal picture would achieve.
6. Pictures can be used at all stage of a learning cycle – for describing the past, for communicating about the present and for envisioning the future.
7. The process of creating pictures helps individuals to sort out their own thoughts and feelings – after which they are able to express themselves more clearly (with or without the picture they created)

The use of 'pictures' in reviewing helps learners to 'see' their experiences and to communicate their experiences to others. Pictures can also enhance the quality of communication throughout the learning cycle.

We all think in pictures – some more than others – depending on our 'preferred learning styles'.

We can use words, tone of voice and gestures to communicate our mental pictures to others. We can also – of course – use pictures to communicate pictures! But many of us get stuck in the groove of communication by words alone – even where a picture would be worth 1,000 words (and might even save a lot of time)

The use of visual communication tools can help people to get out of a verbal rut and to communicate more easily in both words and pictures.

Visuals have universal appeal to all the section of people, from youth to old, north to south, and east to west. Visuals were the common medium to transmit ideas, thoughts, and emotions – the content of heart, mind and soul.

Visuals include illustrations, logo, drawings, painting, and charts. Sometimes spoken or written words are added up to visuals to make a lucid presentation. But what visuals can do alone is not always possible to do only with words. All the signs and symbols discovered on the walls of the cave of pre – historic days are still saying stories greater than a thousand lifetimes. Visuals alone can say a thousand words.

All the visual elements have become the lifeblood in today's world of information, communication and entertainment. In the world of thousands of languages and hundreds of differences in social set up the silent language of visuals is understood by everybody.

How many people read the long budget speech of the finance minister or the performance of a company in a financial year?

In today's competition to communicate more and impressively, charts and graphs are made in a more interesting form as pictographs. Visuals are more easily comprehensible than written words, and visuals do not require any language of understanding.

"Use of Visuals in Advertising."

In obtaining attention, creating impact, stimulating interest from an indifferent audience visuals are used quite frequently. The advertising community has always tried to translate the visual appeal into an effective selling message. Visuals perform the following functions:

(1) Create an atmosphere – visuals help to create an atmosphere or enhance the atmosphere.

(2) Attract attention – can we imagine a newspaper, a magazine, a hoarding advertising without a visual? Surely not even in matrimonial website like "Shadi.com or 'Bharat matrimonial". Visuals play the important part in inviting the viewers to stop and click.

(3) Present the hidden or symbolic form – visuals are symbolic representation of an idea or a thought. A visual of a pigeon of peace, a rose for love.

(4) Use of visuals also increases recalling power and helps in engaging our attention e.g. Amul's butterly girl, Asian Paint gattu, all these visual elements help to command attention and create interest.

The importance of visuals has started a new trend of advertising known as "No copy ADVERTISING"

QUESTION:-

Please provide explanation of concepts relating to Audio and Visual presentations. Is it true that though Audio can explain matters almost properly, an Audio – Visual or even a Visual is much more impact – making?

Answer:

What are the factors that we would consider while purchasing a new mobile? The brand image, opinion of family and friends, features of the mobile phone as per our desire, the color of the phone, etc. Can we judge the product by listening to the description? Or would we purchase it only when we have seen it with our own eyes? Wouldn't we, as intelligent consumers, want to check out the color and features with our own eyes before investing our hard earned money? As a conscious consumer, we would say we should.

A visual is much more impact – making:-

(1) Visuals are more impact making as a single picture can convey more than one message at a time which audio can't do.
(2) Visual aids help you reach your objective by providing emphasis to whatever you said.
(3) Clear pictures multiply the audience level of understanding of the material presented.
(4) They are used to reinforce your message, clarify points and create excitement.
(5) Adds impact and interest to a presentation.
(6) Enables you to appeal to more than one senses at the same time, thereby increasing the audience's understanding and retention level.
(7) With pictures the concepts or ideas you present are no longer simply words – but words plus images and a more clarified message.
(8) We learn through all our 5 senses not just through ears and visuals attack more impactfully on our all 5 senses.

Computer, videodiscs, and interactive videodisc technology are used in many courses to enhance student learning. In the classroom, portable computers linked to an LCD projection panel allow students to see the computer's display on a large screen.

Advantages of Audio Visual Aids.

Audio Visual Aids:

(1) Strengthen the clarity of the speaker's message.
(2) Increase the interest of the speaker's information.
(3) Make a speaker's message easier for listeners to retain.
(4) Enhance the speaker's credibility.
(5) Can improve the speaker's persuasion.
(6) Helps combat stage fright.
(7) Bring deeper understanding to complex subject matter.
(8) Share results of dynamic meetings with others.
(9) Help senior team "see the big picture" and focus attention.
(10) Improve the decision – making process.
(11) Integrate new initiative throughout an organisation.
(12) Speed adoption of major change.
(13) Help everyone picture their role in organsiational transformation.

CONCLUSION

Till now it has been made pretty clear that visuals generate a better effect on the audience as for as retention or remembrance or even enjoyment is considered. Talking about retention we want to sneak in with a research that was conducted in the US to find out the retaining capability of Audio Ads and video Ads. The research proved that after 3 days of watching a visual presentation we remember 65% of it whereas we remember only 10% of an Audio presentation after the same period.

Our study showed that even simple visuals, i.e. Print ads speak better than Simple videos. This is because:-

A. Seeing is believing or rather ....
"A picture is worth a thousand words". This maxim holds true and is universal.

B. Better targeting is possible with visuals because a person will be able to know about the target audience without even hearing anything (just by looking at the product).
E.g. of a SONATA GOLD if shown in the T.V. or even in a magazine then anyone will understand that it is for the Upper Class people. But if this ad is aired in the radio and played .... "Hyundai brings in Hyundai Sonata etc...." then it would have been very difficult even for a very intelligent person to guess about it.

The Final Words

A radio and an Audio Visual ad were shown to the respondents at the beginning of the presentation and a series of questions were given to them after 10 minutes with the following questions –

On Audio –

(1) What was the product?
(2) What was new about the product?
(3) What was the price?

On Video –

(1) What was the Product?
(2) The color of the man's jersey?
(3) Tell us the number of accidents occurred?

It was seen that for "Audio" most of the respondents were able to answer only question (1) correctly, whereas the response was much better for the video part. Hence, it's universal that

"VISUALS SPEAK LOUDER THAN WORDS".

XV

Is the Pen Still Mightier?

Survival of the Print Media in the Electronic Era

With the advent of the electronic media in the form of Radio and Television. Marshall Mcluhan, the Canadian Scholar, had predicted the death of the print media by end of the 20th Century. Since then the new media has expanded to include the Internet or the World Wide Web with numerous sites which carry the latest news, articles, information and almost everything one looks forward to. The Internet need not adhere to rules or regulations and is free to circulate anything that may inhibit radio, television or newspapers to air or publish. The death knell of the print media, so strongly and convincingly sounded by the world's most respected communication and information guru, has now been proved entirely wrong or at least premature.

State of the Indian Press

The Indian media scene, since the early 80s, has been in a state of metamorphosis from a robust scenario in the 70s, when options were limited and the print medium was the single most dominant medium, we find a sudden proliferation of choices in the 80s overriding all other media.

Since 1991, however, the entire scenario has undergone further changes. With growing options in media, the value of the press as a medium started to re - emerge significantly. Qualitatively too, the Press has made tremendous progress which aided its survival in quantitative terms despite

increase in production costs. With great strides in technology, glossy colour printing, innovations in print, multiple editions, split – run facilities and geographical flexibility; it is not surprising that the Press has turned out to be the dominant medium since the 90s.

Whether large or small, about 30,000 newspapers in 16 principal languages with circulations around 231 million copies all over India are the true voices and monitors of the nation. They are, as yet, in spite of the advance of the electronic media, the basic source of most of the daily information and opinion received by the Indian public. At the other end, newspapers are bought and read by the literate elite who are the well – to – do the middle class, and the white and blue colour employees – in short, the educated minority.

The Resurgence of the Press

The last decade and the beginning of the 21st century have witnessed the emergency of the Press in a new role. Hitherto regarded as a recorder of future history, the Press assumed the mantle of the conscience keeper of the nation. One of the reasons for this was the increasing tilt towards investigative journalism. At the same time, however, if the Press really desires to gain acceptability in the new role, it is necessary for it to gain credibility and public confidence by its unbiased approach. In many cases the papers had to retrace their steps and offer apology or regret for having crossed the limits of journalistic propriety. The Press Council of India had to condemn instances of violation of ethical standards by the print media. The Council observed, "The increasing tendency to play God and think the Press can do no wrong is quite disturbing. This not good journalism".

At the other end, the Indian Newspapers Society (INS), with considerable factual data, has focused attention on the variety and truthful dissemination of news and views in representative daily newspapers in the country. The INS Survey shows up Press in India in a favourable light in comparison with those in leading democratic countries such as the UK, Canada, France, Japan and West Germany. The Indian Press, by and large, has pinpointed failings in public life and molded public opinion. The INS survey establishes the complete unbiased nature and fairness in news coverage and editorial comments in the representative Indian newspapers.

The Problem for the print media

The electronic media was attracting more people due to the fact that they didn't need to be literate to understand the Radio or TV messages. Literacy is always a big requirement when it comes to the print media.

Thus, the problem for the print media was that people were not dependent on the newspaper for news with the availability of news on TV and Radio.

This is when the owners of the print media realised the news alone wasn't enough to sell newspapers. They had to find other little things that would impel the public to purchase and read newspapers. The newspapers are no longer seen as just the medium of news alone, but is now seen as a "UTILITY" to keep referring back throughout the day and even later.

Advertising: Get Big, Get Small

The print media have distinct advantage over TV or Radio in the fact that advertising in print is not ephemeral like the TV or Radio spots. Also, more details are possible due to the advantage of space over time. In a newspaper or a magazine or a journal you can have as much space as you want to convey your message and hundreds of big or small ads are accommodated without any discrimination whatsoever. A paper may have the most comprehensive classified advertisements, useful when you want to rent a flat or sell a car – and so the "The Times of India" calls these ads "news you can use". And, therefore, advertising is news too.

But, with markets getting more and more competitive, the advertisers, mainly the big ones, are feeling the heat. In India, as T.N. Ninan, Editor of Business Standard put it "marketing honchos are under-growing pressure to deliver more bang per ad buck". The result is that advertising gets steadily cleverer and more intrusive in the print media.

While competition for circulation between papers has led to a dumping down of content, competition with 24 hour TV news channels has inducted rethinking on news priorities.TV channels no doubt have cut into the advertisement revenues and circulations. Newspapers can no longer attract readers by headlining the latest spot news not to speak of breaking news, that they have already heard and seen on TV. To a great extent, however, brighter headlining, better pictures, more – pages – per rupee have helped. The print media, whether newspapers or journals, are advertising themselves like commodities. Rivalry for circulation and readership – vital for advertisement revenue – has generated claims that hurt the credibility of all print media. Disconcerting indeed, but this is another side of the ongoing tussle between the print and the electronic as well as between print and print.

The Present and the Future

The reasons for the pre – eminence of the press and its continuing survival against the onslaught of "electronic buzz" are both physical as well as psychological. Initially the print media felt acutely nervous and were asking the crucial question: "What is the future of The Fourth Estate? Will it survive effectively in the long run? What kind of publications will survive and what changes are needed in the infrastructure and in the attitude of the Press."

Happily, the Press did not fail. It has won the respect and confidence of its readers with its forthright and imaginative reporting. It has also the record of standing up to the establishment and fearlessly publishing investigative reports and bold editorials in its columns. In – depth coverage and analysis of news and views, special coverage of women, cinema, health, industry, education, agriculture, and finance – in all these, the Press has really been able to combine journalistic talents with visual impact through excellent page make up and good production quality. With strides in technology, the press offers high grade, glossy colour printing; in addition, innovative possibilities in print are abundant which are restrictive in the audio – visual medium.

PROGRESS TASKS

1. Identify the threats that have come to play against the print media in recent times and make an assessment of the advantages of news media in terms of impact and audience acceptance. Do you see any immediate danger of the print media going obsolete?
2. Discuss how the print industry has been able to survive by bringing about far- reaching changes in content as well as in overall image. Can the print media continue to exist without being reduced to entertainment journals or advertisement handouts?
3. Does the newspaper (as well as other forms of print media) enjoy any significant strength to convey communication messages than by Radio or TV? Examine this aspect with total perspective about the relevant issues.

INTRODUCTION

THE PAST

One of the major development in 16th century that altered the course of communication history besides political and socio – economic history was the arrival of printing press to Goa by Portuguese missionary in the year 1556.

In a small town on India's southwest coast an obscure Portuguese printer and his equally obscure Indian assistant opened the earliest and most important technical activity in the history of mass communication in India. But most of the materials printed during this early period were religious text including Bible, hymn books etc. Since these did not touch the economic, political and social lives of the people, printing did not alter the way people communicated and live their lives. The noticeable factors were:

1. The elite class did not want to change their concept of learning directly from the learned Gurus.
2. The scope for popularization of literature through printing was quite limited because of barrier of illiteracy as well as multiplicity of languages.
3. There were manuscript newspapers, especially in the mughal courts, but they were all meant for the emperor, his courtier, military generals and officials.

4. There was a wide gap between elite and the masses in information, education and communication.
5. The different languages of India were not standardized. Anything worth recording was written in Sanskrit and preserved on palm leaves. It was not considered religiously proper to transfer those inscriptions to mechanical printing which would be handled by all and sundry.
6. Printing would defile the sacred texts because the printing ink contained animal fat.

Although the printing press was brought to India in the year 1556, it was in 19th century that printing really got boost with entry of Secrampore Trio in Calcutta and Danish scholars in Tamilnadu. The missionaries got several non religious, secular textbooks printed in presses which included grammars, vocabularies, proverbs, dictionary, and geography.

Historically, the first newspaper was started by James Augustus Hicky on Jan, 29th 1780. It was Bengal Gazette and it was a weekly dealing exclusively with the arrivals, departures and the other social, economic and cultural activities of the small British community in Calcutta, and the head quarter of East India Company. This news paper voiced the grievances of a section of the British residents of Calcutta who were dissatisfied with East India Co's personnel policies and practices. However, Hicky soon ran into hot water for exposing corruption, both at the highest level of company administration and within the superior ranks of British settlers living in Calcutta. In any case, newspaper served small population. It did not have high circulation – perhaps only 350 – 400 copies weekly.

The Present and the Future

Marshall Mcluhan, the Canadian scholar and once referred to as the "Oracle of the Electronic Age", had predicted the death of the print media by the end of the 20th century. As the historical genesis of the Media Industry, the Print Medium still holds center stage, successfully thwarting strong competition from the rapidly growing TV broadcast business, while expanding continuously.

Predictions that TV and new medium would hamper growth of print seem unfounded – India for example, has its number grow by 7 % p.a. in the last decade (culminating in over 30,000 registered dailies). And the growth in overall circulation is estimated to match this figure. Whether large or small about 30,000 newspapers in 16 principal languages with circulation around 231 million copies all over India are the true voices and monitors of the Nation.

Many say gone are the days when one would spend hours in library, when everything is now available with just a click. Web Publishing of Research allows much faster dissemination of ideas than Print Publication. And since Webbed Publications generally are not purchased, they can spread further, into more hands than need them. These factors prophesize the issues of Ownership, Copyright and Originality and will force the Research and Publication community to recast ethical and legal constraints on the usage and sharing of information.

Just out of curiosity, one question. In the next millennium what will researchers call literacy, what languages will students learn? Will students be required to use a new dialect, a kind of Standard Internet English, the unwilling result of so many people writing to each other on computer networks and falling unconsciously into new patterns and conventions introduced like Viruses? What we come to call literacy may move beyond print and text literacy to encompass Computer, Internet and Media literacy.

But most of us agree that there are features texts that can describe our world of ideas and the depth of human experience and emotions better than any other media can. The creative imagination engages with print and text so that readers create their own mental pictures. Reading and writing promote a different kind of cognitive development from the processing of images and sounds, a sort of development that complements other forms of understanding.

Today the scope of the print medium has expanded from reporting news to include Entertainment, Sensationalism and Product Promotion. And judging from the thin line of demarcation between Editorial and Advertising, the Indian Print Medium seem well set to evolve into a vehicle for Entertainment and Product Promotion along with News.

Q.1 Threats that have come to play against the Print media and advantages of new media in terms of impact and audience acceptance. Any immediate danger of the print media going obsolete?

"Threat" the word itself creates an expression of 'danger'. It can as well be a state of challenge. It's a challenge that the print has been facing since the sudden proliferation of choices in various other media. The challenge that were once predicted to be the death knell of print media.

The fiercest threat that print media has been facing today is the emergence of electronic media that has spread like wild fire in the whole world. This new media by creating its newer form has caught the attention and interest of all the age groups. It is true that immediate impact of TV pictures cannot be equalled by press reporting but TV cannot match extensive in - depth coverage of news that printed page can provide. It would take a TV news reader hours to read out the contents on an average newspaper. The multichannel TV had not led to a fall in number and circulation of newspaper in India.

Print media is facing a threat from electronic from media in terms of spontaneity and visuals. Today's print media face the challenge of educating and entertaining the readers so that they can participate fully in the affairs of the country. People prefer to hear the headlines from the day's happenings rather than going through a huge newspaper. Moreover, the immediate impact TV pictures shown live on TV cannot be equalled by press reporting. Today's newspapers are being criticized for serving the consumers and not the readers. The press today is facing various pressures such as technological, financial and professional and so on.

Print media like magazines are affected adversely due to onslaught of TV. The news stories of magazines become obsolete when published fortnightly or monthly.

Magazines are required to constantly try to create a new identity for themselves. There are hardly any studies conducted on impact of print media except the readership survey which throw light on what people prefer to read. Print media in India continue to be largely an urban phenomenon. They are either published in metros, big towns or state capitals. Moreover in a country where literacy rate is so low, the spread of print media and the utilization remains limited compared to other mass media.

Radio

Radio entered the scene in India in the year 1924. Now you could actually hear the things and literacy was not a condition at all. Initially radio started in India with just 6 stations with a total component of 18 transmitters. Music and interactive programmes over the radio made radio a very favourite medium for the people.

Radio is a widely used mass communication medium and has a great potential in dissemination of information as radio signals cover almost entire population. More than 177 radio stations are there across the country. With the advent of transistors this medium has reached the common man in urban and rural area of India though the utilization is more among rural people. It has advantage over the other media like Television and Newspaper in terms of being handy, portable, easily accessible and cheap.

In India, radio with its penetration to the rural areas is becoming a powerful medium for advertisers. It gets 3 % of the national advertising budget. Radio is still a cheap alternative to TV but is no longer the poor medium in advertisement terms. Because radio listening is so widespread, it has prospered as an advertisement medium for reaching local audiences. Moreover, radio serves small highly targeted audiences which make it an excellent advertisement medium for many kinds of specialized products and services.

Before the invasion of TV into our living room, radio was a bright, major, rational, general audience medium. In the zeal of government to promote TV in eighties, radio had been steadily neglected.

It is believed that radio is no longer a potent mass media tool and it has been overshadowed by T.V. In the rural areas, radio has still remained a medium for information and development. It is still a popular medium in rural areas and lower strata of urban society. Survey has shown that TV does not kill radio. There are plenty of evidences showing that after the initial onslaught of TV, radio reestablished itself very firmly. It is not a primitive version of T.V. but it is medium with its own particular strengths. Therefore the strengths of radio must be considered on its own terms.

Television

Amongst all the mass media today, TV attracts the largest number of viewers. Its audience is greater in size than any of the other media audiences. This because it is able to attract the audiences of all age groups, literate and illiterate and of all strata of society. Indian Television has performed different functions as compared to TV in the West. Even today though commercials have entered Indian TV in a big way, its basic purpose has not changed. It continues to perform its functions of national integration and development.

The growth in TV both in technology and reach in the last three decades has been tremendous. It was basically conceived as mass medium and a mass educator for large population scattered in remote and culturally diverse areas. It is supposed to disseminate the message of development and modernization to create awareness for generating public participation. It is expected to support government plans and programmes for bringing about social and economic change and to protect national security as well as advance the cause of national integration. Since TV can transmit not only words but pictures as well, the significance of TV as a medium of mass communication has universally been realized and recognized. In country like India where population and illiteracy are the problems, electronic media provides tremendous reach for dissemination of audio – visual information even in remote areas. India has diverse cultures, religions and traditions. Thus TV can play an important role in developing common understanding among the people and bringing them closer.

Television stimulates and reinforces ideas, beliefs and tendencies already possessed by the viewer. For example TV repeats and thereby reinforces the messages on family planning, importance of girl education, marriage age, environment protection, energy conservation etc. it serves persuasive function. Television has more flexibility and mobility in its coverage due to audio visual presentation. This is the reason why it has become the family medium. It can show landing on Mars, functioning of a heart or division of a cell through animation.

As far as educational message to the masses are concerned, TV can be the most powerful educational medium because it combines speaking, writing, showing. You can only talk to the masses at one time but now you can show them what you mean. Thus, TV presents mass demonstration to thousands of viewers at the same time by moving images; TV fascinates people, demands attention and eventually influences their thought and behavior.

TV audiences have expanded tremendously in India during last 10 years. It is estimated that approximately 660 million households have TV sets. The number of people who can watch TV programme in their own home is about 300 million.

Experts have summarized the pros and cons of growth of TV in India as

Pros	Cons
1. Political will to expand TV services.	1. Use of TV as Propaganda Medium
2. The government intention to use TV for educational development.	2. Lack of local infrastructure to support TV messages.
3. High Advertisement revenues from Doordarshan and Private Channels	3. Entertainment programmes get higher viewer rating than educational shows.
4. Satellite TV can reach rural area.	4. TV encourages socio–economic inequality
	5. Propagation of consumerism especially among socially disadvantaged viewers.

In brief the advantages of TV as a medium are manifold and some of the impactful characteristics are:

1. Excellent quality of production.	1. Creative use of environment and mental make – up of the viewers.
2. Familiar, friendly voices.	2. Animation.
3. Retailers also watch TV.	3. Image building.
4. It is a comprehensive technique.	4. Emotional content.
5. Evocation of experience.	
6. Demonstration.	

Growth of Internet in India

The last decade has seen the birth and growth of Internet in India as a phenomenon that has transformed the life of the people in several respects. Its presence has been universal.

Broad Band Internet Connectivity

Widespread use of "Convergence", however, revolves around next generation applications taking the advantage of increased bandwidth. While a large number of technologies are getting developed for broadband access such as DSL/ ADSL, cable modems, VSAT's, wireless technologies, the mix of deployment would depend upon the market forces and promotional efforts made by the government. International Data Corporation (IDC) has recently carried out a market survey giving the future projections covering interalia, worldwide broadband penetration, outlook as well as possible technology choice.

In India, broadcasting has been a state monopoly with the stress shifting in recent years from expansion of network to technology up-gradation.

The telecommunications sector, on the other hand, witnessed in the last five years a radical transformation from monopoly of operations to a situation of vigorous competition with fast track liberalization of services and infrastructure. Internet, the latest entrant to the field, acquired tremendous acceptance within a short span with a fast and impressive growth. Technology up gradation is now being recognized as an important need. Plans and programmes are being conceived to bring at least half of the television broadcasting to the digital system in the next five or six years. In the telecommunications area, the Department of Telecommunications provided all the services till the opening up started in 1991. In the last about 5 years, the telecommunications sector has experienced a radical transformation from monopoly of operations to a sector facing full and vigorous competition with fast track liberalization of services and infrastructure. The greater harmonization and market opening in telecommunications should now provide a highly fertile environment for growth. This is already bringing benefits to many businesses and consumers with lowering of prices, improved customer service and innovative service offerings. Internet, though the last to emerge on the scene, has acquired tremendous acceptance in India and the growth of internet users has been very impressive. According to NASSCOM there would be about 10 million internet users and more and more in India. It would be interesting to go into the profile of the internet using community presented in a report of the CII's National Sub Committee on IT Enabled Services. According to this report more than 80per cent of the PCs sold in India were for internet access and more than 4 lakh Indian household had internet connection. The dominant use of internet was for "search" (77%) followed by usage for e –mail (73%) and for software downloads (23%). The average use of internet has been about 6 hours a week. The product lines are now in a position to converge through wired and wireless media, and "topple down" old business models and value chains. Various experts think that electronic media has no effect on the print media. According to them the challenges from the electronic medium have in no way hampered the growth of the print segment. The Indian reader still relishes detailed analysis in addition to hourly news bulletin and talk shows.

The 'Press in India Report', prepared by the Registrar of Newspapers in India (RNI), reveals that the total circulation figure of newspapers jumped up from 11,52,53,948 copies in 2001 to more than 16,00,00,000 copies in 2010 - 2011, registering an increase of more than 24 per cent. The figures are constantly displaying an uptrend and may hit 22, 00, 00,000 copies in the next 10 year period.

Q.2 Survival of the print media in the electronic era

Certainly, the last few years of the millennium were nerve – wracking for publishers as they sought to understand the electronic media especially the Internet and its implications for the print media business. But this cannot be seen as an immediate danger to the print media. Interestingly, print media is now available online and many readers read the print communication off the computer screen (contents are electronically fed). The new media has expanded, including the internet or the world wide web with numerous sites that carry the latest news, articles, information and almost everything one looks forward to the internet need not adhere to rules and regulations and is free to circulate anything that may inhibit radio, television or newspaper to air or publish. The internet has lifted the boundaries of access of the print media. The electronic media was attracting the public more due to the fact that they didn't need to be literate to understand the radio or TV messages. The quality of the newspapers also started changing tremendously. New technologies were used for glossy colour printing, innovations in print, multiple editions, split run facilities and geographical flexibility. Due to these changes, the 1990's saw the print media as the most dominant medium.

Isn't it true that material progress and intellectual growth have been based on the printed / written word. This reason is enough to believe why the abiding spells of print media over its audience will survive the challenges of the electronic media. Even after the contents of books in major libraries have been digitalized, libraries have not disappeared. Teaching throughout the campuses in the world continues to be mainly through books and papers. Just as the written / printed words has not replaced the spoken word as the most popular medium of communication, so also electronic media are expected to co – exist with print media.

Print media in India has undergone revolution in the last 20 years. Their role, layout, visual display and reading material have advanced and have resulted in flourishing of print media industry and becoming more challenging and competitive in nature. It has grown enormously in quantity and variety. There is marked advancement in printing, composing, layout and visual display with the advancement in printing technology.

Newspaper has been the leading print medium ever since Johannes Gutenberg started his press in mid fifteenth century. Newspapers as mass media today do not just observe and report but ask, pursue, investigate, doubt and demand. It's true that print cannot compete electronic as far as fastness of news is concerned, but they serve independently as a supplement to these media by offering details of the news with thorough reporting and coverage. Print media like newspaper and magazine offer wider variety of ready material and viewpoints of many people and this provide better comprehension of the affairs and issues.

Another major factor in the development of the Indian language press in recent years has been the introduction of computerized typesetting technology. It has become possible thanks to the new technology, to combine speed in the production with preservation of the identity and aesthetic appeal of the alphabets of Indian languages. Newspapers today have acquired strength in features, photographs, graphics and quality of paper used. Thus newspaper in India is at height of performance. Many of them have circulation close to a million and they have multiple editions. This revolution mainly took place because of modern systems of production and printing.

Commercialization of print

Another major development is commercialization of print media. Newspaper and magazine have two sources of revenue: one from circulation and subscription and another from advertisement revenue. Advertisement revenue which is substantial is generated from sale of space in the publication. Almost 50% to 60 % of space is occupied by ads in major publications. It should be known that financial viability, which requires substantial revenue from ad, is essential for sustaining the freedom and improving the quality of newspaper. Revenue from newspaper has to be supplemented by ads to cover the balance of cost and yield a surplus for growth of qualitative improvement. And then there are some ads, especially classified which are interesting to the readers.

Q.3 Does the newspaper (as well as other forms of print media) enjoy any significant strength to convey advertising massages than by radio or TV? Examine this aspect with total perspective about the relevant issues.

Advertising has played a major role in the development of the newspaper from the early B/W version to its modern contemporary. Advertising provides the revenue that the newspaper requires to keep its price at an affordable level.

Each publication has its readership, which is influenced by its general image. The editorials, news and entertainment offered by a publication form its general image. The better this image, the greater is the acceptance of the advertising message by a reader. However, advertisement effectiveness in a publication varies from reader to reader, from one advertisement to another and from publication to publication.

Local advertising is in fact possible only in newspapers. Barring a few national advertisements, newspapers contain mostly local advertisements. This is one of the biggest advantages, for newspapers provide advertising in a geographically segmented market. Local and regional newspapers offer news about the local community and the region. The advertising message thus delivered in local or community newspapers is most effective.

Newspapers have an advantage over TV or Radio in the fact that advertising in newspapers is not ephemeral like the TV or Radio spots. Newspaper advertisements have the advantage that they are not fleeting like the TV and Radio advertisements. They can be read again and again. Also, more details are possible due to the advantage of Space versus Time.

On TV, you have a few precious seconds, in which you have to convey as much of your message as possible. Even after doing this, you cannot be sure that your target audience has seen the advertisement. Therefore, you have to repeat a few times in order to ensure visibility.

And if you are advertising on a national channel like DD or Star Plus or Sony, you may inadvertently advertise your product to markets you haven't even introduced the product in. This means you do not have geographical selectivity when it comes to popular TV channels.

An advantage with TV used to be that people would rather watch the commercials coming rather than get up and change the channel. But this was truer in earlier years than it is right now. Earlier Television sets generally had to have channels switched manually and also there were not many channels to choose from. But now most TV sets come with remote controls and a large number of channels to choose from, which means people can switch channels from wherever they are sitting as soon as the programme they are watching goes for a commercial break.

It is the same case with the Radio. Radio spots are just a fleeting and could be missed among the general banter going on. Since only sounds can be reproduced in a Radio advertisement there is nothing much to differentiate one advertisement from another.

In a newspaper, you can have as much space as you want to convey your advertising message to the fullest extent and in any innovative way you want. You can easily put teasers in different pages of the same newspaper to attract attention to your main advertisement. Or you may release a string of teaser advertisements across a brief period of time to arouse curiosity and then release the main advertisement. Thus you have a lot of options while advertising in newspapers.

Colour

Colour is one important device that is now helping the newspaper into the new age. Earlier newspapers used to be predominantly in Black and White (B/W), and colour illustrations were a luxury. But nowadays, due to technological advancements, colour illustrations in newspapers are not as rare as they used to be.

Colour in a Black and White world will always draw attention. The change from B/W pictures in newspapers to colour has helped the newspaper to catch the attention of the readers. Most newspapers, even though they may not be printing the whole newspaper in colour, print supplements in colour. The colours brighten up an otherwise drab looking newspaper and get people to read it. Readers expect the newspaper to be more exciting because of the colours. Special articles can be highlighted through the use of colors.

The real effect of colours has been to attract the younger readers. They are used to reading colorful books and have grown up watching Colour

Televisions. Black & White does not interest them. Colour, on the other hand, increase the notice-ability of the newspaper.

Advertisers benefit even more as they can use colours to make their advertisement stand out from the clutter. Colour gives them more options when they are making a print advertisement.

Price

Indian newspapers are the cheapest in the world. The newspapers are themselves responsible for lowering their cover prince, ostensibly to boost circulation, and as a result, to increase advertisement revenues.

Price of the newspaper has had a large role to play in the acceptance of the newspapers. Being daily, high prices would have immediately discouraged readers from buying newspapers. As such, the unit price of newspapers has always been kept low. In India, newspapers are available at as low as Rs. 1.50 each.

Newspapers, especially general newspapers, cannot afford to have higher prices. But, special interesting newspapers, which cater to selective groups, can be priced higher. For example, The Business Standard, The Economic Times and The Financial Express are all business newspapers, which are targeted at business and economic readers. They provide invaluable day to day business information to the businessman and slightly higher prices would be accepted.

The per unit cost of publishing a newspaper comes to almost 20 times the price the reader pays to the vendor. The advertising revenues more than make up this shortfall in price. That is why it is said that advertising helps keep the newspaper independent and unbiased.

If it were not for advertising revenue, the cover price of the regular newspapers would be about 20 times more than the price currently charged form readers. Even now, with all loyalty towards newspaper from readers, if the price were to increase even 5 times, it can be expected that circulation would drop drastically.

Loyalty and Habits

Some newspapers command a certain loyalty from its readers. Readers are so used to reading a certain newspaper that they may not be able to start their day without reading one. The editorship styles and the editorials in a newspaper are the main features that differentiate one newspaper from another. These are also the reasons for which readers prefer one newspaper over another.

Distinct Advantages

The print media has these distinct advantages over television or radio:

1. **Advantage of Space over time:** Advertising in print is not transitory like the one on TV or Radio spots. Also, the ad can be more detailed

as more space is available on newspapers and magazines. Hundreds of ads can be accommodated in a single newspaper. Therefore, 'advertising is news too'.

2. **Smarter Ads in Print:** As the print media faces intense competition from television and radio, ads in the print media are getting cleverer and better than before.

It sounds quite ironical but just as there is competition between print and electronic media, there is equal rivalry between different owners of print media for circulation and readership.

Each tries to overcome marketing stunts of the other by tactics such – as brighter headlining, efficient coverage, better pictures, timely reporting of news, more – page per – rupee, etc.

Conclusion

Hence we had a brief outlook of history of print, threats to print from electronic media and various tools adopted by print to face the challenges imposed by electronic media. In reality it appears that both print as well as electronic are learning from each other by embracing some characteristics of each to survive the new challenges. The general trend of both media seems to rely on direct ad revenues, which is sure to make each one more competitive.

Surely the monopoly of print has ended due to emergence of various new media which have an upper hand in regard to spontaneity and effectiveness but we cannot deny that print has emerged with new fast technology and international newsgathering and of course credibility it enjoys, it's of course not going obsolete.

Finally, the Supreme Court of India, in a very recent comment, hit the nail on the head when it held that the "Special treatment of newspapers has a historical background behind it. The freedom of the press has always been a cherished right in all democratic countries. Newspapers not only purvey news but also ideas, opinion and ideologies besides much else. They are supposed to guard public interest by bringing to fore the misdeed, failings and lapses of the government and other bodies exercising governing power".

XVI

Broadcast Elements Human Voice and Music

We need to first underscore the obvious by recognizing two common elements of both television and radio – they provide for use of that incredible instrument called the human voice, and they allow expression through music. Together, they offer the creator of the broadcast symbol package an impressive array of communication options.

How much easier it is for many of us to remember something we're told rather than something we've read. And, of course, part of this is due to the possibilities of tone, inflection, authority, sympathy, and laughter that are available when one person talks to another. However else they may differ, then, the broadcast media allow advertisers and their message carriers to talk to you – not only as humans, of course, but also as jolly green giants, crickets, cats, frogs, garbage cans, carburetors, and hot dogs.

Sometimes they sing. And rarely if ever have advertisements sung as much. In part that's because all of you grew up on music. Or, as one writer put it, "The Beatles generation has become the buying generation, the 18 to 34-year-old coveted by lifestyle- product companies."

Consider some of the classics:

"When you say Budweiser"

"Fly the Friendly Skies of United"

"Reach out, Reach out and Touch Someone"

"Coke is it"

"Nothing Official about it"

Human voice depiction through prayers.

"I want my Thunder"
"Believe in the Best"
"Love at first drive"
"Dove is not a Soap"
"Mehenga hi sahi magar asli maal"
"Khushi Ke har pal mein"
"Coming for dinner"
"Humara Bajaj"
"Mera Bharat Kahan?"

The primary task facing the TV creative man is how best to get at people's feelings. How can he communicate convincingly with what psychologists call the third ear, with the levels of intuition far beyond reason-where the scales of judgement are weighted by feeling and primitive perceptions? This is the "open Sesame" to believability and persuasion. The intellectual elements-the facts and the arguments-are just a superstructure on the process (often the subconscious process) of achieving conviction. The creative mind in TV advertising has to work both logical and no- rational symbols. This is, after all, what a product image is-the total set of attitudes, the halo of psychological meanings, the association of feelings, the indelibly written aesthetic messages over and above the bare physical qualities.

Composers, copywriters, music directors, engineers, studio musicians, and jingle singers. They are all involved in the creation and execution of mini-melodies that may far outdistance most popular music successes in staying power and – naturally – memorabiity.

Ad Agency Needham, Harper & Steers, notes the following reasons for music's popularity as an advertising vehicle:

Music can get people's attention.
Music can differentiate a brand from others.
Music can make people remember a brand name.
Music can make people remember a brand promise.
Music can add value to a product.
Music can create an atmosphere conducive to selling.
Music can create a winning personality.
Music can glue commercials together.

Overall, the symbol package of television and radio advertisements hold in common the use of the human voice and the full dimensions of instrumental and vocal music. Beyond this, however, they present their own potential and limitations.

Given its sometimes enormous cost as well as its potential impact (tens of millions of people), it is hardly surprising that writing for television has become a coveted art.

A hundred people can be involved in the production of a single television commercial, but, as have seen, the whole process generally begins with the copywriters. The television copywriters' contribution is their ability to think in both advertising terms and the medium's terms. As emphasized earlier, they first need to understand the marketing and communication objectives to be achieved.

Then they draw on the many elements of cinematography- visual, aural, and optical elements-to plan effective television advertisement. They function much as a playwright or a motion picture scriptwriter does. They not only write what the characters in the play are to say but also develop the plot, visualize the scenes, plan the action, and write instructions to the producer, the director, the performers, and technicians who are to make the ideas come alive.

One view is that writing for television is easy because there is so much to work with: sight, sound, motion, and sequential development of an idea. Another view is that such writing is difficult because there are so many variables to learn how to use. Easy or not, writing for television demands knowledge and skills far too specialized to be detailed here. Thus, this brief discussion will deal with some of the more basic elements.

The audio portion of the television commercial can embody the qualities of an effective radio commercial. It can be personal, simple, and direct. More than this, however, the aural must work with the visual. The story unfolds visually with the commentary playing a supporting role; seeing (and hearing) is believing.

Visual elements include the setting – whether a studio set or on location, the visual props, the performers, their movements, gestures and facial expressions. Of course, how the product or idea is to be displayed, demonstrated or conveyed is a vital visual consideration.

All must be considered in terms of their potential meaning to the intended audience. Which symbol will mean what to whom?

The fundamental challenge for the creator of broadcast messages is to choose appropriate symbols to communicate a relevant message to hundreds, thousands or millions of people who she or he has never met and who are not, in general, seeking out the advertisement. Clearly, based on our own recall of television and radio advertisements, the challenges are often met.

Tasks

1. "It is almost impossible to overstate the impact of television on the Indian culture" Do you agree? You may provide your own favorite (or unfavorite) examples.
2. Do you feel that it's likely to be easier or harder to write a successful television advertisement rather than a radio ad? Why?
3. Do you feel that many television and radio ads are potentially annoying? How does this affect the image of the product? Where, as a business professional, you stand on this issue?

FINDINGS AND RECOMMENDATIONS

Task One

Television has become a mainstay of urban and the large rural Indian society, with 98% of Indian urban households having one or more TV sets. With Cable & Satellite Channels, television has a strong impact on our culture.

Television was introduced in India on September 15, 1959 as a pilot project in Delhi, for years no one was really aware that it even existed in India. But today television seems to have taken firm roots in the country. Now TV is regarded more than a source of entertainment. It has become an institutional part of the Indian Society, in such a way that it affects the life of the people and in return is affected by the people's lifestyles.

Television has received this popularity because of its very nature. The advantage that it has over other medium such as radio is that of visuals. With strikingly different combinations of sound, sight, colour, movements & music, it is able to attract attention instantly and the viewer is able to retain the same.

Television has tremendous dramatic capacity; it can make mundane products appear important, exciting and interesting.

For instance, the ad for "Clinic all Clear" antidandruff shampoo in which Sharukh has a double but the real one doesn't have dandruff in his hair. As he has "dhoo dhala" (washed it away) with the clinic antidandruff shampoo.

It can also create a positive association with the sponsor if the advertisement is likeable. This has been the case with "Onida" the devil in the ad did create a positive image with the audience. The energetic writing, unusual visual and edgy humour did the trick.

Because of this nature television receives vast exposure. This enables it to have a large reach, which in turn makes it even more popular. Television is a persuasive medium and thus has a wide impact on the values and lifestyles of the people. This however has its positive and negative sides.

Television today is considered to be a social force that has strong influence on the Indian Culture. TV programmes resemble or rather reflect the very nuances of our society. A housewife can today easily identify with the "Bahu or Saas" relationships in popular serials. Similarly, quite a few stories reflect the growing disloyalty in relationships. Last few years "Star TV", Sony, or Zee TV and quite a few others have occupied a pivotal position in our daily lives.

Television is responsible for reducing the gap between people and a world of glamour. The unreachable film stars or models have become a common face on TV. People now are able to watch various events such as "Film fare awards" or "Miss India Contests" sitting comfortably in their homes. It makes people dream fantasies. One can easily become an owner of a car or win fabulous prizes by participating in different contests. Just dial a number and win "Chappar Phad Ke", or sit face to face with "Amitabh Bachhan" to become a Crorepati. A young girl can look as pretty as the one in commercial by using the same face wash, lotion or soap.

Similarly the eating habits of people are now changing. Soft drinks such as "Coke" & "Pepsi" have replaced water. "Thumps Up" is the drink for grownups. "Kellogs" is the apt name for breakfast and "Cadburys" stands for desert. "Sunflower" & "Dhara" are health & so are the Ice Cream rich in vitamins & calcium. The impact of Television has been tremendous – even the new generations of people are called the "MTV Generation".

TV for many is a source of news and education. It has helped to spread awareness among the people. The messages such as "Donate your Organs". "Keep your city clean". "Help to educate" etc. have been appreciated by the people when communicated through this medium.

The impact of television has been such that at times people have tried to imitate what they see on TV. For instance a teenager got killed when he tried to copy the bungee jumping stunt in the "Thumps Up" ad. It is evident that Television had deeply influenced the behaviour of people and that it is impossible to overstate its impact on the Indian Culture.

Task Two

Let's us see first the elements involved in making the ad in each media, Radio ad requires three primary tools to develop the messages: voice, music and sound effects. Television ad requirements are of audio and video.

The primary requirement for the advertiser, in radio as well as in the TV , is to communicate the message by using the most appropriate symbols. These symbols are to be understood in terms of their potential meaning to the audience when used in communication. In the light of this, it is difficult to categorize TV or radio advertising as hard or easy as compared to each other.

The ads for television are created keeping in mind the virtual nature of the medium. Ads are created using demonstrations, visual props, product close ups, the performers, their movements, gestures, and facial expressions. TV ads have wide scope for creativity – which allows different combinations of sight and sound. The audio and visual elements can be used to present pictures in various ways – appropriate application of testimonials and human emotions, such as fear, humour, fantasy, satire etc. help in making effective ads.

The viewers are more involved and thus build a conviction regarding a product. TV ads are more persuasive and generally have a high recall value. Thus creating television ads may be considered easy.

But in case of TV advertising, the viewer gets involved in the ad and not the product. The audience may like the idea or the message, but might not be influenced to change their buying behaviour. This wastes the efforts of the creator. Also because many elements are involved in TV advertising, it become difficult to effectively coordinate them. In such cases television advertising becomes difficult.

Radio advertising aims to pull the listener "in" from whatever is being done. The success of radio ads depends on how appropriately the ad creates a picture in the mind's "eye" of the listener, by using music, human voice, sound effects and humor. These elements have to be chosen and utilized in such a way that the listener remembers it and is intrigued by it.

In case of radio advertising human emotions have to be projected using the voice of the performer. This may or may not prove to be very persuasive resulting in low retention of the ad. In such respect creating ads for radio becomes harder, since it does not guarantee that the intended picture of the products gets created in the listeners mind. Nonetheless, both radio as well as TV advertising involves a lot of skill and persuasion.

In the overall context, radio ads are more difficult to write than television ads as only with voice the copy writers have to be making the audience convinced, all emotions have to incorporated in the voice itself. Mostly radios are heard when people are doing some other job at the same time. Music and successful jingles to be written that will be remembered by the audience is a challenging task to do. Sound effects, for example, the crash of the sea waves, the clicking of typewriter keys, the cheers of fans at a stadium etc. to create a background and executing it properly is a not easy.

In television ad emotion, action feelings can be showed by the actors but in radio ads all these have to be incorporated in the voice of the speakers. The radio ad is such that it has to create a theatre in the mind of the audience – imagine having to create all visual elements – the scene, the cast, the costumes, and the facial expressions – in the imagination of the audience. Thus all things can be created in the background of a television ad but not for radio ads as the audience is not able to see the actors straightway. So the copywriters of radio ads have a much tougher job to do. In reality, use of imagery can be easy in the television ads than radio ads.

Music plays a vital role in the radio ad as good jingles are often remembered and here the music is used to persuade the consumer to buy. In television ads music plays a background role.

Hence, from above, it appears that it is harder to write a radio ad than a television one.

Task Three

Television and radio ads do tend to get annoying at certain times. People watching or listening to a programme may enjoy often and get absorbed in it. Their absorption is only slightly less than that experienced by people watching a movie in a darkened theater. Advertising often is considered an unwelcome interruption because it disrupts programme viewing or listening.

Hence we often find the more tendencies of viewers to switch channels called zapping, or leaving the room during commercial breaks. Take for example the watching of the event like "Femina Miss India" contest shown on Sony Television. There were about 20 ads minimum in every commercial break. Yes, people do tend to watch the event but the excessive advertising in between made the whole event boring, long, and tedious. When much of the advertisements are of the same sponsors all over again, people generally avoid such ads. And such ads are boring, repetitive and may turn out to be disastrous for the product and the advertiser.

The advertiser should make sure that the ad promises only what the product is capable of delivering, it should not make false claims.

Advertisements that deviate from the actual situation, affect the purchasing behaviour of the consumer. An ad that is deceptive creates a negative impression of the product as well as the brand.

Ambiguous ads also tend to be annoying as it cannot be easily understood by the audience. In absence of simplicity the audiences become indifferent to what is being communicated through that ad.

Ads for certain harmful products at times are labeled as unethical and dangerous. Ads that urge the young people to experiment with drinking and smoking or ads that show dare devil stunts provoking young viewers to imitate them, can be very offending and harmful.

At times advertisements hurt the sentiments of particular sections of society. Advertising that tries to consolidate the stereotyping role of women as primarily sex objects not doing important things and staying at home are very annoying.

Similarly, ads that are obscene and include nudity to attract and advertise a product are very offending. At times such ads may create emotional disturbance among the audience.

In the present situation advertising is used to overcome competition. But most of the time ads are created to make fun of the competitor's product. Such ads don't provide a genuine reason, as to why the consumer should go for that product. Such advertising is very irritating.

The advertisements have a life cycle. At the end of each cycle the broadcast of the ad becomes ineffective. Outdated ads do not influence the audience much. Similarly, ads that are repeated too often become monotonous. As business professionals we need to advertise for our products, because without advertising our products can't survive and succeed in the market. But an ad should not be created for the sake of creating an ad. Emphasis should be laid on what the consumer makes out of it. Yes, we need to advertise but in such way that our product commercials are interesting, intriguing, and likeable and well appreciated by the audiences.

Index

P

Q

R

S